Office of the United Nations High Commissioner for Human Rights
Geneva

Human Rights
A Compilation of
International Instruments

Volume II
Regional Instruments

Unit   Nations
New York a   Geneva, 1997

NOTE

Symbols of United Nations documents are composed of capital letters combined with figures. Mention of such a symbol indicates a reference to a United Nations document.

ST/HR/1/Rev.5
(Vol. II)

UNITED NATIONS PUBLICATION

Sales No. E.97.XIV.1

ISBN 92-1-154124-7
ISSN 0251-7035

Complete set of two volumes: ISBN 92-1-154099-2

CONTENTS

Volume II: Regional Instruments

Page

Introduction

This Compilation is published by the Office of the United Nations High Commissioner for Human Rights in connection with the convening of the 1993 World Conference on Human Rights, in Vienna. The first compilation of international instruments in the field of human rights was issued in 1968. Subsequent editions were issued in 1973,[1] 1978,[2] 1983[3] and 1988,[4] the latter marking the fortieth anniversary of the Universal Declaration of Human Rights.

At its first session in September 1991, the Preparatory Committee of the World Conference adopted decision PC/5 entitled "Studies and documentation for the World Conference", recommending that the General Assembly request the Secretary-General to prepare, *inter alia*, "an update of *A Compilation of International Instruments* and *Status of International Instruments* including also texts of regional instruments on human rights". The Preparatory Committee's decision was endorsed by the General Assembly in its resolution 46/116 of 17 December 1991. In accordance with this request, the present edition, consisting of two volumes, the first devoted to instruments of universal character and the second to regional instruments, was produced.

The first volume, which is published in two parts, contains documents adopted up to 31 March 1993. The list of international instruments has been broadened to include additional United Nations documents and instruments adopted by the International Labour Organisation, the United Nations Educational, Scientific and Cultural Organization and the Office of the United Nations High Commissioner for Refugees. Furthermore, a chapter concerning Humanitarian Law and including the four Geneva Conventions and the Protocols thereto has been added. All the instruments, grouped by subject

---

[1] *Human Rights: A Compilation of International Instruments of the United Nations* (United Nations publication, Sales No. E.73.XIV.2).

[2] *Human Rights: A Compilation of International Instruments* (United Nations publication, Sales No. E.78.XIV.2).

[3] *Human Rights: A Compilation of International Instruments* (United Nations publication, Sales No. E.83.XIV.1).

[4] *Human Rights: A Compilation of International Instruments* (United Nations publication, Sales No. E.88.XIV.1).

1

and organized in chronological order of adoption, appear in a list at the end of each part.

The second volume contains a selection of instruments which have been adopted within the framework of regional intergovernmental organizations up to 31 July 1997. This collection of regional instruments is being issued for the first time. The order of listing of the organizations is that of the dates of their establishment, and that of the instruments is the chronological order of their adoption.

The legal status of the instruments contained in the Compilation varies. Those referred to as *declarations, principles, guidelines, standard rules* and *recommendations* have no binding legal effect.

Nevertheless, these instruments have an undeniable moral force and provide practical guidance to States in their conduct. The value of such instruments rests on their recognition and acceptance by a large number of States, and, even without binding legal effect, they may be seen as declaratory of broadly accepted principles within the international community.

International treaties, which are referred to variously as *covenants, protocols* or *conventions*, are legally binding for those States that ratify or accede to them. Treaties adopted within the United Nations are open for signature and ratification by all States, while those adopted within the framework of regional organizations depend for acceptance on membership of the organization concerned.

A *Chart of Ratifications*, containing the status of all treaties appearing in the first part of the Compilation, is issued by the Office of the High Commissioner for Human Rights every six months. Information on reservations, declarations, observations and notifications relating to the same treaties is contained in the publication *Human Rights: Status of International Instruments*, which is issued—together with the Compilation—every five years.

The two volumes together constitute a comprehensive catalogue of the existing human rights instruments adopted at both universal and regional level. It is hoped that the Compilation will contribute to a wider knowledge and increased awareness of international human rights standards and will be a valuable resource for all those engaged in the promotion and protection of human rights and fundamental freedoms.

A. ORGANIZATION OF AMERICAN STATES

1. American Declaration of the Rights and Duties of Man

Adopted at Bogotá on 2 May 1948

PREAMBLE

All men are born free and equal in dignity and in rights, and, being endowed by nature with reason and conscience, they should conduct themselves as brothers one to another.

The fulfilment of duty by each individual is a prerequisite to the rights of all. Rights and duties are interrelated in every social and political activity of man. While rights exalt individual liberty, duties express the dignity of that liberty.

Duties of a juridical nature presuppose others of a moral nature which support them in principle and constitute their basis.

Inasmuch as spiritual development is the supreme end of human existence and the highest expression thereof, it is the duty of man to serve that end with all his strength and resources.

Since culture is the highest social and historical expression of that spiritual development, it is the duty of man to preserve, practice and foster culture by every means within his power.

And, since moral conduct constitutes the noblest flowering of culture, it is the duty of every man always to hold it in high respect.

CHAPTER ONE

Rights

Article I

RIGHT TO LIFE, LIBERTY AND PERSONAL SECURITY

Every human being has the right to life, liberty and the security of his person.

Article II

Right to equality before the law

All persons are equal before the law and have the rights and duties established in this Declaration, without distinction as to race, sex, language, creed or any other factor.

Article III

Right to religious freedom and worship

Every person has the right freely to profess a religious faith, and to manifest and practice it both in public and in private.

Article IV

Right to freedom of investigation, opinion, expression and dissemination

Every person has the right to freedom of investigation, of opinion, and of the expression and dissemination of ideas, by any medium whatsoever.

Article V

Right to protection of honour, personal reputation, and private and family life

Every person has the right to the protection of the law against abusive attacks upon his honour, his reputation, and his private and family life.

Article VI

Right to a family and to the protection thereof

Every person has the right to establish a family, the basic element of society, and to receive protection therefore.

Article VII

Right to protection for mothers and children

All women, during pregnancy and the nursing period, and all children, have the right to special protection, care and aid.

Article VIII

RIGHT TO RESIDENCE AND MOVEMENT

Every person has the right to fix his residence within the territory of the State of which he is a national, to move about freely within such territory, and not to leave it except by his own will.

Article IX

RIGHT TO INVIOLABILITY OF THE HOME

Every person has the right to the inviolability of his home.

Article X

RIGHT TO THE INVIOLABILITY AND TRANSMISSION OF CORRESPONDENCE

Every person has the right to the inviolability and transmission of his correspondence.

Article XI

RIGHT TO THE PRESERVATION OF HEALTH AND TO WELL-BEING

Every person has the right to the preservation of his health through sanitary and social measures relating to food, clothing, housing and medical care, to the extent permitted by public and community resources.

Article XII

RIGHT TO EDUCATION

Every person has the right to an education, which should be based on the principles of liberty, morality and human solidarity.

Likewise every person has the right to an education that will prepare him to attain a decent life, to raise his standard of living and to be a useful member of society.

The right to an education includes the right to equality of opportunity in every case, in accordance with natural talents, merit and the desire to utilize the resources that the State or the community is in a position to provide.

Every person has the right to receive, free, at least a primary education.

Article XIII

RIGHT TO THE BENEFITS OF CULTURE

Every person has the right to take part in the cultural life of the community, to enjoy the arts, and to participate in the benefits that result from intellectual progress, especially scientific discoveries.

He likewise has the right to the protection of his moral and material interests as regards his inventions or any literary, scientific or artistic works of which he is the author.

Article XIV

RIGHT TO WORK AND TO FAIR REMUNERATION

Every person has the right to work, under proper conditions, and to follow his vocation freely, insofar as existing conditions of employment permit.

Every person who works has the right to receive such remuneration as will, in proportion to his capacity and skill, assure him a standard of living suitable for himself and for his family.

Article XV

RIGHT TO LEISURE TIME AND TO THE USE THEREOF

Every person has the right to leisure time, to wholesome recreation and to the opportunity for advantageous use of his free time to his spiritual, cultural and physical benefit.

Article XVI

RIGHT TO SOCIAL SECURITY

Every person has the right to social security which will protect him from the consequences of unemployment, old age and any disabilities arising from causes beyond his control that make it physically or mentally impossible for him to earn a living.

Article XVII

RIGHT TO RECOGNITION OF JURIDICAL PERSONALITY AND OF CIVIL RIGHTS

Every person has the right to be recognized everywhere as a person having rights and obligations, and to enjoy the basic civil rights.

Article XVIII

RIGHT TO A FAIR TRIAL

Every person may resort to the courts to ensure respect for his legal rights. There should likewise be available to him a simple, brief procedure whereby the courts will protect him from acts of authority that, to his prejudice, violate any fundamental constitutional rights.

Article XIX

RIGHT TO NATIONALITY

Every person has the right to the nationality to which he is entitled by law and to change it, if he so wishes, for the nationality of any other country that is willing to grant it to him.

Article XX

RIGHT TO VOTE AND TO PARTICIPATE IN GOVERNMENT

Every person having legal capacity is entitled to participate in the government of his country, directly or through his representatives, and to take part in popular elections, which shall be by secret ballot, and shall be honest, periodic and free.

Article XXI

RIGHT OF ASSEMBLY

Every person has the right to assemble peaceably with others in a formal public meeting or an informal gathering, in connection with matters of common interest of any nature.

Article XXII

RIGHT OF ASSOCIATION

Every person has the right to associate with others to promote, exercise and protect his legitimate interests of a political, economic, religious, social, cultural, professional, labor-union or other nature.

Article XXIII

RIGHT TO PROPERTY

Every person has a right to own such private property as meets the essential needs of decent living and helps to maintain the dignity of the individual and of the home.

Article XXIV

RIGHT TO PETITION

Every person has the right to submit respectful petitions to any competent authority, for reasons of either general or private interest, and the right to obtain a prompt decision thereon.

Article XXV

RIGHT TO PROTECTION FROM ARBITRARY ARREST

No person may be deprived of his liberty except in the cases and according to the procedures established by pre-existing law.

No person may be deprived of liberty for non-fulfilment of obligations of a purely civil character.

Every individual who has been deprived of his liberty has the right to have the legality of his detention ascertained without delay by a court, and the right to be tried without undue delay, or, otherwise, to be released. He also has the right to humane treatment during the time he is in custody.

Article XXVI

RIGHT TO DUE PROCESS OF LAW

Every accused person is presumed to be innocent until proved guilty.

Every person accused of an offence has the right to be given an impartial and public hearing, and to be tried by courts previously established in accordance with pre-existing laws, and not to receive cruel, infamous or unusual punishment.

Article XXVII

RIGHT OF ASYLUM

Every person has the right, in case of pursuit not resulting from ordinary crimes, to seek and receive asylum in foreign territory, in accordance with the laws of each country and with international agreements.

Article XXVIII

SCOPE OF THE RIGHTS OF MAN

The rights of man are limited by the rights of others, by the security of all, and by the just demands of the general welfare and the advancement of democracy.

CHAPTER TWO

Duties

Article XXIX

DUTIES TO SOCIETY

It is the duty of the individual so to conduct himself in relation to others that each and every one may fully form and develop his personality.

Article XXX

DUTIES TOWARD CHILDREN AND PARENTS

It is the duty of every person to aid, support, educate and protect his minor children, and it is the duty of children to honour their parents always and to aid, support and protect them when they need it.

Article XXXI

DUTY TO RECEIVE INSTRUCTION

It is the duty of every person to acquire at least an elementary education.

Article XXXII

DUTY TO VOTE

It is the duty of every person to vote in the popular elections of the country of which he is a national, when he is legally capable of doing so.

Article XXXIII

DUTY TO OBEY THE LAW

It is the duty of every person to obey the law and other legitimate commands of the authorities of his country and those of the country in which he may be.

Article XXXIV

DUTY TO SERVE THE COMMUNITY AND THE NATION

It is the duty of every able-bodied person to render whatever civil and military service his country may require for its defence and preservation, and, in case of public disaster, to render such services as may be in his power.

It is likewise his duty to hold any public office to which he may be elected by popular vote in the State of which he is a national.

Article XXXV

DUTIES WITH RESPECT TO SOCIAL SECURITY AND WELFARE

It is the duty of every person to cooperate with the State and the community with respect to social security and welfare, in accordance with his ability and with existing circumstances.

Article XXXVI

DUTY TO PAY TAXES

It is the duty of every person to pay the taxes established by law for the support of public services.

Article XXXVII

DUTY TO WORK

It is the duty of every person to work, as far as his capacity and possibilities permit, in order to obtain the means of livelihood or to benefit his community.

Article XXXVIII

DUTY TO REFRAIN FROM POLITICAL ACTIVITIES IN A FOREIGN COUNTRY

It is the duty of every person to refrain from taking part in political activities that, according to law, are reserved exclusively to the citizens of the State in which he is an alien.

2. American Convention on Human Rights: "Pact of San José, Costa Rica"

Adopted at San José, Costa Rica, on 22 November 1969

ENTRY INTO FORCE: 18 July 1978, in accordance with article 74

PREAMBLE

The American states signatory to the present Convention,

Reaffirming their intention to consolidate in this hemisphere, within the framework of democratic institutions, a system of personal liberty and social justice based on respect for the essential rights of man,

Recognizing that the essential rights of man are not derived from one's being a national of a certain state, but are based upon attributes of the human personality, and that they therefore justify international protection in the form of a convention reinforcing or complementing the protection provided by the domestic law of the American states,

Considering that these principles have been set forth in the Charter of the Organization of American States, in the American Declaration of the Rights and Duties of Man, and in the Universal Declaration of Human Rights, and that they have been reaffirmed and refined in other international instruments, worldwide as well as regional in scope,

Reiterating that, in accordance with the Universal Declaration of Human Rights, the ideal of free men enjoying freedom from fear and want can be achieved only if conditions are created whereby everyone may enjoy his economic, social, and cultural rights, as well as his civil and political rights, and

Considering that the Third Special Inter-American Conference (Buenos Aires, 1967) approved the incorporation into the Charter of the Organization itself of broader standards with respect to economic, social, and educational rights and resolved that an inter-American convention on human rights should determine the structure, competence, and procedure of the organs responsible for these matters,

Have agreed upon the following:

PART I.   STATE OBLIGATIONS AND RIGHTS PROTECTED

CHAPTER I.   GENERAL OBLIGATIONS

Article 1.   OBLIGATION TO RESPECT RIGHTS. 1.   The States Parties to this Convention undertake to respect the rights and freedoms recognized herein and to ensure to all persons subject to their jurisdiction the free and full exercise of those rights and freedoms, without any discrimination for reasons of race, color, sex, language, religion, political or other opinion, national or social origin, economic status, birth, or any other social condition.

2.   For the purposes of this Convention, "person" means every human being.

Article 2.   DOMESTIC LEGAL EFFECTS. Where the exercise of any of the rights or freedoms referred to in Article 1 is not already ensured by legislative or other provisions, the States Parties undertake to adopt, in accordance with their constitutional processes and the provisions of this Convention, such legislative or other measures as may be necessary to give effect to those rights or freedoms.

CHAPTER II.   CIVIL AND POLITICAL RIGHTS

Article 3.   RIGHT TO JURIDICAL PERSONALITY. Every person has the right to recognition as a person before the law.

Article 4.   RIGHT TO LIFE. 1.   Every person has the right to have his life respected. This right shall be protected by law, and, in general, from the moment of conception. No one shall be arbitrarily deprived of his life.

2.   In countries that have not abolished the death penalty, it may be imposed only for the most serious crimes and pursuant to a final judgment rendered by a competent court and in accordance with a law establishing such punishment, enacted prior to the commission of the crime. The application of such punishment shall not be extended to crimes to which it does not presently apply.

3.   The death penalty shall not be reestablished in states that have abolished it.

4.   In no case shall capital punishment be inflicted for political offenses or related common crimes.

5.   Capital punishment shall not be imposed upon persons who, at the time the crime was committed, were under 18 years of age or over 70 years of age; nor shall it be applied to pregnant women.

6.   Every person condemned to death shall have the right to apply for amnesty, pardon, or commutation of sentence, which may be granted in all cases. Capital punishment shall not be imposed while such a petition is pending decision by the competent authority.

Article 5.   RIGHT TO HUMANE TREATMENT. 1.   Every person has the right to have his physical, mental, and moral integrity respected.

2.   No one shall be subjected to torture or to cruel, inhuman, or degrading punishment or treatment. All persons deprived of their liberty shall be treated with respect for the inherent dignity of the human person.

3.   Punishment shall not be extended to any person other than the criminal.

4.   Accused persons shall, save in exceptional circumstances, be segregated from convicted persons, and shall be subject to separate treatment appropriate to their status as unconvicted persons.

5.   Minors while subject to criminal proceedings shall be separated from adults and brought before specialized tribunals, as speedily as possible, so that they may be treated in accordance with their status as minors.

6.   Punishments consisting of deprivation of liberty shall have as an essential aim the reform and social readaptation of the prisoners.

Article 6.   FREEDOM FROM SLAVERY. 1.   No one shall be subject to slavery or to involuntary servitude, which are prohibited in all their forms, as are the slave trade and traffic in women.

2.   No one shall be required to perform forced or compulsory labor. This provision shall not be interpreted to mean that, in those countries in which the penalty established for certain crimes is deprivation of liberty at forced labor, the carrying out of such a sentence imposed by a competent court is prohibited. Forced labor shall not adversely affect the dignity or the physical or intellectual capacity of the prisoner.

3.   For the purposes of this article, the following do not constitute forced or compulsory labor:

a. Work or service normally required of a person imprisoned in execution of a sentence or formal decision passed by the competent judicial authority; such work or service shall be carried out under the supervision and control of public authorities, and any persons performing such work or service shall not be placed at the disposal of any private party, company, or juridical person;

b. Military service and, in countries in which conscientious objectors are recognized, national service that the law may provide for in lieu of military service;

c. Service exacted in time of danger or calamity that threatens the existence or the well-being of the community; or *d.* Work or service that forms part of normal civic obligations.

Article 7. RIGHT TO PERSONAL LIBERTY. 1. Every person has the right to personal liberty and security.

2. No one shall be deprived of his physical liberty except for the reasons and under the conditions established beforehand by the constitution of the State Party concerned or by a law established pursuant thereto.

3. No one shall be subject to arbitrary arrest or imprisonment.

4. Anyone who is detained shall be informed of the reasons for his detention and shall be promptly notified of the charge or charges against him.

5. Any person detained shall be brought promptly before a judge or other officer authorized by law to exercise judicial power and shall be entitled to trial within a reasonable time or to be released without prejudice to the continuation of the proceedings. His release may be subject to guarantees to assure his appearance for trial.

6. Anyone who is deprived of his liberty shall be entitled to recourse to a competent court, in order that the court may decide without delay on the lawfulness of his arrest or detention and order his release if the arrest or detention is unlawful. In States Parties whose laws provide that anyone who believes himself to be threatened with deprivation of his liberty is entitled to recourse to a competent court in order that it may decide on the lawfulness of such threat, this remedy may not be restricted or abolished. The interested party or another person on his behalf is entitled to seek these remedies.

7. No one shall be detained for debt. This principle shall not limit the orders of a competent judicial authority issued for nonfulfillment of duties of support.

Article 8. RIGHT TO A FAIR TRIAL. 1. Every person has the right to a hearing, with due guarantees and within a reasonable time, by a competent, independent, and impartial tribunal, previously established by law, in the substantiation of any accusation of a criminal nature made against him or for the determination of his rights and obligations of a civil, labor, fiscal, or any other nature.

2. Every person accused of a criminal offense has the right to be presumed innocent so long as his guilt has not been proven according to law. During the proceedings, every person is entitled, with full equality, to the following minimum guarantees:

a. The right of the accused to be assisted without charge by a translator or interpreter, if he does not understand or does not speak the language of the tribunal or court;

b. Prior notification in detail to the accused of the charges against him;

c. Adequate time and means for the preparation of his defense;

d. The right of the accused to defend himself personally or to be assisted by legal counsel of his own choosing, and to communicate freely and privately with his counsel;

e. The inalienable right to be assisted by counsel provided by the state, paid or not as the domestic law provides, if the accused does not defend himself personally or engage his own counsel within the time period established by law;

f. The right of the defense to examine witnesses present in the court and to obtain the appearance, as witnesses, of experts or other persons who may throw light on the facts;

g. The right not to be compelled to be a witness against himself or to plead guilty; and

h. The right to appeal the judgment to a higher court.

3. A confession of guilt by the accused shall be valid only if it is made without coercion of any kind.

4. An accused person acquitted by a nonappealable judgment shall not be subjected to a new trial for the same cause.

5. Criminal proceedings shall be public, except insofar as may be necessary to protect the interests of justice.

Article 9. FREEDOM FROM *EX POST FACTO* LAWS. No one shall be convicted of any act or omission that did not constitute a criminal offense, under the applicable law, at the time it was committed. A heavier penalty shall not be imposed than the one that was applicable at the time the criminal offense was committed. If subsequent to the commission of the offense the law provides for the imposition of a lighter punishment, the guilty person shall benefit therefrom.

Article 10. RIGHT TO COMPENSATION. Every person has the right to be compensated in accordance with the law in the event he has been sentenced by a final judgment through a miscarriage of justice.

Article 11. RIGHT TO PRIVACY. 1. Everyone has the right to have his honor respected and his dignity recognized.

2. No one may be the object of arbitrary or abusive interference with his private life, his family, his home, or his correspondence, or of unlawful attacks on his honor or reputation.

3. Everyone has the right to the protection of the law against such interference or attacks.

Article 12. FREEDOM OF CONSCIENCE AND RELIGION. 1. Everyone has the right to freedom of conscience and of religion. This right includes freedom to maintain or to change one's religion or beliefs, and freedom to profess or disseminate one's religion or beliefs, either individually or together with others, in public or in private.

2.   No one shall be subject to restrictions that might impair his freedom to maintain or to change his religion or beliefs.

3.   Freedom to manifest one's religion and beliefs may be subject only to the limitations prescribed by law that are necessary to protect public safety, order, health, or morals, or the rights or freedoms of others.

4.   Parents or guardians, as the case may be, have the right to provide for religious and moral education of their children or wards that is in accord with their own convictions.

Article 13.   FREEDOM OF THOUGHT AND EXPRESSION. 1.   Everyone has the right to freedom of thought and expression. This right includes freedom to seek, receive, and impart information and ideas of all kinds, regardless of frontiers, either orally, in writing, in print, in the form of art, or through any other medium of one's choice.

2.   The exercise of the right provided for in the foregoing paragraph shall not be subject to prior censorship but shall be subject to subsequent imposition of liability, which shall be expressly established by law to the extent necessary to ensure:

a.   Respect for the rights or reputations of others; or

b.   The protection of national security, public order, or public health or morals.

3.   The right of expression may not be restricted by indirect methods or means, such as the abuse of government or private controls over newsprint, radio broadcasting frequencies, or equipment used in the dissemination of information, or by any other means tending to impede the communication and circulation of ideas and opinions.

4.   Notwithstanding the provisions of paragraph 2 above, public entertainments may be subject by law to prior censorship for the sole purpose of regulating access to them for the moral protection of childhood and adolescence.

5.   Any propaganda for war and any advocacy of national, racial, or religious hatred that constitute incitements to lawless violence or to any other similar illegal action against any person or group of persons on any grounds including those of race, color, religion, language, or national origin shall be considered as offenses punishable by law.

Article 14.   RIGHT OF REPLY. 1.   Anyone injured by inaccurate or offensive statements or ideas disseminated to the public in general by a legally regulated medium of communication has the right to reply or to make a correction using the same communications outlet, under such conditions as the law may establish.

2.   The correction or reply shall not in any case remit other legal liabilities that may have been incurred.

3.   For the effective protection of honor and reputation, every publisher, and every newspaper, motion picture, radio, and television company, shall have a person responsible who is not protected by immunities or special privileges.

Article 15.   RIGHT OF ASSEMBLY. The right of peaceful assembly, without arms, is recognized. No restrictions may be placed on the exercise of this right other than those imposed in conformity with the law and necessary in a democratic society in the interest of national security, public safety or public order, or to protect public health or morals or the rights or freedoms of others.

Article 16.   FREEDOM OF ASSOCIATION. 1.   Everyone has the right to associate freely for ideological, religious, political, economic, labor, social, cultural, sports, or other purposes.

2.   The exercise of this right shall be subject only to such restrictions established by law as may be necessary in a democratic society, in the interest of national security, public safety or public order, or to protect public health or morals or the rights and freedoms of others.

3.   The provisions of this article do not bar the imposition of legal restrictions, including even deprivation of the exercise of the right of association, on members of the armed forces and the police.

Article 17.   RIGHTS OF THE FAMILY. 1.   The family is the natural and fundamental group unit of society and is entitled to protection by society and the state.

2.   The right of men and women of marriageable age to marry and to raise a family shall be recognized, if they meet the conditions required by domestic laws, insofar as such conditions do not affect the principle of nondiscrimination established in this Convention.

3.   No marriage shall be entered into without the free and full consent of the intending spouses.

4.   The States Parties shall take appropriate steps to ensure the equality of rights and the adequate balancing of responsibilities of the spouses as to marriage, during marriage, and in the event of its dissolution. In case of dissolution, provision shall be made for the necessary protection of any children solely on the basis of their own best interests.

5.   The law shall recognize equal rights for children born out of wedlock and those born in wedlock.

Article 18. RIGHT TO A NAME. Every person has the right to a given name and to the surnames of his parents or that of one of them. The law shall regulate the manner in which this right shall be ensured for all, by the use of assumed names if necessary.

Article 19. RIGHTS OF THE CHILD. Every minor child has the right to the measures of protection required by his condition as a minor on the part of his family, society, and the state.

Article 20. RIGHT TO NATIONALITY. 1. Every person has the right to a nationality.

2. Every person has the right to the nationality of the state in whose territory he was born if he does not have the right to any other nationality.

3. No one shall be arbitrarily deprived of his nationality or of the right to change it.

Article 21. RIGHT TO PROPERTY. 1. Everyone has the right to the use and enjoyment of his property. The law may subordinate such use and enjoyment to the interest of society.

2. No one shall be deprived of his property except upon payment of just compensation, for reasons of public utility or social interest, and in the cases and according to the forms established by law.

3. Usury and any other form of exploitation of man by man shall be prohibited by law.

Article 22. FREEDOM OF MOVEMENT AND RESIDENCE. 1. Every person lawfully in the territory of a State Party has the right to move about in it, and to reside in it subject to the provisions of the law.

2. Every person has the right to leave any country freely, including his own.

3. The exercise of the foregoing rights may be restricted only pursuant to a law to the extent necessary in a democratic society to prevent crime or to protect national security, public safety, public order, public morals, public health, or the rights or freedoms of others.

4. The exercise of the rights recognized in paragraph 1 may also be restricted by law in designated zones for reasons of public interest.

5. No one can be expelled from the territory of the state of which he is a national or be deprived of the right to enter it.

6. An alien lawfully in the territory of a State Party to this Convention may be expelled from it only pursuant to a decision reached in accordance with law.

7. Every person has the right to seek and be granted asylum in a foreign territory, in accordance with the legislation of the state and international conventions, in the event he is being pursued for political offenses or related common crimes.

8. In no case may an alien be deported or returned to a country, regardless of whether or not it is his country of origin, if in that country his right to life or personal freedom is in danger of being violated because of his race, nationality, religion, social status, or political opinions.

9. The collective expulsion of aliens is prohibited.

Article 23. RIGHT TO PARTICIPATE IN GOVERNMENT. 1. Every citizen shall enjoy the following rights and opportunities:

a. To take part in the conduct of public affairs, directly or through freely chosen representatives;

b. To vote and to be elected in genuine periodic elections, which shall be by universal and equal suffrage and by secret ballot that guarantees the free expression of the will of the voters; and

c. To have access, under general conditions of equality, to the public service of his country.

2. The law may regulate the exercise of the rights and opportunities referred to in the preceding paragraph only on the basis of age, nationality, residence, language, education, civil and mental capacity, or sentencing by a competent court in criminal proceedings.

Article 24. RIGHT TO EQUAL PROTECTION. All persons are equal before the law. Consequently, they are entitled, without discrimination, to equal protection of the law.

Article 25. RIGHT TO JUDICIAL PROTECTION. 1. Everyone has the right to simple and prompt recourse, or any other effective recourse, to a competent court or tribunal for protection against acts that violate his fundamental rights recognized by the constitution or laws of the state concerned or by this Convention, even though such violation may have been committed by persons acting in the course of their official duties.

2. The States Parties undertake:

a. To ensure that any person claiming such remedy shall have his right determined by the competent authority provided for by the legal system of the state;

b. To develop the possibilities of judicial remedy; and

c. To ensure that the competent authorities shall enforce such remedies when granted.

CHAPTER III. ECONOMIC, SOCIAL, AND CULTURAL RIGHTS

Article 26. PROGRESSIVE DEVELOPMENT. The States Parties undertake to adopt measures, both internally and through international cooperation, especially those of an economic and technical nature, with a view to achieving progressively, by legislation or other appropriate means, the full realization of the rights implicit in the economic, social, educational, scientific, and cultural standards set forth in the Charter of the Organization of American States as amended by the Protocol of Buenos Aires.

CHAPTER IV. SUSPENSION OF GUARANTEES, INTERPRETATION,
AND APPLICATION

Article 27. SUSPENSION OF GUARANTEES. 1.   In time of war, public danger, or other emergency that threatens the independence or security of a State Party, it may take measures derogating from its obligations under the present Convention to the extent and for the period of time strictly required by the exigencies of the situation, provided that such measures are not inconsistent with its other obligations under international law and do not involve discrimination on the ground of race, color, sex, language, religion, or social origin.

2.   The foregoing provision does not authorize any suspension of the following articles: Article 3 (Right to juridical personality), Article 4 (Right to life), Article 5 (Right to humane treatment), Article 6 (Freedom from slavery), Article 9 (Freedom from *ex post facto* laws), Article 12 (Freedom of conscience and religion), Article 17 (Rights of the family), Article 18 (Right to a name), Article 19 (Rights of the child), Article 20 (Right to nationality), and Article 23 (Right to participate in government), or of the judicial guarantees essential for the protection of such rights.

3.   Any State Party availing itself of the right of suspension shall immediately inform the other States Parties, through the Secretary-General of the Organization of American States, of the provisions the application of which it has suspended, the reasons that gave rise to the suspension, and the date set for the termination of such suspension.

Article 28. FEDERAL CLAUSE. 1.   Where a State Party is constituted as a federal state, the national government of such State Party shall implement all the provisions of the Convention over whose subject matter it exercises legislative and judicial jurisdiction.

2.   With respect to the provisions over whose subject matter the constituent units of the federal state have jurisdiction, the national government shall immediately take suitable measures, in accordance with its constitution

and its laws, to the end that the competent authorities of the constituent units may adopt appropriate provisions for the fulfillment of this Convention.

3. Whenever two or more States Parties agree to form a federation or other type of association, they shall take care that the resulting federal or other compact contains the provisions necessary for continuing and rendering effective the standards of this Convention in the new state that is organized.

Article 29. RESTRICTIONS REGARDING INTERPRETATION. No provision of this Convention shall be interpreted as:

a. Permitting any State Party, group, or person to suppress the enjoyment or exercise of the rights and freedoms recognized in this Convention or to restrict them to a greater extent than is provided for herein;

b. Restricting the enjoyment or exercise of any right or freedom recognized by virtue of the laws of any State Party or by virtue of another convention to which one of the said states is a party;

c. Precluding other rights or guarantees that are inherent in the human personality or derived from representative democracy as a form of government; or

d. Excluding or limiting the effect that the American Declaration of the Rights and Duties of Man and other international acts of the same nature may have.

Article 30. SCOPE OF RESTRICTIONS. The restrictions that, pursuant to this Convention, may be placed on the enjoyment or exercise of the rights or freedoms recognized herein may not be applied except in accordance with laws enacted for reasons of general interest and in accordance with the purpose for which such restrictions have been established.

Article 31. RECOGNITION OF OTHER RIGHTS. Other rights and freedoms recognized in accordance with the procedures established in Articles 76 and 77 may be included in the system of protection of this Convention.

CHAPTER V. PERSONAL RESPONSIBILITIES

Article 32. RELATIONSHIP BETWEEN DUTIES AND RIGHTS. 1. Every person has responsibilities to his family, his community, and mankind.

2. The rights of each person are limited by the rights of others, by the security of all, and by the just demands of the general welfare, in a democratic society.

PART II.   MEANS OF PROTECTION

CHAPTER VI.   COMPETENT ORGANS

Article 33.   The following organs shall have competence with respect to matters relating to the fulfillment of the commitments made by the States Parties to this Convention:

a. The Inter-American Commission on Human Rights, referred to as "the Commission"; and

b. The Inter-American Court of Human Rights, referred to as "the Court".

CHAPTER VII.   INTER-AMERICAN COMMISSION ON HUMAN RIGHTS

Section 1.   ORGANIZATION

Article 34.   The Inter-American Commission on Human Rights shall be composed of seven members, who shall be persons of high moral character and recognized competence in the field of human rights.

Article 35.   The Commission shall represent all the member countries of the Organization of American States.

Article 36.   1.   The members of the Commission shall be elected in a personal capacity by the General Assembly of the Organization from a list of candidates proposed by the governments of the member states.

2.   Each of those governments may propose up to three candidates, who may be nationals of the states proposing them or of any other member state of the Organization of American States. When a slate of three is proposed, at least one of the candidates shall be a national of a state other than the one proposing the slate.

Article 37.   1.   The members of the Commission shall be elected for a term of four years and may be reelected only once, but the terms of three of the members chosen in the first election shall expire at the end of two years. Immediately following that election the General Assembly shall determine the names of those three members by lot.

2.   No two nationals of the same state may be members of the Commission.

Article 38.   Vacancies that may occur on the Commission for reasons other than the normal expiration of a term shall be filled by the Permanent Council of the Organization in accordance with the provisions of the Statute of the Commission.

Article 39. The Commission shall prepare its Statute, which it shall submit to the General Assembly for approval. It shall establish its own Regulations.

Article 40. Secretariat services for the Commission shall be furnished by the appropriate specialized unit of the General Secretariat of the Organization. This unit shall be provided with the resources required to accomplish the tasks assigned to it by the Commission.

Section 2. FUNCTIONS

Article 41. The main function of the Commission shall be to promote respect for and defense of human rights. In the exercise of its mandate, it shall have the following functions and powers:

a. To develop an awareness of human rights among the peoples of America;

b. To make recommendations to the governments of the member states, when it considers such action advisable, for the adoption of progressive measures in favor of human rights within the framework of their domestic law and constitutional provisions as well as appropriate measures to further the observance of those rights;

c. To prepare such studies or reports as it considers advisable in the performance of its duties;

d. To request the governments of the member states to supply it with information on the measures adopted by them in matters of human rights;

e. To respond, through the General Secretariat of the Organization of American States, to inquiries made by the member states on matters related to human rights and, within the limits of its possibilities, to provide those states with the advisory services they request;

f. To take action on petitions and other communications pursuant to its authority, under the provisions of Articles 44 through 51 of this Convention; and

g. To submit an annual report to the General Assembly of the Organization of American States.

Article 42. The States Parties shall transmit to the Commission a copy of each of the reports and studies that they submit annually to the Executive Committees of the Inter-American Economic and Social Council and the Inter-American Council for Education, Science and Culture, in their respective fields, so that the Commission may watch over the promotion of the rights implicit in the economic, social, educational, scientific, and cultural standards set forth in the Charter of the Organization of American States as amended by the Protocol of Buenos Aires.

Article 43. The States Parties undertake to provide the Commission with such information as it may request of them as to the manner in which their domestic law ensures the effective application of any provisions of this Convention.

Section 3. COMPETENCE

Article 44. Any person or group of persons, or any non governmen tal entity legally recognized in one or more member states of the Organization, may lodge petitions with the Commission containing denunciations or complaints of violation of this Convention by a State Party.

Article 45. 1. Any State Party may, when it deposits its instrument of ratification of or adherence to this Convention, or at any later time, declare that it recognizes the competence of the Commission to receive and examine communications in which a State Party alleges that another State Party has committed a violation of a human right set forth in this Convention.

2. Communications presented by virtue of this article may be admitted and examined only if they are presented by a State Party that has made a declaration recognizing the aforementioned competence of the Commission. The Commission shall not admit any communication against a State Party that has not made such a declaration.

3. A declaration concerning recognition of competence may be made to be valid for an indefinite time, for a specified period, or for a specific case.

4. Declarations shall be deposited with the General Secretariat of the Organization of American States, which shall transmit copies thereof to member states of that Organization.

Article 46. 1. Admission by the Commission of a petition or communication lodged in accordance with Articles 44 or 45 shall be subject to the following requirements:

a. That the remedies under domestic law have been pursued and exhausted in accordance with generally recognized principles of international law;

b. That the petition or communication is lodged within a period of six months from the date on which the party alleging violation of his rights was notified of the final judgment;

c. That the subject of the petition or communication is not pending in another international proceeding for settlement; and

d. That, in the case of Article 44, the petition contains the name, nationality, profession, domicile, and signature of the person or persons or of the legal representative of the entity lodging the petition.

2. The provisions of paragraphs 1*a* and 1*b* of this article shall not be applicable when:

a. The domestic legislation of the state concerned does not afford due process of law for the protection of the right or rights that have allegedly been violated;

b. The party alleging violation of his rights has been denied access to the remedies under domestic law or has been prevented from exhausting them; or

c. There has been unwarranted delay in rendering a final judgment under the aforementioned remedies.

Article 47. The Commission shall consider inadmissible any petition or communication submitted under Articles 44 or 45 if:

a. Any of the requirements indicated in Article 46 has not been met;

b. The petition or communication does not state facts that tend to establish a violation of the rights guaranteed by this Convention;

c. The statements of the petitioner or of the state indicate that the petition or communication is manifestly groundless or obviously out of order; or

d. The petition or communication is substantially the same as one previously studied by the Commission or by another international organization.

Section 4. PROCEDURE

Article 48. 1. When the Commission receives a petition or communication alleging violation of any of the rights protected by this Convention, it shall proceed as follows:

a. If it considers the petition or communication admissible, it shall request information from the government of the state indicated as being responsible for the alleged violations and shall furnish that government a transcript of the pertinent portions of the petition or communication. This information shall be submitted within a reasonable period to be determined by the Commission in accordance with the circumstances of each case.

b. After the information has been received, or after the period established has elapsed and the information has not been received, the Commission shall ascertain whether the grounds for the petition or communication still exist. If they do not, the Commission shall order the record to be closed.

c. The Commission may also declare the petition or communication inadmissible or out of order on the basis of information or evidence subsequently received.

d. If the record has not been closed, the Commission shall, with the knowledge of the parties, examine the matter set forth in the petition or communication in order to verify the facts. If necessary and advisable, the Commission shall carry out an investigation, for the effective conduct of which it shall request, and the states concerned shall furnish to it, all necessary facilities.

e. The Commission may request the states concerned to furnish any pertinent information and, if so requested, shall hear oral statements or receive written statements from the parties concerned.

f. The Commission shall place itself at the disposal of the parties concerned with a view to reaching a friendly settlement of the matter on the basis of respect for the human rights recognized in this Convention.

2.   However, in serious and urgent cases, only the presentation of a petition or communication that fulfills all the formal requirements of admissibility shall be necessary in order for the Commission to conduct an investigation with the prior consent of the state in whose territory a violation has allegedly been committed.

Article 49.   If a friendly settlement has been reached in accordance with paragraph 1*f* of Article 48, the Commission shall draw up a report, which shall be transmitted to the petitioner and to the States Parties to this Convention, and shall then be communicated to the Secretary-General of the Organization of American States for publication. This report shall contain a brief statement of the facts and of the solution reached. If any party in the case so requests, the fullest possible information shall be provided to it.

Article 50.   1.   If a settlement is not reached, the Commission shall, within the time limit established by its Statute, draw up a report setting forth the facts and stating its conclusions. If the report, in whole or in part, does not represent the unanimous agreement of the members of the Commission, any member may attach to it a separate opinion. The written and oral statements made by the parties in accordance with paragraph 1*e* of Article 48 shall also be attached to the report.

2.   The report shall be transmitted to the states concerned, which shall not be at liberty to publish it.

3.   In transmitting the report, the Commission may make such proposals and recommendations as it sees fit.

Article 51.   1.   If, within a period of three months from the date of the transmittal of the report of the Commission to the states concerned, the matter has not either been settled or submitted by the Commission or by the state concerned to the Court and its jurisdiction accepted, the Commission may, by the vote of an absolute majority of its members, set forth its opinion and conclusions concerning the question submitted for its consideration.

2.   Where appropriate, the Commission shall make pertinent recommendations and shall prescribe a period within which the state is to take the measures that are incumbent upon it to remedy the situation examined.

3.   When the prescribed period has expired, the Commission shall decide by the vote of an absolute majority of its members whether the state has taken adequate measures and whether to publish its report.

CHAPTER VIII.   INTER-AMERICAN COURT OF HUMAN RIGHTS

Section 1.   ORGANIZATION

Article 52.   1.   The Court shall consist of seven judges, nationals of the member states of the Organization, elected in an individual capacity from among jurists of the highest moral authority and of recognized competence in the field of human rights, who possess the qualifications required for the exercise of the highest judicial functions in conformity with the law of the state of which they are nationals or of the state that proposes them as candidates.

2.   No two judges may be nationals of the same state.

Article 53.   1.   The judges of the Court shall be elected by secret ballot by an absolute majority vote of the States Parties to the Convention, in the General Assembly of the Organization, from a panel of candidates proposed by those states.

2.   Each of the States Parties may propose up to three candidates, nationals of the state that proposes them or of any other member state of the Organization of American States. When a slate of three is proposed, at least one of the candidates shall be a national of a state other than the one proposing the slate.

Article 54.   1.   The judges of the Court shall be elected for a term of six years and may be reelected only once. The term of three of the judges chosen in the first election shall expire at the end of three years. Immediately after the election, the names of the three judges shall be determined by lot in the General Assembly.

2.   A judge elected to replace a judge whose term has not expired shall complete the term of the latter.

3.   The judges shall continue in office until the expiration of their term. However, they shall continue to serve with regard to cases that they have begun to hear and that are still pending, for which purposes they shall not be replaced by the newly elected judges.

Article 55.   1.   If a judge is a national of any of the States Parties to a case submitted to the Court, he shall retain his right to hear that case.

2. If one of the judges called upon to hear a case should be a national of one of the States Parties to the case, any other State Party in the case may appoint a person of its choice to serve on the Court as an *ad hoc* judge.

3. If among the judges called upon to hear a case none is a national of any of the States Parties to the case, each of the latter may appoint an *ad hoc* judge.

4. An *ad hoc* judge shall possess the qualifications indicated in Article 52.

5. If several States Parties to the Convention should have the same interest in a case, they shall be considered as a single party for purposes of the above provisions. In case of doubt, the Court shall decide.

Article 56. Five judges shall constitute a quorum for the transaction of business by the Court.

Article 57. The Commission shall appear in all cases before the Court.

Article 58. 1. The Court shall have its seat at the place determined by the States Parties to the Convention in the General Assembly of the Organization; however, it may convene in the territory of any member state of the Organization of American States when a majority of the Court consider it desirable, and with the prior consent of the state concerned. The seat of the Court may be changed by the States Parties to the Convention in the General Assembly by a two-thirds vote.

2. The Court shall appoint its own Secretary.

3. The Secretary shall have his office at the place where the Court has its seat and shall attend the meetings that the Court may hold away from its seat.

Article 59. The Court shall establish its Secretariat, which shall function under the direction of the Secretary of the Court, in accordance with the administrative standards of the General Secretariat of the Organization in all respects not incompatible with the independence of the Court. The staff of the Court's Secretariat shall be appointed by the Secretary-General of the Organization, in consultation with the Secretary of the Court.

Article 60. The Court shall draw up its Statute which it shall submit to the General Assembly for approval. It shall adopt its own Rules of Procedure.

Section 2. JURISDICTION AND FUNCTIONS

Article 61. 1. Only the States Parties and the Commission shall have the right to submit a case to the Court.

2.   In order for the Court to hear a case, it is necessary that the procedures set forth in Articles 48 to 50 shall have been completed.

Article 62.   1.   A State Party may, upon depositing its instrument of ratification or adherence to this Convention, or at any subsequent time, declare that it recognizes as binding, *ipso facto*, and not requiring special agreement, the jurisdiction of the Court on all matters relating to the interpretation or application of this Convention.

2.   Such declaration may be made unconditionally, on the condition of reciprocity, for a specified period, or for specific cases. It shall be presented to the Secretary-General of the Organization, who shall transmit copies thereof to the other member states of the Organization and to the Secretary of the Court.

3.   The jurisdiction of the Court shall comprise all cases concerning the interpretation and application of the provisions of this Convention that are submitted to it, provided that the States Parties to the case recognize or have recognized such jurisdiction, whether by special declaration pursuant to the preceding paragraphs, or by a special agreement.

Article 63.   1.   If the Court finds that there has been a violation of a right or freedom protected by this Convention, the Court shall rule that the injured party be ensured the enjoyment of his right or freedom that was violated. It shall also rule, if appropriate, that the consequences of the measure or situation that constituted the breach of such right or freedom be remedied and that fair compensation be paid to the injured party.

2.   In cases of extreme gravity and urgency, and when necessary to avoid irreparable damage to persons, the Court shall adopt such provisional measures as it deems pertinent in the matters it has under consideration. With respect to a case not yet submitted to the Court, it may act at the request of the Commission.

Article 64.   1.   The member states of the Organization may consult the Court regarding the interpretation of this Convention or of other treaties concerning the protection of human rights in the American states. Within their spheres of competence, the organs listed in Chapter X of the Charter of the Organization of American States, as amended by the Protocol of Buenos Aires, may in like manner consult the Court.

2.   The Court, at the request of a member state of the Organization, may provide that state with opinions regarding the compatibility of any of its domestic laws with the aforesaid international instruments.

Article 65.   To each regular session of the General Assembly of the Organization of American States the Court shall submit, for the Assembly's consideration, a report on its work during the previous year. It shall specify, in particular, the cases in which a state has not complied with its judgments, making any pertinent recommendations.

Section 3.   PROCEDURE

Article 66.   1.   Reasons shall be given for the judgment of the Court.

2.   If the judgment does not represent in whole or in part the unanimous opinion of the judges, any judge shall be entitled to have his dissenting or separate opinion attached to the judgment.

Article 67.   The judgment of the Court shall be final and not subject to appeal. In case of disagreement as to the meaning or scope of the judgment, the Court shall interpret it at the request of any of the parties, provided the request is made within ninety days from the date of notification of the judgment.

Article 68.   1.   The States Parties to the Convention undertake to comply with the judgment of the Court in any case to which they are parties.

2.   That part of a judgment that stipulates compensatory damages may be executed in the country concerned in accordance with domestic procedure governing the execution of judgments against the state.

Article 69.   The parties to the case shall be notified of the judgment of the Court and it shall be transmitted to the States Parties to the Convention.

CHAPTER IX.   COMMON PROVISIONS

Article 70.   1.   The judges of the Court and the members of the Commission shall enjoy, from the moment of their election and throughout their term of office, the immunities extended to diplomatic agents in accordance with international law. During the exercise of their official function they shall, in addition, enjoy the diplomatic privileges necessary for the performance of their duties.

2.   At no time shall the judges of the Court or the members of the Commission be held liable for any decisions or opinions issued in the exercise of their functions.

Article 71.   The position of judge of the Court or member of the Commission is incompatible with any other activity that might affect the independence or impartiality of such judge or member, as determined in the respective statutes.

Article 72.   The judges of the Court and the members of the Commission shall receive emoluments and travel allowances in the form and under the conditions set forth in their statutes, with due regard for the importance and independence of their office. Such emoluments and travel allowances shall be determined in the budget of the Organization of American States, which shall also include the expenses of the Court and its Secretariat. To this end, the Court shall draw up its own budget and submit it for approval to the General Assembly through the General Secretariat. The latter may not introduce any changes in it.

Article 73.   The General Assembly may, only at the request of the Commission or the Court, as the case may be, determine sanctions to be applied against members of the Commission or judges of the Court when there are justifiable grounds for such action as set forth in the respective statutes. A vote of a two-thirds majority of the member states of the Organization shall be required for a decision in the case of members of the Commission and, in the case of judges of the Court, a two-thirds majority vote of the States Parties to the Convention shall also be required.

PART III.   GENERAL AND TRANSITORY PROVISIONS

CHAPTER X.   SIGNATURE, RATIFICATION, RESERVATIONS, AMENDMENTS, PROTOCOLS, AND DENUNCIATION

Article 74.   1.   This Convention shall be open for signature and ratification by or adherence of any member state of the Organization of American States.

2.   Ratification of or adherence to this Convention shall be made by the deposit of an instrument of ratification or adherence with the General Secretariat of the Organization of American States. As soon as eleven states have deposited their instruments of ratification or adherence, the Convention shall enter into force. With respect to any state that ratifies or adheres thereafter, the Convention shall enter into force on the date of the deposit of its instrument of ratification or adherence.

3.   The Secretary General shall inform all member states of the Organization of the entry into force of the Convention.

Article 75.   This Convention shall be subject to reservations only in conformity with the provisions of the Vienna Convention on the Law of Treaties signed on May 23, 1969.

Article 76.   1.   Proposals to amend this Convention may be submitted to the General Assembly for the action it deems appropriate by any State Party directly, and by the Commission or the Court through the Secretary General.

2.   Amendments shall enter into force for the states ratifying them on the date when two-thirds of the States Parties to this Convention have deposited their respective instruments of ratification. With respect to the other States Parties, the amendments shall enter into force on the dates on which they deposit their respective instruments of ratification.

Article 77.   1.   In accordance with Article 31, any State Party and the Commission may submit proposed protocols to this Convention for consideration by the States Parties at the General Assembly with a view to gradually including other rights and freedoms within its system of protection.

2.   Each protocol shall determine the manner of its entry into force and shall be applied only among the States Parties to it.

Article 78.   1.   The States Parties may denounce this Convention at the expiration of a five-year period starting from the date of its entry into force and by means of notice given one year in advance. Notice of the denunciation shall be addressed to the Secretary General of the Organization, who shall inform the other States Parties.

2.   Such a denunciation shall not have the effect of releasing the State Party concerned from the obligations contained in this Convention with respect to any act that may constitute a violation of those obligations and that has been taken by that state prior to the effective date of denunciation.

CHAPTER XI.   TRANSITORY PROVISIONS

Section 1.   INTER-AMERICAN COMMISSION ON HUMAN RIGHTS

Article 79.   Upon the entry into force of this Convention, the Secretary General shall, in writing, request each member state of the Organization to present, within ninety days, its candidates for membership on the Inter-American Commission on Human Rights. The Secretary General shall prepare a list in alphabetical order of the candidates presented, and transmit it to the member states of the Organization at least thirty days prior to the next session of the General Assembly.

Article 80.   The members of the Commission shall be elected by secret ballot of the General Assembly from the list of candidates referred to in Article 79. The candidates who obtain the largest number of votes and an absolute majority of the votes of the representatives of the member states shall be declared elected. Should it become necessary to have several ballots in order to elect all the members of the Commission, the candidates who receive the smallest number of votes shall be eliminated successively, in the manner determined by the General Assembly.

Section 2. INTER-AMERICAN COURT OF HUMAN RIGHTS

Article 81. Upon the entry into force of this Convention, the Secretary General shall, in writing, request each State Party to present, within ninety days, its candidates for membership on the Inter-American Court of Human Rights. The Secretary General shall prepare a list in alphabetical order of the candidates presented and transmit it to the States Parties at least thirty days prior to the next session of the General Assembly.

Article 82. The judges of the Court shall be elected from the list of candidates referred to in Article 81, by secret ballot of the States Parties to the Convention in the General Assembly. The candidates who obtain the largest number of votes and an absolute majority of the votes of the representatives of the States Parties shall be declared elected. Should it become necessary to have several ballots in order to elect all the judges of the Court, the candidates who receive the smallest number of votes shall be eliminated successively, in the manner determined by the States Parties.

3. Additional Protocol to the American Convention on Human Rights in the Area of Economic, Social and Cultural Rights—"Protocol of San Salvador"

Adopted at San Salvador on 17 November 1988

PREAMBLE

The States Parties to the American Convention on Human Rights—"Pact of San José, Costa Rica",

Reaffirming their intention to consolidate in this hemisphere, within the framework of democratic institutions, a system of personal liberty and social justice based on respect for the essential rights of man;

Recognizing that the essential rights of man are not derived from one's being a national of a certain State, but are based upon attributes of the human person, for which reason they merit international protection in the form of a convention reinforcing or complementing the protection provided by the domestic law of the American States;

Considering the close relationship that exists between economic, social and cultural rights, and civil and political rights, in that the different categories of rights constitute an indivisible whole based on the recognition of the dignity of the human person, for which reason both require permanent protection and promotion if they are to be fully realized, and the violation of some rights in favor of the realization of others can never be justified;

Recognizing the benefits that stem from the promotion and development of cooperation among States and international relations;

Recalling that, in accordance with the Universal Declaration of Human Rights and the American Convention on Human Rights, the ideal of free human beings enjoying freedom from fear and want can only be achieved if conditions are created whereby everyone may enjoy his economic, social and cultural rights as well as his civil and political rights;

Bearing in mind that, although fundamental economic, social and cultural rights have been recognized in earlier international instruments of both world and regional scope, it is essential that those rights be reaffirmed, developed, perfected and protected in order to consolidate in America, on the basis of full respect for the rights of the individual, the democratic representative form of government as well as the right of its peoples to development, self-determination, and the free disposal of their wealth and natural resources; and

Considering that the American Convention on Human Rights provides that draft additional protocols to that Convention may be submitted for consideration to the States Parties, meeting together on the occasion of the General Assembly of the Organization of American States, for the purpose of gradually incorporating other rights and freedoms into the protective system thereof,

Have agreed upon the following Additional Protocol to the American Convention on Human Rights—"Protocol of San Salvador":

Article 1.   Obligation to adopt measures

The States Parties to this Additional Protocol to the American Convention on Human Rights undertake to adopt the necessary measures, both domestically and through cooperation among the States, especially economic and technical, to the extent allowed by their available resources, and taking into account their degree of development, for the purpose of achieving progressively and pursuant to their internal legislations, the full observance of the rights recognized in this Protocol.

Article 2.   Obligation to enact domestic legislation

If the exercise of the rights set forth in this Protocol is not already guaranteed by legislative or other provisions, the States Parties undertake to adopt, in accordance with their constitutional processes and the provisions of this Protocol, such legislative or other measures as may be necessary for making those rights a reality.

Article 3.   Obligation of non-discrimination

The States Parties to this Protocol undertake to guarantee the exercise of the rights set forth herein without discrimination of any kind for reasons related to race, color, sex, language, religion, political or other opinions, national or social origin, economic status, birth or any other social condition.

Article 4.   Inadmissibility of restrictions

A right which is recognized or in effect in a State by virtue of its internal legislation or international conventions may not be restricted or curtailed on the pretext that this Protocol does not recognize the right or recognizes it to a lesser degree.

Article 5. Scope of restrictions and limitations

The States Parties may establish restrictions and limitations on the enjoyment and exercise of the rights established herein by means of laws promulgated for the purpose of preserving the general welfare in a democratic society only to the extent that they are not incompatible with the purpose and reason underlying those rights.

Article 6. Right to work

1. Everyone has the right to work, which includes the opportunity to secure the means for living a dignified and decent existence by performing a freely elected or accepted lawful activity.

2. The States Parties undertake to adopt measures that will make the right to work fully effective, especially with regard to the achievement of full employment, vocational guidance, and the development of technical and vocational training projects, in particular those directed to the disabled. The States Parties also undertake to implement and strengthen programs that help to ensure suitable family care, so that women may enjoy a real opportunity to exercise the right to work.

Article 7. Just, equitable and satisfactory conditions of work

The States Parties to this Protocol recognize that the right to work to which the foregoing article refers presupposes that everyone shall enjoy that right under just, equitable and satisfactory conditions, which the States Parties undertake to guarantee in their internal legislation, particularly with respect to:

a. Remuneration which guarantees, as a minimum, to all workers dignified and decent living conditions for them and their families and fair and equal wages for equal work, without distinction;

b. The right to every worker to follow his vocation and to devote himself to the activity that best fulfils his expectations and to change employment in accordance with the pertinent national regulations;

c. The right of every worker to promotion or upward mobility in his employment, for which purpose account shall be taken of his qualifications, competence, integrity and seniority;

d. Stability of employment, subject to the nature of each industry and occupation and the causes for just separation. In cases of unjustified dismissal, the worker shall have the right to indemnity or to reinstatement on the job or any other benefits provided by domestic legislation;

e. Safety and hygiene at work;

f. The prohibition of night work or unhealthy or dangerous working conditions and, in general, of all work which jeopardizes health, safety or morals, for persons under 18 years of age. As regards minors under the age of 16, the work day shall be subordinated to the provisions regarding compulsory education and in no case shall work constitute an impediment to school attendance or a limitation on benefiting from education received;

g. A reasonable limitation of working hours, both daily and weekly. The days shall be shorter in the case of dangerous or unhealthy work or of night work;

h. Rest, leisure and paid vacations as well as remuneration for national holidays.

Article 8.   *Trade union rights*

1.   The States Parties shall ensure:

a. The right of workers to organize trade unions and to join the union of their choice for the purpose of protecting and promoting their interests. As an extension of that right, the States Parties shall permit trade unions to establish national federations or confederations, or to affiliate with those that already exist, as well as to form international trade union organizations and to affiliate with that of their choice. The States Parties shall also permit trade unions, federations and confederations to function freely;

b. The right to strike.

2.   The exercise of the rights set forth above may be subject only to restrictions established by law, provided that such restrictions are characteristic of a democratic society and necessary for safeguarding public order or for protecting public health or morals or the rights and freedoms of others. Members of the armed forces and the police and of other essential public services shall be subject to limitations and restrictions established by law.

3.   No one may be compelled to belong to a trade union.

Article 9.   *Right to social security*

1.   Everyone shall have the right to social security protecting him from the consequences of old age and of disability which prevents him, physically or mentally, from securing the means for a dignified and decent existence. In the event of the death of a beneficiary, social security benefits shall be applied to his dependents.

2.   In the case of persons who are employed, the right to social security shall cover at least medical care and an allowance or retirement benefit in the case of work accidents or occupational disease and, in the case of women, paid maternity leave before and after childbirth.

Article 10.   Right to health

1.   Everyone shall have the right to health, understood to mean the enjoyment of the highest level of physical, mental and social well-being.

2.   In order to ensure the exercise of the right to health, the States Parties agree to recognize health as a public good and, particularly, to adopt the following measures to ensure that right:

a.   Primary health care, that is, essential health care made available to all individuals and families in the community;

b.   Extension of the benefits of health services to all individuals subject to the State's jurisdiction;

c.   Universal immunization against the principal infectious diseases;

d.   Prevention and treatment of endemic, occupational and other diseases;

e.   Education of the population on the prevention and treatment of health problems; and

f.   Satisfaction of the health needs of the highest risk groups and of those whose poverty makes them the most vulnerable.

Article 11.   Right to a healthy environment

1.   Everyone shall have the right to live in a healthy environment and to have access to basic public services.

2.   The States Parties shall promote the protection, preservation and improvement of the environment.

Article 12.   Right to food

1.   Everyone has the right to adequate nutrition which guarantees the possibility of enjoying the highest level of physical, emotional and intellectual development.

2.   In order to promote the exercise of this right and eradicate malnutrition, the States Parties undertake to improve methods of production, supply and distribution of food, and to this end, agree to promote greater international cooperation in support of the relevant national policies.

Article 13.   Right to education

1.   Everyone has the right to education.

2.   The States Parties to this Protocol agree that education should be directed towards the full development of the human personality and human dignity and should strengthen respect for human rights, ideological pluralism, fundamental freedoms, justice and peace. They further agree that edu-

cation ought to enable everyone to participate effectively in a democratic and pluralistic society and achieve a decent existence and should foster understanding, tolerance and friendship among all nations and all racial, ethnic or religious groups and promote activities for the maintenance of peace.

3.   The States Parties to this Protocol recognize that in order to achieve the full exercise of the right to education:

a.   Primary education should be compulsory and accessible to all without cost;

b.   Secondary education in its different forms, including technical and vocational secondary education, should be made generally available and accessible to all by every appropriate means, and in particular, by the progressive introduction of free education;

c.   Higher education should be made equally accessible to all on the basis of individual capacity, by every appropriate means, and in particular, by the progressive introduction of free education;

d.   Basic education should be encouraged or intensified as far as possible for those persons who have not received or completed the whole cycle of primary instruction;

e.   Programs of special education should be established for the handicapped, so as to provide special instruction and training to persons with physical disabilities or mental deficiencies.

4.   In conformity with the domestic legislation of the States Parties, parents should have the right to select the type of education to be given to their children, provided that it conforms to the principles set forth above.

5.   Nothing in this Protocol shall be interpreted as a restriction of the freedom of individuals and entities to establish and direct educational institutions in accordance with the domestic legislation of the States Parties.

Article 14.   *Right to the benefits of culture*

1.   The States Parties to this Protocol recognize the right of everyone:

a.   To take part in the cultural and artistic life of the community;

b.   To enjoy the benefits of scientific and technological progress;

c.   To benefit from the protection of moral and material interests deriving from any scientific, literary or artistic production of which he is the author.

2.   The steps to be taken by the States Parties to this Protocol to ensure the full exercise of this right shall include those necessary for the conservation, development and dissemination of science, culture and art.

3.   The States Parties to this Protocol undertake to respect the freedom indispensable for scientific research and creative activity.

4.   The States Parties to this Protocol recognize the benefits to be derived from the encouragement and development of international cooperation and relations in the fields of science, arts and culture, and accordingly agree to foster greater international cooperation in these fields.

Article 15.   Right to the formation and the protection of families

1.   The family is the natural and fundamental element of society and ought to be protected by the State, which should see to the improvement of its spiritual and material conditions.

2.   Everyone has the right to form a family, which shall be exercised in accordance with the provisions of the pertinent domestic legislation.

3.   The States Parties hereby undertake to accord adequate protection to the family unit and in particular:

a. To provide special care and assistance to mothers during a reasonable period before and after childbirth;

b. To guarantee adequate nutrition for children at the nursing stage and during school attendance years;

c. To adopt special measures for the protection of adolescents in order to ensure the full development of their physical, intellectual and moral capacities;

d. To undertake special programs of family training so as to help create a stable and positive environment in which children will receive and develop the values of understanding, solidarity, respect and responsibility.

Article 16.   Rights of children

Every child, whatever his parentage, has the right to the protection that his status as a minor requires from his family, society and the State. Every child has the right to grow under the protection and responsibility of his parents; save in exceptional, judicially recognized circumstances, a child of young age ought not to be separated from his mother. Every child has the right to free and compulsory education, at least in the elementary phase, and to continue his training at higher levels of the educational system.

Article 17.   Protection of the elderly

Everyone has the right to special protection in old age. With this in view the States Parties agree to take progressively the necessary steps to make this right a reality and, particularly, to:

a. Provide suitable facilities, as well as food and specialized medical care, for elderly individuals who lack them and are unable to provide them for themselves;

b. Undertake work programs specifically designed to give the elderly the opportunity to engage in a productive activity suited to their abilities and consistent with their vocations or desires;

c. Foster the establishment of social organizations aimed at improving the quality of life for the elderly.

Article 18.   Protection of the handicapped

Everyone affected by a diminution of his physical or mental capacities is entitled to receive special attention designed to help him achieve the greatest possible development of his personality. The States Parties agree to adopt such measures as may be necessary for this purpose and, especially, to:

a. Undertake programs specifically aimed at providing the handicapped with the resources and environment needed for attaining this goal, including work programs consistent with their possibilities and freely accepted by them or their legal representatives, as the case may be;

b. Provide special training to the families of the handicapped in order to help them solve the problems of coexistence and convert them into active agents in the physical, mental and emotional development of the latter;

c. Include the consideration of solutions to specific requirements arising from needs of this group as a priority component of their urban development plans;

d. Encourage the establishment of social groups in which the handicapped can be helped to enjoy a fuller life.

Article 19.   Means of protection

1.   Pursuant to the provisions of this article and the corresponding rules to be formulated for this purpose by the General Assembly of the Organization of American States, the States Parties to this Protocol undertake to submit periodic reports on the progressive measures they have taken to ensure due respect for the rights set forth in this Protocol.

2.   All reports shall be submitted to the Secretary General of the OAS, who shall transmit them to the Inter-American Economic and Social Council and the Inter-American Council for Education, Science and Culture so that they may examine them in accordance with the provisions of this article. The Secretary General shall send a copy of such reports to the Inter-American Commission on Human Rights.

3.   The Secretary General of the Organization of American States shall also transmit to the specialized organizations of the inter-American system of which the States Parties to the present Protocol are members, copies or pertinent portions of the reports submitted, insofar as they relate to

matters within the purview of those organizations, as established by their constituent instruments.

4. The specialized organizations of the inter-American system may submit reports to the Inter-American Economic and Social Council and the Inter-American Council for Education, Science and Culture relative to compliance with the provisions of the present Protocol in their fields of activity.

5. The annual reports submitted to the General Assembly by the Inter-American Economic and Social Council and the Inter-American Council for Education, Science and Culture shall contain a summary of the information received from the States Parties to the present Protocol and the specialized organizations concerning the progressive measures adopted in order to ensure respect for the rights acknowledged in the Protocol itself and the general recommendations they consider to be appropriate in this respect.

6. Any instance in which the rights established in paragraph *a)* of Article 8 and in Article 13 are violated by action directly attributable to a State Party to this Protocol may give rise, through participation of the Inter-American Commission on Human Rights and, when applicable, of the Inter-American Court of Human Rights, to application of the system of individual petitions governed by Articles 44 through 51 and 61 through 69 of the American Convention on Human Rights.

7. Without prejudice to the provisions of the preceding paragraph, the Inter-American Commission on Human Rights may formulate such observations and recommendations as it deems pertinent concerning the status of the economic, social and cultural rights established in the present Protocol in all or some of the States Parties, which it may include in its Annual Report to the General Assembly or in a special report, whichever it considers more appropriate.

8. The Councils and the Inter-American Commission on Human Rights, in discharging the functions conferred upon them in this article, shall take into account the progressive nature of the observance of the rights subject to protection by this Protocol.

Article 20. *Reservations*

The States Parties may, at the time of approval, signature, ratification or accession, make reservations to one or more specific provisions of this Protocol, provided that such reservations are not incompatible with the object and purpose of the Protocol.

Article 21. *Signature, ratification or accession.*
Entry into effect

1. This Protocol shall remain open to signature and ratification or accession by any State Party to the American Convention on Human Rights.

2.   Ratification of or accession to this Protocol shall be effected by depositing an instrument of ratification or accession with the General Secretariat of the Organization of American States.

3.   The Protocol shall enter into effect when eleven States have deposited their respective instruments of ratification or accession.

4.   The Secretary General shall notify all the member States of the Organization of American States of the entry of the Protocol into effect.

Article 22.   Inclusion of other rights and expansion of those recognized

1.   Any State Party and the Inter-American Commission on Human Rights may submit for the consideration of the States Parties meeting on the occasion of the General Assembly proposed amendments to include the recognition of other rights or freedoms or to extend or expand rights or freedoms recognized in this Protocol.

2.   Such amendments shall enter into effect for the States that ratify them on the date of deposit of the instrument of ratification corresponding to the number representing two thirds of the States Parties to this Protocol. For all other States Parties they shall enter into effect on the date on which they deposit their respective instrument of ratification.

4. Protocol to the American Convention on Human Rights to Abolish the Death Penalty

Adopted at Asunción on 8 June 1990

PREAMBLE

The States Parties to this Protocol,

Considering:

That Article 4 of the American Convention on Human Rights recognizes the right to life and restricts the application of the death penalty;

That everyone has the inalienable right to respect for his life, a right that cannot be suspended for any reason;

That the tendency among the American States is to be in favor of abolition of the death penalty;

That application of the death penalty has irrevocable consequences, forecloses the correction of judicial error, and precludes any possibility of changing or rehabilitating those convicted;

That the abolition of the death penalty helps to ensure more effective protection of the right to life;

That an international agreement must be arrived at that will entail a progressive development of the American Convention on Human Rights; and

That States Parties to the American Convention on Human Rights have expressed their intention to adopt an international agreement with a view to consolidating the practice of not applying the death penalty in the Americas,

Have agreed to sign the following Protocol to the American Convention on Human Rights to abolish the death penalty

Article 1

The States Parties to this Protocol shall not apply the death penalty in their territory to any person subject to their jurisdiction.

47

Article 2

1.   No reservations may be made to this Protocol. However, at the time of ratification or accession, the States Parties to this instrument may declare that they reserve the right to apply the death penalty in wartime, in accordance with international law, for extremely serious crimes of a military nature.

2.   The State Party making this reservation shall, upon ratification or accession, inform the Secretary General of the Organization of American States of the pertinent provisions of its national legislation applicable in wartime, as referred to in the preceding paragraph.

3.   Said State Party shall notify the Secretary General of the Organization of American States of the beginning or end of any state of war in effect in its territory.

Article 3

This Protocol shall be open for signature and ratification or accession by any State Party to the American Convention on Human Rights.

Ratification of this Protocol or accession thereto shall be made through the deposit of an instrument of ratification or accession with the General Secretariat of the Organization of American States.

Article 4

This Protocol shall enter into force among the States that ratify or accede to it when they deposit their respective instruments of ratification or accession with the General Secretariat of the Organization of American States.

5. Inter-American Convention to Prevent and Punish Torture

Adopted at Cartagena, Colombia, on 9 December 1985

ENTRY INTO FORCE: 28 February 1987, in accordance with article 22

The American States signatory to the present Convention,

Aware of the provision of the American Convention on Human Rights that no one shall be subjected to torture or to cruel, inhuman, or degrading punishment or treatment;

Reaffirming that all acts of torture or any other cruel, inhuman, or degrading treatment or punishment constitute an offense against human dignity and a denial of the principles set forth in the Charter of the Organization of American States and in the Charter of the United Nations and are violations of the fundamental human rights and freedoms proclaimed in the American Declaration of the Rights and Duties of Man and the Universal Declaration of Human Rights;

Nothing that, in order for the pertinent rules contained in the aforementioned global and regional instruments to take effect, it is necessary to draft an Inter-American Convention that prevents and punishes torture;

Reaffirming their purpose of consolidating in this hemisphere the conditions that make for recognition of and respect for the inherent dignity of man, and ensure the full exercise of his fundamental rights and freedoms,

Have agreed upon the following:

Article 1

The State Parties undertake to prevent and punish torture in accordance with the terms of this Convention.

Article 2

For the purposes of this Convention, torture shall be understood to be any act intentionally performed whereby physical or mental pain or suffering is inflicted on a person for purposes of criminal investigation, as a means of intimidation, as personal punishment, as a preventive measure, as a penalty, or for any other purpose. Torture shall also be understood to be the use of methods upon a person intended to obliterate the personality of the victim or to diminish his physical or mental capacities, even if they do not cause physical pain or mental anguish.

The concept of torture shall not include physical or mental pain or suffering that is inherent in or solely the consequence of lawful measures, provided that they do not include the performance of the acts or use of the methods referred to in this article.

Article 3

The following shall be held guilty of the crime of torture:

a. A public servant or employee who acting in that capacity orders, instigates or induces the use of torture, or who directly commits it or who, being able to prevent it, fails to do so.

b. A person who at the instigation of a public servant or employee mentioned in subparagraph (*a*) orders, instigates or induces the use of torture, directly commits it or is an accomplice thereto.

Article 4

The fact of having acted under orders of a superior shall not provide exemption from the corresponding criminal liability.

Article 5

The existence of circumstances such as a state of war, threat of war, state of siege or of emergency, domestic disturbance or strife, suspension of constitutional guarantees, domestic political instability, or other public emergencies or disasters shall not be invoked or admitted as justification for the crime of torture.

Neither the dangerous character of the detainee or prisoner, nor the lack of security of the prison establishment or penitentiary shall justify torture.

Article 6

In accordance with the terms of Article 1, the States Parties shall take effective measures to prevent and punish torture within their jurisdiction.

The States Parties shall ensure that all acts of torture and attempts to commit torture are offenses under their criminal law and shall make such acts punishable by severe penalties that take into account their serious nature.

The States Parties likewise shall take effective measures to prevent and punish other cruel, inhuman, or degrading treatment or punishment within their jurisdiction.

Article 7

The States Parties shall take measures so that, in the training of police officers and other public officials responsible for the custody of persons temporarily or definitively deprived of their freedom, special emphasis shall be put on the prohibition of the use of torture in interrogation, detention, or arrest.

The States Parties likewise shall take similar measures to prevent other cruel, inhuman, or degrading treatment or punishment.

Article 8

The States Parties shall guarantee that any person making an accusation of having been subjected to torture within their jurisdiction shall have the right to an impartial examination of his case.

Likewise, if there is an accusation or well-grounded reason to believe that an act of torture has been committed within their jurisdiction, the States Parties shall guarantee that their respective authorities will proceed properly and immediately to conduct an investigation into the case and to initiate, whenever appropriate, the corresponding criminal process.

After all the domestic legal procedures of the respective State and the corresponding appeals have been exhausted, the case may be submitted to the international fora whose competence has been recognized by that State.

Article 9

The States Parties undertake to incorporate into their national laws regulations guaranteeing suitable compensation for victims of torture.

None of the provisions of this article shall affect the right to receive compensation that the victim or other persons may have by virtue of existing national legislation.

Article 10

No statement that is verified as having been obtained through torture shall be admissible as evidence in a legal proceeding, except in a legal action taken against a person or persons accused of having elicited it through acts of torture, and only as evidence that the accused obtained such statement by such means.

Article 11

The States Parties shall take the necessary steps to extradite anyone accused of having committed the crime of torture or sentenced for commission of that crime, in accordance with their respective national laws on extradition and their international commitments on this matter.

Article 12

Every State Party shall take the necessary measures to establish its jurisdiction over the crime described in this Convention in the following cases:

   a. When torture has been committed within its jurisdiction;

   b. When the alleged criminal is a national of that State; or

   c. When the victim is a national of that State and it so deems appropriate.

Every State Party shall also take the necessary measures to establish its jurisdiction over the crime described in this Convention when the alleged criminal is within the area under its jurisdiction and it is not appropriate to extradite him in accordance with Article 11.

This Convention does not exclude criminal jurisdiction exercised in accordance with domestic law.

Article 13

The crime referred to in Article 2 shall be deemed to be included among the extraditable crimes in every extradition treaty entered into between States Parties. The States Parties undertake to include the crime of torture as an extraditable offense in every extradition treaty to be concluded between them.

Every State Party that makes extradition conditional on the existence of a treaty may, if it receives a request for extradition from another State Party with which it has no extradition treaty, consider this Convention as the legal basis for extradition in respect of the crime of torture. Extradition shall be subject to the other conditions that may be required by the law of the requested State.

States Parties which do not make extradition conditional on the existence of a treaty shall recognize such crimes as extraditable offenses between themselves, subject to the conditions required by the law of the requested State.

Extradition shall not be granted nor shall the person sought be returned when there are grounds to believe that his life is in danger, that he will be subjected to torture or to cruel, inhuman or degrading treatment, or that he will be tried by special or ad hoc courts in the requesting State.

Article 14

When a State Party does not grant the extradition, the case shall be submitted to its competent authorities as if the crime had been committed within its jurisdiction, for the purposes of investigation, and when appropriate, for criminal action, in accordance with its national law. Any decision adopted by these authorities shall be communicated to the State that has requested the extradition.

Article 15

No provision of this Convention may be interpreted as limiting the right of asylum, when appropriate, nor as altering the obligations of the States Parties in the matter of extradition.

Article 16

This Convention shall not limit the provisions of the American Convention on Human Rights, other conventions on the subject, or the Statutes of the Inter-American Commission on Human Rights, with respect to the crime of torture.

Article 17

The States Parties undertake to inform the Inter-American Commission on Human Rights of any legislative, judicial, administrative, or other measures they adopt in application of this Convention.

In keeping with its duties and responsibilities; the Inter-American Commission on Human Rights will endeavor in its annual report to analyze the existing situation in the member States of the Organization of American States in regard to the prevention and elimination of torture.

Article 18

This Convention is open to signature by the member States of the Organization of American States.

Article 19

This Convention is subject to ratification. The instruments of ratification shall be deposited with the General Secretariat of the Organization of American States.

Article 20

This Convention is open to accession by any other American State. The instruments of accession shall be deposited with the General Secretariat of the Organization of American States.

Article 21

The States Parties may, at the time of approval, signature, ratification, or accession, make reservations to this Convention, provided that such reservations are not incompatible with the object and purpose of the Convention and concern one or more specific provisions.

Article 22

This Convention shall enter into force on the thirtieth day following the date on which the second instrument of ratification is deposited. For each State ratifying or acceding to the Convention after the second instrument of ratification has been deposited, the Convention shall enter into force on the thirtieth day following the date on which that State deposits its instrument of ratification or accession.

Article 23

This Convention shall remain in force indefinitely, but may be denounced by any State Party. The instrument of denunciation shall be deposited with the General Secretariat of the Organization of American States. After one year from the date of deposit of the instrument of denunciation, this Convention shall cease to be in effect for the denouncing State but shall remain in force for the remaining States Parties.

Article 24

The original instrument of this Convention, the English, French, Portuguese and Spanish texts of which are equally authentic, shall be deposited with the General Secretariat of the Organization of American States, which shall send a certified copy to the Secretariat of the United Nations for registration and publication, in accordance with the provisions of Article 102 of the United Nations Charter. The General Secretariat of the Organization of American States shall notify the member States of the Organization and the States that have acceded to the Convention of signatures and of deposits of instruments of ratification, accession and denunciation, as well as reservations, if any.

6. Inter-American Convention on the Forced Disappearance of Persons

The member States of the Organization of American States,

Disturbed by the persistence of the forced disappearance of persons;

Reaffirming that the true meaning of American solidarity and good neighborliness can be none other than that of consolidating in this Hemisphere, in the framework of democratic institutions, a system of individual freedom and social justice based on respect for essential human rights;

Considering that the forced disappearance of persons is an affront to the conscience of the Hemisphere and a grave and abominable offense against the inherent dignity of the human being, and one that contradicts the principles and purposes enshrined in the Charter of the Organization of American States;

Considering that the forced disappearance of persons violates numerous non-derogable and essential human rights enshrined in the American Convention on Human Rights, in the American Declaration of the Rights and Duties of Man, and in the Universal Declaration of Human Rights;

Recalling that the international protection of human rights is in the form of a convention reinforcing or complementing the protection provided by domestic law and is based upon the attributes of the human personality;

Reaffirming that the systematic practice of the forced disappearance of persons constitutes a crime against humanity;

Hoping that this Convention may help to prevent, punish, and eliminate the forced disappearance of persons in the Hemisphere and make a decisive contribution to the protection of human rights and the rule of law,

Resolve to adopt the following Inter-American Convention on the Forced Disappearance of Persons:

Article 1

The States Parties to this Convention undertake:

a. Not to practice, permit, or tolerate the forced disappearance of persons, even in states of emergency or suspension of individual guarantees;

b. To punish within their jurisdictions those persons who commit or attempt to commit the crime of forced disappearance of persons and their accomplices and accessories;

c. To cooperate with one another in helping to prevent, punish and eliminate the forced disappearance of persons;

d. To take legislative, administrative, judicial, and any other measures necessary to comply with the commitments undertaken in this Convention.

Article II

For the purposes of this Convention, forced disappearance is considered to be the act of depriving a person or persons of his or their freedom, in whatever way, perpetrated by agents of the state or by persons or groups of persons acting with the authorization, support, or acquiescence of the state, followed by an absence of information or a refusal to acknowledge that deprivation of freedom or to give information on the whereabouts of that person, thereby impeding his or her recourse to the applicable legal remedies and procedural guarantees.

Article III

The States Parties undertake to adopt, in accordance with their constitutional procedures, the legislative measures that may be needed to define the forced disappearance of persons as an offense and to impose an appropriate punishment commensurate with its extreme gravity. This offense shall be deemed continuous or permanent as long as the fate or whereabouts of the victim has not been determined.

The States Parties may establish mitigating circumstances for persons who have participated in acts constituting forced disappearance when they help to cause the victim to reappear alive or provide information that sheds light on the force disappearance of a person.

Article IV

The acts constituting the forced disappearance of persons shall be considered offenses in every State Party. Consequently, each State Party shall take measures to establish its jurisdiction over such cases in the following instances:

a. When the forced disappearance of persons or any act constituting such offense was committed within its jurisdiction;

b. When the accused is a national of that state;

c. When the victim is a national of that state and that state sees fit to do so.

Every State Party shall, moreover, take the necessary measures to establish its jurisdiction over the crime described in this Convention when the alleged criminal is within its territory and it does not proceed to extradite him.

This Convention does not authorize any State Party to undertake, in the territory of another State Party, the exercise of jurisdiction or the performance of functions that are placed within the exclusive purview of the authorities of that other Party by its domestic law.

Article V

The forced disappearance of persons shall not be considered a political offense for purposes of extradition.

The forced disappearance of persons shall be deemed to be included among the extraditable offenses in every extradition treaty entered into between States Parties.

The States Parties undertake to include the offense of forced disappearance as one which is extraditable in every extradition treaty to be concluded between them in the future.

Every State Party that makes extradition conditional on the existence of a treaty and receives a request for extradition from another State Party with which it has no extradition treaty may consider this Convention as the necessary legal basis for extradition with respect to the offense of forced disappearance.

State Parties which do not make extradition conditional on the existence of a treaty shall recognize such offense as extraditable, subject to the conditions imposed by the law of the requested state.

Extradition shall be subject to the provisions set forth in the constitution and other laws of the requested state.

Article VI

When a State Party does not grant the extradition, the case shall be submitted to its competent authorities as if the offense had been committed within its jurisdiction, for the purposes of investigation and when appropriate, for criminal action, in accordance with its national law. Any decision adopted by these authorities shall be communicated to the state that has requested the extradition.

Article VII

Criminal prosecution for the forced disappearance of persons and the penalty judicially imposed on its perpetrator shall not be subject to statutes of limitations.

However, if there should be a norm of a fundamental character preventing application of the stipulation contained in the previous paragraph, the period of limitation shall be equal to that which applies to the gravest crime in the domestic laws of the corresponding State Party.

Article VIII

The defense of due obedience to superior orders or instructions that stipulate, authorize, or encourage forced disappearance shall not be admitted. All persons who receive such orders have the right and duty not to obey them.

The States Parties shall ensure that the training of public law-enforcement personnel or officials includes the necessary education on the offense of forced disappearance of persons.

Article IX

Persons alleged to be responsible for the acts constituting the offense of forced disappearance of persons may be tried only on the competent jurisdictions of ordinary law in each state, to the exclusion of all other special jurisdictions, particularly military jurisdictions.

The acts constituting forced disappearance shall not be deemed to have been committed in the course of military duties.

Privileges, immunities, or special dispensations shall not be admitted in such trials, without prejudice to the provisions set forth in the Vienna Convention on Diplomatic Relations.

Article X

In no case may exceptional circumstances such as a state of war, the threat of war, internal political instability, or any other public emergency be invoked to justify the forced disappearance of persons. In such cases, the right to expeditious and effective judicial procedures and recourse shall be retained as a means of determining the whereabouts or state of health of a person who has been deprived of freedom, or of identifying the official who ordered or carried out such deprivation of freedom.

In pursuing such procedures or recourse, and in keeping with applicable domestic law, the competent judicial authorities shall have free and immediate access to all detention centers and to each of their units, and to all places where there is reason to believe the disappeared person might be found, including places that are subject to military jurisdiction.

Article XI

Every person deprived of liberty shall be held in an officially recognized place of detention and be brought before a competent judicial authority without delay, in accordance with applicable domestic law.

The State Parties shall establish and maintain official up-to-date registries of their detainees and, in accordance with their domestic law, shall make them available to relatives, judges, attorneys, any other person having a legitimate interest, and other authorities.

Article XII

The States Parties shall give each other mutual assistance in the search for, identification, location, and return of minors who have been removed to another state or detained therein as a consequence of the forced disappearance of their parents or guardians.

Article XIII

For the purposes of this Convention, the processing of petitions or communications presented to the Inter-American Commission on Human Rights alleging the forced disappearance of persons shall be subject to the procedures established in the American Convention on Human Rights and to the Statute and Regulations of the Inter-American Commission on Human Rights and to the Statute and Rules of Procedure of the Inter-American Court of Human Rights, including the provisions on precautionary measures.

Article XIV

Without prejudice to the provisions of the preceding article, when the Inter-American Commission on Human Rights receives a petition or communication regarding an alleged forced disappearance, its Executive Secretariat shall urgently and confidentially address the respective government and shall request that government to provide as soon as possible information as to the whereabouts of the allegedly disappeared person together with any other information it considers pertinent, and such request shall be without prejudice as to the admissibility of the petition.

Article XV

None of the provisions of this Convention shall be interpreted as limiting other bilateral or multilateral treaties or other agreements signed by the Parties.

This Convention shall not apply to the international armed conflicts governed by the 1949 Geneva Convention and its Protocol concerning protection of wounded, sick, and shipwrecked members of the armed forces; and prisoners of war and civilians in time of war.

Article XVI

This Convention is open for signature by the member states of the Organization of American States.

Article XVII

This Convention is subject to ratification. The instruments of ratification shall be deposited with the General Secretariat of the Organization of American States.

Article XVIII

This Convention shall be open to accession by any other state. The instruments of accession shall be deposited with the General Secretariat of the Organization of American States.

Article XIX

The states may make reservations with respect to this Convention when signing, ratifying or acceding to it, unless such reservations are incompatible with the object and purpose of the Convention and as long as they refer to one or more specific provisions.

Article XX

This Convention shall enter into force for the ratifying states on the thirtieth day from the date of deposit of the second instrument of ratification.

For each state ratifying or acceding to the Convention after the second instrument of ratification has been deposited, the Convention shall enter into force on the thirtieth day from the date on which that state deposited its instrument of ratification or accession.

Article XXI

This Convention shall remain in force indefinitely, but may be denounced by any State Party. The instrument of denunciation shall be deposited with the General Secretariat of the Organization of American States. The Convention shall cease to be in effect for the denouncing state and shall remain in force for the other State Parties one year from the date of deposit of the instrument of denunciation.

Article XXII

The original instrument of this Convention, the Spanish, English, Portuguese and French texts of which are equally authentic, shall be deposited with the General Secretariat of the Organization of American States, which shall forward certified copies thereof to the United Nations Secretariat, for registration and publication, in accordance with Article 102 of the Charter of the United Nations. The General Secretariat of the Organization of American States shall notify member states of the Organization and states acceding to the Convention of the signatures and deposit of instruments of ratification, accession or denunciation, as well as of any reservations that may be expressed.

IN WITNESS WHEREOF the undersigned Plenipotentiaries, being duly authorized thereto by their respective governments, have signed this Convention, which shall be called the "Inter-American Convention on the Forced Disappearance of Persons."

DONE in the city of Belen, Brazil, the ninth of June in the year one thousand nine hundred ninety-four.

7. Inter-American Convention on the Prevention, Punishment and Eradication of Violence against Women "Convention of Belem do Para"

The State Parties to this Convention,

Recognizing that full respect for human rights has been enshrined in the American Declaration of the Rights and Duties of Man and the Universal Declaration of Human Rights, and reaffirmed in other international and regional instruments;

Affirming that violence against women constitutes a violation of their human rights and fundamental freedoms, and impairs or nullifies the observance, enjoyment and exercise of such rights and freedoms;

Concerned that violence against women is an offense against human dignity and a manifestation of the historically unequal power relations between women and men;

Recalling the Declaration on the Elimination of Violence against Women, adopted by the Twenty-fifth Assembly of Delegates of the Inter-American Commission of Women, and affirming that violence against women pervades every sector of society regardless of class, race or ethnic group, income, culture, level of education, age or religion and strikes at its very foundations;

Convinced that the elimination of violence against women is essential for their individual and social development and their full and equal participation in all walks of life; and

Convinced that the adoption of a convention on the prevention, punishment and eradication of all forms of violence against women within the framework of the Organization of American States is a positive contribution to protecting the rights of women and eliminating violence against them,

Have agreed to the following:

CHAPTER I

Definition and scope of application

Article 1

For the purposes of this Convention, violence against women shall be understood as any act or conduct, based on gender, which causes death or physical, sexual or psychological harm or suffering to women, whether in the public or the private sphere.

Article 2

Violence against women shall be understood to include physical, sexual and psychological violence:

a. that occurs within the family or domestic unit or within any other interpersonal relationship, whether or not the perpetrator shares or has shared the same residence with the woman, including, among others, rape, battery and sexual abuse;

b. that occurs in the community and is perpetrated by any person, including, among others, rape, sexual abuse, torture, trafficking in persons, forced prostitution, kidnapping and sexual harassment in the workplace, as well as in educational institutions, health facilities or any other place; and

c. that is perpetrated or condoned by the state or its agents regardless of where it occurs.

CHAPTER II

Rights protected

Article 3

Every woman has the right to be free from violence in both the public and private spheres.

Article 4

Every woman has the right to the recognition, enjoyment, exercise and protection of all human rights and freedoms embodied in regional and international human rights instruments. These rights include, among others:

a. The right to have her life respected;

b. The right to have her physical, mental and moral integrity respected;

c. The right to personal liberty and security;

d. The right not to be subjected to torture;

e. The right to have the inherent dignity of her person respected and her family protected;

f. The right to equal protection before the law and of the law;

g. The right to simple and prompt recourse to a competent court for protection against acts that violate her rights;

h. The right to associate freely;

i. The right of freedom to profess her religion and beliefs within the law; and

j. The right to have equal access to the public service of her country and to take part in the conduct of public affairs, including decision-making.

Article 5

Every woman is entitled to the free and full exercise of her civil, political, economic, social and cultural rights, and may rely on the full protection of those rights as embodied in regional and international instruments on human rights. The States Parties recognize that violence against women prevents and nullifies the exercise of these rights.

Article 6

The right of every woman to be free from violence includes, among others:

a. The right of women to be free from all forms of discrimination; and

b. The right of women to be valued and educated free of stereotyped patterns of behavior and social and cultural practices based on concepts of inferiority or subordination.

CHAPTER III

Duties of the States

Article 7

The States Parties condemn all forms of violence against women and agree to pursue, by all appropriate means and without delay, policies to prevent, punish and eradicate such violence and undertake to:

a. refrain from engaging in any act or practice of violence against women and to ensure that their authorities, officials, personnel, agents, and institutions act in conformity with this obligation;

b. apply due diligence to prevent, investigate and impose penalties for violence against women;

c. include in their domestic legislation penal, civil, administrative and any other type of provisions that may be needed to prevent, punish and eradicate violence against women and to adopt appropriate administrative measures where necessary;

d. adopt legal measures to require the perpetrator to refrain from harassing, intimidating or threatening the woman or using any method that harms or endangers her life or integrity, or damages her property;

e. take all appropriate measures, including legislative measures, to amend or repeal existing laws and regulations or to modify legal or customary practices which sustain the persistence and tolerance of violence against women;

f. establish fair and effective legal procedures for women who have been subjected to violence which include, among others, protective measures, a timely hearing and effective access to such procedures;

g. establish the necessary legal and administrative mechanisms to ensure that women subjected to violence have effective access to restitution, reparations or other just and effective remedies; and

h. adopt such legislative or other measures as may be necessary to give effect to this Convention.

Article 8

The States Parties agree to undertake progressively specific measures, including programs:

a. to promote awareness and observance of the right of women to be free from violence, and the right of women to have their human rights respected and protected;

b. to modify social and cultural patterns of conduct of men and women, including the development of formal and informal educational programs appropriate to every level of the educational process, to counteract prejudices, customs and all other practices which are based on the idea of the inferiority or superiority of either of the sexes or on the stereotyped roles for men and women which legitimize or exacerbate violence against women;

c. to promote the education and training of all those involved in the administration of justice, police and other law enforcement officers as well as other personnel responsible for implementing policies for the prevention, punishment and eradication of violence against women;

d. to provide appropriate specialized services for women who have been subjected to violence, through public and private sector agencies, including shelters, counseling services for all family members where appropriate, and care and custody of the affected children;

e. to promote and support governmental and private sector education designed to raise the awareness of the public with respect to the problems of and remedies for violence against women;

f. to provide women who are subjected to violence access to effective readjustment and training programs to enable them to fully participate in public, private and social life;

g. to encourage the communications media to develop appropriate media guidelines in order to contribute to the eradication of violence against women in all its forms, and to enhance respect for the dignity of women;

h. to ensure research and the gathering of statistics and other relevant information relating to the causes, consequences and frequency of violence against women, in order to assess the effectiveness of measures to prevent, punish and eradicate violence against women and to formulate and implement the necessary changes; and

i. to foster international cooperation for the exchange of ideas and experiences and the execution of programs aimed at protecting women who are subjected to violence.

Article 9

With respect to the adoption of the measures in this Chapter, the States Parties shall take special account of the vulnerability of women to violence by reason of, among others, their race or ethnic background or their status as migrants, refugees or displaced persons. Similar consideration shall be given to women subjected to violence while pregnant or who are disabled, of minor age, elderly, socioeconomically disadvantaged, affected by armed conflict or deprived of their freedom.

CHAPTER IV

Inter-American mechanisms of protection

Article 10

In order to protect the right of every woman to be free from violence, the States Parties shall include in their national reports to the Inter-American

Commission of Women information on measures adopted to prevent and prohibit violence against women, and to assist women affected by violence, as well as on any difficulties they observe in applying those measures, and the factors that contribute to violence against women.

Article 11

The States Parties to this Convention and the Inter-American Commission of Women may request of the Inter-American Court of Human Rights advisory opinions on the interpretation of this Convention.

Article 12

Any person or groups of persons, or any non-governmental entity legally recognized in one or more member states of the Organization, may lodge petitions with the Inter-American Commission on Human Rights containing denunciations or complaints of violations of Article 7 of this Convention by a State Party, and the Commission shall consider such claims in accordance with the norms and procedures established by the American Convention on Human Rights and the Statutes and Regulations of the Inter-American Commission on Human Rights for lodging and considering petitions.

CHAPTER V

General provisions

Article 13

No part of this Convention shall be understood to restrict or limit the domestic law of any State Party that affords equal or greater protection and guarantees of the rights of women and appropriate safeguards to prevent and eradicate violence against women.

Article 14

No part of this Convention shall be understood to restrict or limit the American Convention on Human Rights or any other international convention on the subject that provides for equal or greater protection in this area.

Article 15

This Convention is open to signature by all member States of the Organization of American States.

Article 16

This Convention is subject to ratification. The instruments of ratification shall be deposited with the General Secretariat of the Organization of American States.

Article 17

This Convention is open to accession by any other state. Instruments of accession shall be deposited with the General Secretariat of the Organization of American States.

Article 18

Any State may, at the time of approval, signature, ratification, or accession, make reservations to this Convention provided that such reservations are:

a. not incompatible with the object and purpose of the Convention, and

b. not of a general nature and relate to one or more specific provisions.

Article 19

Any State Party may submit to the General Assembly, through the Inter-American Commission of Women, proposals for the amendment of this Convention.

Amendments shall enter into force for the states ratifying them on the date when two-thirds of the States Parties to this Convention have deposited their respective instruments of ratification. With respect to the other States Parties, the amendments shall enter into force on the dates on which they deposit their respective instruments of ratification.

Article 20

If a State Party has two or more territorial units in which the matters dealt with in this Convention are governed by different systems of law, it may, at the time of signature, ratification or accession, declare that this Convention shall extend to all its territorial units or to only one or more of them.

Such a declaration may be amended at any time by subsequent declarations, which shall expressly specify the territorial unit or units to which this Convention applies. Such subsequent declarations shall be transmitted to the General Secretariat of the Organization of American States, and shall enter into force thirty days after the date of their receipt.

Article 21

This Convention shall enter into force on the thirtieth day after the date of deposit of the second instrument of ratification. For each State that ratifies or accedes to the Convention after the second instrument of ratification is deposited, it shall enter into force thirty days after the date on which that State deposited its instrument of ratification or accession.

Article 22

The Secretary General shall inform all member states of the Organization of American States of the entry into force of this Convention.

Article 23

The Secretary General of the Organization of American States shall present an annual report to the member states of the Organization on the status of this Convention, including the signatures, deposits of instruments of ratification and accession, and declarations, and any reservations that may have been presented by the States Parties, accompanied by a report thereon if needed.

Article 24

This Convention shall remain in force indefinitely, but any of the States Parties may denounce it by depositing an instrument to that effect with the General Secretariat of the Organization of American States. One year after the date of deposit of the instrument of denunciation, this Convention shall cease to be in effect for the denouncing State but shall remain in force for the remaining States Parties.

Article 25

The original instrument of this Convention, the English, French, Portuguese and Spanish texts of which are equally authentic, shall be deposited with the General Secretariat of the Organization of American States, which shall send a certified copy to the Secretariat of the United Nations for registration and publication in accordance with the provisions of Article 102 of the United Nations Charter.

IN WITNESS WHEREOF the undersigned Plenipotentiaries, being duly authorized thereto by their respective governments, have signed this Convention, which shall be called the Inter-American Convention on the Prevention, Punishment and Eradication of Violence against Women "Convention of Belém do Pará."

DONE in the city of Belen do Para, Brazil, the ninth of June in the year one thousand nine hundred ninety-four.

B.   COUNCIL OF EUROPE

8. Convention for the Protection of Human Rights and Fundamental Freedoms[1]

Adopted at Rome on 4 November 1950

ENTRY INTO FORCE: 3 September 1953, in accordance with article 66

The Governments signatory hereto, being Members of the Council of Europe,

Considering the Universal Declaration of Human Rights proclaimed by the General Assembly of the United Nations on 10th December 1948;

Considering that this Declaration aims at securing the universal and effective recognition and observance of the rights therein declared;

Considering that the aim of the Council of Europe is the achievement of greater unity between its Members and that one of the methods by which that aim is to be pursued is the maintenance and further realisation of Human Rights and Fundamental Freedoms;

Reaffirming their profound belief in those Fundamental Freedoms which are the foundation of justice and peace in the world and are best maintained on the one hand by an effective political democracy and on the other by a common understanding and observance of the Human Rights upon which they depend;

Being resolved, as the Governments of European countries which are like-minded and have a common heritage of political traditions, ideals, freedom and the rule of law, to take the first steps for the collective enforcement of certain of the rights stated in the Universal Declaration,

Have agreed as follows:

---

[1] Text amended according to the provisions of Protocol No. 3, which entered into force on 21 September 1970, of Protocol No. 5, which entered into force on 20 December 1971, and of Protocol No. 8, which entered into force on 1 January 1990, and comprising also the text of Articles 1 to 4 of Protocol No. 2, which, in accordance with Article 5, paragraph 3, thereof, have been an integral part of the Convention since the entry into force of the Protocol on 21 September 1970.

Article 1

The High Contracting Parties shall secure to everyone within their jurisdiction the rights and freedoms defined in Section I of this Convention.

SECTION I

Article 2

1. Everyone's right to life shall be protected by law. No one shall be deprived of his life intentionally save in the execution of a sentence of a court following his conviction of a crime for which this penalty is provided by law.

2. Deprivation of life shall not be regarded as inflicted in contravention of this Article when it results from the use of force which is no more than absolutely necessary:

   a. in defence of any person from unlawful violence;

   b. in order to effect a lawful arrest or to prevent the escape of a person lawfully detained;

   c. in action lawfully taken for the purpose of quelling a riot or insurrection.

Article 3

No one shall be subjected to torture or to inhuman or degrading treatment or punishment.

Article 4

1. No one shall be held in slavery or servitude.

2. No one shall be required to perform forced or compulsory labour.

3. For the purpose of this Article the term "forced or compulsory labour" shall not include:

   a. any work required to be done in the ordinary course of detention imposed according to the provisions of Article 5 of this Convention or during conditional release from such detention;

   b. any service of a military character or, in case of conscientious objectors in countries where they are recognised, service exacted instead of compulsory military service;

   c. any service exacted in case of an emergency or calamity threatening the life or well-being of the community;

   d. any work or service which forms part of normal civic obligations.

Article 5

1.   Everyone has the right to liberty and security of person.

No one shall be deprived of his liberty save in the following cases and in accordance with a procedure prescribed by law:

a. the lawful detention of a person after conviction by a competent court;

b. the lawful arrest or detention of a person for non-compliance with the lawful order of a court or in order to secure the fulfilment of any obligation prescribed by law;

c. the lawful arrest or detention of a person effected for the purpose of bringing him before the competent legal authority on reasonable suspicion of having committed an offence or when it is reasonably considered necessary to prevent his committing an offence or fleeing after having done so;

d. the detention of a minor by lawful order for the purpose of educational supervision or his lawful detention for the purpose of bringing him before the competent legal authority;

e. the lawful detention of persons for the prevention of the spreading of infectious diseases, of persons of unsound mind, alcoholics or drug addicts or vagrants;

f. the lawful arrest or detention of a person to prevent his effecting an unauthorised entry into the country or of a person against whom action is being taken with a view to deportation or extradition.

2.   Everyone who is arrested shall be informed promptly, in a language which he understands, of the reasons for his arrest and of any charge against him.

3.   Everyone arrested or detained in accordance with the provisions of paragraph 1. *c.* of this Article shall be brought promptly before a judge or other officer authorised by law to exercise judicial power and shall be entitled to trial within a reasonable time or to release pending trial. Release may be conditioned by guarantees to appear for trial.

4.   Everyone who is deprived of his liberty by arrest or detention shall be entitled to take proceedings by which the lawfulness of his detention shall be decided speedily by a court and his release ordered if the detention is not lawful.

5.   Everyone who has been the victim of arrest or detention in contravention of the provisions of this Article shall have an enforceable right to compensation.

Article 6

1. In the determination of his civil rights and obligations or of any criminal charge against him, everyone is entitled to a fair and public hearing within a reasonable time by an independent and impartial tribunal established by law. Judgment shall be pronounced publicly but the press and public may be excluded from all or part of the trial in the interests of morals, public order or national security in a democratic society, where the interests of juveniles or the protection of the private life of the parties so require, or to the extent strictly necessary in the opinion of the court in special circumstances where publicity would prejudice the interests of justice.

2. Everyone charged with a criminal offence shall be presumed innocent until proved guilty according to law.

3. Everyone charged with a criminal offence has the following minimum rights:

a. to be informed promptly, in a language which he understands and in detail, of the nature and cause of the accusation against him;

b. to have adequate time and facilities for the preparation of his defence;

c. to defend himself in person or through legal assistance of his own choosing or, if he has not sufficient means to pay for legal assistance, to be given it free when the interests of justice so require;

d. to examine or have examined witnesses against him and to obtain the attendance and examination of witnesses on his behalf under the same conditions as witnesses against him;

e. to have the free assistance of an interpreter if he cannot understand or speak the language used in court.

Article 7

1. No one shall be held guilty of any criminal offence on account of any act or omission which did not constitute a criminal offence under national or international law at the time when it was committed. Nor shall a heavier penalty be imposed than the one that was applicable at the time the criminal offence was committed.

2. This Article shall not prejudice the trial and punishment of any person for any act or omission which, at the time when it was committed, was criminal according to the general principles of law recognised by civilised nations.

Article 8

1.   Everyone has the right to respect for his private and family life, his home and his correspondence.

2.   There shall be no interference by a public authority with the exercise of this right except such as is in accordance with the law and is necessary in a democratic society in the interests of national security, public safety or the economic well-being of the country, for the prevention of disorder or crime, for the protection of health or morals, or for the protection of the rights and freedoms of others.

Article 9

1.   Everyone has the right to freedom of thought, conscience and religion; this right includes freedom to change his religion or belief and freedom, either alone or in community with others and in public or private, to manifest his religion or belief, in worship, teaching, practice and observance.

2.   Freedom to manifest one's religion or beliefs shall be subject only to such limitations as are prescribed by law and are necessary in a democratic society in the interests of public safety, for the protection of public order, health or morals, or for the protection of the rights and freedoms of others.

Article 10

1.   Everyone has the right to freedom of expression. This right shall include freedom to hold opinions and to receive and impart information and ideas without interference by public authority and regardless of frontiers. This Article shall not prevent States from requiring the licensing of broadcasting, television or cinema enterprises.

2.   The exercise of these freedoms, since it carries with it duties and responsibilities, may be subject to such formalities, conditions, restrictions or penalties as are prescribed by law and are necessary in a democratic society, in the interests of national security, territorial integrity or public safety, for the prevention of disorder or crime, for the protection of health or morals, for the protection of the reputation or rights of others, for preventing the disclosure of information received in confidence, or for maintaining the authority and impartiality of the judiciary.

Article 11

1.   Everyone has the right to freedom of peaceful assembly and to freedom of association with others, including the right to form and to join trade unions for the protection of his interests.

2.   No restrictions shall be placed on the exercise of these rights other than such as are prescribed by law and are necessary in a democratic society in the interests of national security or public safety, for the prevention of disorder or crime, for the protection of health or morals or for the protection of the rights and freedoms of others. This Article shall not prevent the imposition of lawful restrictions on the exercise of these rights by members of the armed forces, of the police or of the administration of the State.

Article 12

Men and women of marriageable age have the right to marry and to found a family, according to the national laws governing the exercise of this right.

Article 13

Everyone whose rights and freedoms as set forth in this Convention are violated shall have an effective remedy before a national authority notwithstanding that the violation has been committed by persons acting in an official capacity.

Article 14

The enjoyment of the rights and freedoms set forth in this Convention shall be secured without discrimination on any ground such as sex, race, colour, language, religion, political or other opinion, national or social origin, association with a national minority, property, birth or other status.

Article 15

1.   In time of war or other public emergency threatening the life of the nation any High Contracting Party may take measures derogating from its obligations under this Convention to the extent strictly required by the exigencies of the situation, provided that such measures are not inconsistent with its other obligations under international law.

2.   No derogation from Article 2, except in respect of deaths resulting from lawful acts of war, or from Articles 3, 4 (paragraph 1) and 7 shall be made under this provision.

3.   Any High Contracting Party availing itself of this right of derogation shall keep the Secretary General of the Council of Europe fully informed of the measures which it has taken and the reasons therefor. It shall also inform the Secretary General of the Council of Europe when such measures have ceased to operate and the provisions of the Convention are again being fully executed.

Article 16

Nothing in Articles 10, 11 and 14 shall be regarded as preventing the High Contracting Parties from imposing restrictions on the political activity of aliens.

Article 17

Nothing in this Convention may be interpreted as implying for any State, group or person any right to engage in any activity or perform any act aimed at the destruction of any of the rights and freedoms set forth herein or at their limitation to a greater extent than is provided for in the Convention.

Article 18

The restrictions permitted under this Convention to the said rights and freedoms shall not be applied for any purpose other than those for which they have been prescribed.

SECTION II

Article 19

To ensure the observance of the engagements undertaken by the High Contracting Parties in the present Convention, there shall be set up:

1.   A European Commission of Human Rights, hereinafter referred to as "the Commission";

2.   A European Court of Human Rights, hereinafter referred to as "the Court".

SECTION III

Article 20

1.   The Commission shall consist of a number of members equal to that of the High Contracting Parties. No two members of the Commission may be nationals of the same State.

2. The Commission shall sit in plenary session. It may, however, set up Chambers, each composed of at least seven members. The Chambers may examine petitions submitted under Article 25 of this Convention which can be dealt with on the basis of established case law or which raise no serious question affecting the interpretation or application of the Convention. Subject to this restriction and to the provisions of paragraph 5 of this Article, the Chambers shall exercise all the powers conferred on the Commission by the Convention.

The member of the Commission elected in respect of a High Contracting Party against which a petition has been lodged shall have the right to sit on a Chamber to which that petition has been referred.

3. The Commission may set up committees, each composed of at least three members, with the power, exercisable by a unanimous vote, to declare inadmissible or strike from its list of cases a petition submitted under Article 25, when such a decision can be taken without further examination.

4. A Chamber or committee may at any time relinquish jurisdiction in favour of the plenary Commission, which may also order the transfer to it of any petition referred to a Chamber or committee.

5. Only the plenary Commission can exercise the following powers:

    a. the examination of applications submitted under Article 24;

    b. the bringing of a case before the Court in accordance with Article 48 *a*;

    c. the drawing up of rules of procedure in accordance with Article 36.

Article 21

1. The members of the Commission shall be elected by the Committee of Ministers by an absolute majority of votes, from a list of names drawn up by the Bureau of the Consultative Assembly; each group of the Representatives of the High Contracting Parties in the Consultative Assembly shall put forward three candidates, of whom two at least shall be its nationals.

2. As far as applicable, the same procedure shall be followed to complete the Commission in the event of other States subsequently becoming Parties to this Convention, and in filling casual vacancies.

3. The candidates shall be of high moral character and must either possess the qualifications required for appointment to high judicial office or be persons of recognised competence in national or international law.

Article 22

1.   The members of the Commission shall be elected for a period of six years. They may be re-elected. However, of the members elected at the first election, the terms of seven members shall expire at the end of three years.

2.   The members whose terms are to expire at the end of the initial period of three years shall be chosen by lot by the Secretary General of the Council of Europe immediately after the first election has been completed.

3.   In order to ensure that, as far as possible, one half of the membership of the Commission shall be renewed every three years, the Committee of Ministers may decide, before proceeding to any subsequent election, that the term or terms of office of one or more members to be elected shall be for a period other than six years but not more than nine and not less than three years.

4.   In cases where more than one term of office is involved and the Committee of Ministers applies the preceding paragraph, the allocation of the terms of office shall be effected by the drawing of lots by the Secretary General, immediately after the election.

5.   A member of the Commission elected to replace a member whose term of office has not expired shall hold office for the remainder of his predecessor's term.

6.   The members of the Commission shall hold office until replaced. After having been replaced, they shall continue to deal with such cases as they already have under consideration.

Article 23

The members of the Commission shall sit on the Commission in their individual capacity. During their term of office they shall not hold any position which is incompatible with their independence and impartiality as members of the Commission or the demands of this office.

Article 24

Any High Contracting Party may refer to the Commission, through the Secretary General of the Council of Europe, any alleged breach of the provisions of the Convention by another High Contracting Party.

Article 25

1.   The Commission may receive petitions addressed to the Secretary General of the Council of Europe from any person, non-governmental or-

ganisation or group of individuals claiming to be the victim of a violation by one of the High Contracting Parties of the rights set forth in this Convention, provided that the High Contracting Party against which the complaint has been lodged has declared that it recognises the competence of the Commission to receive such petitions. Those of the High Contracting Parties who have made such a declaration undertake not to hinder in any way the effective exercise of this right.

2.   Such declarations may be made for a specific period.

3.   The declarations shall be deposited with the Secretary General of the Council of Europe who shall transmit copies thereof to the High Contracting Parties and publish them.

4.   The Commission shall only exercise the powers provided for in this Article when at least six High Contracting Parties are bound by declarations made in accordance with the preceding paragraphs.

Article 26

The Commission may only deal with the matter after all domestic remedies have been exhausted, according to the generally recognised rules of international law, and within a period of six months from the date on which the final decision was taken.

Article 27

1.   The Commission shall not deal with any petition submitted under Article 25 which

   a. is anonymous, or

   b. is substantially the same as a matter which has already been examined by the Commission or has already been submitted to another procedure of international investigation or settlement and if it contains no relevant new information.

2.   The Commission shall consider inadmissible any petition submitted under Article 25 which it considers incompatible with the provisions of the present Convention, manifestly ill-founded, or an abuse of the right of petition.

3.   The Commission shall reject any petition referred to it which it considers inadmissible under Article 26.

Article 28

1.   In the event of the Commission accepting a petition referred to it:

   a. it shall, with a view to ascertaining the facts, undertake together with the representatives of the parties an examination of the petition and, if need be, an investigation, for the effective conduct of which the States concerned shall furnish all necessary facilities, after an exchange of views with the Commission;

b. it shall at the same time place itself at the disposal of the parties concerned with a view to securing a friendly settlement of the matter on the basis of respect for Human Rights as defined in this Convention.

2.   If the Commission succeeds in effecting a friendly settlement, it shall draw up a Report which shall be sent to the States concerned, to the Committee of Ministers and to the Secretary General of the Council of Europe for publication. This Report shall be confined to a brief statement of the facts and of the solution reached.

Article 29

After it has accepted a petition submitted under Article 25, the Commission may nevertheless decide by a majority of two-thirds of its members to reject the petition if, in the course of its examination, it finds that the existence of one of the grounds for non-acceptance provided for in Article 27 has been established.

In such a case, the decision shall be communicated to the parties.

Article 30

1.   The Commission may at any stage of the proceedings decide to strike a petition out of its list of cases where the circumstances lead to the conclusion that:

a. the applicant does not intend to pursue his petition, or

b. the matter has been resolved, or

c. for any other reason established by the Commission, it is no longer justified to continue the examination of the petition.

However, the Commission shall continue the examination of a petition if respect for Human Rights as defined in this Convention so requires.

2.   If the Commission decides to strike a petition out of its list after having accepted it, it shall draw up a Report which shall contain a statement of the facts and the decision striking out the petition together with the reasons therefor. The Report shall be transmitted to the parties, as well as to the Committee of Ministers for information. The Commission may publish it.

3.   The Commission may decide to restore a petition to its list of cases if it considers that the circumstances justify such a course.

Article 31

1.   If the examination of a petition has not been completed in accordance with Articles 28 (paragraph 2), 29 or 30, the Commission shall draw up a Report on the facts and state its opinion as to whether the facts found disclose a breach by the State concerned of its obligations under the Convention. The individual opinions of members of the Commission on this point may be stated in the Report.

2.   The Report shall be transmitted to the Committee of Ministers. It shall also be transmitted to the States concerned, who shall not be at liberty to publish it.

3.   In transmitting the Report to the Committee of Ministers the Commission may make such proposals as it thinks fit.

Article 32

1.   If the question is not referred to the Court in accordance with Article 48 of this Convention within a period of three months from the date of the transmission of the Report to the Committee of Ministers, the Committee of Ministers shall decide by a majority of two-thirds of the members entitled to sit on the Committee whether there has been a violation of the Convention.

2.   In the affirmative case the Committee of Ministers shall prescribe a period during which the High Contracting Party concerned must take the measures required by the decision of the Committee of Ministers.

3.   If the High Contracting Party concerned has not taken satisfactory measures within the prescribed period, the Committee of Ministers shall decide by the majority provided for in paragraph 1 above what effect shall be given to its original decision and shall publish the Report.

4.   The High Contracting Parties undertake to regard as binding on them any decision which the Committee of Ministers may take in application of the preceding paragraphs.

Article 33

The Commission shall meet in camera.

Article 34

Subject to the provisions of Articles 20 (paragraph 3) and 29, the Commission shall take its decisions by a majority of the members present and voting.

Article 35

The Commission shall meet as the circumstances require. The meetings shall be convened by the Secretary General of the Council of Europe.

Article 36

The Commission shall draw up its own rules of procedure.

Article 37

The secretariat of the Commission shall be provided by the Secretary General of the Council of Europe.

SECTION IV

Article 38

The European Court of Human Rights shall consist of a number of judges equal to that of the Members of the Council of Europe. No two judges may be nationals of the same State.

Article 39

1.   The members of the Court shall be elected by the Consultative Assembly by a majority of the votes cast from a list of persons nominated by the Members of the Council of Europe; each Member shall nominate three candidates, of whom two at least shall be its nationals.

2.   As far as applicable, the same procedure shall be followed to complete the Court in the event of the admission of new Members of the Council of Europe, and in filling casual vacancies.

3.   The candidates shall be of high moral character and must either possess the qualifications required for appointment to high judicial office or be jurisconsults of recognised competence.

Article 40

1.   The members of the Court shall be elected for a period of nine years. They may be re-elected. However, of the members elected at the first election the terms of four members shall expire at the end of three years, and the terms of four more members shall expire at the end of six years.

2.   The members whose terms are to expire at the end of the initial periods of three and six years shall be chosen by lot by the Secretary General immediately after the first election has been completed.

3.   In order to ensure that, as far as possible, one third of the membership of the Court shall be renewed every three years, the Consultative Assembly may decide, before proceeding to any subsequent election, that the term or terms of office of one or more members to be elected shall be for a period other than nine years but not more than twelve and not less than six years.

4.   In cases where more than one term of office is involved and the Consultative Assembly applies the preceding paragraph, the allocation of the terms of office shall be effected by the drawing of lots by the Secretary General immediately after the election.

5.   A member of the Court elected to replace a member whose term of office has not expired shall hold office for the remainder of his predecessor's term.

6.   The members of the Court shall hold office until replaced. After having been replaced, they shall continue to deal with such cases as they already have under consideration.

7.   The members of the Court shall sit on the Court in their individual capacity. During their term of office they shall not hold any position which is incompatible with their independence and impartiality as members of the Court or the demands of this office.

Article 41

The Court shall elect its President and one or two Vice-Presidents for a period of three years. They may be re-elected.

Article 42

The members of the Court shall receive for each day of duty a compensation to be determined by the Committee of Ministers.

Article 43

For the consideration of each case brought before it the Court shall consist of a Chamber composed of nine judges. There shall sit as an *ex officio* member of the Chamber the judge who is a national of any State Party concerned, or, if there is none, a person of its choice who shall sit in the capacity of judge; the names of the other judges shall be chosen by lot by the President before the opening of the case.

Article 44

Only the High Contracting Parties and the Commission shall have the right to bring a case before the Court.

Article 45

The jurisdiction of the Court shall extend to all cases concerning the interpretation and application of the present Convention which the High Contracting Parties or the Commission shall refer to it in accordance with Article 48.

Article 46

1.   Any of the High Contracting Parties may at any time declare that it recognises as compulsory *ipso facto* and without special agreement the jurisdiction of the Court in all matters concerning the interpretation and application of the present Convention.

2.   The declarations referred to above may be made unconditionally or on condition of reciprocity on the part of several or certain other High Contracting Parties or for a specified period.

3.   These declarations shall be deposited with the Secretary General of the Council of Europe who shall transmit copies thereof to the High Contracting Parties.

Article 47

The Court may only deal with a case after the Commission has acknowledged the failure of efforts for a friendly settlement and within the period of three months provided for in Article 32.

Article 48

The following may bring a case before the Court, provided that the High Contracting Party concerned, if there is only one, or the High Contracting Parties concerned, if there is more than one, are subject to the compulsory jurisdiction of the Court or, failing that, with the consent of the High Contracting Party concerned, if there is only one, or of the High Contracting Parties concerned if there is more than one:

   a.   the Commission;

   b.   a High Contracting Party whose national is alleged to be a victim;

   c.   a High Contracting Party which referred the case to the Commission;

   d.   a High Contracting Party against which the complaint has been lodged.

Article 49

In the event of dispute as to whether the Court has jurisdiction, the matter shall be settled by the decision of the Court.

Article 50

If the Court finds that a decision or a measure taken by a legal authority or any other authority of a High Contracting Party is completely or partially in conflict with the obligations arising from the present Convention, and if the internal law of the said Party allows only partial reparation to be made for the consequences of this decision or measure, the decision of the Court shall, if necessary, afford just satisfaction to the injured party.

Article 51

1.   Reasons shall be given for the judgment of the Court.

2.   If the judgment does not represent in whole or in part the unanimous opinion of the judges, any judge shall be entitled to deliver a separate opinion.

Article 52

The judgment of the Court shall be final.

Article 53

The High Contracting Parties undertake to abide by the decision of the Court in any case to which they are parties.

Article 54

The judgment of the Court shall be transmitted to the Committee of Ministers which shall supervise its execution.

Article 55

The Court shall draw up its own rules and shall determine its own procedure.

Article 56

1.   The first election of the members of the Court shall take place after the declarations by the High Contracting Parties mentioned in Article 46 have reached a total of eight.

2.   No case can be brought before the Court before this election.

SECTION V

Article 57

On receipt of a request from the Secretary General of the Council of Europe any High Contracting Party shall furnish an explanation of the manner in which its internal law ensures the effective implementation of any of the provisions of this Convention.

Article 58

The expenses of the Commission and the Court shall be borne by the Council of Europe.

Article 59

The members of the Commission and of the Court shall be entitled, during the discharge of their functions, to the privileges and immunities provided for in Article 40 of the Statute of the Council of Europe and in the agreements made thereunder.

Article 60

Nothing in this Convention shall be construed as limiting or derogating from any of the human rights and fundamental freedoms which may be ensured under the laws of any High Contracting Party or under any other agreement to which it is a Party.

Article 61

Nothing in this Convention shall prejudice the powers conferred on the Committee of Ministers by the Statute of the Council of Europe.

Article 62

The High Contracting Parties agree that, except by special agreement, they will not avail themselves of treaties, conventions or declarations in force between them for the purpose of submitting, by way of petition, a dispute arising out of the interpretation or application of this Convention to a means of settlement other than those provided for in this Convention.

Article 63

1.   Any State may at the time of its ratification or at any time thereafter declare by notification addressed to the Secretary General of the Coun-

cil of Europe that the present Convention shall extend to all or any of the territories for whose international relations it is responsible.

2. The Convention shall extend to the territory or territories named in the notification as from the thirtieth day after the receipt of this notification by the Secretary General of the Council of Europe.

3. The provisions of this Convention shall be applied in such territories with due regard, however, to local requirements.

4. Any State which has made a declaration in accordance with paragraph 1 of this article may at any time thereafter declare on behalf of one or more of the territories to which the declaration relates that it accepts the competence of the Commission to receive petitions from individuals, non-governmental organisations or groups of individuals in accordance with Article 25 of the present Convention.

Article 64

1. Any State may, when signing this Convention or when depositing its instrument of ratification, make a reservation in respect of any particular provision of the Convention to the extent that any law then in force in its territory is not in conformity with the provision. Reservations of a general character shall not be permitted under this Article.

2. Any reservation made under this Article shall contain a brief statement of the law concerned.

Article 65

1. A High Contracting Party may denounce the present Convention only after the expiry of five years from the date on which it became a Party to it and after six months' notice contained in a notification addressed to the Secretary General of the Council of Europe, who shall inform the other High Contracting Parties.

2. Such a denunciation shall not have the effect of releasing the High Contracting Party concerned from its obligations under this Convention in respect of any act which, being capable of constituting a violation of such obligations, may have been performed by it before the date at which the denunciation became effective.

3. Any High Contracting Party which shall cease to be a Member of the Council of Europe shall cease to be a Party to this Convention under the same conditions.

4. The Convention may be denounced in accordance with the provisions of the preceding paragraphs in respect of any territory to which it has been declared to extend under the terms of Article 63.

Article 66

1. This Convention shall be open to the signature of the Members of the Council of Europe. It shall be ratified. Ratifications shall be deposited with the Secretary General of the Council of Europe.

2. The present Convention shall come into force after the deposit of ten instruments of ratification.

3. As regards any signatory ratifying subsequently, the Convention shall come into force at the date of the deposit of its instrument of ratification.

4. The Secretary General of the Council of Europe shall notify all the Members of the Council of Europe of the entry into force of the Convention, the names of the High Contracting Parties who have ratified it, and the deposit of all instruments of ratification which may be effected subsequently.

DONE at Rome this 4th day of November 1950 in English and French, both texts being equally authentic, in a single copy which shall remain deposited in the archives of the Council of Europe. The Secretary General shall transmit certified copies to each of the signatories.

9. Protocol No. 1 to the Convention for the Protection of Human Rights and Fundamental Freedoms, securing certain rights and freedoms other than those already included in the Convention

Adopted at Paris on 20 March 1952

ENTRY INTO FORCE: 18 May 1954, in accordance with article 6

The Governments signatory hereto, being Members of the Council of Europe,

Being resolved to take steps to ensure the collective enforcement of certain rights and freedoms other than those already included in Section I of the Convention for the Protection of Human Rights and Fundamental Freedoms signed at Rome on 4th November, 1950 (hereinafter referred to as "the Convention"),

Have agreed as follows:

Article 1

Every natural or legal person is entitled to the peaceful enjoyment of his possessions. No one shall be deprived of his possessions except in the public interest and subject to the conditions provided for by law and by the general principles of international law.

The preceding provisions shall not, however, in any way impair the right of a State to enforce such laws as it deems necessary to control the use of property in accordance with the general interest or to secure the payment of taxes or other contributions or penalties.

Article 2

No person shall be denied the right to education. In the exercise of any functions which it assumes in relation to education and to teaching, the State shall respect the right of parents to ensure such education and teaching in conformity with their own religious and philosophical convictions.

Article 3

The High Contracting Parties undertake to hold free elections at reasonable intervals by secret ballot, under conditions which will ensure the free expression of the opinion of the people in the choice of the legislature.

Article 4

Any High Contracting Party may at the time of signature or ratification or at any time thereafter communicate to the Secretary-General of the Council of Europe a declaration stating the extent to which it undertakes that the provisions of the present Protocol shall apply to such of the territories for the international relations of which it is responsible as are named therein.

Any High Contracting Party which has communicated a declaration in virtue of the preceding paragraph may from time to time communicate a further declaration modifying the terms of any former declaration or terminating the application of the provisions of this Protocol in respect of any territory.

A declaration made in accordance with this Article shall be deemed to have been made in accordance with paragraph 1 of Article 63 of the Convention.

Article 5

As between the High Contracting Parties the provisions of Articles 1, 2, 3 and 4 of this Protocol shall be regarded as additional Articles to the Convention and all the provisions of the Convention shall apply accordingly.

Article 6

This Protocol shall be open for signature by the Members of the Council of Europe, who are the signatories of the Convention; it shall be ratified at the same time as or after the ratification of the Convention. It shall enter into force after the deposit of ten instruments of ratification. As regards any signatory ratifying subsequently, the Protocol shall enter into force at the date of the deposit of its instrument of ratification.

The instruments of ratification shall be deposited with the Secretary-General of the Council of Europe, who will notify all Members of the names of those who have ratified.

DONE at Paris on the 20th day of March 1952, in English and French, both texts being equally authentic, in a single copy which shall remain deposited in the archives of the Council of Europe. The Secretary-General shall transmit certified copies to each of the signatory Governments.

10. Protocol No. 2 to the Convention for the Protection of Human Rights and Fundamental Freedoms, conferring upon the European Court of Human Rights competence to give advisory opinions

Adopted at Strasbourg on 6 May 1963

ENTRY INTO FORCE: 21 September 1970, in accordance with article 5

The member States of the Council of Europe signatory hereto:

Having regard to the provisions of the Convention for the Protection of Human Rights and Fundamental Freedoms signed at Rome on 4th November 1950 (hereinafter referred to as "the Convention") and, in particular, Article 19 instituting, among other bodies, a European Court of Human Rights (hereinafter referred to as "the Court");

Considering that it is expedient to confer upon the Court competence to give advisory opinions subject to certain conditions;

Have agreed as follows:

Article 1

1. The Court may, at the request of the Committee of Ministers, give advisory opinions on legal questions concerning the interpretation of the Convention and the Protocols thereto.

2. Such opinions shall not deal with any question relating to the content or scope of the rights or freedoms defined in Section I of the Convention and in the Protocols thereto, or with any other question which the Commission, the Court or the Committee of Ministers might have to consider in consequence of any such proceedings as could be instituted in accordance with the Convention.

3. Decisions of the Committee of Ministers to request an advisory opinion of the Court shall require a two-thirds majority vote of the representatives entitled to sit on the Committee.

Article 2

The Court shall decide whether a request for an advisory opinion submitted by the Committee of Ministers is within its consultative competence as defined in Article 1 of this Protocol.

Article 3

1. For the consideration of requests for an advisory opinion, the Court shall sit in plenary session.

2. Reasons shall be given for advisory opinions of the Court.

3. If the advisory opinion does not represent in whole or in part the unanimous opinion of the judges, any judge shall be entitled to deliver a separate opinion.

4. Advisory opinions of the Court shall be communicated to the Committee of Ministers.

Article 4

The powers of the Court under Article 55 of the Convention shall extend to the drawing up of such rules and the determination of such procedure as the Court may think necessary for the purposes of this Protocol.

Article 5

1. This Protocol shall be open to signature by member States of the Council of Europe, signatories to the Convention, who may become Parties to it by:

(a) signature without reservation in respect of ratification or acceptance;

(b) signature with reservation in respect of ratification or acceptance, followed by ratification or acceptance.

Instruments of ratification or acceptance shall be deposited with the Secretary-General of the Council of Europe.

2. This Protocol shall enter into force as soon as all States Parties to the Convention shall have become Parties to the Protocol, in accordance with the provisions of paragraph 1 of this Article.

3. From the date of the entry into force of this Protocol, Articles 1 to 4 shall be considered an integral part of the Convention.

4. The Secretary-General of the Council of Europe shall notify the member States of the Council of:

(a) any signature without reservation in respect of ratification or acceptance;

(b) any signature with reservation in respect of ratification or acceptance;

(c) the deposit of any instrument of ratification or acceptance;

(*d*) the date of entry into force of this Protocol in accordance with paragraph 2 of this Article.

IN WITNESS WHEREOF, the undersigned, being duly authorised thereto, have signed this Protocol.

DONE at Strasbourg, this 6th day of May 1963, in English and in French, both texts being equally authoritative, in a single copy which shall remain deposited in the archives of the Council of Europe. The Secretary-General shall transmit certified copies to each of the signatory States.

11. Protocol No. 4 to the Convention for the Protection of Human Rights and Fundamental Freedoms, securing certain rights and freedoms other than those already included in the Convention and in the First Protocol thereto

Adopted at Strasbourg on 16 September 1963

ENTRY INTO FORCE: 2 May 1968, in accordance with article 7

The Governments signatory hereto, being Members of the Council of Europe,

Being resolved to take steps to ensure the collective enforcement of certain rights and freedoms other than those already included in Section I of the Convention for the Protection of Human Rights and Fundamental Freedoms signed at Rome on 4th November 1950 (hereinafter referred to as the "Convention") and in Articles 1 to 3 of the First Protocol to the Convention, signed at Paris on 20th March 1952,

Have agreed as follows:

Article 1

No one shall be deprived of his liberty merely on the ground of inability to fulfil a contractual obligation.

Article 2

1. Everyone lawfully within the territory of a State shall, within that territory, have the right to liberty of movement and freedom to choose his residence.

2. Everyone shall be free to leave any country, including his own.

3. No restrictions shall be placed on the exercise of these rights other than such as are in accordance with law and are necessary in a democratic society in the interests of national security or public safety, for the maintenance of *ordre public*, for the prevention of crime, for the protection of health or morals, or for the protection of the rights and freedoms of others.

4. The rights set forth in paragraph 1 may also be subject, in particular areas, to restrictions imposed in accordance with law and justified by the public interest in a democratic society.

Article 3

1.   No one shall be expelled, by means either of an individual or of a collective measure, from the territory of the State of which he is a national.

2.   No one shall be deprived of the right to enter the territory of the State of which he is a national.

Article 4

Collective expulsion of aliens is prohibited.

Article 5

1.   Any High Contracting Party may, at the time of signature or ratification of this Protocol, or at any time thereafter, communicate to the Secretary-General of the Council of Europe a declaration stating the extent to which it undertakes that the provisions of this Protocol shall apply to such of the territories for the international relations of which it is responsible as are named therein.

2.   Any High Contracting Party which has communicated a declaration in virtue of the preceding paragraph may, from time to time, communicate a further declaration modifying the terms of any former declaration or terminating the application of the provisions of this Protocol in respect of any territory.

3.   A declaration made in accordance with this Article shall be deemed to have been made in accordance with paragraph 1 of Article 63 of the Convention.

4.   The territory of any State to which this Protocol applies by virtue of ratification or acceptance by that State, and each territory to which this Protocol is applied by virtue of a declaration by that State under this Article, shall be treated as separate territories for the purpose of the references in Articles 2 and 3 to the territory of a State.

Article 6

1.   As between the High Contracting Parties the provisions of Articles 1 to 5 of this Protocol shall be regarded as additional Articles to the Convention, and all the provisions of the Convention shall apply accordingly.

2.   Nevertheless, the right of individual recourse recognised by a declaration made under Article 25 of the Convention, or the acceptance of the compulsory jurisdiction of the Court by a declaration made under Article 46 of the Convention, shall not be effective in relation to this Protocol unless

the High Contracting Party concerned has made a statement recognising such right, or accepting such jurisdiction, in respect of all or any of Articles 1 to 4 of the Protocol.

Article 7

1. This Protocol shall be open for signature by the Members of the Council of Europe who are the signatories of the Convention; it shall be ratified at the same time as or after the ratification of the Convention. It shall enter into force after the deposit of five instruments of ratification. As regards any signatory ratifying subsequently, the Protocol shall enter into force at the date of the deposit of its instrument of ratification.

2. The instruments of ratification shall be deposited with the Secretary-General of the Council of Europe, who will notify all Members of the names of those who have ratified.

IN WITNESS WHEREOF, the undersigned, being duly authorised thereto, have signed this Protocol.

DONE at Strasbourg, this 16th day of September 1963, in English and in French, both texts being equally authoritative, in a single copy which shall remain deposited in the archives of the Council of Europe. The Secretary-General shall transmit certified copies to each of the signatory States.

12. Protocol No. 6 to the Convention for the Protection of Human Rights and Fundamental Freedoms concerning the abolition of the death penalty

Adopted at Strasbourg on 28 April 1983

ENTRY INTO FORCE: 1 March 1985, in accordance with article 8

The member States of the Council of Europe, signatory to this Protocol to the Convention for the Protection of Human Rights and Fundamental Freedoms, signed at Rome on 4 November 1950 (hereinafter referred to as "the Convention"),

Considering that the evolution that has occurred in several member States of the Council of Europe expresses a general tendency in favour of abolition of the death penalty;

Have agreed as follows:

Article 1

The death penalty shall be abolished. No one shall be condemned to such penalty or executed.

Article 2

A State may make provision in its law for the death penalty in respect of acts committed in time of war or of imminent threat of war; such penalty shall be applied only in the instances laid down in the law and in accordance with its provisions. The State shall communicate to the Secretary General of the Council of Europe the relevant provisions of that law.

Article 3

No derogation from the provisions of this Protocol shall be made under Article 15 of the Convention.

Article 4

No reservation may be made under Article 64 of the Convention in respect of the provisions of this Protocol.

Article 5

1.   Any State may at the time of signature or when depositing its instrument of ratification, acceptance or approval, specify the territory or territories to which this Protocol shall apply.

2.   Any State may at any later date, by a declaration addressed to the Secretary General of the Council of Europe, extend the application of this Protocol to any other territory specified in the declaration. In respect of such territory the Protocol shall enter into force on the first day of the month following the date of receipt of such declaration by the Secretary General.

3.   Any declaration made under the two preceding paragraphs may, in respect of any territory specified in such declaration, be withdrawn by a notification addressed to the Secretary General. The withdrawal shall become effective on the first day of the month following the date of receipt of such notification by the Secretary General.

Article 6

As between the States Parties the provisions of Articles 1 to 5 of this Protocol shall be regarded as additional Articles to the Convention and all the provisions of the Convention shall apply accordingly.

Article 7

The Protocol shall be open for signature by the member States of the Council of Europe, signatories to the Convention. It shall be subject to ratification, acceptance or approval. A member State of the Council of Europe may not ratify, accept or approve this Protocol unless it has, simultaneously or previously, ratified the Convention. Instruments of ratification, acceptance or approval shall be deposited with the Secretary General of the Council of Europe.

Article 8

1.   This Protocol shall enter into force on the first day of the month following the date on which five member States of the Council of Europe have expressed their consent to be bound by the Protocol in accordance with the provisions of Article 7.

2.   In respect of any member State which subsequently expresses its consent to be bound by it, the Protocol shall enter into force on the first day of the month following the date of the deposit of the instrument of ratification, acceptance or approval.

Article 9

The Secretary General of the Council of Europe shall notify the member States of the Council of:

    a. any signature;

    b. the deposit of any instrument of ratification, acceptance or approval;

    c. any date of entry into force of this Protocol in accordance with Articles 5 and 8;

    d. any other act, notification or communication relating to this Protocol.

IN WITNESS WHEREOF the undersigned, being duly authorised thereto, have signed this Protocol.

DONE at Strasbourg, this 28th day of April 1983, in English and French, both texts being equally authentic, in a single copy which shall be deposited in the archives of the Council of Europe. The Secretary General of the Council of Europe shall transmit certified copies to each member State of the Council of Europe.

13. Protocol No. 7 to the Convention for the Protection of Human Rights and Fundamental Freedoms

Adopted at Strasbourg on 22 November 1984

ENTRY INTO FORCE: 1 November 1988, in accordance with article 9

The member States of the Council of Europe signatory hereto,

Being resolved to take further steps to ensure the collective enforcement of certain rights and freedoms by means of the Convention for the Protection of Human Rights and Fundamental Freedoms signed at Rome on 4 November 1950 (hereinafter referred to as "the Convention"),

Have agreed as follows:

Article 1

1.   An alien lawfully resident in the territory of a State shall not be expelled therefrom except in pursuance of a decision reached in accordance with law and shall be allowed:

a. to submit reasons against his expulsion,

b. to have his case reviewed, and

c. to be represented for these purposes before the competent authority or a person or persons designated by that authority.

2.   An alien may be expelled before the exercise of his rights under paragraph 1. *a, b* and *c* of this Article, when such expulsion is necessary in the interests of public order or is grounded on reasons of national security.

Article 2

1.   Everyone convicted of a criminal offence by a tribunal shall have the right to have his conviction or sentence reviewed by a higher tribunal. The exercise of this right, including the grounds on which it may be exercised, shall be governed by law.

2.   This right may be subject to exceptions in regard to offences of a minor character, as prescribed by law, or in cases in which the person concerned was tried in the first instance by the highest tribunal or was convicted following an appeal against acquittal.

Article 3

When a person has by a final decision been convicted of a criminal offence and when subsequently his conviction has been reversed, or he has been pardoned, on the ground that a new or newly discovered fact shows conclusively that there has been a miscarriage of justice, the person who has suffered punishment as a result of such conviction shall be compensated according to the law or the practice of the State concerned, unless it is proved that the non-disclosure of the unknown fact in time is wholly or partly attributable to him.

Article 4

1.   No one shall be liable to be tried or punished again in criminal proceedings under the jurisdiction of the same State for an offence for which he has already been finally acquitted or convicted in accordance with the law and penal procedure of that State.

2.   The provisions of the preceding paragraph shall not prevent the reopening of the case in accordance with the law and penal procedure of the State concerned, if there is evidence of new or newly discovered facts, or if there has been a fundamental defect in the previous proceedings, which could affect the outcome of the case.

3.   No derogation from this Article shall be made under Article 15 of the Convention.

Article 5

Spouses shall enjoy equality of rights and responsibilities of a private law character between them, and in their relations with their children, as to marriage, during marriage and in the event of its dissolution. This Article shall not prevent States from taking such measures as are necessary in the interests of the children.

Article 6

1.   Any State may at the time of signature or when depositing its instrument of ratification, acceptance or approval, specify the territory or territories to which this Protocol shall apply and state the extent to which it undertakes that the provisions of this Protocol shall apply to such territory or territories.

2.   Any State may at any later date, by a declaration addressed to the Secretary General of the Council of Europe, extend the application of this Protocol to any other territory specified in the declaration. In respect of such territory the Protocol shall enter into force on the first day of the month fol-

lowing the expiration of a period of two months after the date of receipt by the Secretary General of such declaration.

3.   Any declaration made under the two preceding paragraphs may, in respect of any territory specified in such declaration, be withdrawn or modified by a notification addressed to the Secretary General. The withdrawal or modification shall become effective on the first day of the month following the expiration of a period of two months after the date of receipt of such notification by the Secretary General.

4.   A declaration made in accordance with this Article shall be deemed to have been made in accordance with paragraph 1 of Article 63 of the Convention.

5.   The territory of any State to which this Protocol applies by virtue of ratification, acceptance or approval by that State, and each territory to which this Protocol is applied by virtue of a declaration by that State under this Article, may be treated as separate territories for the purpose of the reference in Article 1 to the territory of a State.

Article 7

1.   As between the States Parties, the provisions of Articles 1 to 6 of this Protocol shall be regarded as additional Articles to the Convention, and all the provisions of the Convention shall apply accordingly.

2.   Nevertheless, the right of individual recourse recognised by a declaration made under Article 25 of the Convention, or the acceptance of the compulsory jurisdiction of the Court by a declaration made under Article 46 of the Convention, shall not be effective in relation to this Protocol unless the State concerned has made a statement recognising such right, or accepting such jurisdiction in respect of Articles 1 to 5 of this Protocol.

Article 8

This Protocol shall be open for signature by member States of the Council of Europe which have signed the Convention. It is subject to ratification, acceptance or approval. A member State of the Council of Europe may not ratify, accept or approve this Protocol without previously or simultaneously ratifying the Convention. Instruments of ratification, acceptance or approval shall be deposited with the Secretary General of the Council of Europe.

Article 9

1.   This Protocol shall enter into force on the first day of the month following the expiration of a period of two months after the date on which

seven member States of the Council of Europe have expressed their consent to be bound by the Protocol in accordance with the provisions of Article 8.

2. In respect of any member State which subsequently expresses its consent to be bound by it, the Protocol shall enter into force on the first day of the month following the expiration of a period of two months after the date of the deposit of the instrument of ratification, acceptance or approval.

Article 10

The Secretary General of the Council of Europe shall notify all the member States of the Council of Europe of:

 a. any signature;

 b. the deposit of any instrument of ratification, acceptance or approval;

 c. any date of entry into force of this Protocol in accordance with Articles 6 and 9;

 d. any other act, notification or declaration relating to this Protocol.

IN WITNESS WHEREOF the undersigned, being duly authorised thereto, have signed this Protocol.

DONE at Strasbourg, this 22nd day of November 1984, in English and French, both texts being equally authentic, in a single copy which shall be deposited in the archives of the Council of Europe. The Secretary General of the Council of Europe shall transmit certified copies to each member State of the Council of Europe.

14. Protocol No. 9 to the Convention for the Protection of Human Rights and Fundamental Freedoms

Adopted at Rome on 6 November 1990

The member States of the Council of Europe, signatories to this Protocol to the Convention for the Protection of Human Rights and Fundamental Freedoms, signed at Rome on 4 November 1950 (hereinafter referred to as "the Convention"),

Being resolved to make further improvements to the procedure under the Convention,

Have agreed as follows:

Article 1

For Parties to the Convention which are bound by this Protocol, the Convention shall be amended as provided in Articles 2 to 5.

Article 2

Article 31, paragraph 2, of the Convention, shall read as follows:

"2. The Report shall be transmitted to the Committee of Ministers. The Report shall also be transmitted to the States concerned and, if it deals with a petition submitted under Article 25, the applicant. The States concerned and the applicant shall not be at liberty to publish it."

Article 3

Article 44 of the Convention shall read as follows:

"Only the High Contracting Parties, the Commission, and persons, non-governmental organisations or groups of individuals having submitted a petition under Article 25 shall have the right to bring a case before the Court."

Article 4

Article 45 of the Convention shall read as follows:

"The jurisdiction of the Court shall extend to all cases concerning the interpretation and application of the present Convention which are referred to it in accordance with Article 48.''

Article 5

Article 48 of the Convention shall read as follows:

"1.   The following may refer a case to the Court, provided that the High Contracting Party concerned, if there is only one, or the High Contracting Parties concerned, if there is more than one, are subject to the compulsory jurisdiction of the Court or, failing that, with the consent of the High Contracting Party concerned, if there is only one, or of the High Contracting Parties concerned if there is more than one:

"*a.*   the Commission;

"*b.*   a High Contracting Party whose national is alleged to be a victim;

"*c.*   a High Contracting Party which referred the case to the Commission;

"*d.*   a High Contracting Party against which the complaint has been lodged;

"*e.*   the person, non-governmental organisation or group of individuals having lodged the complaint with the Commission.

"2.   If a case is referred to the Court only in accordance with paragraph 1. *e*, it shall first be submitted to a panel composed of three members of the Court. There shall sit as an ex officio member of the panel the judge who is elected in respect of the High Contracting Party against which the complaint has been lodged, or, if there is none, a person of its choice who shall sit in the capacity of judge. If the complaint has been lodged against more than one High Contracting Party, the size of the panel shall be increased accordingly.

"If the case does not raise a serious question affecting the interpretation or application of the Convention and does not for any other reason warrant consideration by the Court, the panel may, by a unanimous vote, decide that it shall not be considered by the Court. In that event, the Committee of Ministers shall decide, in accordance with the provisions of Article 32, whether there has been a violation of the Convention.''

Article 6

1.   This Protocol shall be open for signature by member States of the Council of Europe signatories to the Convention, which may express their consent to be bound by:

a. signature without reservation as to ratification, acceptance or approval; or

b. signature subject to ratification, acceptance or approval, followed by ratification, acceptance or approval.

2. The instruments of ratification, acceptance or approval shall be deposited with the Secretary General of the Council of Europe.

Article 7

1. This Protocol shall enter into force on the first day of the month following the expiration of a period of three months after the date on which ten member States of the Council of Europe have expressed their consent to be bound by the Protocol in accordance with the provisions of Article 6.

2. In respect of any member State which subsequently expresses its consent to be bound by it, the Protocol shall enter into force on the first day of the month following the expiration of a period of three months after the date of signature or of the deposit of the instrument of ratification, acceptance or approval.

Article 8

The Secretary General of the Council of Europe shall notify all the member States of the Council of Europe of:

a. any signature;

b. the deposit of any instrument of ratification, acceptance or approval;

c. any date of entry into force of this Protocol in accordance with Article 7;

d. any other act, notification or declaration relating to this Protocol.

IN WITNESS WHEREOF the undersigned, being duly authorised thereto, have signed this Protocol.

DONE at Rome, this 6th day of November 1990, in English and French, both texts being equally authentic, in a single copy which shall be deposited in the archives of the Council of Europe. The Secretary General of the Council of Europe shall transmit certified copies to each member State of the Council of Europe.

15. Protocol No. 10 to the Convention for the Protection of Human Rights and Fundamental Freedoms

Adopted at Strasbourg on 25 March 1992

The member States of the Council of Europe, signatories to this Protocol to the Convention for the Protection of Human Rights and Fundamental Freedoms, signed at Rome on 4 November 1950 (hereinafter referred to as "the Convention"),

Considering that it is advisable to amend Article 32 of the Convention with a view to the reduction of the two-thirds majority provided therein,

Have agreed as follows:

Article 1

The words "of two-thirds" shall be deleted from paragraph 1 of Article 32 of the Convention.

Article 2

1. This Protocol shall be open for signature by member States of the Council of Europe signatories to the Convention, which may express their consent to be bound by:

a. signature without reservation as to ratification, acceptance or approval; or

b. signature subject to ratification, acceptance or approval, followed by ratification, acceptance or approval.

2. Instruments of ratification, acceptance or approval shall be deposited with the Secretary General of the Council of Europe.

Article 3

This Protocol shall enter into force on the first day of the month following the expiration of a period of three months after the date on which all Parties to the Convention have expressed their consent to be bound by the Protocol in accordance with the provisions of Article 2.

Article 4

The Secretary General of the Council of Europe shall notify the member States of the Council of:

a. any signature;

b. the deposit of any instrument of ratification, acceptance or approval;

c. the date of entry into force of this Protocol in accordance with Article 3;

d. any other act, notification or communication relating to this Protocol.

IN WITNESS WHEREOF the undersigned, being duly authorised thereto, have signed this Protocol.

DONE at Strasbourg, this 25th day of March 1992, in English and French, both texts being equally authentic, in a single copy which shall be deposited in the archives of the Council of Europe. The Secretary General of the Council of Europe shall transmit certified copies to each member State of the Council of Europe.

16. Protocol No. 11 to the Convention for the Protection of Human Rights and Fundamental Freedoms, restructuring the control machinery established thereby

Adopted at Strasbourg on 11 May 1994

The member States of the Council of Europe, signatories to this Protocol to the Convention for the Protection of Human Rights and Fundamental Freedoms, signed at Rome on 4 November 1950 (hereinafter referred to as "The Convention"),

Considering the urgent need to restructure the control machinery established by the Convention in order to maintain and improve the efficiency of its protection of human rights and fundamental freedoms, mainly in view of the increase in the number of applications and the growing membership of the Council of Europe;

Considering that it is therefore desirable to amend certain provisions of the Convention with a view, in particular, to replacing the existing European Commission and Court of Human Rights with a new permanent Court;

Having regard to Resolution No. 1 adopted at the European Ministerial Conference on Human Rights, held in Vienna on 19 and 20 March 1985;

Having regard to Recommendation 1194 (1992), adopted by the Parliamentary Assembly of the Council of Europe on 6 October 1992;

Having regard to the decision taken on reform of the Convention control machinery by the Heads of State and Government of the Council of Europe member States in the Vienna Declaration on 9 October 1993,

Have agreed as follows:

Article 1

The existing text of Sections II to IV of the Convention (Articles 19 to 56) and Protocol No. 2 conferring upon the European Court of Human Rights competence to give advisory opinions shall be replaced by the following Section II of the Convention (Articles 19 to 51):

"Section II—European Court of Human Rights

Article 19—Establishment of the Court

To ensure the observance of the engagements undertaken by the High Contracting Parties in the Convention and the protocols thereto, there shall be set up a European Court of Human Rights, hereinafter referred to as "the Court". It shall function on a permanent basis.

Article 20—Number of judges

The Court shall consist of a number of judges equal to that of the High Contracting Parties.

Article 21—Criteria for office

1. The judges shall be of high moral character and must either possess the qualifications required for appointment to high judicial office or be jurisconsults of recognised competence.

2. The judges shall sit on the Court in their individual capacity.

3. During their term of office the judges shall not engage in any activity which is incompatible with their independence, impartiality or with the demands of a full-time office; all questions arising from the application of this paragraph shall be decided by the Court.

Article 22—Election of judges

1. The judges shall be elected by the Parliamentary Assembly with respect to each High Contracting Party by a majority of votes cast from a list of three candidates nominated by the High Contracting Party.

2. The same procedure shall be followed to complete the Court in the event of the accession of new High Contracting Parties and in filling casual vacancies.

Article 23—Terms of office

1. The judges shall be elected for a period of six years. They may be re-elected. However, the terms of office of one-half of the judges elected at the first election shall expire at the end of three years.

2. The judges whose terms of office are to expire at the end of the initial period of three years shall be chosen by lot by the Secretary General of the Council of Europe immediately after their election.

3. In order to ensure that, as far as possible, the terms of office of one-half of the judges are renewed every three years, the Parliamentary Assembly may decide, before proceeding to any subsequent election, that the term or terms of office of one or more judges to be elected shall be for a period other than six years but not more than nine and not less than three years.

4. In cases where more than one term of office is involved and where the Parliamentary Assembly applies the preceding paragraph, the allocation of the terms of office shall be effected by a drawing of lots by the Secretary General of the Council of Europe immediately after the election.

5. A judge elected to replace a judge whose term of office has not expired shall hold office for the remainder of his predecessor's term.

6. The terms of office of judges shall expire when they reach the age of 70.

7. The judges shall hold office until replaced. They shall, however, continue to deal with such cases as they already have under consideration.

Article 24—Dismissal

No judge may be dismissed from his office unless the other judges decide by a majority of two-thirds that he has ceased to fulfil the required conditions.

Article 25—Registry and legal secretaries

The Court shall have a registry, the functions and organisation of which shall be laid down in the rules of the Court. The Court shall be assisted by legal secretaries.

Article 26—Plenary Court

The plenary Court shall

    a. elect its President and one or two Vice-Presidents for a period of three years; they may be re-elected;

    b. set up Chambers, constituted for a fixed period of time;

    c. elect the Presidents of the Chambers of the Court; they may be re-elected;

    d. adopt the rules of the Court; and

    e. elect the Registrar and one or more Deputy Registrars.

Article 27—Committees, Chambers and Grand Chamber

1. To consider cases brought before it, the Court shall sit in committees of three judges, in Chambers of seven judges and in a Grand Chamber of seventeen judges. The Court's Chambers shall set up committees for a fixed period of time.

2. There shall sit as an *ex officio* member of the Chamber and the Grand Chamber the judge elected in respect of the State Party concerned or, if there is none or if he is unable to sit, a person of its choice who shall sit in the capacity of judge.

3. The Grand Chamber shall also include the President of the Court, the Vice-Presidents, the Presidents of the Chambers and other judges chosen in accordance with the rules of the Court. When a case is referred to the Grand Chamber under Article 43, no judge from the Chamber which rendered the judgment shall sit in the Grand Chamber, with the exception of the President of the Chamber and the judge who sat in respect of the State Party concerned.

Article 28—Declarations of inadmissibility by committees

A committee may, by a unanimous vote, declare inadmissible or strike out of its list of cases an individual application submitted under Article 34 where such a decision can be taken without further examination. The decision shall be final.

Article 29—Decisions by Chambers on admissibility and merits

1. If no decision taken under Article 28, a Chamber shall decide on the admissibility and merits of individual applications submitted under Article 34.

2. A Chamber shall decide on the admissibility and merits of inter-State applications submitted under Article 33.

3. The decision on admissibility shall be taken separately unless the Court, in exceptional cases, decides otherwise.

Article 30—Relinquishment of jurisdiction to the Grand Chamber

Where a case pending before a Chamber raises a serious question affecting the interpretation of the Convention or the protocols thereto, or where the resolution of a question before the Chamber might have a result inconsistent with a judgment previously delivered by the Court, the Chamber may, at any time before it has rendered its judgment, relinquish jurisdiction in favour of the Grand Chamber, unless one of the parties to the case objects.

Article 31—Powers of the Grand Chamber

The Grand Chamber shall

    a. determine applications submitted either under Article 33 or Article 34 when a Chamber has relinquished jurisdiction under Article 30 or when the case has been referred to it under Article 43; and

    b. consider requests for advisory opinions submitted under Article 47.

Article 32—Jurisdiction of the Court

1. The jurisdiction of the Court shall extend to all matters concerning the interpretation and application of the Convention and the protocols thereto which are referred to it as provided in Articles 33, 34 and 47.

2. In the event of dispute as to whether the Court has jurisdiction, the Court shall decide.

Article 33—Inter-State cases

Any High Contracting Party may refer to the Court any alleged breach of the provisions of the Convention and the protocols thereto by another High Contracting Party.

Article 34—Individual applications

The Court may receive applications from any person, non-governmental organisation or group of individuals claiming to be the victim of a violation by one of the High Contracting Parties of the rights set forth in the Convention or the protocols thereto. The High Contracting Parties undertake not to hinder in any way the effective exercise of this right.

Article 35—Admissibility criteria

1. The Court may only deal with the matter after all domestic remedies have been exhausted, according to the generally recognised rules of international law, and within a period of six months from the date on which the final decision was taken.

2. The Court shall not deal with any individual application submitted under Article 34 that

    a. is anonymous; or

b. is substantially the same as a matter that has already been examined by the Court or has already been submitted to another procedure of international investigation or settlement and contains no relevant new information.

3. The Court shall declare inadmissible any individual application submitted under Article 34 which it considers incompatible with the provisions of the Convention or the protocols thereto, manifestly ill-founded, or an abuse of the right of application.

4. The Court shall reject any application which it considers inadmissible under this Article. It may do so at any stage of the proceedings.

Article 36—Third-party intervention

1. In all cases before a Chamber or the Grand Chamber, a High Contracting Party one of whose nationals is an applicant shall have the right to submit written comments and to take part in hearings.

2. The President of the Court may, in the interest of the proper administration of justice, invite any High Contracting Party which is not a party to the proceedings or any person concerned who is not the applicant to submit written comments or take part in hearings.

Article 37—Striking out applications

1. The Court may at any stage of the proceedings decide to strike an application out of its list of cases where the circumstances lead to the conclusion that

   a. the applicant does not intend to pursue his application; or

   b. the matter has been resolved; or

   c. for any other reason established by the Court, it is no longer justified to continue the examination of the application.

However, the Court shall continue the examination of the application if respect for human rights as defined in the Convention and the protocols thereto so requires.

2. The Court may decide to restore an application to its list of cases if it considers that the circumstances justify such a course.

Article 38—Examination of the case and friendly settlement proceedings

1. If the Court declares the application admissible, it shall

    a. pursue the examination of the case, together with the representatives of the parties, and if need be, undertake an investigation, for the effective conduct of which the States concerned shall furnish all necessary facilities;

    b. place itself at the disposal of the parties concerned with a view to securing a friendly settlement of the matter on the basis of respect for human rights as defined in the Convention and the protocols thereto.

2. Proceedings conducted under paragraph 1.*b* shall be confidential.

Article 39—Finding of a friendly settlement

If a friendly settlement is effected, the Court shall strike the case out of its list by means of a decision which shall be confined to a brief statement of the facts and of the solution reached.

Article 40—Public hearings and access to documents

1. Hearings shall be public unless the Court in exceptional circumstances decides otherwise.

2. Documents deposited with the Registrar shall be accessible to the public unless the President of the Court decides otherwise.

Article 41—Just satisfaction

If the Court finds that there has been a violation of the Convention or the protocols thereto, and if the internal law of the High Contracting Party concerned allows only partial reparation to be made, the Court shall, if necessary, afford just satisfaction to the injured party.

Article 42—Judgments of Chambers

Judgments of Chambers shall become final in accordance with the provisions of Article 44, paragraph 2.

Article 43—Referral to the Grand Chamber

1. Within a period of three months from the date of the judgment of the Chamber, any party to the case may, in exceptional cases, request that the case be referred to the Grand Chamber.

2. A panel of five judges of the Grand Chamber shall accept the request if the case raises a serious question affecting the interpretation or application of the Convention or the protocols thereto, or a serious issue of general importance.

3. If the panel accepts the request, the Grand Chamber shall decide the case by means of a judgment.

Article 44—Final judgments

1. The judgment of the Grand Chamber shall be final.

2. The judgment of a Chamber shall become final

    a. when the parties declare that they will not request that the case be referred to the Grand Chamber; or

    b. three months after the date of the judgment, if reference of the case to the Grand Chamber has not been requested; or

    c. when the panel of the Grand Chamber rejects the request to refer under Article 43.

3. The final judgment shall be published.

Article 45—Reasons for judgments and decisions

1. Reasons shall be given for judgments as well as for decisions declaring applications admissible or inadmissible.

2. If a judgment does not represent, in whole or in part, the unanimous opinion of the judges, any judge shall be entitled to deliver a separate opinion.

Article 46—Binding force and execution of judgments

1. The High Contracting Parties undertake to abide by the final judgment of the Court in any case to which they are parties.

2. The final judgment of the Court shall be transmitted to the Committee of Ministers, which shall supervise its execution.

Article 47—Advisory opinions

1. The Court may, at the request of the Committee of Ministers, give advisory opinions on legal questions concerning the interpretation of the Convention and the protocols thereto.

2. Such opinions shall not deal with any question relating to the content or scope of the rights or freedoms defined in Section I of the Convention and the protocols thereto, or with any other question which the Court or the Committee of Ministers might have to consider in consequence of any such proceedings as could be instituted in accordance with the Convention.

3. Decisions of the Committee of Ministers to request an advisory opinion of the Court shall require a majority vote of the representatives entitled to sit on the Committee.

Article 48—Advisory jurisdiction of the Court

The Court shall decide whether a request for an advisory opinion submitted by the Committee of Ministers is within its competence as defined in Article 47.

Article 49—Reasons for advisory opinions

1. Reasons shall be given for advisory opinions of the Court.

2. If the advisory opinion does not represent, in whole or in part, the unanimous opinion of the judges, any judge shall be entitled to deliver a separate opinion.

3. Advisory opinions of the Court shall be communicated to the Committee of Ministers.

Article 50—Expenditure on the Court

The expenditure on the Court shall be borne by the Council of Europe.

Article 51—Privileges and immunities of judges

The judges shall be entitled, during the exercise of their functions, to the privileges and immunities provided for in Article 40 of the Statute of the Council of Europe and in the agreements made thereunder.''

Article 2

1. Section V of the Convention shall become Section III of the Convention; Article 57 of the Convention shall become Article 52 of the Convention; Articles 58 and 59 of the Convention shall be deleted, and Articles 60 to 66 of the Convention shall become Articles 53 to 59 of the Convention respectively.

2. Section I of the Convention shall be entitled ''Rights and freedoms'' and new Section III of the Convention shall be entitled ''Miscellaneous provisions''. Articles 1 to 18 and new Articles 52 to 59 of the Convention shall be provided with headings, as listed in the appendix to this Protocol.

3. In new Article 56, in paragraph 1, the words '', subject to paragraph 4 of this Article,'' shall be inserted after the word ''shall''; in paragraph 4, the words ''Commission to receive petitions'' and ''in accordance

with Article 25 of the present Convention'' shall be replaced by the words ''Court to receive applications'' and ''as provided in Article 34 of the Convention'' respectively. In new Article 58, paragraph 4, the words ''Article 63'' shall be replaced by the words ''Article 56''.

4. The Protocol to the Convention shall be amended as follows

a. the Articles shall be provided with the headings listed in the appendix to the present Protocol; and

b. in Article 4, last sentence, the words ''of Article 63'' shall be replaced by the words ''of Article 56''.

5. Protocol No. 4 shall be amended as follows

a. the Articles shall be provided with the headings listed in the appendix to the present Protocol;

b. in Article 5, paragraph 3, the words ''of Article 63'' shall be replaced by the words ''of Article 56''; a new paragraph 5 shall be added, which shall read

''Any State which has made a declaration in accordance with paragraph 1 or 2 of this Article may at any time thereafter declare on behalf of one or more of the territories to which the declaration relates that it accepts the competence of the Court to receive applications from individuals, non-governmental organisations or groups of individuals as provided in Article 34 of the Convention in respect of all or any of Articles 1 to 4 of this Protocol.''; and

c. paragraph 2 of Article 6 shall be deleted.

6. Protocol No. 6 shall be amended as follows

a. the Articles shall be provided with the headings listed in the appendix to the present Protocol; and

b. in Article 4 the words ''under Article 64'' shall be replaced by the words ''under Article 57''.

7. Protocol No. 7 shall be amended as follows

a. the Articles shall be provided with the headings listed in the appendix to the present Protocol;

b. in Article 6, paragraph 4, the words ''of Article 63'' shall be replaced by the words ''of Article 56''; a new paragraph 6 shall be added, which shall read

''Any State which has made a declaration in accordance with paragraph 1 or 2 of this Article may at any time thereafter declare on behalf of one or more of the territories to which the declaration relates that it accepts the competence of the Court to receive applications from individuals, non-governmental organisations or groups of individuals as provided in Article 34 of the Convention in respect of Articles 1 to 5 of this Protocol.''; and

c. paragraph 2 of Article 7 shall be deleted.

8.   Protocol No. 9 shall be repealed.

Article 3

1.   This Protocol shall be open for signature by member States of the Council of Europe signatories to the Convention, which may express their consent to be bound by

a. signature without reservation as to ratification, acceptance or approval; or

b. signature subject to ratification, acceptance or approval, followed by ratification, acceptance or approval.

2.   The instruments of ratification, acceptance or approval shall be deposited with the Secretary General of the Council of Europe.

Article 4

This Protocol shall enter into force on the first day of the month following the expiration of a period of one year after the date on which all Parties to the Convention have expressed their consent to be bound by the Protocol in accordance with the provisions of Article 3. The election of new judges may take place, and any further necessary steps may be taken to establish the new Court, in accordance with the provisions of this Protocol from the date on which all Parties to the Convention have expressed their consent to be bound by the Protocol.

Article 5

1.   Without prejudice to the provisions in paragraphs 3 and 4 below, the terms of office of the judges, members of the Commission, Registrar and Deputy Registrar shall expire at the date of entry into force of this Protocol.

2.   Applications pending before the Commission which have not been declared admissible at the date of the entry into force of this Protocol shall be examined by the Court in accordance with the provisions of this Protocol.

3.   Applications which have been declared admissible at the date of entry into force of this Protocol shall continue to be dealt with by members of the Commission within a period of one year thereafter. Any applications the examination of which has not been completed within the aforesaid period shall be transmitted to the Court which shall examine them as admissible cases in accordance with the provisions of this Protocol.

4. With respect to applications in which the Commission, after the entry into force of this Protocol, has adopted a report in accordance with former Article 31 of the Convention, the report shall be transmitted to the parties, who shall not be at liberty to publish it. In accordance with the provisions applicable prior to the entry into force of this Protocol, a case may be referred to the Court. The panel of the Grand Chamber shall determine whether one of the Chambers or the Grand Chamber shall decide the case. If the case is decided by a Chamber, the decision of the Chamber shall be final. Cases not referred to the Court shall be dealt with by the Committee of Ministers acting in accordance with the provisions of former Article 32 of the Convention.

5. Cases pending before the Court which have not been decided at the date of entry into force of this Protocol shall be transmitted to the Grand Chamber of the Court, which shall examine them in accordance with the provisions of this Protocol.

6. Cases pending before the Committee of Ministers which have not been decided under former Article 32 of the Convention at the date of entry into force of this Protocol shall be completed by the Committee of Ministers acting in accordance with that Article.

Article 6

Where a High Contracting Party had made a declaration recognising the competence of the Commission or the jurisdiction of the Court under former Article 25 or 46 of the Convention with respect to matters arising after or based on facts occurring subsequent to any such declaration, this limitation shall remain valid for the jurisdiction of the Court under this Protocol.

Article 7

The Secretary General of the Council of Europe shall notify the member States of the Council of

a. any signature;

b. the deposit of any instrument of ratification, acceptance or approval;

c. the date of entry into force of this Protocol or of any of its provisions in accordance with Article 4; and

d. any other act, notification or communication relating to this Protocol.

IN WITNESS WHEREOF the undersigned, being duly authorised thereto, have signed this Protocol.

DONE at Strasbourg, this 11th day of May 1994 in English and French, both texts being equally authentic, in a single copy which shall be deposited in the archives of the Council of Europe. The Secretary General of the Council of Europe shall transmit certified copies to each member State of the Council of Europe

APPENDIX

Headings of articles to be inserted into the text of the Convention for the Protection of Human Rights and Fundamental Freedoms and its protocols*

Article 1—Obligation to respect human rights

Article 2—Right to life

Article 3—Prohibition of torture

Article 4—Prohibition of slavery and forced labour

Article 5—Right to liberty and security

Article 6—Right to a fair trial

Article 7—No punishment without law

Article 8—Right to respect for private and family life

Article 9—Freedom of thought, conscience and religion

Article 10—Freedom of expression

Article 11—Freedom of assembly and association

Article 12—Right to marry

Article 13—Right to an effective remedy

Article 14—Prohibition of discrimination

Article 15—Derogation in time of emergency

Article 16—Restrictions on political activity of aliens

Article 17—Prohibition of abuse of rights

Article 18—Limitation on use of restrictions on rights

[. . .]

Article 52—Enquiries by the Secretary General

Article 53—Safeguard for existing human rights

Article 54—Powers of the Committee of Ministers

Article 55—Exclusion of other means of dispute settlement

Article 56—Territorial application

---

* Headings have already been added to new Articles 19 to 51 of the Convention by the present Protocol.

Protocol No. 7

17. European Agreement relating to Persons Participating in Proceedings at the European Court of Human Rights

Adopted at Strasbourg on 5 March 1996

The member States of the Council of Europe, signatories hereto,

Having regard to the Convention for the Protection of Human Rights and Fundamental Freedoms, signed at Rome on 4 November 1950 (hereinafter referred to as "the Convention");

Recalling the European Agreement relating to Persons Participating in Proceedings of the European Commission and Court of Human Rights, signed at London on 6 May 1969;

Having regard to Protocol No. 11 to the Convention, restructuring the control machinery established thereby, signed at Strasbourg on 11 May 1994 (hereinafter referred to as "Protocol No. 11 to the Convention"), which establishes a permanent European Court of Human Rights (hereinafter referred to as "the Court") to replace the European Commission and Court of Human Rights;

Considering, in the light of this development, that it is advisable for the better fulfilment of the purposes of the Convention that persons taking part in proceedings before the Court be accorded certain immunities and facilities by a new Agreement, the European Agreement relating to Persons Participating in Proceedings of the European Court of Human Rights (hereinafter referred to as "this Agreement"),

Have agreed as follows:

Article 1

1. The persons to whom this Agreement applies are:

a. any persons taking part in proceedings instituted before the Court as parties, their representatives and advisers;

b. witnesses and experts called upon by the Court and other persons invited by the President of the Court to take part in proceedings.

2. For the purposes of this Agreement, the term "Court" shall include committees, chambers, a panel of the Grand Chamber, the Grand Chamber and the judges. The term "taking part in proceedings" shall in-

clude making communications with a view to a complaint against a State Party to the Convention.

3. If in the course of the exercise by the Committee of Ministers of its functions under Article 46, paragraph 2, of the Convention, any person mentioned in paragraph 1 above is called upon to appear before, or to submit written statements to the Committee of Ministers, the provisions of this Agreement shall apply in relation to him.

Article 2

1. The persons referred to in paragraph 1 of Article 1 of this Agreement shall have immunity from legal process in respect of oral or written statements made, or documents or other evidence submitted by them before or to the Court.

2. This immunity does not apply to communication outside the Court of any such statements, documents or evidence submitted to the Court.

Article 3

1. The Contracting Parties shall respect the right of the persons referred to in paragraph 1 of Article 1 of this Agreement to correspond freely with the Court.

2. As regards persons under detention, the exercise of this right shall in particular imply that:

a. their correspondence shall be despatched and delivered without undue delay and without alteration;

b. such persons shall not be subject to disciplinary measures in any form on account of any communication sent through the proper channels to the Court;

c. such persons shall have the right to correspond, and consult out of hearing of other persons, with a lawyer qualified to appear before the courts of the country where they are detained in regard to an application to the Court, or any proceedings resulting therefrom.

3. In application of the preceding paragraphs, there shall be no interference by a public authority except such as is in accordance with the law and is necessary in a democratic society in the interests of national security, for the detection or prosecution of a criminal offence or for the protection of health.

Article 4

1. *a.* The Contracting Parties undertake not to hinder the free movement and travel, for the purpose of attending and returning from proceedings before the Court, of persons referred to in paragraph 1 of Article 1 of this Agreement.

b. No restrictions shall be placed on their movement and travel other than such as are in accordance with the law and necessary in a democratic society in the interests of national security or public safety, for the maintenance of *ordre public*, for the prevention of crime, for the protection of health or morals, or for the protection of the rights and freedoms of others.

2. *a.* Such persons shall not, in countries of transit and in the country where the proceedings take place, be prosecuted or detained or be subjected to any other restriction of their personal liberty in respect of acts or convictions prior to the commencement of the journey.

b. Any Contracting Party may, at the time of signature, ratification, acceptance or approval of this Agreement, declare that the provisions of this paragraph will not apply to its own nationals. Such a declaration may be withdrawn at any time by means of a notification addressed to the Secretary General of the Council of Europe.

3. The Contracting Parties undertake to re-admit on his return to their territory any such person who commenced his journey in the said territory.

4. The provisions of paragraphs 1 and 2 of this Article shall cease to apply when the person concerned has had, for a period of fifteen consecutive days from the date when his presence is no longer required by the Court, the opportunity of returning to the country from which his journey commenced.

5. Where there is any conflict between the obligations of a Contracting Party resulting from paragraph 2 of this Article and those resulting from a Council of Europe convention or from an extradition treaty or other treaty concerning mutual assistance in criminal matters with other Contracting Parties, the provisions of paragraph 2 of this Article shall prevail.

Article 5

1. Immunities and facilities are accorded to the persons referred to in paragraph 1 of Article 1 of this Agreement solely in order to ensure for them the freedom of speech and the independence necessary for the discharge of their functions, tasks or duties, or the exercise of their rights in relation to the Court.

2. *a.* The Court shall alone be competent to waive, in whole or in part, the immunity provided for in paragraph 1 of Article 2 of this Agreement; it has not only the right but the duty to waive immunity in any case

where, in its opinion, such immunity would impede the course of justice and waiver in whole or in part would not prejudice the purpose defined in paragraph 1 of this Article.

b. The immunity may be waived by the Court, either *ex officio* or at the request of any Contracting Party or of any person concerned.

c. Decisions waiving immunity or refusing the waiver shall be accompanied by a statement of reasons.

3. If a Contracting Party certifies that waiver of the immunity provided for in paragraph 1 of Article 2 of this Agreement is necessary for the purpose of proceedings in respect of an offence against national security, the Court shall waive immunity to the extent specified in the certificate.

4. In the event of the discovery of a fact which might, by its nature, have a decisive influence and which at the time of the decision refusing waiver of immunity was unknown to the author of the request, the latter may make a new request to the Court.

Article 6

Nothing in this Agreement shall be construed as limiting or derogating from any of the obligations assumed by the Contracting Parties under the Convention or its protocols.

Article 7

1. This Agreement shall be open for signature by the member States of the Council of Europe, which may express their consent to be bound by;

a. signature without reservation as to ratification, acceptance or approval; or

b. signature, subject to ratification, acceptance or approval, followed by ratification, acceptance or approval.

2. Instruments of ratification, acceptance or approval shall be deposited with the Secretary General of the Council of Europe.

Article 8

1. This Agreement shall enter into force on the first day of the month following the expiration of a period of one month after the date on which ten member States of the Council of Europe have expressed their consent to be bound by the Agreement in accordance with the provisions of Article 7 or on the date of entry into force of Protocol No. 11 to the Convention, whichever is the later.

2. In respect of any member State which subsequently expresses its consent to be bound by it, this Agreement shall enter into force on the first day of the month following the expiration of a period of one month after the date of such signature or of the deposit of the instrument of ratification, acceptance or approval.

Article 9

1. Any Contracting State may, when depositing its instrument of ratification, acceptance or approval or at any later date, by declaration addressed to the Secretary General of the Council of Europe, extend this Agreement to any territory or territories specified in the declaration and for whose international relations it is responsible or on whose behalf it is authorised to give undertakings.

2. This Agreement shall enter into force for any territory or territories specified in a declaration made pursuant to paragraph 1 on the first day of the month following the expiration of one month after the date of receipt of the declaration by the Secretary General.

3. Any declaration made pursuant to paragraph 1 may, in respect of any territory mentioned in such declaration, be withdrawn according to the procedure laid down for denunciation in Article 10 of this Agreement.

Article 10

1. This Agreement shall remain in force indefinitely.

2. Any Contracting Party may, insofar as it is concerned, denounce this Agreement by means of a notification addressed to the Secretary General of the Council of Europe.

3. Such denunciation shall take effect six months after the date of receipt by the Secretary General of such notification. Such denunciation shall not have the effect of releasing the Contracting Parties concerned from any obligation which may have arisen under this Agreement in relation to any person referred to in paragraph 1 of Article 1.

Article 11

The Secretary General of the Council of Europe shall notify the member States of the Council of:

a. any signature;

b. the deposit of any instrument of ratification, acceptance or approval;

c. any date of entry into force of this Agreement in accordance with Articles 8 and 9 thereof;

d. any other act, notification or communication relating to this Agreement.

IN WITNESS WHEREOF the undersigned, being duly authorised thereto, have signed this Agreement.

DONE at Strasbourg, this 5th day of March 1996, in English and French, both texts being equally authentic, in a single copy which shall be deposited in the archives of the Council of Europe. The Secretary General of the Council of Europe shall transmit certified copies to each member State of the Council of Europe.

18. European Agreement on Regulations Governing the Movement of Persons between Member States of the Council of Europe

Adopted at Paris on 13 December 1957

ENTRY INTO FORCE: 1 January 1958, in accordance with article 9

The Governments signatory hereto, being Members of the Council of Europe,

Desirous of facilitating personal travel between their countries,

Have agreed as follows:

Article 1

(1) Nationals of the Contracting Parties, whatever their country of residence, may enter or leave the territory of another Party by all frontiers on presentation of one of the documents listed in the Appendix to this Agreement, which is an integral part thereof.

(2) The facilities mentioned in paragraph (1) above shall be available only for visits of not more than three months' duration.

(3) Valid passports and visas may be required for all visits of more than three months' duration or whenever the territory of another Party is entered for the purpose of pursuing a gainful activity.

(4) For the purposes of this Agreement, the term "territory" of a Contracting Party shall have the meaning assigned to it by such a Party in a declaration addressed to the Secretary-General of the Council of Europe for communication to all other Contracting Parties.

Article 2

To the extent that one or more Contracting Parties deem necessary, the frontier shall be crossed only at authorised points.

Article 3

The foregoing provisions shall in no way prejudice the laws and regulations governing visits by aliens to the territory of any Contracting Party.

Article 4

This Agreement shall not prejudice the provisions of any domestic law and bilateral or multilateral treaties, conventions or agreements now in force or which may hereafter enter into force, whereby more favourable terms are applied to the nationals of other Contracting Parties in respect of the crossing of frontiers.

Article 5

Each Contracting Party shall allow the holder of any of the documents mentioned in the list drawn up by it and embodied in the Appendix to this Agreement to re-enter its territory without formality even if his nationality is under dispute.

Article 6

Each Contracting Party reserves the right to forbid nationals of another Party whom it considers undesirable to enter or stay in its territory.

Article 7

Each Contracting Party reserves the option, on grounds relating to *ordre public*, security or public health, to delay the entry into force of this Agreement or order the temporary suspension thereof in respect of all or some of the other Parties, except insofar as the provisions of Article 5 are concerned. This measure shall immediately be notified to the Secretary-General of the Council of Europe, who shall inform the other Parties. The same procedure shall apply as soon as this measure ceases to be operative.

A Contracting Party which avails itself of either of the options mentioned in the preceding paragraph may not claim the application of this Agreement by another Party save insofar as it also applies it in respect of that Party.

Article 8

This Agreement shall be open to the signature of the Members of the Council of Europe, who may become Parties to it either by:

(*a*) signature without reservation in respect of ratification;

(*b*) signature with reservation in respect of ratification followed by ratification.

Instruments of ratification shall be deposited with the Secretary-General of the Council of Europe.

Article 9

This Agreement shall enter into force on the first day of the month following the date on which three Members of the Council shall, in accordance with Article 8, have signed the Agreement without reservation in respect of ratification or shall have ratified it.

In the case of any Member who shall subsequently sign the Agreement without reservation in respect of ratification or shall ratify it, the Agreement shall enter into force on the first day of the month following such signature or the deposit of the instrument of ratification.

Article 10

After entry into force of this Agreement, the Committee of Ministers of the Council of Europe may invite any non-Member State to accede to it. Such accession shall take effect on the first day of the month following the deposit of the instrument of accession with the Secretary-General of the Council of Europe.

Article 11

Any Government wishing to sign or accede to this Agreement which has not yet drawn up its list of the documents mentioned in Article 1, paragraph (1), and appearing in the Appendix, shall submit a list of such documents to the Contracting Parties through the Secretary-General of the Council of Europe. This list shall be considered to be approved by all the Contracting Parties and shall be added to the Appendix to this Agreement if no objection is raised within two months of its transmission by the Secretary-General.

The same procedure shall apply if a signatory Government wishes to alter the list of documents drawn up by it and embodied in the Appendix.

Article 12

The Secretary-General of the Council of Europe shall notify Members of the Council and acceding States:

(a) of the date of entry into force of this Agreement and the names of any Members who have signed without reservation in respect of ratification or who have ratified it;

(b) of the deposit of any instrument of accession in accordance with Article 10;

(c) of any notification received in accordance with Article 13 and of its effective date.

Article 13

Any Contracting Party may terminate its own application of the Agreement by giving three months' notice to that effect to the Secretary-General of the Council of Europe.

IN WITNESS WHEREOF the undersigned, being duly authorised thereto, have signed this Convention.

DONE at Paris, this 13th day of December 1957, in English and French, both texts being equally authentic, in a single copy which shall remain deposited in the archives of the Council of Europe. The Secretary-General of the Council of Europe shall transmit certified copies to the signatory Governments.

19. European Agreement on the Abolition of Visas for Refugees

Adopted at Strasbourg on 20 April 1959

ENTRY INTO FORCE: 3 September 1960, in accordance with article 9

The Governments signatory hereto, being Members of the Council of Europe,

Desirous of facilitating travel for refugees residing in their territory,

Have agreed as follows:

Article 1

1. Refugees lawfully resident in the territory of a Contracting Party shall be exempt, under the terms of this Agreement and subject to reciprocity, from the obligation to obtain visas for entering or leaving the territory of another Party by any frontier, provided that:

(a) they hold a valid travel document issued in accordance with the Convention on the Status of Refugees of 28th July 1951 or the Agreement relating to the issue of a travel document to refugees of 15th October 1946, by the authorities of the Contracting Party in whose territory they are lawfully resident;

(b) their visit is of not more than three months' duration.

2. A visa may be required for a stay of longer than three months or for the purpose of taking up gainful employment in the territory of another Contracting Party.

Article 2

For the purposes of the present Agreement the "territory" of a Contracting Party shall have the meaning assigned to it by this Party in a declaration addressed to the Secretary-General of the Council of Europe.

Article 3

To the extent that one or more Contracting Parties deem necessary, the frontier shall be crossed only at authorised points.

Article 4

1.   The provisions of this Agreement shall be without prejudice to the laws or regulations governing visits by aliens to the territory of any Contracting Party.

2.   Each Contracting Party reserves the right to prohibit persons it deems to be undesirable from entering or staying in its territory.

Article 5

Refugees who have entered the territory of a Contracting Party by virtue of the present Agreement shall be re-admitted at any time to the territory of the Contracting Party by whose authorities the travel document was issued, at the simple request of the first-mentioned Party, except where this Party has authorised the persons concerned to settle in its territory.

Article 6

This Agreement shall not prejudice the provisions of any municipal law or bilateral or multilateral treaties, conventions or agreements now in force or which may hereafter enter into force, whereby more favourable terms are applied to refugees lawfully resident in the territory of a Contracting Party in respect of the crossing of frontiers.

Article 7

1.   Each Contracting Party reserves the option, for reasons of *ordre public*, security or public health, to delay the entry into force of this Agreement, or order the temporary suspension thereof in respect of all or some of the other Parties, except in so far as the provisions of Article 5 are concerned. The Secretary-General of the Council of Europe shall immediately be informed when any such measure is taken and again when it ceases to be operative.

2.   A Contracting Party which avails itself of either of the options provided for in the foregoing paragraph may not claim the application of this Agreement by another Party save in so far as it also applies it in respect of that Party.

Article 8

This Agreement shall be open to the signature of Members of the Council of Europe, who may become Parties thereto either by:

(a)   signature without reservation in respect of ratification, or (*b*) signature with reservation in respect of ratification, followed by ratification.

Instruments of ratification shall be deposited with the Secretary-General of the Council of Europe.

Article 9

1. The Agreement shall enter into force one month after the date on which three Members of the Council, in accordance with Article 8, shall have signed the Agreement without reservation in respect of ratification or shall have ratified it.

2. In the case of any Member who shall subsequently sign the Agreement without reservation in respect of ratification, or shall ratify it, the Agreement shall enter into force one month after the date of such signature or the date of deposit of the instrument of ratification.

Article 10

After this Agreement has entered into force the Committee of Ministers of the Council of Europe may, by unanimous vote, invite any Government not a Member of the Council, which is party either to the Convention on the Status of Refugees of 28th July 1951 or to the Agreement relating to the issue of a travel document to refugees of 15th October 1946, to accede to this Agreement. Such accession shall take effect one month after the date of deposit of the instrument of accession with the Secretary-General of the Council of Europe.

Article 11

The Secretary-General of the Council of Europe shall notify Member States of the Council and States acceding to this Agreement:

(*a*) of every signature, with any reservations in respect of ratification, of the deposit of each instrument of ratification, and of the date on which the Agreement enters into force;

(*b*) of the deposit of any instrument of accession in accordance with Article 10;

(*c*) of any notification or declaration received in accordance with Articles 2, 7 and 12, and the date on which it takes effect.

Article 12

Any Contracting Party may terminate its own application of the Agreement by giving three months' notice to that effect to the Secretary-General of the Council of Europe.

IN WITNESS WHEREOF the undersigned, being duly authorised thereto, have signed this Agreement.

DONE at Strasbourg, this 20th day of April 1959, in English and French, both texts being equally authoritative, in a single copy which shall remain deposited in the archives of the Council of Europe. The Secretary-General shall transmit certified copies to the signatory Governments.

20. European Social Charter

Adopted at Turin on 18 October 1961

ENTRY INTO FORCE: 26 February 1965, in accordance with article 35

The Governments signatory hereto, being Members of the Council of Europe,

Considering that the aim of the Council of Europe is the achievement of greater unity between its Members for the purpose of safeguarding and realising the ideals and principles which are their common heritage and of facilitating their economic and social progress, in particular by the maintenance and further realisation of human rights and fundamental freedoms;

Considering that in the European Convention for the Protection of Human Rights and Fundamental Freedoms signed at Rome on 4th November 1950, and the Protocol thereto signed at Paris on 20th March 1952, the member States of the Council of Europe agreed to secure to their populations the civil and political rights and freedoms therein specified;

Considering that the enjoyment of social rights should be secured without discrimination on grounds of race, colour, sex, religion, political opinion, national extraction or social origin;

Being resolved to make every effort in common to improve the standard of living and to promote the social well-being of both their urban and rural populations by means of appropriate institutions and action,

Have agreed as follows:

PART I

The Contracting Parties accept as the aim of their policy, to be pursued by all appropriate means, both national and international in character, the attainment of conditions in which the following rights and principles may be effectively realised:

1.   Everyone shall have the opportunity to earn his living in an occupation freely entered upon.

2.   All workers have the right to just conditions of work.

3.   All workers have the right to safe and healthy working conditions.

4.   All workers have the right to a fair remuneration sufficient for a decent standard of living for themselves and their families.

5.   All workers and employers have the right to freedom of association in national or international organisations for the protection of their economic and social interests.

6.   All workers and employers have the right to bargain collectively.

7.   Children and young persons have the right to a special protection against the physical and moral hazards to which they are exposed.

8.   Employed women, in case of maternity, and other employed women as appropriate, have the right to a special protection in their work.

9.   Everyone has the right to appropriate facilities for vocational guidance with a view to helping him choose an occupation suited to his personal aptitude and interests.

10.   Everyone has the right to appropriate facilities for vocational training.

11.   Everyone has the right to benefit from any measures enabling him to enjoy the highest possible standard of health attainable.

12.   All workers and their dependants have the right to social security.

13.   Anyone without adequate resources has the right to social and medical assistance.

14.   Everyone has the right to benefit from social welfare services.

15.   Disabled persons have the right to vocational training, rehabilitation and resettlement, whatever the origin and nature of their disability.

16.   The family as a fundamental unit of society has the right to appropriate social, legal and economic protection to ensure its full development.

17.   Mothers and children, irrespective of marital status and family relations, have the right to appropriate social and economic protection.

18.   The nationals of any one of the Contracting Parties have the right to engage in any gainful occupation in the territory of any one of the others on a footing of equality with the nationals of the latter, subject to restrictions based on cogent economic or social reasons.

19.   Migrant workers who are nationals of a Contracting Party and their families have the right to protection and assistance in the territory of any other Contracting Party.

PART II

The Contracting Parties undertake, as provided for in Part III, to consider themselves bound by the obligations laid down in the following Articles and paragraphs.

Article 1

THE RIGHT TO WORK

With a view to ensuring the effective exercise of the right to work, the Contracting Parties undertake:

1.   to accept as one of their primary aims and responsibilities the achievement and maintenance of as high and stable a level of employment as possible, with a view to the attainment of full employment;

2.   to protect effectively the right of the worker to earn his living in an occupation freely entered upon;

3.   to establish or maintain free employment services for all workers;

4.   to provide or promote appropriate vocational guidance, training and rehabilitation.

Article 2

THE RIGHT TO JUST CONDITIONS OF WORK

With a view to ensuring the effective exercise of the right to just conditions of work, the Contracting Parties undertake:

1.   to provide for reasonable daily and weekly working hours, the working week to be progressively reduced to the extent that the increase of productivity and other relevant factors permit;

2.   to provide for public holidays with pay;

3.   to provide for a minimum of two weeks' annual holiday with pay;

4.   to provide for additional paid holidays or reduced working hours for workers engaged in dangerous or unhealthy occupations as prescribed;

5.   to ensure a weekly rest period which shall, as far as possible, coincide with the day recognised by tradition or custom in the country or region concerned as a day of rest.

Article 3

THE RIGHT TO SAFE AND HEALTHY WORKING CONDITIONS

With a view to ensuring the effective exercise of the right to safe and healthy working conditions, the Contracting Parties undertake:

1. to issue safety and health regulations;

2. to provide for the enforcement of such regulations by measures of supervision;

3. to consult, as appropriate, employers' and workers' organisations on measures intended to improve industrial safety and health.

Article 4

THE RIGHT TO A FAIR REMUNERATION

With a view to ensuring the effective exercise of the right to a fair remuneration, the Contracting Parties undertake:

1. to recognise the right of workers to a remuneration such as will give them and their families a decent standard of living;

2. to recognise the right of workers to an increased rate of remuneration for overtime work, subject to exceptions in particular cases;

3. to recognise the right of men and women workers to equal pay for work of equal value;

4. to recognise the right of all workers to a reasonable period of notice for termination of employment;

5. to permit deductions from wages only under conditions and to the extent prescribed by national laws or regulations or fixed by collective agreements or arbitration awards.

The exercise of these rights shall be achieved by freely concluded collective agreements, by statutory wage-fixing machinery, or by other means appropriate to national conditions.

Article 5

THE RIGHT TO ORGANISE

With a view to ensuring or promoting the freedom of workers and employers to form local, national or international organisations for the protection of their economic and social interests and to join those organisations, the Contracting Parties undertake that national law shall not be such as to impair, nor shall it be so applied as to impair, this freedom. The extent to which the guarantees provided for in this Article shall apply to the police shall be determined by national laws or regulations. The principle governing the application to the members of the armed forces of these guarantees and the extent to which they shall apply to persons in this category shall equally be determined by national laws or regulations.

Article 6

THE RIGHT TO BARGAIN COLLECTIVELY

With a view to ensuring the effective exercise of the right to bargain collectively, the Contracting Parties undertake:

1. to promote joint consultation between workers and employers;

2. to promote, where necessary and appropriate, machinery for voluntary negotiations between employers or employers' organisations and workers' organisations, with a view to the regulation of terms and conditions of employment by means of collective agreements;

3. to promote the establishment and use of appropriate machinery for conciliation and voluntary arbitration for the settlement of labour disputes;

and recognise:

4. the right of workers and employers to collective action in cases of conflicts of interest, including the right to strike, subject to obligations that might arise out of collective agreements previously entered into.

Article 7

THE RIGHT OF CHILDREN AND YOUNG PERSONS TO PROTECTION

With a view to ensuring the effective exercise of the right of children and young persons to protection, the Contracting Parties undertake:

1. to provide that the minimum age of admission to employment shall be 15 years, subject to exceptions for children employed in prescribed light work without harm to their health, morals or education;

2. to provide that a higher minimum age of admission to employment shall be fixed with respect to prescribed occupations regarded as dangerous or unhealthy;

3. to provide that persons who are still subject to compulsory education shall not be employed in such work as would deprive them of the full benefit of their education;

4. to provide that the working hours of persons under 16 years of age shall be limited in accordance with the needs of their development, and particularly with their need for vocational training;

5. to recognise the right of young workers and apprentices to a fair wage or other appropriate allowances;

6. to provide that the time spent by young persons in vocational training during the normal working hours with the consent of the employer shall be treated as forming part of the working day;

7. to provide that employed persons under 18 years of age shall be entitled to not less than three weeks' annual holiday with pay;

8. to provide that persons under 18 years of age shall not be employed in night work with the exception of certain occupations provided for by national laws or regulations;

9. to provide that persons under 18 years of age employed in occupations prescribed by national laws or regulations shall be subject to regular medical control;

10. to ensure special protection against physical and moral dangers to which children and young persons are exposed, and particularly against those resulting directly or indirectly from their work.

Article 8

THE RIGHT OF EMPLOYED WOMEN TO PROTECTION

With a view to ensuring the effective exercise of the right of employed women to protection, the Contracting Parties undertake:

1. to provide either by paid leave, by adequate social security benefits or by benefits from public funds for women to take leave before and after childbirth up to a total of at least 12 weeks;

2. to consider it as unlawful for an employer to give a woman notice of dismissal during her absence on maternity leave or to give her notice of dismissal at such a time that the notice would expire during such absence;

3. to provide that mothers who are nursing their infants shall be entitled to sufficient time off for this purpose;

4. (a) to regulate the employment of women workers on night work in industrial employment;

(b) to prohibit the employment of women workers in underground mining and, as appropriate, on all other work which is unsuitable for them by reason of its dangerous, unhealthy, or arduous nature.

Article 9

THE RIGHT TO VOCATIONAL GUIDANCE

With a view to ensuring the effective exercise of the right to vocational guidance, the Contracting Parties undertake to provide or promote, as necessary, a service which will assist all persons, including the handicapped, to solve problems related to occupational choice and progress, with due regard to the individual's characteristics and their relation to occupational opportunity: this assistance should be available free of charge, both to young persons, including school children, and to adults.

Article 10

THE RIGHT TO VOCATIONAL TRAINING

With a view to ensuring the effective exercise of the right to vocational training, the Contracting Parties undertake:

1. to provide or promote, as necessary, the technical and vocational training of all persons, including the handicapped, in consultation with employers' and workers' organisations, and to grant facilities for access to higher technical and university education, based solely on individual aptitude;

2. to provide or promote a system of apprenticeship and other systematic arrangements for training young boys and girls in their various employments;

3. to provide or promote, as necessary:

(a) adequate and readily available training facilities for adult workers;

(b) special facilities for the re-training of adult workers needed as a result of technological development or new trends in employment;

4. to encourage the full utilisation of the facilities provided by appropriate measures such as:

(a) reducing or abolishing any fees or charges;

(b) granting financial assistance in appropriate cases;

(c) including in the normal working hours time spent on supplementary training taken by the worker, at the request of his employer, during employment;

(d) ensuring, through adequate supervision, in consultation with the employers' and workers' organisations, the efficiency of apprenticeship and other training arrangements for young workers, and the adequate protection of young workers generally.

Article 11

THE RIGHT TO PROTECTION OF HEALTH

With a view to ensuring the effective exercise of the right to protection of health, the Contracting Parties undertake, either directly or in cooperation with public or private organisations, to take appropriate measures designed *inter alia*:

1. to remove as far as possible the causes of ill-health;

2. to provide advisory and educational facilities for the promotion of health and the encouragement of individual responsibility in matters of health;

3. to prevent as far as possible epidemic, endemic and other diseases.

Article 12

THE RIGHT TO SOCIAL SECURITY

With a view to ensuring the effective exercise of the right to social security, the Contracting Parties undertake:

1. to establish or maintain a system of social security;

2. to maintain the social security system at a satisfactory level at least equal to that required for ratification of International Labour Convention (No. 102) Concerning Minimum Standards of Social Security;

3. to endeavour to raise progressively the system of social security to a higher level;

4. to take steps, by the conclusion of appropriate bilateral and multilateral agreements, or by other means, and subject to the conditions laid down in such agreements, in order to ensure:

(*a*) equal treatment with their own nationals of the nationals of other Contracting Parties in respect of social security rights, including the retention of benefits arising out of social security legislation, whatever movements the persons protected may undertake between the territories of the Contracting Parties;

(*b*) the granting, maintenance and resumption of social security rights by such means as the accumulation of insurance or employment periods completed under the legislation of each of the Contracting Parties.

Article 13

THE RIGHT TO SOCIAL AND MEDICAL ASSISTANCE

With a view to ensuring the effective exercise of the right to social and medical assistance, the Contracting Parties undertake:

1. to ensure that any person who is without adequate resources and who is unable to secure such resources either by his own efforts or from other sources, in particular by benefits under a social security scheme, be granted adequate assistance, and, in case of sickness, the care necessitated by his condition;

2. to ensure that persons receiving such assistance shall not, for that reason, suffer from a diminution of their political or social rights;

3. to provide that everyone may receive by appropriate public or private services such advice and personal help as may be required to prevent, to remove, or to alleviate personal or family want;

4. to apply the provisions referred to in paragraphs 1, 2 and 3 of this Article on an equal footing with their nationals to nationals of other Contracting Parties lawfully within their territories, in accordance with their obligations under the European Convention on Social and Medical Assistance, signed at Paris on 11th December 1953.

Article 14

THE RIGHT TO BENEFIT FROM SOCIAL WELFARE SERVICES

With a view to ensuring the effective exercise of the right to benefit from social welfare services, the Contracting Parties undertake:

1. to promote or provide services which, by using methods of social work, would contribute to the welfare and development of both individuals and groups in the community, and to their adjustment to the social environment;

2. to encourage the participation of individuals and voluntary or other organisations in the establishment and maintenance of such services.

Article 15

THE RIGHT OF PHYSICALLY OR MENTALLY DISABLED PERSONS
TO VOCATIONAL TRAINING, REHABILITATION AND SOCIAL RESETTLEMENT

With a view to ensuring the effective exercise of the right of the physically or mentally disabled to vocational training, rehabilitation and resettlement, the Contracting Parties undertake:

1. to take adequate measures for the provision of training facilities, including, where necessary, specialised institutions, public or private;

2. to take adequate measures for the placing of disabled persons in employment, such as specialised placing services, facilities for sheltered employment and measures to encourage employers to admit disabled persons to employment.

Article 16

THE RIGHT OF THE FAMILY TO SOCIAL, LEGAL AND ECONOMIC PROTECTION

With a view to ensuring the necessary conditions for the full development of the family, which is a fundamental unit of society, the Contracting Parties undertake to promote the economic, legal and social protection of family life by such means as social and family benefits, fiscal arrangements, provision of family housing, benefits for the newly married, and other appropriate means.

Article 17

THE RIGHT OF MOTHERS AND CHILDREN TO SOCIAL AND ECONOMIC PROTECTION

With a view to ensuring the effective exercise of the right of mothers and children to social and economic protection, the Contracting Parties will take all appropriate and necessary measures to that end, including the establishment or maintenance of appropriate institutions or services.

Article 18

THE RIGHT TO ENGAGE IN A GAINFUL OCCUPATION IN THE TERRITORY OF OTHER CONTRACTING PARTIES

With a view to ensuring the effective exercise of the right to engage in a gainful occupation in the territory of any other Contracting Party, the Contracting Parties undertake:

1. to apply existing regulations in a spirit of liberality;

2. to simplify existing formalities and to reduce or abolish chancery dues and other charges payable by foreign workers or their employers;

3. to liberalise, individually or collectively, regulations governing the employment of foreign workers;

and recognise:

4. the right of their nationals to leave the country to engage in a gainful occupation in the territories of the other Contracting Parties.

Article 19

THE RIGHT OF MIGRANT WORKERS AND THEIR FAMILIES
TO PROTECTION AND ASSISTANCE

With a view to ensuring the effective exercise of the right of migrant workers and their families to protection and assistance in the territory of any other Contracting Party, the Contracting Parties undertake:

1.   to maintain or to satisfy themselves that there are maintained adequate and free services to assist such workers, particularly in obtaining accurate information, and to take all appropriate steps, so far as national laws and regulations permit, against misleading propaganda relating to emigration and immigration;

2.   to adopt appropriate measures within their own jurisdiction to facilitate the departure, journey and reception of such workers and their families, and to provide, within their own jurisdiction, appropriate services for health, medical attention and good hygienic conditions during the journey;

3.   to promote co-operation, as appropriate, between social services, public and private, in emigration and immigration countries;

4.   to secure for such workers lawfully within their territories, insofar as such matters are regulated by law or regulations or are subject to the control of administrative authorities, treatment not less favourable than that of their own nationals in respect of the following matters:

(a)   remuneration and other employment and working conditions;

(b)   membership of trade unions and enjoyment of the benefits of collective bargaining;

(c)   accommodation;

5.   to secure for such workers lawfully within their territories treatment not less favourable than that of their own nationals with regard to employment taxes, dues or contributions payable in respect of employed persons;

6.   to facilitate as far as possible the reunion of the family of a foreign worker permitted to establish himself in the territory;

7.   to secure for such workers lawfully within their territories treatment not less favourable than that of their own nationals in respect of legal proceedings relating to matters referred to in this Article;

8.   to secure that such workers lawfully residing within their territories are not expelled unless they endanger national security or offend against public interest or morality;

9.   to permit, within legal limits, the transfer of such parts of the earnings and savings of such workers as they may desire;

10. to extend the protection and assistance provided for in this Article to self-employed migrants insofar as such measures apply.

PART III

Article 20

UNDERTAKINGS

1. Each of the Contracting Parties undertakes:

(*a*) to consider Part I of this Charter as a declaration of the aims which it will pursue by all appropriate means, as stated in the introductory paragraph of that Part;

(*b*) to consider itself bound by at least five of the following Articles of Part II of this Charter: Articles 1, 5, 6, 12, 13, 16 and 19;

(*c*) in addition to the Articles selected by it in accordance with the preceding sub-paragraph, to consider itself bound by such a number of Articles or numbered paragraphs of Part II of the Charter as it may select, provided that the total number of Articles or numbered paragraphs by which it is bound is not less than 10 articles or 45 numbered paragraphs.

2. The Articles or paragraphs selected in accordance with sub-paragraphs (*b*) and (*c*) of paragraph 1 of this Article shall be notified to the Secretary-General of the Council of Europe at the time when the instrument of ratification or approval of the Contracting Party concerned is deposited.

3. Any Contracting Party may, at a later date, declare by notification to the Secretary-General that it considers itself bound by any Articles or any numbered paragraphs of Part II of the Charter which it has not already accepted under the terms of paragraph 1 of this Article. Such undertakings subsequently given shall be deemed to be an integral part of the ratification or approval, and shall have the same effect as from the thirtieth day after the date of the notification.

4. The Secretary-General shall communicate to all the signatory Governments and to the Director-General of the International Labour Office any notification which he shall have received pursuant to this Part of the Charter.

5. Each Contracting Party shall maintain a system of labour inspection appropriate to national conditions.

PART IV

Article 21

REPORTS CONCERNING ACCEPTED PROVISIONS

The Contracting Parties shall send to the Secretary-General of the Council of Europe a report at two-yearly intervals, in a form to be determined by the Committee of Ministers, concerning the application of such provisions of Part II of the Charter as they have accepted.

Article 22

REPORTS CONCERNING PROVISIONS WHICH ARE NOT ACCEPTED

The Contracting Parties shall send to the Secretary-General, at appropriate intervals as requested by the Committee of Ministers, reports relating to the provisions of Part II of the Charter which they did not accept at the time of their ratification or approval or in a subsequent notification. The Committee of Ministers shall determine from time to time in respect of which provisions such reports shall be requested and the form of the reports to be provided.

Article 23

COMMUNICATION OF COPIES

1. Each Contracting Party shall communicate copies of its reports referred to in Articles 21 and 22 to such of its national organisations as are members of the international organisations of employers and trade unions to be invited under Article 27, paragraph 2, to be represented at meetings of the Sub-committee of the Governmental Social Committee.

2. The Contracting Parties shall forward to the Secretary-General any comments on the said reports received from these national organisations, if so requested by them.

Article 24

EXAMINATION OF THE REPORTS

The reports sent to the Secretary-General in accordance with Articles 21 and 22 shall be examined by a Committee of Experts, who shall have also before them any comments forwarded to the Secretary-General in accordance with paragraph 2 of Article 23.

Article 25

COMMITTEE OF EXPERTS

1. The Committee of Experts shall consist of not more than seven members appointed by the Committee of Ministers from a list of independent experts of the highest integrity and of recognised competence in international social questions, nominated by the Contracting Parties.

2. The members of the Committee shall be appointed for a period of six years. They may be reappointed. However, of the members first appointed, the terms of office of two members shall expire at the end of four years.

3. The members whose terms of office are to expire at the end of the initial period of four years shall be chosen by lot by the Committee of Ministers immediately after the first appointment has been made.

4. A member of the Committee of Experts appointed to replace a member whose term of office has not expired shall hold office for the remainder of his predecessor's term.

Article 26

PARTICIPATION OF THE INTERNATIONAL LABOUR ORGANISATION

The International Labour Organisation shall be invited to nominate a representative to participate in a consultative capacity in the deliberations of the Committee of Experts.

Article 27

SUB-COMMITTEE OF THE GOVERNMENTAL SOCIAL COMMITTEE

1. The reports of the Contracting Parties and the conclusions of the Committee of Experts shall be submitted for examination to a Sub-Committee of the Governmental Social Committee of the Council of Europe.

2. The Sub-committee shall be composed of one representative of each of the Contracting Parties. It shall invite no more than two international organisations of employers and no more than two international trade union organisations as it may designate to be represented as observers in a consultative capacity at its meetings. Moreover, it may consult no more than two representatives of international non-governmental organisations having consultative status with the Council of Europe, in respect of questions with which the organisations are particularly qualified to deal, such as social welfare, and the economic and social protection of the family.

3. The sub-committee shall present to the Committee of Ministers a report containing its conclusions and append the report of the Committee of Experts.

Article 28

CONSULTATIVE ASSEMBLY

The Secretary-General of the Council of Europe shall transmit to the Consultative Assembly the conclusions of the Committee of Experts. The Consultative Assembly shall communicate its views on these conclusions to the Committee of Ministers.

Article 29

COMMITTEE OF MINISTERS

By a majority of two-thirds of the members entitled to sit on the Committee, the Committee of Ministers may, on the basis of the report of the Sub-committee, and after consultation with the Consultative Assembly, make to each Contracting Party any necessary recommendations.

PART V

Article 30

DEROGATIONS IN TIME OF WAR OR PUBLIC EMERGENCY

1. In time of war or other public emergency threatening the life of the nation any Contracting Party may take measures derogating from its obligations under this Charter to the extent strictly required by the exigencies of the situation, provided that such measures are not inconsistent with its other obligations under international law.

2. Any Contracting Party which has availed itself of this right of derogation shall, within a reasonable lapse of time, keep the Secretary-General of the Council of Europe fully informed of the measures taken and of the reasons therefor. It shall likewise inform the Secretary-General when such measures have ceased to operate and the provisions of the Charter which it has accepted are again being fully executed.

3. The Secretary-General shall in turn inform other Contracting Parties and the Director-General of the International Labour Office of all communications received in accordance with paragraph 2 of this Article.

Article 31

RESTRICTIONS

1.   The rights and principles set forth in Part I when effectively realised, and their effective exercise as provided for in Part II, shall not be subject to any restrictions or limitations not specified in those Parts, except such as are prescribed by law and are necessary in a democratic society for the protection of the rights and freedoms of others or for the protection of public interest, national security, public health, or morals.

2.   The restrictions permitted under this Charter to the rights and obligations set forth herein shall not be applied for any purpose other than that for which they have been prescribed.

Article 32

RELATIONS BETWEEN THE CHARTER AND DOMESTIC LAW
OR INTERNATIONAL AGREEMENTS

The provisions of this Charter shall not prejudice the provisions of domestic law or of any bilateral or multilateral treaties, conventions or agreements which are already in force, or may come into force, under which more favourable treatment would be accorded to the persons protected.

Article 33

IMPLEMENTATION BY COLLECTIVE AGREEMENTS

1.   In member States where the provisions of paragraphs 1, 2, 3, 4 and 5 of Article 2, paragraphs 4, 6 and 7 of Article 7 and paragraphs 1, 2, 3 and 4 of Article 10 of Part II of this Charter are matters normally left to agreements between employers or employers' organisations and workers' organisations, or are normally carried out otherwise than by law, the undertakings of those paragraphs may be given and compliance with them shall be treated as effective if their provisions are applied through such agreements or other means to the great majority of the workers concerned.

2.   In member States where these provisions are normally the subject of legislation, the undertakings concerned may likewise be given, and compliance with them shall be regarded as effective if the provisions are applied by law to the great majority of the workers concerned.

Article 34

TERRITORIAL APPLICATION

1.   This Charter shall apply to the metropolitan territory of each Contracting Party. Each signatory Government may, at the time of signature or of the deposit of its instrument of ratification or approval, specify, by declaration addressed to the Secretary-General of the Council of Europe, the territory which shall be considered to be its metropolitan territory for this purpose.

2.   Any Contracting Party may, at the time of ratification or approval of this Charter or at any time thereafter, declare by notification addressed to the Secretary-General of the Council of Europe, that the Charter shall extend in whole or in part to a non-metropolitan territory or territories specified in the said declaration for whose international relations it is responsible or for which it assumes international responsibility. It shall specify in the declaration the Articles or paragraphs of Part II of the Charter which it accepts as binding in respect of the territories named in the declaration.

3.   The Charter shall extend to the territory or territories named in the aforesaid declaration as from the thirtieth day after the date on which the Secretary-General shall have received notification of such declaration.

4.   Any Contracting Party may declare at a later date by notification addressed to the Secretary-General of the Council of Europe that, in respect of one or more of the territories to which the Charter has been extended in accordance with paragraph 2 of this Article, it accepts as binding any Articles or any numbered paragraphs which it has not already accepted in respect of that territory or territories. Such undertakings subsequently given shall be deemed to be an integral part of the original declaration in respect of the territory concerned, and shall have the same effect as from the thirtieth day after the date of the notification.

5.   The Secretary-General shall communicate to the other signatory Governments and to the Director-General of the International Labour Office any notification transmitted to him in accordance with this Article.

Article 35

SIGNATURE, RATIFICATION AND ENTRY INTO FORCE

1.   This Charter shall be open for signature by the Members of the Council of Europe. It shall be ratified or approved. Instruments of ratification or approval shall be deposited with the Secretary-General of the Council of Europe.

2.   This Charter shall come into force as from the thirtieth day after the date of deposit of the fifth instrument of ratification or approval.

3. In respect of any signatory Government ratifying subsequently, the Charter shall come into force as from the thirtieth day after the date of deposit of its instrument of ratification or approval.

4. The Secretary-General shall notify all the Members of the Council of Europe and the Director-General of the International Labour Office of the entry into force of the Charter, the names of the Contracting Parties which have ratified or approved it and the subsequent deposit of any instruments of ratification or approval.

Article 36

AMENDMENTS

Any Member of the Council of Europe may propose amendments to this Charter in a communication addressed to the Secretary-General of the Council of Europe. The Secretary-General shall transmit to the other Members of the Council of Europe any amendments so proposed, which shall then be considered by the Committee of Ministers and submitted to the Consultative Assembly for opinion. Any amendments approved by the Committee of Ministers shall enter into force as from the thirtieth day after all the Contracting Parties have informed the Secretary-General of their acceptance. The Secretary-General shall notify all the Members of the Council of Europe and the Director-General of the International Labour Office of the entry into force of such amendments.

Article 37

DENUNCIATION

1. Any Contracting Party may denounce this Charter only at the end of a period of five years from the date on which the Charter entered into force for it, or at the end of any successive period of two years, and, in each case, after giving six months' notice to the Secretary-General of the Council of Europe, who shall inform the other Parties and the Director-General of the International Labour Office accordingly. Such denunciation shall not affect the validity of the Charter in respect of the other Contracting Parties provided that at all times there are not less than five such Contracting Parties.

2. Any Contracting Party may, in accordance with the provisions set out in the preceding paragraph, denounce any Article or paragraph of Part II of the Charter accepted by it provided that the number of Articles or paragraphs by which this Contracting Party is bound shall never be less than 10 in the former case and 45 in the latter and that this number of Articles or paragraphs shall continue to include the Articles selected by the Contracting Party among those to which special reference is made in Article 20, paragraph 1, sub-paragraph (b).

3.   Any Contracting Party may denounce the present Charter or any of the Articles or paragraphs of Part II of the Charter, under the conditions specified in paragraph 1 of this Article in respect of any territory to which the said Charter is applicable by virtue of a declaration made in accordance with paragraph 2 of Article 34.

Article 38

APPENDIX

The Appendix to this Charter shall form an integral part of it.

IN WITNESS WHEREOF, the undersigned, being duly authorised thereto, have signed this Charter.

DONE at Turin, this 18th day of October 1961, in English and French, both texts being equally authoritative, in a single copy which shall be deposited within the archives of the Council of Europe. The Secretary-General shall transmit certified copies to each of the Signatories.

APPENDIX TO THE SOCIAL CHARTER

SCOPE OF THE SOCIAL CHARTER IN TERMS OF PERSONS PROTECTED

1.   Without prejudice to Article 12, paragraph 4 and Article 13, paragraph 4, the persons covered by Articles 1 to 17 include foreigners only insofar as they are nationals of other Contracting Parties lawfully resident or working regularly within the territory of the Contracting Party concerned, subject to the understanding that these Articles are to be interpreted in the light of the provisions of Articles 18 and 19.

This interpretation would not prejudice the extension of similar facilities to other persons by any of the Contracting Parties.

2.   Each Contracting Party will grant to refugees as defined in the Convention relating to the Status of Refugees, signed at Geneva on 28th July 1951, and lawfully staying in its territory, treatment as favourable as possible, and in any case not less favourable than under the obligations accepted by the Contracting Party under the said Convention and under any other existing international instruments applicable to those refugees.

Part I		*Part II*
PARAGRAPH 18	and	ARTICLE 18, PARAGRAPH 1

It is understood that these provisions are not concerned with the question of entry into the territories of the Contracting Parties and do not prejudice the provisions of the European Convention on Establishment, signed at Paris on 13th December 1955.

Part II

ARTICLE 1, PARAGRAPH 2

This provision shall not be interpreted as prohibiting or authorising any union security clause or practice.

ARTICLE 4, PARAGRAPH 4

This provision shall be so understood as not to prohibit immediate dismissal for any serious offence.

ARTICLE 4, PARAGRAPH 5

It is understood that a Contracting Party may give the undertaking required in this paragraph if the great majority of workers are not permitted to suffer deductions from wages either by law or through collective agreements or arbitration awards, the exceptions being those persons not so covered.

ARTICLE 6, PARAGRAPH 4

It is understood that each Contracting Party may, insofar as it is concerned, regulate the exercise of the right to strike by law, provided that any further restriction that this might place on the right can be justified under the terms of Article 31.

ARTICLE 7, PARAGRAPH 8

It is understood that a Contracting Party may give the undertaking required in this paragraph if it fulfils the spirit of the undertaking by providing by law that the great majority of persons under 18 years of age shall not be employed in night work.

ARTICLE 12, PARAGRAPH 4

The words "and subject to the conditions laid down in such agreements" in the introduction to this paragraph are taken to imply *inter alia* that with regard to benefits which are available independently of any insurance contribution a Contracting Party may require the completion of a prescribed period of residence before granting such benefits to nationals of other Contracting Parties.

ARTICLE 13, PARAGRAPH 4

Governments not Parties to the European Convention on Social and Medical Assistance may ratify the Social Charter in respect of this paragraph provided that they grant to nationals of other Contracting Parties a treatment which is in conformity with the provisions of the said Convention.

ARTICLE 19, PARAGRAPH 6

For the purpose of this provision, the term "family of a foreign worker" is understood to mean at least his wife and dependent children under the age of 21 years.

Part III

It is understood that the Charter contains legal obligations of an international character, the application of which is submitted solely to the supervision provided for in Part IV thereof.

ARTICLE 20, PARAGRAPH 1

It is understood that the "numbered paragraphs" may include Articles consisting of only one paragraph.

Part V

ARTICLE 30

The term "in time of war or other public emergency" shall be so understood as to cover also the threat of war.

21.   Additional Protocol to the European Social Charter

Adopted at Strasbourg on 5 May 1988

ENTRY INTO FORCE: 4 September 1992, in accordance with article 10

PREAMBLE

The member States of the Council of Europe signatory hereto,

Resolved to take new measures to extend the protection of the social and economic rights guaranteed by the European Social Charter, opened for signature in Turin on 18 October 1961 (hereinafter referred to as "the Charter"),

Have agreed as follows:

PART I

The Parties accept as the aim of their policy to be pursued by all appropriate means, both national and international in character, the attainment of conditions in which the following rights and principles may be effectively realised:

1.   All workers have the right to equal opportunities and equal treatment in matters of employment and occupation without discrimination on the grounds of sex.

2.   Workers have the right to be informed and to be consulted within the undertaking.

3.   Workers have the right to take part in the determination and improvement of the working conditions and working environment in the undertaking.

4.   Every elderly person has the right to social protection.

PART II

The Parties undertake, as provided for in Part III, to consider themselves bound by the obligations laid down in the following articles:

Article 1

*Right to equal opportunities and equal treatment in matters of
employment and occupation without discrimination on the grounds of sex*

1.   With a view to ensuring the effective exercise of the right to equal
opportunities and equal treatment in matters of employment and occupation
without discrimination on the grounds of sex, the Parties undertake to recognise that right and to take appropriate measures to ensure or promote its application in the following fields:

—access to employment, protection against dismissal and occupational
resettlement;

—vocational guidance, training, retraining and rehabilitation;

—terms of employment and working conditions including remuneration;

—career development including promotion.

2.   Provisions concerning the protection of women, particularly as regards pregnancy, confinement and the post-natal period, shall not be deemed
to be discrimination as referred to in paragraph 1 of this Article.

3.   Paragraph 1 of this Article shall not prevent the adoption of specific measures aimed at removing de facto inequalities.

4.   Occupational activities which, by reason of their nature or the
context in which they are carried out, can be entrusted only to persons of a
particular sex may be excluded from the scope of this Article or some of its
provisions.

Article 2

Right to information and consultation

1.   With a view to ensuring the effective exercise of the right of
workers to be informed and consulted within the undertaking, the Parties undertake to adopt or encourage measures enabling workers or their representatives, in accordance with national legislation and practice:

a. to be informed regularly or at the appropriate time and in a comprehensible way about the economic and financial situation of the undertaking employing them, on the understanding that the disclosure of certain information which could be prejudicial to the undertaking may be refused or
subject to confidentiality; and

b. to be consulted in good time on proposed decisions which could
substantially affect the interests of workers, particularly on those decisions
which could have an important impact on the employment situation in the
undertaking.

2.   The Parties may exclude from the field of application of paragraph 1 of this Article those undertakings employing less than a certain number of workers to be determined by national legislation or practice.

Article 3

Right to take part in the determination and improvement of the working conditions and working environment

1.   With a view to ensuring the effective exercise of the right of workers to take part in the determination and improvement of the working conditions and working environment in the undertaking, the Parties undertake to adopt or encourage measures enabling workers or their representatives, in accordance with national legislation and practice, to contribute:

a. to the determination and the improvement of the working conditions, work organisation and working environment;

b. to the protection of health and safety within the undertaking;

c. to the organisation of social and socio-cultural services and facilities within the undertaking;

d. to the supervision of the observance of regulations on these matters.

2.   The Parties may exclude from the field of application of paragraph 1 of this Article those undertakings employing less than a certain number of workers to be determined by national legislation or practice.

Article 4

Right of elderly persons to social protection

With a view to ensuring the effective exercise of the right of elderly persons to social protection, the Parties undertake to adopt or encourage, either directly or in co-operation with public or private organisations, appropriate measures designed in particular:

1.   to enable elderly persons to remain full members of society for as long as possible, by means of:

a. adequate resources enabling them to lead a decent life and play an active part in public, social and cultural life;

b. provision of information about services and facilities available for elderly persons and their opportunities to make use of them;

2.   to enable elderly persons to choose their life-style freely and to lead independent lives in their familiar surroundings for as long as they wish and are able, by means of:

    a. provision of housing suited to their needs and their state of health or of adequate support for adapting their housing;

    b. the health care and the services necessitated by their state;

    3. to guarantee elderly persons living in institutions appropriate support, while respecting their privacy, and participation in decisions concerning living conditions in the institution.

PART III

Article 5

Undertakings

    1. Each of the Parties undertakes:

    a. to consider Part I of this Protocol as a declaration of the aims which it will pursue by all appropriate means, as stated in the introductory paragraph of that Part;

    b. to consider itself bound by one or more articles of Part II of this Protocol.

    2. The article or articles selected in accordance with sub-paragraph *b* of paragraph 1 of this Article shall be notified to the Secretary General of the Council of Europe at the time when the instrument of ratification, acceptance or approval of the Contracting State concerned is deposited.

    3. Any Party may, at a later date, declare by notification to the Secretary General that it considers itself bound by any articles of Part II of this Protocol which it has not already accepted under the terms of paragraph 1 of this Article. Such undertakings subsequently given shall be deemed to be an integral part of the ratification, acceptance or approval, and shall have the same effect as from the thirtieth day after the date of the notification.

PART IV

Article 6

Supervision of compliance with the undertakings given

    The Parties shall submit reports on the application of those provisions of Part II of this Protocol which they have accepted in the reports submitted by virtue of Article 21 of the Charter.

PART V

Article 7

Implementation of the undertakings given

1.   The relevant provisions of Articles 1 to 4 of Part II of this Protocol may be implemented by:

a. laws or regulations;

b. agreements between employers or employers' organisations and workers' organisations;

c. a combination of those two methods; or

d. other appropriate means.

2.   Compliance with the undertakings deriving from Articles 2 and 3 of Part II of this Protocol shall be regarded as effective if the provisions are applied, in accordance with paragraph 1 of this Article, to the great majority of the workers concerned.

Article 8

Relations between the Charter and this Protocol

1.   The provisions of this Protocol shall not prejudice the provisions of the Charter.

2.   Articles 22 to 32 and Article 36 of the Charter shall apply, mutatis mutandis, to this Protocol.

Article 9

Territorial application

1.   This Protocol shall apply to the metropolitan territory of each Party. Any State may, at the time of signature or when depositing its instrument of ratification, acceptance or approval, specify by declaration addressed to the Secretary General of the Council of Europe the territory which shall be considered to be its metropolitan territory for this purpose.

2.   Any Contracting State may, at the time of ratification, acceptance or approval of this Protocol or at any time thereafter, declare by notification addressed to the Secretary General of the Council of Europe that the Protocol shall extend in whole or in part to a non-metropolitan territory or territories specified in the said declaration for whose international relations it is responsible or for which it assumes international responsibility. It shall specify in the declaration the article or articles of Part II of the Protocol which it accepts as binding in respect of the territories named in the declaration.

3.   This Protocol shall enter into force in respect of the territory or territories named in the aforesaid declaration as from the thirtieth day after the date on which the Secretary General shall have notification of such declaration.

4.   Any Party may declare at a later date by notification addressed to the Secretary General of the Council of Europe that, in respect of one or more of the territories to which this Protocol has been extended in accordance with paragraph 2 of this Article, it accepts as binding any articles which it has not already accepted in respect of that territory or territories. Such undertakings subsequently given shall be deemed to be an integral part of the original declaration in respect of the territory concerned, and shall have the same effect as from the thirtieth day after the date on which the Secretary General shall have notification of such declaration.

Article 10

Signature, ratification, acceptance, approval and entry into force

1.   This Protocol shall be open for signature by member States of the Council of Europe who are signatories to the Charter. It is subject to ratification, acceptance or approval. No member State of the Council of Europe shall ratify, accept or approve this Protocol except at the same time as or after ratification of the Charter. Instruments of ratification, acceptance or approval shall be deposited with the Secretary General of the Council of Europe.

2.   This Protocol shall enter into force on the thirtieth day after the date of deposit of the third instrument of ratification, acceptance or approval.

3.   In respect of any signatory State ratifying subsequently, this Protocol shall come into force as from the thirtieth day after the date of deposit of its instrument of ratification, acceptance or approval.

Article 11

Denunciation

1.   Any Party may denounce this Protocol only at the end of a period of five years from the date on which the Protocol entered into force for it, or at the end of any successive period of two years, and, in each case, after giving six months' notice to the Secretary General of the Council of Europe. Such denunciation shall not affect the validity of the Protocol in respect of the other Parties provided that at all times there are not less than three such Parties.

2.   Any Party may, in accordance with the provisions set out in the preceding paragraph, denounce any article of Part II of this Protocol ac-

cepted by it, provided that the number of articles by which this Party is bound shall never be less than one.

3.   Any Party may denounce this Protocol or any of the articles of Part II of the Protocol, under the conditions specified in paragraph 1 of this Article, in respect of any territory to which the Protocol is applicable by virtue of a declaration made in accordance with paragraphs 2 and 4 of Article 9.

4.   Any Party bound by the Charter and this Protocol which denounces the Charter in accordance with the provisions of paragraph 1 of Article 37 thereof, will be considered to have denounced the Protocol likewise.

Article 12

Notifications

The Secretary General of the Council of Europe shall notify the member States of the Council and the Director General of the International Labour Office of:

   a. any signature;

   b. the deposit of any instrument of ratification, acceptance or approval;

   c. any date of entry into force of this Protocol in accordance with Articles 9 and 10;

   d. any other act, notification or communication relating to this Protocol.

Article 13

Appendix

The Appendix to this Protocol shall form an integral part of it.

IN WITNESS WHEREOF the undersigned, being duly authorised thereto, have signed this Protocol.

DONE at Strasbourg, this 5th day of May 1988, in English and French, both texts being equally authentic, in a single copy which shall be deposited in the archives of the Council of Europe. The Secretary General of the Council of Europe shall transmit certified copies to each member State of the Council of Europe.

Scope of the Protocol in terms of persons protected

1. The persons covered by Articles 1 to 4 include foreigners only insofar as they are nationals of other Parties lawfully resident or working regularly within the territory of the Party concerned subject to the understanding that these articles are to be interpreted in the light of the provisions of Articles 18 and 19 of the Charter.

This interpretation would not prejudice the extension of similar facilities to other persons by any of the Parties.

2. Each Party will grant to refugees as defined in the Convention relating to the Status of Refugees, signed at Geneva on 28 July 1951, and in the Protocol of 31 January 1967, and lawfully staying in its territory, treatment as favourable as possible and in any case not less favourable than under the obligations accepted by the Party under the said instruments and under any other existing international instruments applicable to those refugees.

3. Each Party will grant to stateless persons as defined in the Convention on the Status of Stateless Persons done at New York on 28 September 1954, and lawfully staying in its territory, treatment as favourable as possible and in any case not less favourable than under the obligations accepted by the Party under the said instrument and under any other existing international instruments applicable to those stateless persons.

Article 1

It is understood that social security matters, as well as other provisions relating to unemployment benefit, old age benefit and survivor's benefit, may be excluded from the scope of this Article.

Article 1, paragraph 4

This provision is not to be interpreted as requiring the Parties to embody in laws or regulations a list of occupations which, by reason of their nature or the context in which they are carried out, may be reserved to persons of a particular sex.

Articles 2 and 3

1. For the purpose of the application of these articles, the term "workers' representatives" means persons who are recognised as such under national legislation or practice.

2. The term "national legislation and practice" embraces as the case may be, in addition to laws and regulations, collective agreements, other

agreements between employers and workers' representatives, customs, as well as relevant case law.

3. For the purpose of the application of these articles, the term "undertaking" is understood as referring to a set of tangible and intangible components, with or without legal personality, formed to produce goods or provide services for financial gain and with power to determine its own market policy.

4. It is understood that religious communities and their institutions may be excluded from the application of these articles, even if these institutions are "undertakings" within the meaning of paragraph 3. Establishments pursuing activities which are inspired by certain ideals or guided by certain moral concepts, ideals and concepts which are protected by national legislation, may be excluded from the application of these articles to such an extent as is necessary to protect the orientation of the undertaking.

5. It is understood that where in a State the rights set out in Articles 2 and 3 are exercised in the various establishments of the undertaking, the Party concerned is to be considered as fulfilling the obligations deriving from these provisions.

Article 3

This provision affects neither the powers and obligations of States as regards the adoption of health and safety regulations for work-places, nor the powers and responsibilities of the bodies in charge of monitoring their application.

The terms "social and socio-cultural services and facilities" are understood as referring to the social and/or cultural facilities for workers provided by some undertakings such as welfare assistance, sports fields, rooms for nursing mothers, libraries, children's holiday camps, etc.

Article 4, paragraph 1

For the purpose of the application of this paragraph, the term "for as long as possible" refers to the elderly person's physical, psychological and intellectual capacities.

Article 7

It is understood that workers excluded in accordance with paragraph 2 of Article 2 and paragraph 2 of Article 3 are not taken into account in establishing the number of workers concerned.

22. Protocol amending the European Social Charter

Adopted at Turin on 21 October 1991

The member States of the Council of Europe, signatory to this Protocol to the European Social Charter, opened for signature in Turin on 18 October 1961 (hereinafter referred to as "the Charter"),

Being resolved to take some measures to improve the effectiveness of the Charter, and particularly the functioning of its supervisory machinery;

Considering therefore that it is desirable to amend certain provisions of the Charter,

Have agreed as follows:

Article 1

Article 23 of the Charter shall read as follows:

"Article 23—Communication of copies of reports and comments

1. When sending to the Secretary General a report pursuant to Articles 21 and 22, each Contracting Party shall forward a copy of that report to such of its national organisations as are members of the international organisations of employers and trade unions invited, under Article 27, paragraph 2, to be represented at meetings of the Governmental Committee. Those organisations shall send to the Secretary General any comments on the reports of the Contracting Parties. The Secretary General shall send a copy of those comments to the Contracting Parties concerned, who might wish to respond.

2. The Secretary General shall forward a copy of the reports of the Contracting Parties to the international non-governmental organisations which have consultative status with the Council of Europe and have particular competence in the matters governed by the present Charter.

3. The reports and comments referred to in Articles 21 and 22 and in the present article shall be made available to the public on request."

Article 2

Article 24 of the Charter shall read as follows:

"Article 24—Examination of the reports

1. The reports sent to the Secretary General in accordance with Articles 21 and 22 shall be examined by a Committee of Independent Experts constituted pursuant to Article 25. The committee shall also have before it any comments forwarded to the Secretary General in accordance with paragraph 1 of Article 23. On completion of its examination, the Committee of Independent Experts shall draw up a report containing its conclusions.

2. With regard to the reports referred to in Article 21, the Committee of Independent Experts shall assess from a legal standpoint the compliance of national law and practice with the obligations arising from the Charter for the Contracting Parties concerned.

3. The Committee of Independent Experts may address requests for additional information and clarification directly to Contracting Parties. In this connection the Committee of Independent Experts may also hold, if necessary, a meeting with the representatives of a Contracting Party, either on its own initiative or at the request of the Contracting Party concerned. The organisations referred to in paragraph 1 of Article 23 shall be kept informed.

4. The conclusions of the Committee of Independent Experts shall be made public and communicated by the Secretary General to the Governmental Committee, to the Parliamentary Assembly and to the organisations which are mentioned in paragraph 1 of Article 23 and paragraph 2 of Article 27."

Article 3

Article 25 of the Charter shall read as follows:

"Article 25—Committee of Independent Experts

1. The Committee of Independent Experts shall consist of at least nine members elected by the Parliamentary Assembly by a majority of votes cast from a list of experts of the highest integrity and of recognised competence in national and international social questions, nominated by the Contracting Parties. The exact number of members shall be determined by the Committee of Ministers.

2. The members of the committee shall be elected for a period of six years. They may stand for re-election once.

3.   A member of the Committee of Independent Experts elected to replace a member whose term of office has not expired shall hold office for the remainder of his predecessor's term.

4.   The members of the committee shall sit in their individual capacity. Throughout their term of office, they may not perform any function incompatible with the requirements of independence, impartiality and availability inherent in their office.''

Article 4

Article 27 of the Charter shall read as follows:

''Article 27—Governmental Committee

1.   The reports of the Contracting Parties, the comments and information communicated in accordance with paragraphs 1 of Article 23 and 3 of Article 24, and the reports of the Committee of Independent Experts shall be submitted to a Governmental Committee.

2.   The committee shall be composed of one representative of each of the Contracting Parties. It shall invite no more than two international organisations of employers and no more than two international trade union organisations to send observers in a consultative capacity to its meetings. Moreover, it may consult representatives of international non-governmental organisations which have consultative status with the Council of Europe and have particular competence in the matters governed by the present Charter.

3.   The Governmental Committee shall prepare the decisions of the Committee of Ministers. In particular, in the light of the reports of the Committee of Independent Experts and of the Contracting Parties, it shall select, giving reasons for its choice, on the basis of social, economic and other policy considerations the situations which should, in its view, be the subject of recommendations to each Contracting Party concerned, in accordance with Article 28 of the Charter. It shall present to the Committee of Ministers a report which shall be made public.

4.   On the basis of its findings on the implementation of the Social Charter in general, the Governmental Committee may submit proposals to the Committee of Ministers aiming at studies to be carried out on social issues and on articles of the Charter which possibly might be updated.''

Article 5

Article 28 of the Charter shall read as follows:

"Article 28—Committee of Ministers

1. The Committee of Ministers shall adopt, by a majority of two-thirds of those voting, with entitlement to voting limited to the Contracting Parties, on the basis of the report of the Governmental Committee, a resolution covering the entire supervision cycle and containing individual recommendations to the Contracting Parties concerned.

2. Having regard to the proposals made by the Governmental Committee pursuant to paragraph 4 of Article 27, the Committee of Ministers shall take such decisions as it deems appropriate."

Article 6

Article 29 of the Charter shall read as follows:

"Article 29—Parliamentary Assembly

The Secretary General of the Council of Europe shall transmit to the Parliamentary Assembly, with a view to the holding of periodical plenary debates, the reports of the Committee of Independent Experts and of the Governmental Committee, as well as the resolutions of the Committee of Ministers."

Article 7

1. This Protocol shall be open for signature by member States of the Council of Europe signatories to the Charter, which may express their consent to be bound by:

a. signature without reservation as to ratification, acceptance or approval; or

b. signature subject to ratification, acceptance or approval, followed by ratification, acceptance or approval.

2. Instruments of ratification, acceptance or approval shall be deposited with the Secretary General of the Council of Europe.

Article 8

This Protocol shall enter into force on the thirtieth day after the date on which all Contracting Parties to the Charter have expressed their consent to be bound by the Protocol in accordance with the provisions of Article 7.

Article 9

The Secretary General of the Council of Europe shall notify the member States of the Council of :

    a. any signature;

    b. the deposit of any instrument of ratification, acceptance or approval;

    c. the date of entry into force of this Protocol in accordance with Article 8;

    d. any other act, notification or communication relating to this Protocol.

IN WITNESS WHEREOF the undersigned, being duly authorised thereto, have signed this Protocol.

DONE at Turin, this 21st day of October 1991, in English and French, both texts being equally authentic, in a single copy which shall be deposited in the archives of the Council of Europe. The Secretary General of the Council of Europe shall transmit certified copies to each member State of the Council of Europe.

23. Additional Protocol to the European Social Charter Providing for a System of Collective Complaints

Adopted at Strasbourg on 9 November 1995

PREAMBLE

The member States of the Council of Europe, signatories to this Protocol to the European Social Charter, opened for signature in Turin on 18 October 1961 (hereinafter referred to as "the Charter");

Resolved to take new measures to improve the effective enforcement of the social rights guaranteed by the Charter;

Considering that this aim could be achieved in particular by the establishment of a collective complaints procedure, which, *inter alia*, would strengthen the participation of management and labour and of non-governmental organisations,

Have agreed as follows:

Article 1

The Contracting Parties to this Protocol recognise the right of the following organisations to submit complaints alleging unsatisfactory application of the Charter:

a. international organisations of employers and trade unions referred to in paragraph 2 of Article 27 of the Charter;

b. other international non-governmental organisations which have consultative status with the Council of Europe and have been put on a list established for this purpose by the Governmental Committee;

c. representative national organisations of employers and trade unions within the jurisdiction of the Contracting Party against which they have lodged a complaint.

Article 2

1. Any Contracting State may also, when it expresses its consent to be bound by this Protocol, in accordance with the provisions of Article 13, or at any moment thereafter, declare that it recognises the right of any other

representative national non-governmental organisation within its jurisdiction which has particular competence in the matters governed by the Charter, to lodge complaints against it.

2.   Such declarations may be made for a specific period.

3.   The declarations shall be deposited with the Secretary General of the Council of Europe who shall transmit copies thereof to the Contracting Parties and publish them.

Article 3

The international non-governmental organisations and the national non-governmental organisations referred to in Article 1.*b* and Article 2 respectively may submit complaints in accordance with the procedure prescribed by the aforesaid provisions only in respect of those matters regarding which they have been recognised as having particular competence.

Article 4

The complaint shall be lodged in writing, relate to a provision of the Charter accepted by the Contracting Party concerned and indicate in what respect the latter has not ensured the satisfactory application of this provision.

Article 5

Any complaint shall be addressed to the Secretary General who shall acknowledge receipt of it, notify it to the Contracting Party concerned and immediately transmit it to the Committee of Independent Experts.

Article 6

The Committee of Independent Experts may request the Contracting Party concerned and the organisation which lodged the complaint to submit written information and observations on the admissibility of the complaint within such time-limit as it shall prescribe.

Article 7

1.   If it decides that a complaint is admissible, the Committee of Independent Experts shall notify the Contracting Parties to the Charter through the Secretary General. It shall request the Contracting Party concerned and the organisation which lodged the complaint to submit, within such time-limits as it shall prescribe, all relevant written explanations or information, and the other Contracting Parties to this Protocol, the comments they wish to submit, within the same time-limit.

2. If the complaint has been lodged by a national organisation of employers or a national trade union or by another national or international non-governmental organisation, the Committee of Independent Experts shall notify the international organisations of employers or trade unions referred to in paragraph 2 of Article 27 of the Charter, through the Secretary General, and invite them to submit observations within such time-limit as it shall prescribe.

3. On the basis of the explanations, information or observations submitted under paragraphs 1 and 2 above, the Contracting Party concerned and the organisation which lodged the complaint may submit any additional written information or observations within such time-limit as the Committee of Independent Experts shall prescribe.

4. In the course of the examination of the complaint, the Committee of Independent Experts may organise a hearing with the representatives of the parties.

Article 8

1. The Committee of Independent Experts shall draw up a report in which it shall describe the steps taken by it to examine the complaint and present its conclusions as to whether or not the Contracting Party concerned has ensured the satisfactory application of the provision of the Charter referred to in the complaint.

2. The report shall be transmitted to the Committee of Ministers. It shall also be transmitted to the organisation that lodged the complaint and to the Contracting Parties to the Charter, which shall not be at liberty to publish it.

It shall be transmitted to the Parliamentary Assembly and made public at the same time as the resolution referred to in Article 9 or no later than four months after it has been transmitted to the Committee of Ministers.

Article 9

1. On the basis of the report of the Committee of Independent Experts, the Committee of Ministers shall adopt a resolution by a majority of those voting. If the Committee of Independent Experts finds that the Charter has not been applied in a satisfactory manner, the Committee of Ministers shall adopt, by a majority of two-thirds of those voting, a recommendation addressed to the Contracting Party concerned. In both cases, entitlement to voting shall be limited to the Contracting Parties to the Charter.

2. At the request of the Contracting Party concerned, the Committee of Ministers may decide, where the report of the Committee of Independent

Experts raises new issues, by a two-thirds majority of the Contracting Parties to the Charter, to consult the Governmental Committee.

Article 10

The Contracting Party concerned shall provide information on the measures it has taken to give effect to the Committee of Ministers' recommendation, in the next report which it submits to the Secretary General under Article 21 of the Charter.

Article 11

Articles 1 to 10 of this Protocol shall apply also to the articles of Part II of the first Additional Protocol to the Charter in respect of the States Parties to that Protocol, to the extent that these articles have been accepted.

Article 12

The States Parties to this Protocol consider that the first paragraph of the appendix to the Charter, relating to Part III, reads as follows:

"It is understood that the Charter contains legal obligations of an international character, the application of which is submitted solely to the supervision provided for in Part IV thereof and in the provisions of this Protocol."

Article 13

1. This Protocol shall be open for signature by member States of the Council of Europe signatories to the Charter, which may express their consent to be bound by:

a. signature without reservation as to ratification, acceptance or approval; or

b. signature subject to ratification, acceptance or approval, followed by ratification, acceptance or approval.

2. A member State of the Council of Europe may not express its consent to be bound by this Protocol without previously or simultaneously ratifying the Charter.

3. Instruments of ratification, acceptance or approval shall be deposited with the Secretary General of the Council of Europe.

Article 14

1. This Protocol shall enter into force on the first day of the month following the expiration of a period of one month after the date on which five member States of the Council of Europe have expressed their consent to be bound by the Protocol in accordance with the provisions of Article 13.

2. In respect of any member State which subsequently expresses its consent to be bound by it, the Protocol shall enter into force on the first day of the month following the expiration of a period of one month after the date of the deposit of the instrument of ratification, acceptance or approval.

Article 15

1. Any Party may at any time denounce this Protocol by means of a notification addressed to the Secretary General of the Council of Europe.

2. Such denunciation shall become effective on the first day of the month following the expiration of a period of twelve months after the date of receipt of such notification by the Secretary General.

Article 16

The Secretary General of the Council of Europe shall notify all the member States of the Council of:

    a. any signature;

    b. the deposit of any instrument of ratification, acceptance or approval;

    c. the date of entry into force of this Protocol in accordance with Article 14;

    d. any other act, notification or declaration relating to this Protocol.

IN WITNESS WHEREOF the undersigned, being duly authorised thereto, have signed this Protocol.

DONE at Strasbourg, this 9th day of November 1995, in English and French, both texts being equally authentic, in a single copy which shall be deposited in the archives of the Council of Europe. The Secretary General of the Council of Europe shall transmit certified copies to each member State of the Council of Europe.

24. European Social Charter
(revised)

Adopted at Strasbourg on 3 May 1996

PREAMBLE

The Governments signatory hereto, being members of the Council of Europe,

Considering that the aim of the Council of Europe is the achievement of greater unity between its members for the purpose of safeguarding and realising the ideals and principles which are their common heritage and of facilitating their economic and social progress, in particular by the maintenance and further realisation of human rights and fundamental freedoms;

Considering that in the European Convention for the Protection of Human Rights and Fundamental Freedoms signed at Rome on 4 November 1950, and the Protocols thereto, the member States of the Council of Europe agreed to secure to their populations the civil and political rights and freedoms therein specified;

Considering that in the European Social Charter opened for signature in Turin on 18 October 1961 and the Protocols thereto, the member States of the Council of Europe agreed to secure to their populations the social rights specified therein in order to improve their standard of living and their social well-being;

Recalling that the Ministerial Conference on Human Rights held in Rome on 5 November 1990 stressed the need, on the one hand, to preserve the indivisible nature of all human rights, be they civil, political, economic, social or cultural and, on the other hand, to give the European Social Charter fresh impetus;

Resolved, as was decided during the Ministerial Conference held in Turin on 21 and 22 October 1991, to update and adapt the substantive contents of the Charter in order to take account in particular of the fundamental social changes which have occurred since the text was adopted;

Recognising the advantage of embodying in a Revised Charter, designed progressively to take the place of the European Social Charter, the rights guaranteed by the Charter as amended, the rights guaranteed by the Additional Protocol of 1988 and to add new rights,

Have agreed as follows:

Part I

The Parties accept as the aim of their policy, to be pursued by all appropriate means both national and international in character, the attainment of conditions in which the following rights and principles may be effectively realised:

1.   Everyone shall have the opportunity to earn his living in an occupation freely entered upon.

2.   All workers have the right to just conditions of work.

3.   All workers have the right to safe and healthy working conditions.

4.   All workers have the right to a fair remuneration sufficient for a decent standard of living for themselves and their families.

5.   All workers and employers have the right to freedom of association in national or international organisations for the protection of their economic and social interests.

6.   All workers and employers have the right to bargain collectively.

7.   Children and young persons have the right to a special protection against the physical and moral hazards to which they are exposed.

8.   Employed women, in case of maternity, have the right to a special protection.

9.   Everyone has the right to appropriate facilities for vocational guidance with a view to helping him choose an occupation suited to his personal aptitude and interests.

10.   Everyone has the right to appropriate facilities for vocational training.

11.   Everyone has the right to benefit from any measures enabling him to enjoy the highest possible standard of health attainable.

12.   All workers and their dependents have the right to social security.

13.   Anyone without adequate resources has the right to social and medical assistance.

14.   Everyone has the right to benefit from social welfare services.

15.   Disabled persons have the right to independence, social integration and participation in the life of the community.

16.   The family as a fundamental unit of society has the right to appropriate social, legal and economic protection to ensure its full development.

17.   Children and young persons have the right to appropriate social, legal and economic protection.

18.   The nationals of any one of the Parties have the right to engage in any gainful occupation in the territory of any one of the others on a footing of equality with the nationals of the latter, subject to restrictions based on cogent economic or social reasons.

19.   Migrant workers who are nationals of a Party and their families have the right to protection and assistance in the territory of any other Party.

20.   All workers have the right to equal opportunities and equal treatment in matters of employment and occupation without discrimination on the grounds of sex.

21.   Workers have the right to be informed and to be consulted within the undertaking.

22.   Workers have the right to take part in the determination and improvement of the working conditions and working environment in the undertaking.

23.   Every elderly person has the right to social protection.

24.   All workers have the right to protection in cases of termination of employment.

25.   All workers have the right to protection of their claims in the event of the insolvency of their employer.

26.   All workers have the right to dignity at work.

27.   All persons with family responsibilities and who are engaged or wish to engage in employment have a right to do so without being subject to discrimination and as far as possible without conflict between their employment and family responsibilities.

28.   Workers' representatives in undertakings have the right to protection against acts prejudicial to them and should be afforded appropriate facilities to carry out their functions.

29.   All workers have the right to be informed and consulted in collective redundancy procedures.

30.   Everyone has the right to protection against poverty and social exclusion.

31.   Everyone has the right to housing.

Part II

The Parties undertake, as provided for in Part III, to consider themselves bound by the obligations laid down in the following articles and paragraphs.

Article 1—The right to work

With a view to ensuring the effective exercise of the right to work, the Parties undertake:

1. to accept as one of their primary aims and responsibilities the achievement and maintenance of as high and stable level of employment as possible, with a view to the attainment of full employment;

2. to protect effectively the right of the worker to earn his living in an occupation freely entered upon;

3. to establish or maintain free employment services for all workers;

4. to provide or promote appropriate vocational guidance, training and rehabilitation.

Article 2—The right to just conditions of work

With a view to ensuring the effective exercise of the right to just conditions of work, the Parties undertake:

1. to provide for reasonable daily and weekly working hours, the working week to be progressively reduced to the extent that the increase of productivity and other relevant factors permit;

2. to provide for public holidays with pay;

3. to provide for a minimum of four weeks' annual holiday with pay;

4. to eliminate risks in inherently dangerous or unhealthy occupations, and where it has not yet been possible to eliminate or reduce sufficiently these risks, to provide for either a reduction of working hours or additional paid holidays for workers engaged in such occupations;

5. to ensure a weekly rest period which shall, as far as possible, coincide with the day recognised by tradition or custom in the country or region concerned as a day of rest;

6. to ensure that workers are informed in written form, as soon as possible, and in any event not later than two months after the date of commencing their employment, of the essential aspects of the contract or employment relationship;

7. to ensure that workers performing night work benefit from measures which take account of the special nature of the work.

Article 3—The right to safe and healthy working conditions

With a view to ensuring the effective exercise of the right to safe and healthy working conditions, the Parties undertake, in consultation with employers' and workers' organisations:

1. to formulate, implement and periodically review a coherent national policy on occupational safety, occupational health and the working environment. The primary aim of this policy shall be to improve occupational safety and health and to prevent accidents and injury to health arising out of, linked with or occurring in the course of work, particularly by minimising the causes of hazards inherent in the working environment;

2. to issue safety and health regulations;

3. to provide for the enforcement of such regulations by measures of supervision;

4. to promote the progressive development of occupational health services for all workers with essentially preventive and advisory functions.

Article 4—The right to a fair remuneration

With a view to ensuring the effective exercise of the right to a fair remuneration, the Parties undertake:

1. to recognise the right of workers to a remuneration such as will give them and their families a decent standard of living;

2. to recognise the right of workers to an increased rate of remuneration for overtime work, subject to exceptions in particular cases;

3. to recognise the right of men and women workers to equal pay for work of equal value;

4. to recognise the right of all workers to a reasonable period of notice for termination of employment;

5. to permit deductions from wages only under conditions and to the extent prescribed by national laws or regulations or fixed by collective agreements or arbitration awards.

The exercise of these rights shall be achieved by freely concluded collective agreements, by statutory wage-fixing machinery, or by other means appropriate to national conditions.

Article 5—The right to organise

With a view to ensuring or promoting the freedom of workers and employers to form local, national or international organisations for the protection of their economic and social interests and to join those organisations, the Parties undertake that national law shall not be such as to impair, nor shall it be so applied as to impair, this freedom. The extent to which the guarantees provided for in this article shall apply to the police shall be determined by national laws or regulations. The principle governing the application to the members of the armed forces of these guarantees and the extent to which they shall apply to persons in this category shall equally be determined by national laws or regulations.

Article 6—*The right to bargain collectively*

With a view to ensuring the effective exercise of the right to bargain collectively, the Parties undertake:

1.   to promote joint consultation between workers and employers;

2.   to promote, where necessary and appropriate, machinery for voluntary negotiations between employers or employers' organisations and workers' organisations, with a view to the regulation of terms and conditions of employment by means of collective agreements;

3.   to promote the establishment and use of appropriate machinery for conciliation and voluntary arbitration for the settlement of labour disputes;

and recognise:

4.   the right of workers and employers to collective action in cases of conflicts of interest, including the right to strike, subject to obligations that might arise out of collective agreements previously entered into.

Article 7—*The right of children and young persons to protection*

With a view to ensuring the effective exercise of the right of children and young persons to protection, the Parties undertake:

1.   to provide that the minimum age of admission to employment shall be 15 years, subject to exceptions for children employed in prescribed light work without harm to their health, morals or education;

2.   to provide that the minimum age of admission to employment shall be 18 years with respect to prescribed occupations regarded as dangerous or unhealthy;

3.   to provide that persons who are still subject to compulsory education shall not be employed in such work as would deprive them of the full benefit of their education;

4.   to provide that the working hours of persons under 18 years of age shall be limited in accordance with the needs of their development, and particularly with their need for vocational training;

5. to recognise the right of young workers and apprentices to a fair wage or other appropriate allowances;

6. to provide that the time spent by young persons in vocational training during the normal working hours with the consent of the employer shall be treated as forming part of the working day;

7. to provide that employed persons of under 18 years of age shall be entitled to a minimum of four weeks' annual holiday with pay;

8. to provide that persons under 18 years of age shall not be employed in night work with the exception of certain occupations provided for by national laws or regulations;

9. to provide that persons under 18 years of age employed in occupations prescribed by national laws or regulations shall be subject to regular medical control;

10. to ensure special protection against physical and moral dangers to which children and young persons are exposed, and particularly against those resulting directly or indirectly from their work.

Article 8—The right of employed women to protection of maternity

With a view to ensuring the effective exercise of the right of employed women to the protection of maternity, the Parties undertake:

1. to provide either by paid leave, by adequate social security benefits or by benefits from public funds for employed women to take leave before and after childbirth up to a total of at least fourteen weeks;

2. to consider it as unlawful for an employer to give a woman notice of dismissal during the period from the time she notifies her employer that she is pregnant until the end of her maternity leave, or to giver her notice of dismissal at such a time that the notice would expire during such a period;

3. to provide that mothers who are nursing their infants shall be entitled to sufficient time off for this purpose;

4. to regulate the employment in night work of pregnant women, women who have recently given birth and women nursing their infants;

5. to prohibit the employment of pregnant women, women who have recently given birth or who are nursing their infants in underground mining and all other work which is unsuitable by reason of its dangerous, unhealthy or arduous nature and to take appropriate measures to protect the employment rights of these women.

Article 9—The right to vocational guidance

With a view to ensuring the effective exercise of the right to vocational guidance, the Parties undertake to provide or promote, as necessary, a service which will assist all persons, including the handicapped, to solve problems related to occupational choice and progress, with due regard to the individual's characteristics and their relation to occupational opportunity: this assistance should be available free of charge, both to young persons, including schoolchildren, and to adults.

Article 10—The right to vocational training

With a view to ensuring the effective exercise of the right to vocational training, the Parties undertake:

1. to provide or promote, as necessary, the technical and vocational training of all persons, including the handicapped, in consultation with employers' and workers' organisations, and to grant facilities for access to higher technical and university education, based solely on individual aptitude;

2. to provide or promote a system of apprenticeship and other systematic arrangements for training young boys and girls in their various employments;

3. to provide or promote, as necessary:

    a. adequate and readily available training facilities for adult workers;

    b. special facilities for the retraining of adult workers needed as a result of technological development or new trends in employment;

4. to provide or promote, as necessary, special measures for the retraining and reintegration of the long-term unemployed;

5. to encourage the full utilisation of the facilities provided by appropriate measures such as:

    a. reducing or abolishing any fees or charges;

    b. granting financial assistance in appropriate cases;

    c. including in the normal working hours time spent on supplementary training taken by the worker, at the request of his employer, during employment;

    d. ensuring, through adequate supervision, in consultation with the employers' and workers' organisations, the efficiency of apprenticeship and other training arrangements for young workers, and the adequate protection of young workers generally.

Article 11—The right to protection of health

With a view to ensuring the effective exercise of the right to protection of health, the Parties undertake, either directly or in co-operation with public or private organisations, to take appropriate measures designed *inter alia*:

1. to remove as far as possible the causes of ill-health;

2. to provide advisory and educational facilities for the promotion of health and the encouragement of individual responsibility in matters of health;

3. to prevent as far as possible epidemic, endemic and other diseases, as well as accidents.

Article 12—The right to social security

With a view to ensuring the effective exercise of the right to social security, the Parties undertake:

1. to establish or maintain a system of social security;

2. to maintain the social security system at a satisfactory level at least equal to that necessary for the ratification of the European Code of Social Security;

3. to endeavour to raise progressively the system of social security to a higher level.

4. to take steps, by the conclusion of appropriate bilateral and multilateral agreements or by other means, and subject to the conditions laid down in such agreements, in order to ensure:

a. equal treatment with their own nationals of the nationals of other Parties in respect of social security rights, including the retention of benefits arising out of social security legislation, whatever movements the persons protected may undertake between the territories of the Parties;

b. the granting, maintenance and resumption of social security rights by such means as the accumulation of insurance or employment periods completed under the legislation of each of the Parties.

Article 13—The right to social and medical assistance

With a view to ensuring the effective exercise of the right to social and medical assistance, the Parties undertake;

1. to ensure that any person who is without adequate resources and who is unable to secure such resources either by his own efforts or from other sources, in particular by benefits under a social security scheme, be

granted adequate assistance, and, in case of sickness, the care necessitated by his condition;

2.   to ensure that persons receiving such assistance shall not, for that reason, suffer from a diminution of their political or social rights;

3.   to provide that everyone may receive by appropriate public or private services such advice and personal help as may be required to prevent, to remove, or to alleviate personal or family want;

4.   to apply the provisions referred to in paragraphs 1, 2 and 3 of this article on an equal footing with their nationals to nationals of other Parties lawfully within their territories, in accordance with their obligations under the European Convention on Social and Medical Assistance, signed at Paris on 11 December 1953.

Article 14—The right to benefit from social welfare services

With a view to ensuring the effective exercise of the right to benefit from social welfare services, the Parties undertake:

1.   to promote or provide services which, by using methods of social work, would contribute to the welfare and development of both individuals and groups in the community, and to their adjustment to the social environment;

2.   to encourage the participation of individuals and voluntary or other organisations in the establishment and maintenance of such services.

Article 15—The right of persons with disabilities to independence, social integration and participation in the life of the community

With a view to ensuring to persons with disabilities, irrespective of age and the nature and origin of their disabilities, the effective exercise of the right to independence, social integration and participation in the life of the community, the Parties undertake, in particular:

1.   to take the necessary measures to provide persons with disabilities with guidance, education and vocational training in the framework of general schemes wherever possible or, where this is not possible, through specialised bodies, public or private;

2.   to promote their access to employment through all measures tending to encourage employers to hire and keep in employment persons with disabilities in the ordinary working environment and to adjust the working conditions to the needs of the disabled or, where this is not possible by reason of the disability, by arranging for or creating sheltered employment according to the level of disability. In certain cases, such measures may require recourse to specialised placement and support services;

3. to promote their full social integration and participation in the life of the community in particular through measures, including technical aids, aiming to overcome barriers to communication and mobility and enabling access to transport, housing, cultural activities and leisure.

Article 16—The right of the family to social, legal and economic protection

With a view to ensuring the necessary conditions for the full development of the family, which is a fundamental unit of society, the Parties undertake to promote the economic, legal and social protection of family life by such means as social and family benefits, fiscal arrangements, provision of family housing, benefits for the newly married and other appropriate means.

Article 17—The right of children and young persons to social, legal and economic protection

With a view to ensuring the effective exercise of the right of children and young persons to grow up in an environment which encourages the full development of their personality and of their physical and mental capacities, the Parties undertake, either directly or in co-operation with public and private organisations, to take all appropriate and necessary measures designed:

1. *a.* to ensure that children and young persons, taking account of the rights and duties of their parents, have the care, the assistance, the education and the training they need, in particular by providing for the establishment or maintenance of institutions and services sufficient and adequate for this purpose;

b. to protect children and young persons against negligence, violence or exploitation;

c. to provide protection and special aid from the state for children and young persons temporarily or definitely deprived of their family's support;

2. to provide to children and young persons a free primary and secondary education as well as to encourage regular attendance at schools.

Article 18—The right to engage in a gainful occupation in the territory of other Parties

With a view to ensuring the effective exercise of the right to engage in a gainful occupation in the territory of any other Party, the Parties undertake:

1. to apply existing regulations in a spirit of liberality;

2. to simplify existing formalities and to reduce or abolish chancery dues and other charges payable by foreign workers or their employers,

3. to liberalise, individually or collectively, regulations governing the employment of foreign workers,

and recognise:

4. the right of their nationals to leave the country to engage in a gainful occupation in the territories of the other Parties.

Article 19—The right of migrant workers and their families to protection and assistance

With a view to ensuring the effective exercise of the right of migrant workers and their families to protection and assistance in the territory of any other Party, the Parties undertake:

1. to maintain or to satisfy themselves that there are maintained adequate and free services to assist such workers, particularly in obtaining accurate information, and to take all appropriate steps, so far as national laws and regulations permit, against misleading propaganda relating to emigration and immigration;

2. to adopt appropriate measures within their own jurisdiction to facilitate the departure, journey and reception of such workers and their families, and to provide, within their own jurisdiction, appropriate services for health, medical attention and good hygienic conditions during the journey;

3. to promote co-operation, as appropriate, between social services, public and private, in emigration and immigration countries;

4. to secure for such workers lawfully within their territories, insofar as such matters are regulated by law or regulations or are subject to the control of administrative authorities, treatment not less favourable than that of their own nationals in respect of the following matters;

a. remuneration and other employment and working conditions;

b. membership of trade unions and enjoyment of the benefits of collective bargaining;

c. accommodation;

5. to secure for such workers lawfully within their territories treatment not less favourable than that of their own nationals with regard to employment taxes, dues or contributions payable in respect of employed persons;

6. to facilitate as far as possible the reunion of the family of a foreign worker permitted to establish himself in the territory;

7.   to secure for such workers lawfully within their territories treatment not less favourable than that of their own nationals in respect of legal proceedings relating to matters referred to in this article;

8.   to secure that such workers lawfully residing within their territories are not expelled unless they endanger national security or offend against public interest or morality;

9.   to permit, within legal limits, the transfer of such parts of the earnings and savings of such workers as they may desire;

10.   to extend the protection and assistance provided for in this article to self-employed migrants insofar as such measures apply;

11.   to promote and facilitate the teaching of the national language of the receiving state or, if there are several, one of these languages, to migrant workers and members of their families;

12.   to promote and facilitate, as far as practicable, the teaching of the migrant worker's mother tongue to the children of the migrant worker.

Article 20—The right to equal opportunities and equal treatment in matters of employment and occupation without discrimination on the grounds of sex

With a view to ensuring the effective exercise of the right to equal opportunities and equal treatment in matters of employment and occupation without discrimination on the grounds of sex, the Parties undertake to recognise that right and to take appropriate measures to ensure or promote its application in the following fields:

a. access to employment, protection against dismissal and occupational reintegration;

b. vocational guidance, training, retraining and rehabilitation;

c. terms of employment and working conditions, including remuneration;

d. career development, including promotion.

Article 21—The right to information and consultation

With a view to ensuring the effective exercise of the right of workers to be informed and consulted within the undertaking, the Parties undertake to adopt or encourage measures enabling workers or their representatives, in accordance with national legislation and practice:

a. to be informed regularly or at the appropriate time and in a comprehensible way about the economic and financial situation of the undertaking employing them, on the understanding that the disclosure of certain information which could be prejudicial to the undertaking may be refused or subject to confidentiality; and

b. to be consulted in good time on proposed decisions which could substantially affect the interests of workers, particularly on those decisions which could have an important impact on the employment situation in the undertaking.

Article 22—The right to take part in the determination and improvement of the working conditions and working environment

With a view to ensuring the effective exercise of the right of workers to take part in the determination and improvement of the working conditions and working environment in the undertaking, the Parties undertake to adopt or encourage measures enabling workers or their representatives, in accordance with national legislation and practice, to contribute:

a. to the determination and the improvement of the working conditions, work organisation and working environment;

b. to the protection of health and safety within the undertaking;

c. to the organisation of socio and socio-cultural services and facilities within the undertaking;

d. to the supervision of the observance of regulations on these matters.

Article 23—The right of elderly persons to social protection

With a view to ensuring the effective exercise of the right of elderly persons to social protection, the Parties undertake to adopt or encourage, either directly or in co-operation with public or private organisations, appropriate measures designed in particular:

—to enable elderly persons to remain full members of society for as long as possible, by means of:

a. adequate resources enabling them to lead a decent life and play an active part in public, social and cultural life;

b. provision of information about services and facilities available for elderly persons and their opportunities to make use of them;

—to enable elderly persons to choose their life-style freely and to lead independent lives in their familiar surroundings for as long as they wish and are able, by means of:

a. provision of housing suited to their needs and their state of health or of adequate support for adapting their housing;

b. the health care and the services necessitated by their state;

—to guarantee elderly persons living in institutions appropriate support, while respecting their privacy, and participation in decisions concerning living conditions in the institution.

Article 24—The right to protection in cases of termination of employment

With a view to ensuring the effective exercise of the right of workers to protection in cases of termination of employment, the Parties undertake to recognise:

a. the right of all workers not to have their employment terminated without valid reasons for such termination connected with their capacity or conduct or based on the operational requirements of the undertaking, establishment or service;

b. the right of workers whose employment is terminated without a valid reason to adequate compensation or other appropriate relief.

To this end the Parties undertake to ensure that a worker who considers that his employment has been terminated without a valid reason shall have the right to appeal to an impartial body.

Article 25—The right of workers to the protection of their claims in the event of the insolvency of their employer

With a view to ensuring the effective exercise of the right of workers to the protection of their claims in the event of the insolvency of their employer, the Parties undertake to provide that workers' claims arising from contracts of employment or employment relationships be guaranteed by a guarantee institution or by any other effective form of protection.

Article 26—The right to dignity at work

With a view to ensuring the effective exercise of the right of all workers to protection of their dignity at work, the Parties undertake, in consultation with employers' and workers' organisations:

1. to promote awareness, information and prevention of sexual harassment in the workplace or in relation to work and to take all appropriate measures to protect workers from such conduct.

2. to promote awareness, information and prevention of recurrent reprehensible or distinctly negative and offensive actions directed against individual workers in the workplace or in relation to work and to take all appropriate measures to protect workers from such conduct.

*Article 27—The right of workers with family responsibilities to
equal opportunities and equal treatment*

With a view to ensuring the exercise of the right to equality of opportunity and treatment for men and women workers with family responsibilities and between such workers and other workers, the Parties undertake:

1. to take appropriate measures:

   a. to enable workers with family responsibilities to enter and remain in employment, as well as to re-enter employment after an absence due to those responsibilities, including measures in the field of vocational guidance and training;

   b. to take account of their needs in terms of conditions of employment and social security;

   c. to develop or promote services, public or private, in particular child daycare services and other childcare arrangements;

2. to provide a possibility for either parent to obtain, during a period after maternity leave, parental leave to take care of a child, the duration and conditions of which should be determined by national legislation, collective agreements or practice;

3. to ensure that family responsibilities shall not, as such, constitute a valid reason for termination of employment.

*Article 28—The right of workers' representatives to protection in the
undertaking and facilities to be accorded to them*

With a view to ensuring the effective exercise of the right of workers' representatives to carry out their functions, the Parties undertake to ensure that in the undertaking:

   a. they enjoy effective protection against acts prejudicial to them, including dismissal, based on their status or activities as workers' representatives within the undertaking;

   b. they are afforded such facilities as may be appropriate in order to enable them to carry out their functions promptly and efficiently, account being taken of the industrial relations system of the country and the needs, size and capabilities of the undertaking concerned.

Article 29—The right to information and consultation
in collective redundancy procedures

With a view to ensuring the effective exercise of the right of workers to be informed and consulted in situations of collective redundancies, the Parties undertake to ensure that employers shall inform and consult workers' representatives, in good time prior to such collective redundancies, on ways and means of avoiding collective redundancies or limiting their occurrence and mitigating their consequences, for example by recourse to accompanying social measures aimed, in particular, at aid for the redeployment or retraining of the workers concerned.

Article 30—The right to protection against poverty and social exclusion

With a view to ensuring the effective exercise of the right to protection against poverty and social exclusion, the Parties undertake:

a. to take measures within the framework of an overall and co-ordinated approach to promote the effective access of persons who live or risk living in a situation of social exclusion or poverty, as well as their families, to, in particular, employment, housing, training, education, culture and social and medical assistance;

b. to review these measures with a view to their adaptation if necessary.

Article 31—The right to housing

With a view to ensuring the effective exercise of the right to housing, the Parties undertake to take measures designed:

1. to promote access to housing of an adequate standard;

2. to prevent and reduce homelessness with a view to its gradual elimination;

3. to make the price of housing accessible to those without adequate resources.

Part III

Article A—Undertakings

1. Subject to the provisions of Article B below, each of the Parties undertakes:

a. to consider Part I of this Charter as a declaration of the aims which it will pursue by all appropriate means, as stated in the introductory paragraph of that part;

b. to consider itself bound by at least six of the following nine articles of Part II of this Charter: Articles 1, 5, 6, 7, 12, 13, 16, 19 and 20;

c. to consider itself bound by an additional number of articles or numbered paragraphs of Part II of the Charter which it may select, provided that the total number of articles or numbered paragraphs by which it is bound is not less than sixteen articles or sixty-three numbered paragraphs.

2.   The articles or paragraphs selected in accordance with sub-paragraphs *b* and *c* of paragraph 1 of this article shall be notified to the Secretary General of the Council of Europe at the time when the instrument of ratification, acceptance or approval is deposited.

3.   Any Party may, at a later date, declare by notification addressed to the Secretary General that it considers itself bound by any articles or any numbered paragraphs of Part II of the Charter which it has not already accepted under the terms of paragraph 1 of this article. Such undertakings subsequently given shall be deemed to be an integral part of the ratification, acceptance or approval and shall have the same effect as from the first day of the month following the expiration of a period of one month after the date of the notification.

4.   Each Party shall maintain a system of labour inspection appropriate to national conditions.

Article B—Links with the European Social Charter and the 1988 Additional Protocol

1.   No Contracting Party to the European Social Charter or Party to the Additional Protocol of 5 May 1988 may ratify, accept or approve this Charter without considering itself bound by at least the provisions corresponding to the provisions of the European Social Charter and, where appropriate, of the Additional Protocol, to which it was bound.

2.   Acceptance of the obligations of any provision of this Charter shall, from the date of entry into force of those obligations for the Party concerned, result in the corresponding provision of the European Social Charter and, where appropriate, of its Additional Protocol of 1988 ceasing to apply to the Party concerned in the event of that Party being bound by the first of those instruments or by both instruments.

Part IV

Article C—Supervision of the implementation of the undertakings contained in this Charter

The implementation of the legal obligations contained in this Charter shall be submitted to the same supervision as the European Social Charter.

Article D—Collective complaints

1. The provisions of the Additional Protocol to the European Social Charter providing for a system of collective complaints shall apply to the undertakings given in this Charter for the States which have ratified the said Protocol.

2. Any State which is not bound by the Additional Protocol to the European Social Charter providing for a system of collective complaints may when depositing its instrument of ratification, acceptance or approval of this Charter or at any time thereafter, declare by notification addressed to the Secretary General of the Council of Europe, that it accepts the supervision of its obligations under this Charter following the procedure provided for in the said Protocol.

Part V

Article E—Non-discrimination

The enjoyment of the rights set forth in this Charter shall be secured without discrimination on any ground such as race, colour, sex, language, religion, political or other opinion, national extrication or social origin, health, association with a national minority, birth or other status.

Article F—Derogations in time of war or public emergency

1. In time of war or other public emergency threatening the life of the nation any Party may take measures derogating from its obligations under this Charter to the extent strictly required by the exigencies of the situation, provided that such measures are not inconsistent with its other obligations under international law.

2. Any Party which has availed itself of this right of derogation shall, within a reasonable lapse of time, keep the Secretary General of the Council of Europe fully informed of the measures taken and of the reasons therefor. It shall likewise inform the Secretary General when such measures have

ceased to operate and the provisions of the Charter which it has accepted are again being fully executed.

Article G—Restrictions

1.   The rights and principles set forth in Part I when effectively realised, and their effective exercise as provided for in Part II, shall not be subject to any restrictions or limitations not specified in those parts, except such as are prescribed by law and are necessary in a democratic society for the protection of the rights and freedoms of others or for the protection of public interest, national security, public health, or morals.

2.   The restrictions permitted under this Charter to the rights and obligations set forth herein shall not be applied for any purpose other than that for which they have been prescribed.

Article H—Relations between the Charter and domestic law or international agreements

The provisions of this Charter shall not prejudice the provisions of domestic law or of any bilateral or multilateral treaties, conventions or agreements which are already in force, or may come into force, under which more favourable treatment would be accorded to the persons protected.

Article I—Implementation of the undertakings given

1.   Without prejudice to the methods of implementation foreseen in these articles the relevant provisions of Articles 1 to 31 of Part II of this Charter shall be implemented by:

a.   laws or regulations;

b.   agreements between employers or employers' organisations and workers' organisations;

c.   a combination of those two methods;

d.   other appropriate means.

2.   Compliance with the undertakings deriving from the provisions of paragraphs 1, 2, 3, 4, 5 and 7 of Article 2, paragraphs 4, 6 and 7 of Article 7, paragraphs 1, 2, 3 and 5 of Article 10 and Articles 21 and 22 of Part II of this Charter shall be regarded as effective if the provisions are applied, in accordance with paragraph 1 of this article, to the great majority of the workers concerned.

Article J—Amendments

1.   Any amendment to Parts I and II of this Charter with the purpose of extending the rights guaranteed in this Charter as well as any amendment to Parts III to VI, proposed by a Party or by the Governmental Committee, shall be communicated to the Secretary General of the Council of Europe and forwarded by the Secretary General to the Parties to this Charter.

2.   Any amendment proposed in accordance with the provisions of the preceding paragraph shall be examined by the Governmental Committee which shall submit the text adopted to the Committee of Ministers for approval after consultation with the Parliamentary Assembly. After its approval by the Committee of Ministers this text shall be forwarded to the Parties for acceptance.

3.   Any amendment to Part I and to Part II of this Charter shall enter into force, in respect of those Parties which have accepted it, on the first day of the month following the expiration of a period of one month after the date on which three Parties have informed the Secretary General that they have accepted it.

In respect of any Party which subsequently accepts it, the amendment shall enter into force on the first day of the month following the expiration of a period of one month after the date on which that Party has informed the Secretary General of its acceptance.

4.   Any amendment to Parts III to VI of this Charter shall enter into force on the first day of the month following the expiration of a period of one month after the date on which all Parties have informed the Secretary General that they have accepted it.

Part VI

Article K—Signature, ratification and entry into force

1.   This Charter shall be open for signature by the member States of the Council of Europe. It shall be subject to ratification, acceptance or approval. Instruments of ratification, acceptance or approval shall be deposited with the Secretary General of the Council of Europe.

2.   This Charter shall enter into force on the first day of the month following the expiration of a period of one month after the date on which three member States of the Council of Europe have expressed their consent to be bound by this Charter in accordance with the preceding paragraph.

3.   In respect of any member State which subsequently expresses its consent to be bound by this Charter, it shall enter into force on the first day

of the month following the expiration of a period of one month after the date of the deposit of the instrument of ratification, acceptance or approval.

Article L—Territorial application

1. This Charter shall apply to the metropolitan territory of each Party. Each signatory may, at the time of signature or of the deposit of its instrument of ratification, acceptance or approval, specify, by declaration addressed to the Secretary General of the Council of Europe, the territory which shall be considered to be its metropolitan territory for this purpose.

2. Any signatory may, at the time of signature or of the deposit of its instrument of ratification, acceptance or approval, or at any time thereafter, declare by notification addressed to the Secretary General of the Council of Europe, that the Charter shall extend in whole or in part to a non-metropolitan territory or territories specified in the said declaration for whose international relations it is responsible or for which it assumes international responsibility. It shall specify in the declaration the articles or paragraphs of Part II of the Charter which it accepts as binding in respect of the territories named in the declaration.

3. The Charter shall extend its application to the territory or territories named in the aforesaid declaration as from the first day of the month following the expiration of a period of one month after the date of receipt of the notification of such declaration by the Secretary General.

4. Any Party may declare at a later date by notification addressed to the Secretary General of the Council of Europe that, in respect of one or more of the territories to which the Charter has been applied in accordance with paragraph 2 of this article, it accepts as binding any articles or any numbered paragraphs which it has not already accepted in respect of that territory or territories. Such undertakings subsequently given shall be deemed to be an integral part of the original declaration in respect of the territory concerned, and shall have the same effect as from the first day of the month following the expiration of a period of one month after the date of receipt of such notification by the Secretary General.

Article M—Denunciation

1. Any Party may denounce this Charter only at the end of a period of five years from the date on which the Charter entered into force for it, or at the end of any subsequent period of two years, and in either case after giving six months' notice to the Secretary General of the Council of Europe who shall inform the other Parties accordingly.

2. Any Party may, in accordance with the provisions set out in the preceding paragraph, denounce any article or paragraph of Part II of the

Charter accepted by it provided that the number of articles or paragraphs by which this Party is bound shall never be less than sixteen in the former case and sixty-three in the latter and that this number of articles or paragraphs shall continue to include the articles selected by the Party among those to which special reference is made in Article A, paragraph 1, sub-paragraph *b*.

3. Any Party may denounce the present Charter or any of the articles or paragraphs of Part II of the Charter under the conditions specified in paragraph 1 of this article in respect of any territory to which the said Charter is applicable, by virtue of a declaration made in accordance with paragraph 2 of Article L.

Article N—Appendix

The appendix to this Charter shall form an integral part of it.

Article O—Notifications

The Secretary General of the Council of Europe shall notify the member States of the Council and the Director General of the International Labour Office of:

a. any signature;

b. the deposit of any instrument of ratification, acceptance or approval;

c. any date of entry into force of this Charter in accordance with Article K;

d. any declaration made in application of Articles A, paragraphs 2 and 3, D, paragraphs 1 and 2, F, paragraph 2, L, paragraphs 1, 2, 3 and 4;

e. any amendment in accordance with Article J;

f. any denunciation in accordance with Article M;

g. any other act, notification or communication relating to this Charter.

IN WITNESS WHEREOF, the undersigned, being duly authorised thereto, have signed this revised Charter.

DONE at Strasbourg, this 3rd day of May 1996, in English and French, both texts being equally authentic, in a single copy which shall be deposited in the archives of the Council of Europe. The Secretary General of the Council of Europe shall transmit certified copies to each member State of the Council of Europe and to the Director General of the International Labour Office.

APPENDIX TO THE REVISED EUROPEAN SOCIAL CHARTER

SCOPE OF THE REVISED EUROPEAN SOCIAL CHARTER IN TERMS OF PERSONS PROTECTED

1. Without prejudice to Article 12, paragraph 4, and Article 13, paragraph 4, the persons covered by Articles 1 to 17 and 20 to 31 include foreigners only in so far as they are nationals of other Parties lawfully resident or working regularly within the territory of the Party concerned, subject to the understanding that these articles are to be interpreted in the light of the provisions of Articles 18 and 19.

This interpretation would not prejudice the extension of similar facilities to other persons by any of the Parties.

2. Each Party will grant to refugees as defined in the Convention relating to the Status of Refugees, signed in Geneva on 28 July 1951 and in the Protocol of 31 January 1967, and lawfully staying in its territory, treatment as favourable as possible, and in any case not less favourable than under the obligations accepted by the Party under the said convention and under any other existing international instruments applicable to those refugees.

3. Each Party will grant to stateless persons as defined in the Convention on the Status of Stateless Persons done in New York on 28 September 1954 and lawfully staying in its territory, treatment as favourable as possible and in any case not less favourable than under the obligations accepted by the Party under the said instrument and under any other existing international instruments applicable to those stateless persons.

Part I, paragraph 18, and Part II, Article 18, paragraph 1

It is understood that these provisions are not concerned with the question of entry into the territories of the Parties and do not prejudice the provisions of the European Convention on Establishment, signed in Paris on 13 December 1955.

Part II

Article 1, paragraph 2

This provision shall not be interpreted as prohibiting or authorising any union security clause or practice.

Article 2, paragraph 6

Parties may provided that this provision shall not apply:

a. to workers having a contract or employment relationship with a total duration not exceeding one month and/or with a working week not exceeding eight hours;

b. where the contract or employment relationship is of a casual and/or specific nature, provided, in these cases, that its non-application is justified by objective considerations.

Article 3, paragraph 4

It is understood that for the purposes of this provision the functions, organisations and conditions of operation of these services shall be determined by national laws or regulations, collective agreements or other means appropriate to national conditions.

Article 4, paragraph 4

This provision shall be so understood as not to prohibit immediate dismissal for any serious offence.

Article 4, paragraph 5

It is understood that a Party may give the undertaking required in this paragraph if the great majority of workers are not permitted to suffer deductions from wages either by law or through collective agreements or arbitration awards, the exceptions being those persons not so covered.

Article 6, paragraph 4

It is understood that each Party may, insofar as it is concerned, regulate the exercise of the right to strike by law, provided that any further restriction that this might place on the right can be justified under the terms of Article G.

Article 7, paragraph 2

This provision does not prevent Parties from providing in their legislation that young persons not having reached the minimum age laid down may perform work in so far as it is absolutely necessary for their vocational training where such work is carried out in accordance with conditions prescribed by the competent authority and measures are taken to protect the health and safety of these young persons.

Article 7, paragraph 8

It is understood that a Party may give the undertaking required in this paragraph if it fulfils the spirit of the undertaking by providing by law that the great majority of persons under eighteen years of age shall not be employed in night work.

Article 8, paragraph 2

This provision shall not be interpreted as laying down an absolute prohibition. Exceptions could be made, for instance, in the following cases:

a. if an employed woman has been guilty of misconduct which justifies breaking off the employment relationship;

b. if the undertaking concerned ceases to operate;

c. if the period prescribed in the employment contract has expired.

Article 12, paragraph 4

The words "and subject to the conditions laid down in such agreements" in the introduction to this paragraph are taken to imply *inter alia* that with regard to benefits which are available independently of any insurance contribution, a Party may require the completion of a prescribed period of residence before granting such benefits to nationals of other Parties.

Article 13, paragraph 4

Governments not Parties to the European Convention on Social and Medical Assistance may ratify the Charter in respect of this paragraph provided that they grant to nationals of other Parties a treatment which is in conformity with the provisions of the said convention.

Article 16

It is understood that the protection afforded in this provision covers single-parent families.

Article 17

It is understood that this provision covers all persons below the age of 18 years, unless under the law applicable to the child majority is attained earlier, without prejudice to the other specific provisions provided by the Charter, particularly Article 7.

This does not imply an obligation to provide compulsory education up to the above-mentioned age.

Article 19, paragraph 6

For the purpose of applying this provision, the term "family of a foreign worker" is understood to mean at least the worker's spouse and unmarried children, as long as the latter are considered to be minors by the receiving State and are dependent on the migrant worker.

Article 20

1.   It is understood that social security matters, as well as other provisions relating to unemployment benefit, old age benefit and survivor's benefit, may be excluded from the scope of this article.

2.   Provisions concerning the protection of women, particularly as regards pregnancy, confinement and the post-natal period, shall not be deemed to be discrimination as referred to in this article.

3.   This article shall not prevent the adoption of specific measures aimed at removing *de facto* inequalities.

4.   Occupational activities which, by reason of their nature or the context in which they are carried out, can be entrusted only to persons of a particular sex may be excluded from the scope of this article or some of its provisions. This provision is not to be interpreted as requiring the Parties to embody in laws or regulations a list of occupations which, by reason of their nature or the context in which they are carried out, may be reserved to persons of a particular sex.

Articles 21 and 22

1.   For the purpose of the application of these articles, the term "workers' representatives" means persons who are recognised as such under national legislation or practice.

2.   The terms "national legislation and practice" embrace as the case may be, in addition to laws and regulations, collective agreements, other agreements between employers and workers' representatives, customs as well as relevant case law.

3.   For the purpose of the application of these articles, the term "undertaking" is understood as referring to a set of tangible and intangible components, with or without legal personality, formed to produce goods or provide services for financial gain and with power to determine its own market policy.

4.   It is understood that religious communities and their institutions may be excluded from the application of these articles, even if these institutions are "undertakings" within the meaning of paragraph 3. Establishments pursuing activities which are inspired by certain ideals or guided by certain

moral concepts, ideals and concepts which are protected by national legislation, may be excluded from the application of these articles to such an extent as is necessary to protect the orientation of the undertaking.

5. It is understood that where in a state the rights set out in these articles are exercised in the various establishments of the undertaking, the Party concerned is to be considered as fulfilling the obligations deriving from these provisions.

6. The Parties may exclude from the field of application of these articles, those undertakings employing less than a certain number of workers, to be determined by national legislation or practice.

Article 22

1. This provision affects neither the powers and obligations of states as regards the adoption of health and safety regulations for workplaces, nor the powers and responsibilities of the bodies in charge of monitoring their application.

2. The terms "social and socio-cultural services and facilities" are understood as referring to the social and/or cultural facilities for workers provided by some undertakings such as welfare assistance, sports fields, rooms for nursing mothers, libraries, children's holiday camps, etc.

Article 23, paragraph 1

For the purpose of the application of this paragraph, the term "for as long as possible" refers to the elderly person's physical, psychological and intellectual capacities.

Article 24

1. It is understood that for the purposes of this article the terms "termination of employment" and "terminated" means termination of employment at the initiative of the employer.

2. It is understood that this article covers all workers but that a Party may exclude from some or all of its protection the following categories of employed persons:

a. workers engaged under a contract of employment for a specified period of time or a specified task;

b. workers undergoing a period of probation or a qualifying period of employment, provided that this is determined in advance and is of a reasonable duration;

c. workers engaged on a casual basis for a short period.

3. For the purpose of this article the following, in particular, shall not constitute valid reasons for termination of employment:

   a. trade union membership or participation in union activities outside working hours, or, with the consent of the employer, within working hours;

   b. seeking office as, acting or having acted in the capacity of a workers' representative;

   c. the filing of a complaint or the participation in proceedings against an employer involving alleged violation of laws or regulations or recourse to competent administrative authorities;

   d. race, colour, sex, marital status, family responsibilities, pregnancy, religion, political opinion, national extraction or social origin;

   e. maternity or parental leave;

   f. temporary absence from work due to illness or injury.

4. It is understood that compensation or other appropriate relief in case of termination of employment without valid reasons shall be determined by national laws or regulations, collective agreements or other means appropriate to national conditions.

Article 25

1. It is understood that the competent national authority may, by way of exemption and after consulting organisations of employers and workers, exclude certain categories of workers from the protection provided in this provision by reason of the special nature of their employment relationship.

2. It is understood that the definition of the term "insolvency" must be determined by national law and practice.

3. The workers' claims covered by this provision shall include at least:

   a. the workers' claims for wages relating to a prescribed period, which shall not be less than three months under a privilege system and eight weeks under a guarantee system, prior to the insolvency or to the termination of employment;

   b. the workers' claims for holiday pay due as a result of work performed during the year in which the insolvency or the termination of employment occurred;

   c. the workers' claims for amounts due in respect of other types of paid absence relating to a prescribed period, which shall not be less than three months under a privilege system and eight weeks under a guarantee system, prior to the insolvency or the termination of the employment.

4. National laws or regulations may limit the protection of workers' claims to a prescribed amount, which shall be of a socially acceptable level.

Article 26

It is understood that this article does not require that legislation be enacted by the Parties.

It is understood that paragraph 2 does not cover sexual harassment.

Article 27

It is understood that this article applies to men and women workers with family responsibilities in relation to their dependent children as well as in relation to other members of their immediate family who clearly need their care or support where such responsibilities restrict their possibilities of preparing for, entering, participating in or advancing in economic activity. The terms "dependent children" and "other members of their immediate family who clearly need their care and support" mean persons defined as such by the national legislation of the Party concerned.

Articles 28 and 29

For the purpose of the application of this article, the term "workers' representatives" means persons who are recognised as such under national legislation or practice.

Part III

It is understood that the Charter contains legal obligations of an international character, the application of which is submitted solely to the supervision provided for in Part IV thereof.

Article A, paragraph 1

It is understood that the numbered paragraphs may include articles consisting of only one paragraph.

Article B, paragraph 2

For the purpose of paragraph 2 of Article B, the provisions of the revised Charter correspond to the provisions of the Charter with the same article or paragraph number with the exception of:

a. Article 3, paragraph 2, of the revised Charter which corresponds to Article 3, paragraphs 1 and 3, of the Charter;

b. Article 3, paragraph 3, of the revised Charter which corresponds to Article 3, paragraphs 2 and 3, of the Charter;

c. Article 10, paragraph 5, of the revised Charter which corresponds to Article 10, paragraph 4, of the Charter;

d. Article 17, paragraph 1, of the revised Charter which corresponds to Article 17 of the Charter.

Part V

Article E

A differential treatment based on an objective and reasonable justification shall not be deemed discriminatory.

Article F

The terms "in time of war or other public emergency" shall be so understood as to cover also the *threat* of war.

Article I

It is understood that workers excluded in accordance with the appendix to Articles 21 and 22 are not taken into account in establishing the number of workers concerned.

Article J

The term "amendment" shall be extended so as to cover also the addition of new articles to the Charter.

25. European Convention on the Legal Status of Children Born out of Wedlock

Adopted at Strasbourg on 15 October 1975

The member States of the Council of Europe, signatory hereto,

Considering that the aim of the Council of Europe is to achieve a greater unity between its Members, in particular by the adoption of common rules in the field of law;

Noting that in a great number of member States efforts have been, or are being, made to improve the legal status of children born out of wedlock by reducing the differences between their legal status and that of children born in wedlock which are to the legal or social disadvantage of the former;

Recognising that wide disparities in the laws of member States in this field still exist;

Believing that the situation of children born out of wedlock should be improved and that the formulation of certain common rules concerning their legal status would assist this objective and at the same time would contribute to a harmonisation of the laws of the member States in this field;

Considering however that it is necessary to allow progressive stages for those States which consider themselves unable to adopt immediately certain rules of this Convention,

Have agreed as follows:

Article 1

Each Contracting Party undertakes to ensure the conformity of its law with the provisions of this Convention and to notify the Secretary General of the Council of Europe of the measures taken for that purpose.

Article 2

Maternal affiliation of every child born out of wedlock shall be based solely on the fact of the birth of the child.

Article 3

Paternal affiliation of every child born out of wedlock may be evidenced or established by voluntary recognition or by judicial decision.

Article 4

The voluntary recognition of paternity may not be opposed or contested insofar as the internal law provides for these procedures unless the person seeking to recognise or having recognised the child is not the biological father.

Article 5

In actions relating to paternal affiliation scientific evidence which may help to establish or disprove paternity shall be admissible.

Article 6

1.   The father and mother of a child born out of wedlock shall have the same obligation to maintain the child as if it were born in wedlock.

2.   Where a legal obligation to maintain a child born in wedlock falls on certain members of the family of the father or mother, this obligation shall also apply for the benefit of a child born out of wedlock.

Article 7

1.   Where the affiliation of a child born out of wedlock has been established as regards both parents, parental authority may not be attributed automatically to the father alone.

2.   There shall be power to transfer parental authority; cases of transfer shall be governed by the internal law.

Article 8

Where the father or mother of a child born out of wedlock does not have parental authority over or the custody of the child, that parent may obtain a right of access to the child in appropriate cases.

Article 9

A child born out of wedlock shall have the same right of succession in the estate of its father and its mother and of a member of its father's or mother's family as if it had been born in wedlock.

Article 10

The marriage between the father and mother of a child born out of wedlock shall confer on the child the legal status of a child born in wedlock.

Article 11

1. This Convention shall be open to signature by the member States of the Council of Europe. It shall be subject to ratification, acceptance or approval. Instruments of ratification, acceptance or approval shall be deposited with the Secretary General of the Council of Europe.

2. This Convention shall enter into force three months after the date of the deposit of the third instrument of ratification, acceptance or approval.

3. In respect of a signatory State ratifying, accepting or approving subsequently, the Convention shall come into force three months after the date of the deposit of its instrument of ratification, acceptance or approval.

Article 12

1. After the entry into force of this Convention, the Committee of Ministers of the Council of Europe may invite any non-member State to accede to this Convention.

2. Such accession shall be effected by depositing with the Secretary General of the Council of Europe an instrument of accession which shall take effect three months after the date of its deposit.

Article 13

1. Any State may, at the time of signature, or when depositing its instrument of ratification, acceptance, approval or accession, specify the territory or territories to which this Convention shall apply.

2. Any State may, when depositing its instrument of ratification, acceptance, approval or accession or at any later date, by declaration addressed to the Secretary General of the Council of Europe, extend this Convention to any other territory or territories specified in the declaration and for whose international relations it is responsible or on whose behalf it is authorised to give undertakings.

3. Any declaration made in pursuance of the preceding paragraph may, in respect of any territory mentioned in such declaration, be withdrawn according to the procedure laid down in Article 15 of this Convention.

Article 14

1.   Any State may, at the time of signature, or when depositing its instrument of ratification, acceptance, approval or accession or when making a declaration in accordance with paragraph 2 of Article 13 of this Convention, make not more than three reservations in respect of the provisions of Articles 2 to 10 of the Convention.

Reservations of a general nature shall not be permitted; each reservation may not affect more than one provision.

2.   A reservation shall be valid for five years from the entry into force of this Convention for the Contracting Party concerned. It may be renewed for successive periods of five years by means of a declaration addressed to the Secretary General of the Council of Europe before the expiration of each period.

3.   Any Contracting Party may wholly or partly withdraw a reservation it has made in accordance with the foregoing paragraphs by means of a declaration addressed to the Secretary General of the Council of Europe, which shall become effective as from the date of its receipt.

Article 15

1.   Any Contracting Party may, insofar as it is concerned, denounce this Convention by means of a notification addressed to the Secretary General of the Council of Europe.

2.   Such denunciation shall take effect six months after the date of receipt by the Secretary General of such notification.

Article 16

The Secretary General of the Council of Europe shall notify the member States of the Council and any State which has acceded to this Convention of:

a.   any signature;

b.   any deposit of an instrument of ratification, acceptance, approval or accession;

c.   any date of entry into force of this Convention in accordance with Article 11 thereof;

d.   any notification received in pursuance of the provisions of Article 1;

e.   any declaration received in pursuance of the provisions of paragraphs 2 and 3 of Article 13;

f. any reservation made in pursuance of the provisions of paragraph 1 of Article 14;

g. the renewal of any reservation carried out in pursuance of the provisions of paragraph 2 of Article 14;

h. the withdrawal of any reservation carried out in pursuance of the provisions of paragraph 3 of Article 14;

i. any notification received in pursuance of the provisions of Article 15 and the date on which denunciation takes effect.

IN WITNESS WHEREOF, the undersigned, being duly authorised thereto, have signed this Convention.

DONE at Strasbourg, this 15th day of October 1975, in English and in French, both texts being equally authoritative, in a single copy which shall remain deposited in the archives of the Council of Europe. The Secretary General of the Council of Europe shall transmit certified copies to each of the signatory and acceding States.

26. European Convention on the Legal Status of Migrant Workers

Adopted at Strasbourg on 24 November 1977

The member States of the Council of Europe, signatory hereto,

Considering that the aim of the Council of Europe is to achieve a greater unity between its Members for the purpose of safeguarding and realising the ideals and principles which are their common heritage and facilitating their economic and social progress while respecting human rights and fundamental freedoms;

Considering that the legal status of migrant workers who are nationals of Council of Europe member States should be regulated so as to ensure that as far as possible they are treated no less favourably than workers who are nationals of the receiving State in all aspects of living and working conditions;

Being resolved to facilitate the social advancement of migrant workers and members of their families;

Affirming that the rights and privileges which they grant to each other's nationals are conceded by virtue of the close association uniting the member States of the Council of Europe by means of its Statute,

Have agreed as follows:

CHAPTER I

Article 1

Definition

1. For the purpose of this Convention, the term "migrant worker" shall mean a national of a Contracting Party who has been authorised by another Contracting Party to reside in its territory in order to take up paid employment.

2. This Convention shall not apply to:

a. frontier workers;

b. artists, other entertainers and sportsmen engaged for a short period and members of a liberal profession;

c. seamen;

d. persons undergoing training;

e. seasonal workers; seasonal migrant workers are those who, being nationals of a Contracting Party, are employed on the territory of another Contracting Party in an activity dependent on the rhythm of the seasons, on the basis of a contract for a specified period or for specified employment;

f. workers, who are nationals of a Contracting Party, carrying out specific work in the territory of another Contracting Party on behalf of an undertaking having its registered office outside the territory of that Contracting Party.

CHAPTER II

Article 2

Forms of recruitment

1.   The recruitment of prospective migrant workers may be carried out either by named or by unnamed request and in the latter case shall be effected through the intermediary of the official authority in the State of origin if such an authority exists and, where appropriate, through the intermediary of the official authority of the receiving State.

2.   The administrative costs of recruitment, introduction and placing, when these operations are carried out by an official authority, shall not be borne by the prospective migrant worker.

Article 3

Medical examination and vocational test

1.   Recruitment of prospective migrant workers may be preceded by a medical examination and a vocational test.

2.   The medical examination and the vocational test are intended to establish whether the prospective migrant worker is physically and mentally fit and technically qualified for the job offered to him and to make certain that his state of health does not endanger public health.

3.   Arrangements for the reimbursement of expenses connected with the medical examination and vocational test shall be laid down when appropriate by bilateral agreements, so as to ensure that such expenses do not fall upon the prospective migrant worker.

4.   A migrant worker to whom an individual offer of employment is made shall not be required, otherwise than on grounds of fraud, to undergo a vocational test except at the employer's request.

Article 4

Right of exit—Right to admission—Administrative formalities

1.   Each Contracting Party shall guarantee the following rights to migrant workers:

—the right to leave the territory of the Contracting Party of which they are nationals;

—the right to admission to the territory of a Contracting Party in order to take up paid employment after being authorised to do so and obtaining the necessary papers.

2.   These rights shall be subject to such limitations as are prescribed by legislation and are necessary for the protection of national security, public order, public health or morals.

3.   The papers required of the migrant worker for emigration and immigration shall be issued as expeditiously as possible free of charge or on payment of an amount not exceeding their administrative cost.

Article 5

Formalities and procedure relating to the work contract

Every migrant worker accepted for employment shall be provided prior to departure for the receiving State with a contract of employment or a definite offer of employment, either of which may be drawn up in one or more of the languages in use in the State of origin and in one or more of the languages in use in the receiving State. The use of at least one language of the State of origin and one language of the receiving State shall be compulsory in the case of recruitment by an official authority or an officially recognised employment bureau.

Article 6

Information

1.   The Contracting Parties shall exchange and provide for prospective migrants appropriate information on their residence, conditions of and opportunities for family reunion, the nature of the job, the possibility of a new work contract being concluded after the first has lapsed, the qualifications required, working and living conditions (including the cost of living), remuneration, social security, housing, food, the transfer of savings, travel, and on deductions made from wages in respect of contributions for social protection and social security, taxes and other charges. Information may also be provided on the cultural and religious conditions in the receiving State.

2.   In the case of recruitment through an official authority of the receiving State, such information shall be provided, before his departure, in a language which the prospective migrant worker can understand, to enable him to take a decision in full knowledge of the facts. The translation, where necessary, of such information into a language that the prospective migrant worker can understand shall be provided as a general rule by the State of origin.

3.   Each Contracting Party undertakes to adopt the appropriate steps to prevent misleading propaganda relating to emigration and immigration.

Article 7

Travel

1.   Each Contracting Party undertakes to ensure, in the case of official collective recruitment, that the cost of travel to the receiving State shall never be borne by the migrant worker. The arrangements for payment shall be determined under bilateral agreements, which may also extend these measures to families and to workers recruited individually.

2.   In the case of migrant workers and their families in transit through the territory of one Contracting Party en route to the receiving State, or on their return journey to the State of origin, all steps shall be taken by the competent authorities of the transit State to expedite their journey and prevent administrative delays and difficulties.

3.   Each Contracting Party shall exempt from import duties and taxes at the time of entry into the receiving State and of the final return to the State of origin and in transit:

a. the personal effects and movable property of migrant workers and members of their family belonging to their household;

b. a reasonable quantity of hand-tools and portable equipment necessary for the occupation to be engaged in.

The exemptions referred to above shall be granted in accordance with the laws or regulations in force in the States concerned.

CHAPTER III

Article 8

Work permit

1.   Each Contracting Party which allows a migrant worker to enter its territory to take up paid employment shall issue or renew a work permit for

him (unless he is exempt from this requirement), subject to the conditions laid down in its legislation.

2.   However, a work permit issued for the first time may not as a rule bind the worker to the same employer or the same locality for a period longer than one year.

3.   In case of renewal of the migrant worker's work permit, this should as a general rule be for a period of at least one year, insofar as the current state and development of the employment situation permits.

Article 9

Residence permit

1.   Where required by national legislation, each Contracting Party shall issue residence permits to migrant workers who have been authorised to take up paid employment on their territory under conditions laid down in this Convention.

2.   The residence permit shall in accordance with the provisions of national legislation be issued and, if necessary, renewed for a period as a general rule at least as long as that of the work permit. When the work permit is valid indefinitely, the residence permit shall as a general rule be issued and, if necessary, renewed for a period of at least one year. It shall be issued and renewed free of charge or for a sum covering administrative costs only.

3.   The provisions of this Article shall also apply to members of the migrant worker's family who are authorised to join him in accordance with Article 12 of this Convention.

4.   If a migrant worker is no longer in employment, either because he is temporarily incapable of work as a result of illness or accident or because he is involuntarily unemployed, this being duly confirmed by the competent authorities, he shall be allowed for the purpose of the application of Article 25 of this Convention to remain on the territory of the receiving State for a period which should not be less than five months.

Nevertheless, no Contracting Party shall be bound, in the case provided for in the above sub-paragraph, to allow a migrant worker to remain for a period exceeding the period of payment of the unemployment allowance.

5.   The residence permit, issued in accordance with the provisions of paragraphs 1 to 3 of this Article, may be withdrawn:

     a.   for reasons of national security, public policy or morals;

b. if the holder refuses, after having been duly informed of the consequences of such refusal, to comply with the measures prescribed for him by an official medical authority with a view to the protection of public health;

c. if a condition essential to its issue or validity is not fulfilled.

Each Contracting Party nevertheless undertakes to grant to migrant workers whose residence permits have been withdrawn an effective right to appeal, in accordance with the procedure for which provision is made in its legislation, to a judicial or administrative authority.

Article 10

Reception

1. After arrival in the receiving State, migrant workers and members of their families shall be given all appropriate information and advice as well as all necessary assistance for their settlement and adaptation.

2. For this purpose, migrant workers and members of their families shall be entitled to help and assistance from the social services of the receiving State or from bodies working in the public interest in the receiving State and to help from the consular authorities of their State of origin. Moreover, migrant workers shall be entitled, on the same basis as national workers, to help and assistance from the employment services. However, each Contracting Party shall endeavour to ensure that special social services are available, whenever the situation so demands, to facilitate or co-ordinate the reception of migrant workers and their families.

3. Each Contracting Party undertakes to ensure that migrant workers and members of their families can worship freely, in accordance with their faith; each Contracting Party shall facilitate such worship, within the limit of available means.

Article 11

Recovery of sums due in respect of maintenance

1. The status of migrant workers must not interfere with the recovery of sums due in respect of maintenance to persons in the State of origin to whom they have maintenance obligations arising from a family relationship, parentage, marriage or affinity, including a maintenance obligation in respect of a child who is not legitimate.

2. Each Contracting Party shall take the steps necessary to ensure the recovery of sums due in respect of such maintenance, making use as far as possible of the form adopted by the Committee of Ministers of the Council of Europe.

3. As far as possible, each Contracting Party shall take steps to appoint a single national or regional authority to receive and despatch applications for sums due in respect of maintenance provided for in paragraph 1 above.

4. This Article shall not affect existing or future bilateral or multilateral agreements.

Article 12

Family reunion

1. The spouse of a migrant worker who is lawfully employed in the territory of a Contracting Party and the unmarried children thereof, as long as they are considered to be minors by the relevant law of the receiving State, who are dependent on the migrant worker, are authorised on conditions analogous to those which this Convention applies to the admission of migrant workers and according to the admission procedure prescribed by such law or by international agreements to join the migrant worker in the territory of a Contracting Party, provided that the latter has available for the family housing considered as normal for national workers in the region where the migrant worker is employed. Each Contracting Party may make the giving of authorisation conditional upon a waiting period which shall not exceed twelve months.

2. Any State may, at any time, by declaration addressed to the Secretary General of the Council of Europe, which shall take effect one month after the date of its receipt, make the family reunion referred to in paragraph 1 above further conditional upon the migrant worker having steady resources sufficient to meet the needs of his family.

3. Any State may, at any time, by declaration addressed to the Secretary General of the Council of Europe, which shall take effect one month after the date of its receipt, derogate temporarily from the obligation to give the authorisation provided for in paragraph 1 above, for one or more parts of its territory which it shall designate in its declaration, on the condition that these measures do not conflict with obligations under other international instruments. The declaration shall state the special reasons justifying the derogation with regard to receiving capacity.

Any State availing itself of this possibility of derogation shall keep the Secretary General of the Council of Europe fully informed of the measures which it has taken and shall ensure that these measures are published as soon as possible. It shall also inform the Secretary General of the Council of Europe when such measures cease to operate and the provisions of the Convention are again being fully executed.

The derogation shall not, as a general rule, affect requests for family reunion submitted to the competent authorities, before the declaration is addressed to the Secretary General, by migrant workers already established in the part of the territory concerned.

Article 13

Housing

1. Each Contracting Party shall accord to migrant workers, with regard to access to housing and rents, treatment not less favourable than that accorded to its own nationals, insofar as this matter is covered by domestic laws and regulations.

2. Each Contracting Party shall ensure that the competent national authorities carry out inspections in appropriate cases in collaboration with the respective consular authorities, acting within their competence, to ensure that standards of fitness of accommodation are kept up for migrant workers as for its own nationals.

3. Each Contracting Party undertakes to protect migrant workers against exploitation in respect of rents, in accordance with its laws and regulations on the matter.

4. Each Contracting Party shall ensure, by the means available to the competent national authorities, that the housing of the migrant worker shall be suitable.

Article 14

Pretraining—Schooling—Linguistic training—Vocational training and retraining

1. Migrant workers and members of their families officially admitted to the territory of a Contracting Party shall be entitled, on the same basis and under the same conditions as national workers, to general education and vocational training and retraining and shall be granted access to higher education according to the general regulations governing admission to respective institutions in the receiving State.

2. To promote access to general and vocational schools and to vocational training centres, the receiving State shall facilitate the teaching of its language or, if there are several, one of its languages to migrant workers and members of their families.

3. For the purpose of the application of paragraphs 1 and 2 above, the granting of scholarships shall be left to the discretion of each Contracting Party which shall make efforts to grant the children of migrant workers

living with their families in the receiving State—in accordance with the provisions of Article 12 of this Convention—the same facilities in this respect as the receiving State's nationals.

4. The workers' previous attainments, as well as diplomas and vocational qualifications acquired in the State of origin, shall be recognised by each Contracting Party in accordance with arrangements laid down in bilateral and multilateral agreements.

5. The Contracting Parties concerned, acting in close co-operation, shall endeavour to ensure that the vocational training and retraining schemes, within the meaning of this Article, cater as far as possible for the needs of migrant workers with a view to their return to their State of origin.

Article 15

Teaching of the migrant worker's mother tongue

The Contracting Parties concerned shall take action by common accord to arrange, so far as practicable, for the migrant worker's children, special courses for the teaching of the migrant worker's mother tongue, to facilitate, inter alia, their return to their State of origin.

Article 16

Conditions of work

1. In the matter of conditions of work, migrant workers authorised to take up employment shall enjoy treatment not less favourable than that which applies to national workers by virtue of legislative or administrative provisions, collective labour agreements or custom.

2. It shall not be possible to derogate by individual contract from the principle of equal treatment referred to in the foregoing paragraph.

Article 17

Transfer of savings

1. Each Contracting Party shall permit, according to the arrangements laid down by its legislation, the transfer of all or such parts of the earnings and savings of migrant workers as the latter may wish to transfer.

This provision shall apply also to the transfer of sums due by migrant workers in respect of maintenance. The transfer of sums due by migrant workers in respect of maintenance shall on no account be hindered or prevented.

2.   Each Contracting Party shall permit, under bilateral agreements or by any other means, the transfer of such sums as remain due to migrant workers when they leave the territory of the receiving State.

Article 18

Social security

1.   Each Contracting Party undertakes to grant within its territory, to migrant workers and members of their families, equality of treatment with its own nationals in the matter of social security, subject to conditions required by national legislation and by bilateral or multilateral agreements already concluded or to be concluded between the Contracting Parties concerned.

2.   The Contracting Parties shall moreover endeavour to secure to migrant workers and members of their families the conservation of rights in course of acquisition and acquired rights, as well as provision of benefits abroad, through bilateral and multilateral agreements.

Article 19

Social and medical assistance

Each Contracting Party undertakes to grant within its territory, to migrant workers and members of their families who are lawfully present in its territory, social and medical assistance on the same basis as nationals in accordance with the obligations it has assumed by virtue of other international agreements and in particular of the European Convention on Social and Medical Assistance of 1953.

Article 20

Industrial accidents and occupational diseases—Industrial hygiene

1.   With regard to the prevention of industrial accidents and occupational diseases and to industrial hygiene, migrant workers shall enjoy the same rights and protection as national workers, in application of the laws of a Contracting Party and collective agreements and having regard to their particular situation.

2.   A migrant worker who is victim of an industrial accident or who has contracted an occupational disease in the territory of the receiving State shall benefit from occupational rehabilitation on the same basis as national workers.

Article 21

Inspection of working conditions

Each Contracting Party shall inspect or provide for inspection of the conditions of work of migrant workers in the same manner as for national workers. Such inspection shall be carried out by the competent bodies or institutions of the receiving State and by any other authority authorised by the receiving State.

Article 22

Death

Each Contracting Party shall take care, within the framework of its laws and, if need be, within the framework of bilateral agreements, that steps are taken to provide all help and assistance necessary for the transport to the State of origin of the bodies of migrant workers deceased as the result of an industrial accident.

Article 23

Taxation on earnings

1. In the matter of earnings and without prejudice to the provisions on double taxation contained in agreements already concluded or which may in future be concluded between Contracting Parties, migrant workers shall not be liable, in the territory of a Contracting Party, to duties, charges, taxes or contributions of any description whatsoever either higher or more burdensome than those imposed on nationals in similar circumstances. In particular, they shall be entitled to deductions or exemptions from taxes or charges and to all allowances, including allowances for dependants.

2. The Contracting Parties shall decide between themselves, by bilateral or multilateral agreements on double taxation, what measures might be taken to avoid double taxation on the earnings of migrant workers.

Article 24

Expiry of contract and discharge

1. On the expiry of a work contract concluded for a specified period at the end of the period agreed on and in the case of anticipated cancellation of such a contract or cancellation of a work contract for an unspecified period, migrant workers shall be accorded treatment not less favourable than that accorded to national workers under the provisions of national legislation or collective labour agreements.

2.   In the event of individual or collective dismissal, migrant workers shall receive the treatment applicable to national workers under national legislation or collective labour agreements, particularly as regards the form and period of notice, the compensation provided for in legislation or agreements or such as may be due in cases of unwarranted cancellation of their work contracts.

Article 25

Re-employment

1.   If a migrant worker loses his job for reasons beyond his control, such as redundancy or prolonged illness, the competent authority of the receiving State shall facilitate his re-employment in accordance with the laws and regulations of that State.

2.   To this end the receiving State shall promote the measures necessary to ensure, as far as possible, the vocational retraining and occupational rehabilitation of the migrant worker in question, provided that he intends to continue in employment in the State concerned afterwards.

Article 26

Right of access to the courts and administrative authorities in the receiving State

1.   Each Contracting Party shall secure to migrant workers treatment not less favourable than that of its own nationals in respect of legal proceedings. Migrant workers shall be entitled, under the same conditions as nationals, to full legal and judicial protection of their persons and property and of their rights and interests; in particular, they shall have, in the same manner as nationals, the right of access to the competent courts and administrative authorities, in accordance with the law of the receiving State, and the right to obtain the assistance of any person of their choice who is qualified by the law of that State, for instance in disputes with employers, members of their families or third parties. The rules of private international law of the receiving State shall not be affected by this Article.

2.   Each Contracting Party shall provide migrant workers with legal assistance on the same conditions as for their own nationals and, in the case of civil or criminal proceedings, the possibility of obtaining the assistance of an interpreter where they cannot understand or speak the language used in court.

Article 27

Use of employment services

Each Contracting Party recognises the right of migrant workers and of the members of their families officially admitted to its territory to make use of employment services under the same conditions as national workers subject to the legal provisions and regulations and administrative practice, including conditions of access, in force in that State.

Article 28

Exercise of the right to organise

Each Contracting Party shall allow to migrant workers the right to organise for the protection of their economic and social interests on the conditions provided for by national legislation for its own nationals.

Article 29

Participation in the affairs of the undertaking

Each Contracting Party shall facilitate as far as possible the participation of migrant workers in the affairs of the undertaking on the same conditions as national workers.

CHAPTER IV

Article 30

Return home

1. Each Contracting Party shall, as far as possible, take appropriate measures to assist migrant workers and their families on the occasion of their final return to their State of origin, and in particular the steps referred to in paragraphs 2 and 3 of Article 7 of this Convention. The provision of financial assistance shall be left to the discretion of each Contracting Party.

2. To enable migrant workers to know, before they set out on their return journey, the conditions on which they will be able to resettle in their State of origin, this State shall communicate to the receiving State, which shall keep available for those who request it, information regarding in particular:

—possibilities and conditions of employment in the State of origin;

—financial aid granted for economic reintegration;

—the maintenance of social security rights acquired abroad;

—steps to be taken to facilitate the finding of accommodation;

—equivalence accorded to occupational qualifications obtained abroad and any tests to be passed to secure their official recognition;

—equivalence accorded to educational qualifications, so that migrant workers' children can be admitted to schools without down-grading.

CHAPTER V

Article 31

Conservation of acquired rights

No provision of this Convention may be interpreted as justifying less favourable treatment than that enjoyed by migrant workers under the national legislation of the receiving State or under bilateral and multilateral agreements to which that State is a Contracting Party.

Article 32

Relations between this Convention and the laws of the Contracting Parties or international agreements

The provisions of this Convention shall not prejudice the provisions of the laws of the Contracting Parties or of any bilateral or multilateral treaties, conventions, agreements or arrangements, as well as the steps taken to implement them, which are already in force, or may come into force, and under which more favourable treatment has been, or would be, accorded to the persons protected by the Convention.

Article 33

Application of the Convention

1. A Consultative Committee shall be set up within a year of the entry into force of this Convention.

2. Each Contracting Party shall appoint a representative to the Consultative Committee. Any other member State of the Council of Europe may be represented by an observer with the right to speak.

3. The Consultative Committee shall examine any proposals submitted to it by one of the Contracting Parties with a view to facilitating or improving the application of the Convention, as well as any proposal to amend it.

4. The opinions and recommendations of the Consultative Committee shall be adopted by a majority of the members of the Committee; how-

ever, proposals to amend the Convention shall be adopted unanimously by the members of the Committee.

5.   The opinions, recommendations and proposals of the Consultative Committee referred to above shall be addressed to the Committee of Ministers of the Council of Europe, which shall decide on the action to be taken.

6.   The Consultative Committee shall be convened by the Secretary General of the Council of Europe and shall meet, as a general rule, at least once every two years and, in addition, whenever at least two Contracting Parties or the Committee of Ministers so requests. The Committee shall also meet at the request of one Contracting Party whenever the provisions of paragraph 3 of Article 12 are applied.

7.   The Consultative Committee shall draw up periodically, for the attention of the Committee of Ministers, a report containing information regarding the laws and regulations in force in the territory of the Contracting Parties in respect of matters provided for in this Convention.

CHAPTER VI

Article 34

Signature, ratification and entry into force

1.   This Convention shall be open to signature by the member States of the Council of Europe. It shall be subject to ratification, acceptance or approval. Instruments of ratification, acceptance or approval shall be deposited with the Secretary General of the Council of Europe.

2.   This Convention shall enter into force on the first day of the third month following the date of the deposit of the fifth instrument of ratification, acceptance or approval.

3.   In respect of a signatory State ratifying, approving or accepting subsequently, the Convention shall enter into force on the first day of the third month following the date of the deposit of its instrument of ratification, acceptance or approval.

Article 35

Territorial scope

1.   Any State may, at the time of signature or when depositing its instrument of ratification, acceptance or approval or at any later date, by declaration addressed to the Secretary General of the Council of Europe, extend the application of this Convention to all or any of the territories for whose

international relations it is responsible or on whose behalf it is authorised to give undertakings.

2.   Any declaration made in pursuance of the preceding paragraph may, in respect of any territory mentioned in such declaration, be withdrawn. Such withdrawal shall take effect six months after receipt by the Secretary General of the Council of Europe of the declaration of withdrawal.

Article 36

Reservations

1.   Any State may, at the time of signature or when depositing its instrument of ratification, acceptance or approval, make one or more reservations which may relate to no more than nine articles of Chapters II to IV inclusive, other than Articles 4, 8, 9, 12, 16, 17, 20, 25, 26.

2.   Any State may, at any time, wholly or partly withdraw a reservation it has made in accordance with the foregoing paragraph by means of a declaration addressed to the Secretary General of the Council of Europe, which shall become effective as from the date of its receipt.

Article 37

Denunciation of the Convention

1.   Each Contracting Party may denounce this Convention by notification addressed to the Secretary General of the Council of Europe, which shall take effect six months after the date of its receipt.

2.   No denunciation may be made within five years of the date of the entry into force of the Convention in respect of the Contracting Party concerned.

3.   Each Contracting Party which ceases to be a Member of the Council of Europe shall cease to be a Party to this Convention six months after the date on which it loses its quality as a Member of the Council of Europe.

Article 38

Notifications

The Secretary General of the Council of Europe shall notify the member States of the Council of:

    a. any signature;

    b. the deposit of any instrument of ratification, acceptance or approval;

    c. any notification received in respect of paragraphs 2 and 3 of Article 12;

    d. any date of entry into force of this Convention in accordance with Article 34 thereof;

    e. any declaration received in pursuance of the provisions of Article 35;

    f. any reservation made in pursuance of the provisions of paragraph 1 of Article 36;

    g. withdrawal of any reservation carried out in pursuance of the provisions of paragraph 2 of Article 36;

    h. any notification received in pursuance of the provisions of Article 37 and the date on which denunciation takes place.

    IN WITNESS WHEREOF, the undersigned, being duly authorised thereto, have signed this Convention.

    DONE at Strasbourg, this 24th day of November 1977, in English and in French, both texts being equally authoritative, in a single copy which shall remain deposited in the archives of the Council of Europe. The Secretary General of the Council of Europe shall transmit certified copies to each of the signatory States.

27. European Agreement on Transfer of Responsibility for Refugees

Adopted at Strasbourg on 16 October 1980

The member States of the Council of Europe, signatory hereto,

Considering that the aim of the Council of Europe is to achieve a greater unity between its Members;

Wishing to further improve the situation of refugees in member States of the Council of Europe;

Desirous of facilitating the application of Article 28 of the Convention relating to the Status of Refugees of 28 July 1951 and paragraphs 6 and 11 of its Schedule, in particular as regards the situation where a refugee has lawfully taken up residence in the territory of another Contracting Party;

Concerned especially to specify, in a liberal and humanitarian spirit, the conditions on which the responsibility for issuing a travel document is transferred from one Contracting Party to another;

Considering that it is desirable to regulate this question in a uniform manner between the member States of the Council of Europe,

Have agreed as follows:

Article 1

For the purposes of this Agreement:

a. "refugee" means a person to whom the Convention relating to the Status of Refugees of 28 July 1951 or, as the case may be, the Protocol relating to the Status of Refugees of 31 January 1967 applies;

b. "travel document" means the travel document issued by virtue of the above-mentioned Convention;

c. "first State" means a State, Party to this Agreement, which has issued such a travel document;

d. "second State" means another State, Party to this Agreement, in which a refugee, holder of a travel document issued by the first State, is present.

235

Article 2

1.   Responsibility shall be considered to be transferred on the expiry of a period of two years of actual and continuous stay in the second State with the agreement of its authorities or earlier if the second State has permitted the refugee to remain in its territory either on a permanent basis or for a period exceeding the validity of the travel document.

This period of two years shall run from the date of admission of the refugee to the territory of the second State or, if such a date cannot be established, from the date on which he presents himself to the authorities of the second State.

2.   For the calculation of the period specified in paragraph 1 of this Article:

a.   stays authorised solely for the purpose of studies, training or medical care shall not be taken into account;

b.   periods of imprisonment of the refugee imposed in connection with a criminal conviction shall not be taken into account;

c.   periods during which the refugee is allowed to remain in the territory of the second State pending an appeal against a decision of refusal of residence or of removal from the territory shall only be taken into account if the decision on the appeal is favourable to the refugee;

d.   periods during which the refugee leaves on a temporary basis the territory of the second State for not more than three consecutive months or, on more than one occasion, for not more than six months in total, shall be taken into account, such absences not being deemed to interrupt or suspend the stay.

3.   Responsibility shall also be deemed to be transferred if readmission of the refugee to the first State can no longer be requested under Article 4.

Article 3

1.   Until the date of transfer of responsibility, the travel document shall be extended or renewed by the first State.

2.   The refugee shall not be required to leave the second State to obtain the extension or renewal of his travel document and may for this purpose apply to diplomatic missions or consular posts of the first State.

Article 4

1.   As long as transfer of responsibility has not occurred in accordance with Article 2, paragraphs 1 and 2, the refugee shall be readmitted to the territory of the first State at any time, even after the expiry of the travel

document. In the latter case readmission shall occur on the simple request of the second State, on condition that the request is made during the six months following the expiry of the travel document.

2. If the authorities of the second State do not know the whereabouts of the refugee and for this reason are not able to make the request mentioned in paragraph 1 during the six months following the expiry of the travel document, that request must be made within the six months following the time at which the whereabouts of the refugee become known to the second State, but in no case later than two years after the expiry of the travel document.

Article 5

1. From the date of transfer of responsibility:

a. the responsibility of the first State to extend or renew the travel document of the refugee shall cease;

b. the second State shall be responsible for issuing a new travel document to the refugee.

2. The second State shall inform the first State that transfer of responsibility has taken place.

Article 6

After the date of transfer of responsibility, the second State shall, in the interest of family reunification and for humanitarian reasons, facilitate the admission to its territory of the refugee's spouse and minor or dependent children.

Article 7

The competent authorities of the Parties may communicate directly with each other as regards the application of this Agreement. These authorities shall be specified by each State, when expressing its consent to be bound by the Agreement, by means of a notification addressed to the Secretary General of the Council of Europe.

Article 8

1. Nothing in this Agreement shall impair any rights and benefits which have been or which may be granted to refugees independently of this Agreement.

2. None of the provisions of this Agreement shall be interpreted as preventing a Party from extending the benefits of this Agreement to persons who do not fulfil the conditions laid down.

3.   The provisions of bilateral agreements concluded between Parties relating to the transfer of responsibility for the issuing of Convention travel documents or to the readmission of refugees in the absence of such a transfer shall cease to be applicable from the date of entry into force of this Agreement between those Parties. Rights and benefits acquired or in the course of being acquired by refugees under such agreements shall not be affected.

Article 9

1.   This Agreement shall be open for signature by the member States of the Council of Europe, which may express their consent to be bound by:

a. signature without reservation as to ratification, acceptance or approval, or

b. signature subject to ratification, acceptance or approval, followed by ratification, acceptance or approval.

2.   Instruments of ratification, acceptance or approval shall be deposited with the Secretary General of the Council of Europe.

Article 10

1.   This Agreement shall enter into force on the first day of the month following the expiration of a period of one month after the date on which two member States of the Council of Europe have expressed their consent to be bound by the Agreement, in accordance with the provisions of Article 9.

2.   In respect of any member State which subsequently expresses its consent to be bound by it, the Agreement shall enter into force on the first day of the month following the expiration of a period of one month after the date of signature or of the deposit of the instrument of ratification, acceptance or approval.

Article 11

1.   After the entry into force of this Agreement, the Committee of Ministers of the Council of Europe may invite any State not a member of the Council which is a Party to the Convention relating to the Status of Refugees of 28 July 1951 or, as the case may be, the Protocol relating to the Status of Refugees of 31 January 1967, to accede to the Agreement. The decision to invite shall be taken by the majority provided for by Article 20.*d* of the Statute and by the unanimous vote of the representatives of the Contracting States entitled to sit on the Committee.

2.   In respect of any acceding State, the Agreement shall enter into force on the first day of the month following the expiration of a period of

one month after the date of deposit of the instrument of accession with the Secretary General of the Council of Europe.

Article 12

1. Any State may at the time of signature or when depositing its instrument of ratification, acceptance, approval or accession, specify the territory or territories to which this Agreement shall apply.

2. Any State may at any later date, by a declaration addressed to the Secretary General of the Council of Europe, extend the application of this Agreement to any other territory specified in the declaration. In respect of such territory the Agreement shall enter into force on the first day of the month following the expiration of a period of one month after the date of receipt by the Secretary General of such declaration.

3. Any declaration made under the two preceding paragraphs may, in respect of any territory specified in such declaration, be withdrawn by a notification addressed to the Secretary General. The withdrawal shall become effective on the first day of the month following the expiration of a period of six months after the date of receipt of such notification by the Secretary General.

Article 13

Without prejudice to the provisions of Article 12, this Agreement shall apply to each Party subject to the same limitations and reservations applicable to its obligations under the Convention relating to the Status of Refugees of 28 July 1951 or, as the case may be, the Protocol relating to the Status of Refugees of 31 January 1967.

Article 14

1. Any State may, at the time of signature or when depositing its instrument of ratification, acceptance, approval or accession, declare that it avails itself of one or both of the reservations provided for in the Annex to this Agreement. No other reservation may be made.

2. Any Contracting State which has made a reservation under the preceding paragraph may wholly or partly withdraw it by means of a notification addressed to the Secretary General of the Council of Europe. The withdrawal shall take effect on the date of receipt of such notification by the Secretary General.

3. A Party which has made a reservation in respect of any provision of this Agreement may not claim the application of that provision by any

other Party; it may, however, if its reservation is partial or conditional, claim the application of that provision insofar as it has itself accepted it.

Article 15

1.   Difficulties with regard to the interpretation and application of this Agreement shall be settled by direct consultation between the competent administrative authorities and, if the need arises, through diplomatic channels.

2.   Any dispute between Parties concerning the interpretation or application of this Agreement which it has not been possible to settle by negotiation or other means shall, at the request of any party to the dispute, be referred to arbitration. Each party shall nominate an arbitrator and the two arbitrators shall nominate a referee. If any party has not nominated its arbitrator within the three months following the request for arbitration, he shall be nominated at the request of the other party by the President of the European Court of Human Rights. If the latter should be a national of one of the parties to the dispute, this duty shall be carried out by the Vice-President of the Court, or, if the Vice-President is a national of one of the parties to the dispute, by the most senior judge of the Court not being a national of one of the parties to the dispute. The same procedure shall be observed if the arbitrators cannot agree on the choice of referee.

The arbitration tribunal shall lay down its own procedure. Its decisions shall be taken by majority vote. Its award shall be final.

Article 16

1.   Any Party may at any time denounce this Agreement by means of a notification addressed to the Secretary General of the Council of Europe.

2.   Such denunciation shall become effective on the first day of the month following the expiration of a period of six months after the date of receipt of the notification by the Secretary General.

3.   Rights and benefits acquired or in the course of being acquired by refugees under this Agreement shall not be affected in the event of the Agreement being denounced.

Article 17

The Secretary General of the Council of Europe shall notify the member States of the Council and any State which has acceded to this Agreement of:

a.   any signature;

b. the deposit of any instrument of ratification, acceptance, approval or accession;

c. any date of entry into force of this Agreement in accordance with Articles 10, 11 and 12;

d. any other act, notification or communication relating to this Agreement.

IN WITNESS WHEREOF the undersigned, being duly authorised thereto, have signed this Agreement.

DONE at Strasbourg, the 16th day of October 1980, in English and in French, both texts being equally authentic, in a single copy which shall be deposited in the archives of the Council of Europe. The Secretary General of the Council of Europe shall transmit certified copies to each member State of the Council of Europe and to any State invited to accede to this Agreement.

ANNEX

Reservations

Under paragraph 1 of Article 14 of this Agreement, any State may declare:

1.   that insofar as it is concerned, transfer of responsibility under the provisions of paragraph 1 of Article 2 shall not occur for the reason that it has authorised the refugee to stay in its territory for a period exceeding the validity of the travel document solely for the purposes of studies or training.

2.   that it will not accept a request for readmission presented on the basis of the provisions of paragraph 2 of Article 4.

28. Convention for the Protection of Individuals with regard to Automatic Processing of Personal Data

Adopted at Strasbourg on 28 January 1981

PREAMBLE

The member States of the Council of Europe, signatory hereto,

Considering that the aim of the Council of Europe is to achieve greater unity between its Members, based in particular on respect for the rule of law, as well as human rights and fundamental freedoms;

Considering that it is desirable to extend the safeguards for everyone's rights and fundamental freedoms, and in particular the right to the respect for privacy, taking account of the increasing flow across frontiers of personal data undergoing automatic processing;

Reaffirming at the same time their commitment to freedom of information regardless of frontiers;

Recognising that it is necessary to reconcile the fundamental values of the respect for privacy and the free flow of information between peoples,

Have agreed as follows:

CHAPTER I.—GENERAL PROVISIONS

Article 1

Object and purpose

The purpose of this Convention is to secure in the territory of each Party for every individual, whatever his nationality or residence, respect for his rights and fundamental freedoms, and in particular his right to privacy, with regard to automatic processing of personal data relating to him ("data protection").

Article 2

Definitions

For the purposes of this Convention:

a. "personal data" means any information relating to an identified or identifiable individual ("data subject");

b. "automated data file" means any set of data undergoing automatic processing;

c. "automatic processing" includes the following operations if carried out in whole or in part by automated means: storage of data, carrying out of logical and/or arithmetical operations on those data, their alteration, erasure, retrieval or dissemination;

d. "controller of the file" means the natural or legal person, public authority, agency or any other body who is competent according to the national law to decide what should be the purpose of the automated data file, which categories of personal data should be stored and which operations should be applied to them.

Article 3

Scope

1.   The Parties undertake to apply this Convention to automated personal data files and automatic processing of personal data in the public and private sectors.

2.   Any State may, at the time of signature or when depositing its instrument of ratification, acceptance, approval or accession, or at any later time, give notice by a declaration addressed to the Secretary General of the Council of Europe:

a. that it will not apply this Convention to certain categories of automated personal data files, a list of which will be deposited. In this list it shall not include, however, categories of automated data files subject under its domestic law to data protection provisions. Consequently, it shall amend this list by a new declaration whenever additional categories of automated personal data files are subjected to data protection provisions under its domestic law;

b. that it will also apply this Convention to information relating to groups of persons, associations, foundations, companies, corporations and any other bodies consisting directly or indirectly of individuals, whether or not such bodies possess legal personality;

c. that it will also apply this Convention to personal data files which are not processed automatically.

3.   Any State which has extended the scope of this Convention by any of the declarations provided for in sub-paragraph 2.*b* or *c* above may give notice in the said declaration that such extensions shall apply only to certain categories of personal data files, a list of which will be deposited.

4. Any Party which has excluded certain categories of automated personal data files by a declaration provided for in sub-paragraph 2.*a* above may not claim the application of this Convention to such categories by a Party which has not excluded them.

5. Likewise, a Party which has not made one or other of the extensions provided for in sub-paragraphs 2.*b* and *c* above may not claim the application of this Convention on these points with respect to a Party which has made such extensions.

6. The declarations provided for in paragraph 2 above shall take effect from the moment of the entry into force of the Convention with regard to the State which has made them if they have been made at the time of signature or deposit of its instrument of ratification, acceptance, approval or accession, or three months after their receipt by the Secretary General of the Council of Europe if they have been made at any later time. These declarations may be withdrawn, in whole or in part, by a notification addressed to the Secretary General of the Council of Europe. Such withdrawals shall take effect three months after the date of receipt of such notification.

CHAPTER II.—BASIC PRINCIPLES FOR DATA PROTECTION

Article 4

Duties of the Parties

1. Each Party shall take the necessary measures in its domestic law to give effect to the basic principles for data protection set out in this chapter.

2. These measures shall be taken at the latest at the time of entry into force of this Convention in respect of that Party.

Article 5

Quality of data

Personal data undergoing automatic processing shall be:

a. obtained and processed fairly and lawfully;

b. stored for specified and legitimate purposes and not used in a way incompatible with those purposes;

c. adequate, relevant and not excessive in relation to the purposes for which they are stored;

d. accurate and, where necessary, kept up to date;

e. preserved in a form which permits identification of the data subjects for no longer than is required for the purpose for which those data are stored.

Article 6

Special categories of data

Personal data revealing racial origin, political opinions or religious or other beliefs, as well as personal data concerning health or sexual life, may not be processed automatically unless domestic law provides appropriate safeguards. The same shall apply to personal data relating to criminal convictions.

Article 7

Data security

Appropriate security measures shall be taken for the protection of personal data stored in automated data files against accidental or unauthorised destruction or accidental loss as well as against unauthorised access, alteration or dissemination.

Article 8

Additional safeguards for the data subject

Any person shall be enabled:

a. to establish the existence of an automated personal data file, its main purposes, as well as the identity and habitual residence or principal place of business of the controller of the file;

b. to obtain at reasonable intervals and without excessive delay or expense confirmation of whether personal data relating to him are stored in the automated data file as well as communication to him of such data in an intelligible form;

c. to obtain, as the case may be, rectification or erasure of such data if these have been processed contrary to the provisions of domestic law giving effect to the basic principles set out in Articles 5 and 6 of this Convention;

d. to have a remedy if a request for confirmation or, as the case may be, communication, rectification or erasure as referred to in paragraphs *b* and *c* of this article is not complied with.

Article 9

Exceptions and restrictions

1. No exception to the provisions of Articles 5, 6 and 8 of this Convention shall be allowed except within the limits defined in this article.

2. Derogation from the provisions of Articles 5, 6 and 8 of this Convention shall be allowed when such derogation is provided for by the law of the Party and constitutes a necessary measure in a democratic society in the interests of:

    a. protecting State security, public safety, the monetary interests of the State or the suppression of criminal offences;

    b. protecting the data subject or the rights and freedoms of others.

3. Restrictions on the exercise of the rights specified in Article 8, paragraphs *b*, *c* and *d*, may be provided by law with respect to automated personal data files used for statistics or for scientific research purposes when there is obviously no risk of an infringement of the privacy of the data subjects.

Article 10

Sanctions and remedies

Each Party undertakes to establish appropriate sanctions and remedies for violations of provisions of domestic law giving effect to the basic principles for data protection set out in this chapter.

Article 11

Extended protection

None of the provisions of this chapter shall be interpreted as limiting or otherwise affecting the possibility for a Party to grant data subjects a wider measure of protection than that stipulated in this Convention.

CHAPTER III.—TRANSBORDER DATA FLOWS

Article 12

Transborder flows of personal data and domestic law

1. The following provisions shall apply to the transfer across national borders, by whatever medium, of personal data undergoing automatic processing or collected with a view to their being automatically processed.

2.   A Party shall not, for the sole purpose of the protection of privacy, prohibit or subject to special authorisation transborder flows of personal data going to the territory of another Party.

3.   Nevertheless, each Party shall be entitled to derogate from the provisions of paragraph 2:

a. insofar as its legislation includes specific regulations for certain categories of personal data or of automated personal data files, because of the nature of those data or those files, except where the regulations of the other Party provide an equivalent protection;

b. when the transfer is made from its territory to the territory of a non-Contracting State through the intermediary of the territory of another Party, in order to avoid such transfers resulting in circumvention of the legislation of the Party referred to at the beginning of this paragraph.

CHAPTER IV.—MUTUAL ASSISTANCE

Article 13

Co-operation between Parties

1.   The Parties agree to render each other mutual assistance in order to implement this Convention.

2.   For that purpose:

a. each Party shall designate one or more authorities, the name and address of each of which it shall communicate to the Secretary General of the Council of Europe;

b. each Party which has designated more than one authority shall specify in its communication referred to in the previous sub-paragraph the competence of each authority.

3.   An authority designated by a Party shall at the request of an authority designated by another Party:

a. furnish information on its law and administrative practice in the field of data protection;

b. take, in conformity with its domestic law and for the sole purpose of protection of privacy, all appropriate measures for furnishing factual information relating to specific automatic processing carried out in its territory, with the exception however of the personal data being processed.

Article 14

Assistance to data subjects resident abroad

1.   Each Party shall assist any person resident abroad to exercise the rights conferred by its domestic law giving effect to the principles set out in Article 8 of this Convention.

2.   When such a person resides in the territory of another Party he shall be given the option of submitting his request through the intermediary of the authority designated by that Party.

3.   The request for assistance shall contain all the necessary particulars, relating *inter alia* to:

a.   the name, address and any other relevant particulars identifying the person making the request;

b.   the automated personal data file to which the request pertains, or its controller;

c.   the purpose of the request.

Article 15

Safeguards concerning assistance rendered by designated authorities

1.   An authority designated by a Party which has received information from an authority designated by another Party either accompanying a request for assistance or in reply to its own request for assistance shall not use that information for purposes other than those specified in the request for assistance.

2.   Each Party shall see to it that the persons belonging to or acting on behalf of the designated authority shall be bound by appropriate obligations of secrecy or confidentiality with regard to that information.

3.   In no case may a designated authority be allowed to make under Article 14, paragraph 2, a request for assistance on behalf of a data subject resident abroad, of its own accord and without the express consent of the person concerned.

Article 16

Refusal of requests for assistance

A designated authority to which a request for assistance is addressed under Articles 13 or 14 of this Convention may not refuse to comply with it unless:

a.   the request is not compatible with the powers in the field of data protection of the authorities responsible for replying;

b. the request does not comply with the provisions of this Convention;

c. compliance with the request would be incompatible with the sovereignty, security or public policy (*ordre public*) of the Party by which it was designated, or with the rights and fundamental freedoms of persons under the jurisdiction of that Party.

Article 17

Costs and procedures of assistance

1. Mutual assistance which the Parties render each other under Article 13 and assistance they render to data subjects abroad under Article 14 shall not give rise to the payment of any costs or fees other than those incurred for experts and interpreters. The latter costs or fees shall be borne by the Party which has designated the authority making the request for assistance.

2. The data subject may not be charged costs or fees in connection with the steps taken on his behalf in the territory of another Party other than those lawfully payable by residents of that Party.

3. Other details concerning the assistance relating in particular to the forms and procedures and the languages to be used shall be established directly between the Parties concerned.

CHAPTER V.—CONSULTATIVE COMMITTEE

Article 18

Composition of the Committee

1. A Consultative Committee shall be set up after the entry into force of this Convention.

2. Each Party shall appoint a representative to the Committee and a deputy representative. Any member State of the Council of Europe which is not a Party to the Convention shall have the right to be represented on the Committee by an observer.

3. The Consultative Committee may, by unanimous decision, invite any non-member State of the Council of Europe which is not a Party to the Convention to be represented by an observer at a given meeting.

Article 19

Functions of the Committee

The Consultative Committee:

a. may make proposals with a view to facilitating or improving the application of the Convention;

b. may make proposals for amendment of this Convention in accordance with Article 21;

c. shall formulate its opinion on any proposal for amendment of this Convention which is referred to it in accordance with Article 21, paragraph 3;

d. may, at the request of a Party, express an opinion on any question concerning the application of this Convention.

Article 20

Procedure

1. The Consultative Committee shall be convened by the Secretary General of the Council of Europe. Its first meeting shall be held within twelve months of the entry into force of this Convention. It shall subsequently meet at least once every two years and in any case when one-third of the representatives of the Parties request its convocation.

2. A majority of representatives of the Parties shall constitute a quorum for a meeting of the Consultative Committee.

3. After each of its meetings, the Consultative Committee shall submit to the Committee of Ministers of the Council of Europe a report on its work and on the functioning of the Convention.

4. Subject to the provisions of this Convention, the Consultative Committee shall draw up its own Rules of Procedure.

CHAPTER VI.—AMENDMENTS

Article 21

Amendments

1. Amendments to this Convention may be proposed by a Party, the Committee of Ministers of the Council of Europe or the Consultative Committee.

2. Any proposal for amendment shall be communicated by the Secretary General of the Council of Europe to the member States of the Council

of Europe and to every non-member State which has acceded to or has been invited to accede to this Convention in accordance with the provisions of Article 23.

3.   Moreover, any amendment proposed by a Party or the Committee of Ministers shall be communicated to the Consultative Committee, which shall submit to the Committee of Ministers its opinion on that proposed amendment.

4.   The Committee of Ministers shall consider the proposed amendment and any opinion submitted by the Consultative Committee and may approve the amendment.

5.   The text of any amendment approved by the Committee of Ministers in accordance with paragraph 4 of this article shall be forwarded to the Parties for acceptance.

6.   Any amendment approved in accordance with paragraph 4 of this article shall come into force on the thirtieth day after all Parties have informed the Secretary General of their acceptance thereof.

CHAPTER VII.—FINAL CLAUSES

Article 22

Entry into force

1.   This Convention shall be open for signature by the member States of the Council of Europe. It is subject to ratification, acceptance or approval. Instruments of ratification, acceptance or approval shall be deposited with the Secretary General of the Council of Europe.

2.   This Convention shall enter into force on the first day of the month following the expiration of a period of three months after the date on which five member States of the Council of Europe have expressed their consent to be bound by the Convention in accordance with the provisions of the preceding paragraph.

3.   In respect of any member State which subsequently expresses its consent to be bound by it, the Convention shall enter into force on the first day of the month following the expiration of a period of three months after the date of the deposit of the instrument of ratification, acceptance or approval.

Article 23

Accession by non-member States

1. After the entry into force of this Convention, the Committee of Ministers of the Council of Europe may invite any State not a member of the Council of Europe to accede to this Convention by a decision taken by the majority provided for in Article 20.*d* of the Statute of the Council of Europe and by the unanimous vote of the representatives of the Contracting States entitled to sit on the Committee.

2. In respect of any acceding State, the Convention shall enter into force on the first day of the month following the expiration of a period of three months after the date of deposit of the instrument of accession with the Secretary General of the Council of Europe.

Article 24

Territorial clause

1. Any State may at the time of signature or when depositing its instrument of ratification, acceptance, approval or accession specify the territory or territories to which this Convention shall apply.

2. Any State may at any later date, by a declaration addressed to the Secretary General of the Council of Europe, extend the application of this Convention to any other territory specified in the declaration. In respect of such territory the Convention shall enter into force on the first day of the month following the expiration of a period of three months after the date of receipt of such declaration by the Secretary General.

3. Any declaration made under the two preceding paragraphs may, in respect of any territory specified in such declaration, be withdrawn by a notification addressed to the Secretary General. The withdrawal shall become effective on the first day of the month following the expiration of a period of six months after the date of receipt of such notification by the Secretary General.

Article 25

Reservations

No reservation may be made in respect of the provisions of this Convention.

Article 26

Denunciation

1.   Any Party may at any time denounce this Convention by means of a notification addressed to the Secretary General of the Council of Europe.

2.   Such denunciation shall become effective on the first day of the month following the expiration of a period of six months after the date of re ceipt of the notification by the Secretary General.

Article 27

Notifications

The Secretary General of the Council of Europe shall notify the member States of the Council and any State which has acceded to this Convention of:

   a. any signature;

   b. the deposit of any instrument of ratification, acceptance, approval or accession;

   c. any date of entry into force of this Convention in accordance with Articles 22, 23 and 24;

   d. any other act, notification or communication relating to this Convention.

IN WITNESS WHEREOF the undersigned, being duly authorised thereto, have signed this Convention.

DONE at Strasbourg, the 28th day of January 1981, in English and in French, both texts being equally authoritative, in a single copy which shall remain deposited in the archives of the Council of Europe. The Secretary General of the Council of Europe shall transmit certified copies to each member State of the Council of Europe and to any State invited to accede to this Convention.

29.   Convention on the Transfer of Sentenced Persons

Adopted at Strasbourg on 21 March 1983

The member States of the Council of Europe and the other States, signatory hereto,

Considering that the aim of the Council of Europe is to achieve a greater unity between its Members;

Desirous of further developing international co-operation in the field of criminal law;

Considering that such co-operation should further the ends of justice and the social rehabilitation of sentenced persons;

Considering that these objectives require that foreigners who are deprived of their liberty as a result of their commission of a criminal offence should be given the opportunity to serve their sentences within their own society; and

Considering that this aim can best be achieved by having them transferred to their own countries,

Have agreed as follows:

Article 1

Definitions

For the purposes of this Convention:

a. "sentence" means any punishment or measure involving deprivation of liberty ordered by a court for a limited or unlimited period of time on account of a criminal offence;

b. "judgment" means a decision or order of a court imposing a sentence;

c. "sentencing State" means the State in which the sentence was imposed on the person who may be, or has been, transferred;

d. "administering State" means the State to which the sentenced person may be, or has been, transferred in order to serve his sentence.

Article 2

General principles

1.   The Parties undertake to afford each other the widest measure of co-operation in respect of the transfer of sentenced persons in accordance with the provisions of this Convention.

2.   A person sentenced in the territory of a Party may be transferred to the territory of another Party, in accordance with the provisions of this Convention, in order to serve the sentence imposed on him. To that end, he may express his interest to the sentencing State or to the administering State in being transferred under this Convention.

3.   Transfer may be requested by either the sentencing State or the administering State.

Article 3

Conditions for transfer

1.   A sentenced person may be transferred under this Convention only on the following conditions:

a. if that person is a national of the administering State;

b. if the judgment is final;

c. if, at the time of receipt of the request for transfer, the sentenced person still has at least six months of the sentence to serve or if the sentence is indeterminate;

d. if the transfer is consented to by the sentenced person or, where in view of his age or his physical or mental condition one of the two States considers it necessary, by the sentenced person's legal representative;

e. if the acts or omissions on account of which the sentence has been imposed constitute a criminal offence according to the law of the administering State or would constitute a criminal offence if committed on its territory; and

f. if the sentencing and administering States agree to the transfer.

2.   In exceptional cases, Parties may agree to a transfer even if the time to be served by the sentenced person is less than that specified in paragraph 1. *c.*

3.   Any State may, at the time of signature or when depositing its instrument of ratification, acceptance, approval or accession, by a declaration addressed to the Secretary General of the Council of Europe, indicate that it intends to exclude the application of one of the procedures provided in Article 9.1. *a* and *b* in its relations with other Parties.

4.   Any State may, at any time, by a declaration addressed to the Secretary General of the Council of Europe, define, as far as it is concerned, the term "national" for the purposes of this Convention.

Article 4

Obligation to furnish information

1.   Any sentenced person to whom this Convention may apply shall be informed by the sentencing State of the substance of this Convention.

2.   If the sentenced person has expressed an interest to the sentencing State in being transferred under this Convention, that State shall so inform the administering State as soon as practicable after the judgment becomes final.

3.   The information shall include:

    a.   the name, date and place of birth of the sentenced person;

    b.   his address, if any, in the administering State;

    c.   a statement of the facts upon which the sentence was based;

    d.   the nature, duration and date of commencement of the sentence.

4.   If the sentenced person has expressed his interest to the administering State, the sentencing State shall, on request, communicate to that State the information referred to in paragraph 3 above.

5.   The sentenced person shall be informed, in writing, of any action taken by the sentencing State or the administering State under the preceding paragraphs, as well as of any decision taken by either State on a request for transfer.

Article 5

Requests and replies

1.   Requests for transfer and replies shall be made in writing.

2.   Requests shall be addressed by the Ministry of Justice of the requesting State to the Ministry of Justice of the requested State. Replies shall be communicated through the same channels.

3.   Any Party may, by a declaration addressed to the Secretary General of the Council of Europe, indicate that it will use other channels of communication.

4.   The requested State shall promptly inform the requesting State of its decision whether or not to agree to the requested transfer.

Article 6

Supporting documents

1. The administering State, if requested by the sentencing State, shall furnish it with:

a. a document or statement indicating that the sentenced person is a national of that State;

b. a copy of the relevant law of the administering State which provides that the acts or omissions on account of which the sentence has been imposed in the sentencing State constitute a criminal offence according to the law of the administering State, or would constitute a criminal offence if committed on its territory;

c. a statement containing the information mentioned in Article 9.2.

2. If a transfer is requested, the sentencing State shall provide the following documents to the administering State, unless either State has already indicated that it will not agree to the transfer:

a. a certified copy of the judgment and the law on which it is based;

b. a statement indicating how much of the sentence has already been served, including information on any pre-trial detention, remission, and any other factor relevant to the enforcement of the sentence;

c. a declaration containing the consent to the transfer as referred to in Article 3.1. *d*; and

d. whenever appropriate, any medical or social reports on the sentenced person, information about his treatment in the sentencing State, and any recommendation for his further treatment in the administering State.

3. Either State may ask to be provided with any of the documents or statements referred to in paragraphs 1 or 2 above before making a request for transfer or taking a decision on whether or not to agree to the transfer.

Article 7

Consent and its verification

1. The sentencing State shall ensure that the person required to give consent to the transfer in accordance with Article 3.1. *d* does so voluntarily and with full knowledge of the legal consequences thereof. The procedure for giving such consent shall be governed by the law of the sentencing State.

2. The sentencing State shall afford an opportunity to the administering State to verify, through a consul or other official agreed upon with the administering State, that the consent is given in accordance with the conditions set out in paragraph 1 above.

Article 8

Effect of transfer for sentencing State

1. The taking into charge of the sentenced person by the authorities of the administering State shall have the effect of suspending the enforcement of the sentence in the sentencing State.

2. The sentencing State may no longer enforce the sentence if the administering State considers enforcement of the sentence to have been completed.

Article 9

Effect of transfer for administering State

1. The competent authorities of the administering State shall:

a. continue the enforcement of the sentence immediately or through a court or administrative order, under the conditions set out in Article 10, or

b. convert the sentence, through a judicial or administrative procedure, into a decision of that State, thereby substituting for the sanction imposed in the sentencing State a sanction prescribed by the law of the administering State for the same offence, under the conditions set out in Article 11.

2. The administering State, if requested, shall inform the sentencing State before the transfer of the sentenced person as to which of these procedures it will follow.

3. The enforcement of the sentence shall be governed by the law of the administering State and that State alone shall be competent to take all appropriate decisions.

4. Any State which, according to its national law, cannot avail itself of one of the procedures referred to in paragraph 1 to enforce measures imposed in the territory of another Party on persons who for reasons of mental condition have been held not criminally responsible for the commission of the offence, and which is prepared to receive such persons for further treatment may, by way of a declaration addressed to the Secretary General of the Council of Europe, indicate the procedures it will follow in such cases.

Article 10

Continued enforcement

1. In the case of continued enforcement, the administering State shall be bound by the legal nature and duration of the sentence as determined by the sentencing State.

2.   If, however, this sentence is by its nature or duration incompatible with the law of the administering State, or its law so requires, that State may, by a court or administrative order, adapt the sanction to the punishment or measure prescribed by its own law for a similar offence. As to its nature, the punishment or measure shall, as far as possible, correspond with that imposed by the sentence to be enforced. It shall not aggravate, by its nature or duration, the sanction imposed in the sentencing State, nor exceed the maximum prescribed by the law of the administering State.

Article 11

Conversion of sentence

1.   In the case of conversion of sentence, the procedures provided for by the law of the administering State apply. When converting the sentence, the competent authority:

a.   shall be bound by the findings as to the facts insofar as they appear explicitly or implicitly from the judgment imposed in the sentencing State;

b.   may not convert a sanction involving deprivation of liberty to a pecuniary sanction;

c.   shall deduct the full period of deprivation of liberty served by the sentenced person; and

d.   shall not aggravate the penal position of the sentenced person, and shall not be bound by any minimum which the law of the administering State may provide for the offence or offences committed.

2.   If the conversion procedure takes place after the transfer of the sentenced person, the administering State shall keep that person in custody or otherwise ensure his presence in the administering State pending the outcome of that procedure.

Article 12

Pardon, amnesty, commutation

Each Party may grant pardon, amnesty or commutation of the sentence in accordance with its Constitution or other laws.

Article 13

Review of judgment

The sentencing State alone shall have the right to decide on any application for review of the judgment.

Article 14

Termination of enforcement

The administering State shall terminate enforcement of the sentence as soon as it is informed by the sentencing State of any decision or measure as a result of which the sentence ceases to be enforceable.

Article 15

Information on enforcement

The administering State shall provide information to the sentencing State concerning the enforcement of the sentence:

a. when it considers enforcement of the sentence to have been completed;

b. if the sentenced person has escaped from custody before enforcement of the sentence has been completed; or

c. if the sentencing State requests a special report.

Article 16

Transit

1.   A Party shall, in accordance with its law, grant a request for transit of a sentenced person through its territory if such a request is made by another Party and that State has agreed with another Party or with a third State to the transfer of that person to or from its territory.

2.   A Party may refuse to grant transit:

a. if the sentenced person is one of its nationals, or

b. if the offence for which the sentence was imposed is not an offence under its own law.

3.   Requests for transit and replies shall be communicated through the channels referred to in the provisions of Article 5.2 and 3.

4.   A Party may grant a request for transit of a sentenced person through its territory made by a third State if that State has agreed with another Party to the transfer to or from its territory.

5.   The Party requested to grant transit may hold the sentenced person in custody only for such time as transit through its territory requires.

6.   The Party requested to grant transit may be asked to give an assurance that the sentenced person will not be prosecuted, or, except as provided in the preceding paragraph, detained, or otherwise subjected to any restriction on his liberty in the territory of the transit State for any offence commit-

ted or sentence imposed prior to his departure from the territory of the sentencing State.

7.   No request for transit shall be required if transport is by air over the territory of a Party and no landing there is scheduled. However, each State may, by a declaration addressed to the Secretary General of the Council of Europe at the time of signature or of deposit of its instrument of ratification, acceptance, approval or accession, require that it be notified of any such transit over its territory.

Article 17

Language and costs

1.   Information under Article 4, paragraphs 2 to 4, shall be furnished in the language of the Party to which it is addressed or in one of the official languages of the Council of Europe.

2.   Subject to paragraph 3 below, no translation of requests for transfer or of supporting documents shall be required.

3.   Any State may, at the time of signature or when depositing its instrument of ratification, acceptance, approval or accession, by a declaration addressed to the Secretary General of the Council of Europe, require that requests for transfer and supporting documents be accompanied by a translation into its own language or into one of the official languages of the Council of Europe or into such one of these languages as it shall indicate. It may on that occasion declare its readiness to accept translations in any other language in addition to the official language or languages of the Council of Europe.

4.   Except as provided in Article 6.2.*a*, documents transmitted in application of this Convention need not be certified.

5.   Any costs incurred in the application of this Convention shall be borne by the administering State, except costs incurred exclusively in the territory of the sentencing State.

Article 18

Signature and entry into force

1.   This Convention shall be open for signature by the member States of the Council of Europe and non-member States which have participated in its elaboration. It is subject to ratification, acceptance or approval. Instruments of ratification, acceptance or approval shall be deposited with the Secretary General of the Council of Europe.

2.   This Convention shall enter into force on the first day of the month following the expiration of a period of three months after the date on which three member States of the Council of Europe have expressed their consent to be bound by the Convention in accordance with the provisions of paragraph 1.

3.   In respect of any signatory State which subsequently expresses its consent to be bound by it, the Convention shall enter into force on the first day of the month following the expiration of a period of three months after the date of the deposit of the instrument of ratification, acceptance or approval.

Article 19

Accession by non-member States

1.   After the entry into force of this Convention, the Committee of Ministers of the Council of Europe, after consulting the Contracting States, may invite any State not a member of the Council and not mentioned in Article 18.1 to accede to this Convention, by a decision taken by the majority provided for in Article 20.*d* of the Statute of the Council of Europe and by the unanimous vote of the representatives of the Contracting States entitled to sit on the Committee.

2.   In respect of any acceding State, the Convention shall enter into force on the first day of the month following the expiration of a period of three months after the date of deposit of the instrument of accession with the Secretary General of the Council of Europe.

Article 20

Territorial application

1.   Any State may at the time of signature or when depositing its instrument of ratification, acceptance, approval or accession, specify the territory or territories to which this Convention shall apply.

2.   Any State may at any later date, by a declaration addressed to the Secretary General of the Council of Europe, extend the application of this Convention to any other territory specified in the declaration. In respect of such territory the Convention shall enter into force on the first day of the month following the expiration of a period of three months after the date of receipt of such declaration by the Secretary General.

3.   Any declaration made under the two preceding paragraphs may, in respect of any territory specified in such declaration, be withdrawn by a notification addressed to the Secretary General. The withdrawal shall become effective on the first day of the month following the expiration of a

period of three months after the date of receipt of such notification by the Secretary General.

Article 21

Temporal application

This Convention shall be applicable to the enforcement of sentences imposed either before or after its entry into force.

Article 22

Relationship to other Conventions and Agreements

1. This Convention does not affect the rights and undertakings derived from extradition treaties and other treaties on international cooperation in criminal matters providing for the transfer of detained persons for purposes of confrontation or testimony.

2. If two or more Parties have already concluded an agreement or treaty on the transfer of sentenced persons or otherwise have established their relations in this matter, or should they in future do so, they shall be entitled to apply that agreement or treaty or to regulate those relations accordingly, in lieu of the present Convention.

3. The present Convention does not affect the right of States party to the European Convention on the International Validity of Criminal Judgments to conclude bilateral or multilateral agreements with one another on matters dealt with in that Convention in order to supplement its provisions or facilitate the application of the principles embodied in it.

4. If a request for transfer falls within the scope of both the present Convention and the European Convention on the International Validity of Criminal Judgments or another agreement or treaty on the transfer of sentenced persons, the requesting State shall, when making the request, indicate on the basis of which instrument it is made.

Article 23

Friendly settlement

The European Committee on Crime Problems of the Council of Europe shall be kept informed regarding the application of this Convention and shall do whatever is necessary to facilitate a friendly settlement of any difficulty which may arise out of its application.

Article 24

Denunciation

1.   Any Party may at any time denounce this Convention by means of a notification addressed to the Secretary General of the Council of Europe.

2.   Such denunciation shall become effective on the first day of the month following the expiration of a period of three months after the date of receipt of the notification by the Secretary General.

3.   The present Convention shall, however, continue to apply to the enforcement of sentences of persons who have been transferred in conformity with the provisions of the Convention before the date on which such a denunciation takes effect.

Article 25

Notifications

The Secretary General of the Council of Europe shall notify the member States of the Council of Europe, the non-member States which have participated in the elaboration of this Convention and any State which has acceded to this Convention of:

   a.   any signature;

   b.   the deposit of any instrument of ratification, acceptance, approval or accession;

   c.   any date of entry into force of this Convention in accordance with Articles 18.2 and 3, 19.2 and 20.2 and 3;

   d.   any other act, declaration, notification or communication relating to this Convention.

IN WITNESS WHEREOF the undersigned, being duly authorised thereto, have signed this Convention.

DONE at Strasbourg, this 21st day of March 1983, in English and French, both texts being equally authentic, in a single copy which shall be deposited in the archives of the Council of Europe. The Secretary General of the Council of Europe shall transmit certified copies to each member State of the Council of Europe, to the non-member States which have participated in the elaboration of this Convention, and to any State invited to accede to it.

30. European Convention for the Prevention of Torture and Inhuman or Degrading Treatment or Punishment

Adopted at Strasbourg on 26 November 1987

ENTRY INTO FORCE: 1 February 1989, in accordance with article 19

The member States of the Council of Europe, signatory hereto,

Having regard to the provisions of the Convention for the Protection of Human Rights and Fundamental Freedoms;

Recalling that, under Article 3 of the same Convention, "no one shall be subjected to torture or to inhuman or degrading treatment or punishment";

Noting that the machinery provided for in that Convention operates in relation to persons who allege that they are victims of violations of Article 3;

Convinced that the protection of persons deprived of their liberty against torture and inhuman or degrading treatment or punishment could be strengthened by non-judicial means of a preventive character based on visits,

Have agreed as follows:

CHAPTER I

Article 1

There shall be established a European Committee for the Prevention of Torture and Inhuman or Degrading Treatment or Punishment (hereinafter referred to as "the Committee"). The Committee shall, by means of visits, examine the treatment of persons deprived of their liberty with a view to strengthening, if necessary, the protection of such persons from torture and from inhuman or degrading treatment or punishment.

Article 2

Each Party shall permit visits, in accordance with this Convention, to any place within its jurisdiction where persons are deprived of their liberty by a public authority.

Article 3

In the application of this Convention, the Committee and the competent national authorities of the Party concerned shall co-operate with each other.

CHAPTER II

Article 4

1. The Committee shall consist of a number of members equal to that of the Parties.

2. The members of the Committee shall be chosen from among persons of high moral character, known for their competence in the field of human rights or having professional experience in the areas covered by this Convention.

3. No two members of the Committee may be nationals of the same State.

4. The members shall serve in their individual capacity, shall be independent and impartial, and shall be available to serve the Committee effectively.

Article 5

1. The members of the Committee shall be elected by the Committee of Ministers of the Council of Europe by an absolute majority of votes, from a list of names drawn up by the Bureau of the Consultative Assembly of the Council of Europe; each national delegation of the Parties in the Consultative Assembly shall put forward three candidates, of whom two at least shall be its nationals.

2. The same procedure shall be followed in filling casual vacancies.

3. The members of the Committee shall be elected for a period of four years. They may only be re-elected once. However, among the members elected at the first election, the terms of three members shall expire at the end of two years. The members whose terms are to expire at the end of the initial period of two years shall be chosen by lot by the Secretary General of the Council of Europe immediately after the first election has been completed.

Article 6

1. The Committee shall meet in camera. A quorum shall be equal to the majority of its members. The decisions of the Committee shall be taken

by a majority of the members present, subject to the provisions of Article 10, paragraph 2.

2. The Committee shall draw up its own rules of procedure.

3. The Secretariat of the Committee shall be provided by the Secretary General of the Council of Europe.

CHAPTER III

Article 7

1. The Committee shall organise visits to places referred to in Article 2. Apart from periodic visits, the Committee may organise such other visits as appear to it to be required in the circumstances.

2. As a general rule, the visits shall be carried out by at least two members of the Committee. The Committee may, if it considers it necessary, be assisted by experts and interpreters.

Article 8

1. The Committee shall notify the Government of the Party concerned of its intention to carry out a visit. After such notification, it may at any time visit any place referred to in Article 2.

2. A Party shall provide the Committee with the following facilities to carry out its task:

  a. access to its territory and the right to travel without restriction;

  b. full information on the places where persons deprived of their liberty are being held;

  c. unlimited access to any place where persons are deprived of their liberty, including the right to move inside such places without restriction;

  d. other information available to the Party which is necessary for the Committee to carry out its task. In seeking such information, the Committee shall have regard to applicable rules of national law and professional ethics.

3. The Committee may interview in private persons deprived of their liberty.

4. The Committee may communicate freely with any person whom it believes can supply relevant information.

5. If necessary, the Committee may immediately communicate observations to the competent authorities of the Party concerned.

Article 9

1.   In exceptional circumstances, the competent authorities of the Party concerned may make representations to the Committee against a visit at the time or to the particular place proposed by the Committee. Such representations may only be made on grounds of national defence, public safety, serious disorder in places where persons are deprived of their liberty, the medical condition of a person or that an urgent interrogation relating to a serious crime is in progress.

2.   Following such representations, the Committee and the Party shall immediately enter into consultations in order to clarify the situation and seek agreement on arrangements to enable the Committee to exercise its functions expeditiously. Such arrangements may include the transfer to another place of any person whom the Committee proposed to visit. Until the visit takes place, the Party shall provide information to the Committee about any person concerned.

Article 10

1.   After each visit, the Committee shall draw up a report on the facts found during the visit, taking account of any observations which may have been submitted by the Party concerned. It shall transmit to the latter its report containing any recommendations it considers necessary. The Committee may consult with the Party with a view to suggesting, if necessary, improvements in the protection of persons deprived of their liberty.

2.   If the Party fails to co-operate or refuses to improve the situation in the light of the Committee's recommendations, the Committee may decide, after the Party has had an opportunity to make known its views, by a majority of two-thirds of its members to make a public statement on the matter.

Article 11

1.   The information gathered by the Committee in relation to a visit, its report and its consultations with the Party concerned shall be confidential.

2.   The Committee shall publish its report, together with any comments of the Party concerned, whenever requested to do so by that Party.

3.   However, no personal data shall be published without the express consent of the person concerned.

Article 12

Subject to the rules of confidentiality in Article 11, the Committee shall every year submit to the Committee of Ministers a general report on its activities which shall be transmitted to the Consultative Assembly and made public.

Article 13

The members of the Committee, experts and other persons assisting the Committee are required, during and after their terms of office, to maintain the confidentiality of the facts or information of which they have become aware during the discharge of their functions.

Article 14

1.   The names of persons assisting the Committee shall be specified in the notification under Article 8, paragraph 1.

2.   Experts shall act on the instructions and under the authority of the Committee. They shall have particular knowledge and experience in the areas covered by this Convention and shall be bound by the same duties of independence, impartiality and availability as the members of the Committee.

3.   A Party may exceptionally declare that an expert or other person assisting the Committee may not be allowed to take part in a visit to a place within its jurisdiction.

CHAPTER IV

Article 15

Each Party shall inform the Committee of the name and address of the authority competent to receive notifications to its Government, and of any liaison officer it may appoint.

Article 16

The Committee, its members and experts referred to in Article 7, paragraph 2, shall enjoy the privileges and immunities set out in the Annex to this Convention.

Article 17

1. This Convention shall not prejudice the provisions of domestic law or any international agreement which provide greater protection for persons deprived of their liberty.

2. Nothing in this Convention shall be construed as limiting or derogating from the competence of the organs of the European Convention on Human Rights or from the obligations assumed by the Parties under that Convention.

3. The Committee shall not visit places which representatives or delegates of Protecting Powers or the International Committee of the Red Cross effectively visit on a regular basis by virtue of the Geneva Conventions of 12 August 1949 and the Additional Protocols of 8 June 1977 thereto.

Chapter V

Article 18

This Convention shall be open for signature by the member States of the Council of Europe. It is subject to ratification, acceptance or approval. Instruments of ratification, acceptance or approval shall be deposited with the Secretary General of the Council of Europe.

Article 19

1. This Convention shall enter into force on the first day of the month following the expiration of a period of three months after the date on which seven member States of the Council of Europe have expressed their consent to be bound by the Convention in accordance with the provisions of Article 18.

2. In respect of any member State which subsequently expresses its consent to be bound by it, the Convention shall enter into force on the first day of the month following the expiration of a period of three months after the date of the deposit of the instrument of ratification, acceptance or approval.

Article 20

1. Any State may at the time of signature or when depositing its instrument of ratification, acceptance or approval, specify the territory or territories to which this Convention shall apply.

2.   Any State may at any later date, by a declaration addressed to the Secretary General of the Council of Europe, extend the application of this Convention to any other territory specified in the declaration. In respect of such territory the Convention shall enter into force on the first day of the month following the expiration of a period of three months after the date of receipt of such declaration by the Secretary General.

3.   Any declaration made under the two preceding paragraphs may, in respect of any territory specified in such declaration, be withdrawn by a notification addressed to the Secretary General. The withdrawal shall become effective on the first day of the month following the expiration of a period of three months after the date of receipt of such notification by the Secretary General.

Article 21

No reservation may be made in respect of the provisions of this Convention.

Article 22

1.   Any Party may, at any time, denounce this Convention by means of a notification addressed to the Secretary General of the Council of Europe.

2.   Such denunciation shall become effective on the first day of the month following the expiration of a period of twelve months after the date of receipt of the notification by the Secretary General.

Article 23

The Secretary General of the Council of Europe shall notify the member States of the Council of Europe of:

a.   any signature;

b.   the deposit of any instrument of ratification, acceptance or approval;

c.   any date of entry into force of this Convention in accordance with Articles 19 and 20;

d.   any other act, notification or communication relating to this Convention, except for action taken in pursuance of Articles 8 and 10.

IN WITNESS WHEREOF the undersigned, being duly authorised thereto, have signed this Convention.

DONE at Strasbourg, the 26 November 1987, in English and French, both texts being equally authentic, in a single copy which shall be deposited in the archives of the Council of Europe. The Secretary General of the Council of Europe shall transmit certified copies to each member State of the Council of Europe.

ANNEX

Privileges and immunities
(Article 16)

1.   For the purpose of this Annex, references to members of the Committee shall be deemed to include references to experts mentioned in Article 7, paragraph 2.

2.   The members of the Committee shall, while exercising their functions and during journeys made in the exercise of their functions, enjoy the following privileges and immunities:

a. immunity from personal arrest or detention and from seizure of their personal baggage and, in respect of words spoken or written and all acts done by them in their official capacity, immunity from legal process of every kind;

b. exemption from any restrictions on their freedom of movement on exit from and return to their country of residence, and entry into and exit from the country in which they exercise their functions, and from alien registration in the country which they are visiting or through which they are passing in the exercise of their functions.

3.   In the course of journeys undertaken in the exercise of their functions, the members of the Committee shall, in the matter of customs and exchange control, be accorded:

a. by their own Government, the same facilities as those accorded to senior officials travelling abroad on temporary official duty;

b. by the Governments of other Parties, the same facilities as those accorded to representatives of foreign Governments on temporary official duty.

4.   Documents and papers of the Committee, in so far as they relate to the business of the Committee, shall be inviolable.

The official correspondence and other official communications of the Committee may not be held up or subjected to censorship.

5.   In order to secure for the members of the Committee complete freedom of speech and complete independence in the discharge of their duties, the immunity from legal process in respect of words spoken or written and all acts done by them in discharging their duties shall continue to be ac-

corded, notwithstanding that the persons concerned are no longer engaged in the discharge of such duties.

6. Privileges and immunities are accorded to the members of the Committee, not for the personal benefit of the individuals themselves but in order to safeguard the independent exercise of their functions. The Committee alone shall be competent to waive the immunity of its members; it has not only the right, but is under a duty, to waive the immunity of one of its members in any case where, in its opinion, the immunity would impede the course of justice, and where it can be waived without prejudice to the purpose for which the immunity is accorded.

31. Protocol No. 1 to the European Convention for the Prevention of Torture and Inhuman or Degrading Treatment or Punishment

Adopted at Strasbourg on 4 November 1993

The member States of the Council of Europe, signatories to this Protocol to the European Convention for the Prevention of Torture and Inhuman or Degrading Treatment or Punishment, signed at Strasbourg on 26 November 1987 (hereinafter referred to as "the Convention",

Considering that non-member States of the Council of Europe should be allowed to accede to the Convention at the invitation of the Committee of Ministers,

Have agreed as follows:

Article 1

A sub-paragraph shall be added to Article 5, paragraph 1, of the Convention as follows:

"Where a member is to be elected to the Committee in respect of a non-member State of the Council of Europe, the Bureau of the Consultative Assembly shall invite the Parliament of that State to put forward three candidates, of whom two at least shall be its nationals. The election by the Committee of Ministers shall take place after consultation with the Party concerned."

Article 2

Article 12 of the Convention shall read as follows:

"Subject to the rules of confidentiality in Article 11, the Committee shall every year submit to the Committee of Ministers a general report on its activities which shall be transmitted to the Consultative Assembly and to any non-member State of the Council of Europe which is a party to the Convention, and made public."

Article 3

The text of Article 18 of the Convention shall become paragraph 1 of that article and shall be supplemented by the following second paragraph:

"2.   The Committee of Ministers of the Council of Europe may invite any non-member State of the Council of Europe to accede to the Convention."

Article 4

In paragraph 2 of Article 19 of the Convention, the word "member" shall be deleted and the words "or approval", shall be replaced by "approval or accession."

Article 5

In paragraph 1 of Article 20 of the Convention, the words "or approval" shall be replaced by "approval or accession,".

Article 6

1.   The introductory sentence of Article 23 of the Convention shall read as follows:

"The Secretary General of the Council of Europe shall notify the member States and any non-member State of the Council of Europe party to the Convention of."

2.   In Article 23.b of the Convention, the words "or approval;" shall be replaced by "approval or accession;".

Article 7

1.   This Protocol shall be open for signature by member States of the Council of Europe signatories to the Convention, which may express their consent to be bound by:

a.   signature without reservation as to ratification, acceptance or approval; or

b.   signature subject to ratification, acceptance or approval, followed by ratification, acceptance or approval.

2.   Instruments of ratification, acceptance or approval shall be deposited with the Secretary General of the Council of Europe.

Article 8

This Protocol shall enter into force on the first day of the month following the expiration of a period of three months after the date on which all Parties to the Convention have expressed their consent to be bound by the Protocol, in accordance with the provisions of Article 7.

Article 9

The Secretary General of the Council of Europe shall notify the member States of the Council of Europe of:

a. any signature;

b. the deposit of any instrument of ratification, acceptance or approval;

c. the date of entry into force of this Protocol, in accordance with Article 8;

d. any other act, notification or communication relating to this Protocol.

IN WITNESS WHEREOF, the undersigned, being duly authorised thereto, have signed this Protocol.

DONE at Strasbourg this 4th day of November 1993, in English and French, both texts being equally authentic, in a single copy which shall be deposited in the archives of the Council of Europe. The Secretary General of the Council of Europe shall transmit certified copies to each member State of the Council of Europe.

32. Protocol No. 2 to the European Convention for the Prevention of Torture and Inhuman or Degrading Treatment or Punishment

Adopted at Strasbourg on 4 November 1993

The States, signatories to this Protocol to the European Convention for the Prevention of Torture and Inhuman or Degrading Treatment or Punishment, signed at Strasbourg on 26 November 1987 (hereinafter referred to as "the Convention"),

Convinced of the advisability of enabling members of the European Committee for the Prevention of Torture and Inhuman and Degrading Treatment or Punishment (hereinafter referred to as "the Committee") to be re-elected twice;

Also considering the need to guarantee an orderly renewal of the membership of the Committee,

Have agreed as follows:

Article 1

1. In Article 5, paragraph 3, the second sentence shall read as follows:

"They may be re-elected twice."

2. Article 5 of the Convention shall be supplemented by the following paragraphs 4 and 5:

"4. In order to ensure that, as far as possible, one half of the membership of the Committee shall be renewed every two years, the Committee of Ministers may decide, before proceeding to any subsequent election, that the term or terms of office of one or more members to be elected shall be for a period other than four years but not more than six and not less than two years.

5. In cases where more than one term of office is involved and the Committee of Ministers applies the preceding paragraph, the allocation of the terms of office shall be effected by the drawing of lots by the Secretary General, immediately after the election."

Article 2

1.   This Protocol shall be open for signature by States signatories to the Convention or acceding thereto, which may express their consent to be bound by:

a. signature without reservation as to ratification, acceptance or approval; or

b. signature subject to ratification, acceptance or approval, followed by ratification, acceptance or approval.

2.   Instruments of ratification, acceptance or approval shall be deposited with the Secretary General of the Council of Europe.

Article 3

This Protocol shall enter into force on the first day of the month following the expiration of a period of three months after the date on which all Parties to the Convention have expressed their consent to be bound by the Protocol, in accordance with the provisions of Article 2.

Article 4

The Secretary General of the Council of Europe shall notify the member States of the Council of Europe and non-member States Parties to the Convention of:

a. any signature;

b. the deposit of any instrument of ratification, acceptance or approval;

c. the date of any entry into force of this Protocol, in accordance with Article 3;

d. any other act, notification or communication relating to this Protocol.

IN WITNESS WHEREOF, the undersigned, being duly authorised thereto, have signed this Protocol.

DONE at Strasbourg, this 4th day of November 1993, in English and French, both texts being equally authentic, in a single copy which shall be deposited in the archives of the Council of Europe. The Secretary General of the Council of Europe shall transmit certified copies to each member State of the Council of Europe.

33. Convention on the Participation of Foreigners in Public Life at Local Level

Adopted at Strasbourg on 5 February 1992

PREAMBLE

The member States of the Council of Europe, signatory hereto,

Considering that the aim of the Council of Europe is to achieve a greater unity between its members for the purpose of safeguarding and realising the ideals and principles which are their common heritage, and facilitating their economic and social progress while respecting human rights and fundamental freedoms;

Reaffirming their commitment to the universal and indivisible nature of human rights and fundamental freedoms based on the dignity of all human beings;

Having regard to Articles 10, 11, 16 and 60 of the Convention for the Protection of Human Rights and Fundamental Freedoms;

Considering that the residence of foreigners on the national territory is now a permanent feature of European societies;

Considering that foreign residents generally have the same duties as citizens at local level;

Aware of the active participation of foreign residents in the life of the local community and the development of its prosperity, and convinced of the need to improve their integration into the local community, especially by enhancing the possibilities for them to participate in local public affairs,

Have agreed as follows:

Part I

Article 1

1. Each Party shall apply the provisions of Chapters A, B, and C.

279

However, any Contracting State may declare, when depositing its instrument of ratification, acceptance, approval or accession, that it reserves the right not to apply the provisions of either Chapter B or Chapter C or both.

2.   Each Party which has declared that it will apply one or two chapters only may, at any subsequent time, notify the Secretary General that it agrees to apply the provisions of the chapter or chapters which it had not accepted at the moment of depositing its instrument of ratification, acceptance, approval or accession.

Article 2

For the purposes of this Convention, the term "foreign residents" means persons who are not nationals of the State and who are lawfully resident on its territory.

Chapter A—Freedoms of expression, assembly and association

Article 3

Each Party undertakes, subject to the provisions of Article 9, to guarantee to foreign residents, on the same terms as to its own nationals:

a. the right to freedom of expression; this right shall include freedom to hold opinions and to receive and impart information and ideas without interference by public authority and regardless of frontiers. This article shall not prevent States from requiring the licensing of broadcasting, television or cinema enterprises;

b. the right to freedom of peaceful assembly and to freedom of association with others, including the right to form and to join trade unions for the protection of their interests. In particular, the right to freedom of association shall imply the right of foreign residents to form local associations of their own for purposes of mutual assistance, maintenance and expression of their cultural identity or defence of their interests in relation to matters falling within the province of the local authority, as well as the right to join any association.

Article 4

Each Party shall endeavour to ensure that reasonable efforts are made to involve foreign residents in public inquiries, planning procedures and other processes of consultation on local matters.

Chapter B—Consultative bodies to represent foreign residents at local level

Article 5

1. Each Party undertakes, subject to the provisions of Article 9, paragraph 1:

a. to ensure that there are no legal or other obstacles to prevent local authorities in whose area there is a significant number of foreign residents from setting up consultative bodies or making other appropriate institutional arrangements designed:

    i. to form a link between themselves and such residents,

    ii. to provide a forum for the discussion and formulation of the opinions, wishes and concerns of foreign residents on matters which particularly affect them in relation to local public life, including the activities and responsibilities of the local authority concerned, and

    iii. to foster their general integration into the life of the community;

b. to encourage and facilitate the establishment of such consultative bodies or the making of other appropriate institutional arrangements for the representation of foreign residents by local authorities in whose area there is a significant number of foreign residents.

2. Each Party shall ensure that representatives of foreign residents participating in the consultative bodies or other institutional arrangements referred to in paragraph 1 can be elected by the foreign residents in the local authority area or appointed by individual associations of foreign residents.

Chapter C—Right to vote in local authority elections

Article 6

1. Each Party undertakes, subject to the provisions of Article 9, paragraph 1, to grant to every foreign resident the right to vote and to stand for election in local authority elections, provided that he fulfils the same legal requirements as apply to nationals and furthermore has been a lawful and habitual resident in the State concerned for the five years preceding the elections.

2. However, a Contracting State may declare, when depositing its instrument of ratification, acceptance, approval or accession, that it intends to confine the application of paragraph 1 to the right to vote only.

Article 7

Each Party may, either unilaterally or by bilateral or multilateral agreement, stipulate that the residence requirements laid down in Article 6 are satisfied by a shorter period of residence.

Part II

Article 8

Each Party shall endeavour to ensure that information is available to foreign residents concerning their rights and obligations in relation to local public life.

Article 9

1. In time of war or other public emergency threatening the life of the nation, the rights accorded to foreign residents under Part I may be subjected to further restrictions to the extent strictly required by the exigencies of the situation, provided that such restrictions are not inconsistent with the Party's other obligations under international law.

2. As the right recognised by Article 3.*a* carries with it duties and responsibilities, it may be subject to such formalities, conditions, restrictions or penalties as are prescribed by law and are necessary in a democratic society, in the interests of national security, territorial integrity or public safety, for the prevention of disorder or crime, for the protection of health or morals, for the protection of the reputation or rights of others, for preventing the disclosure of information received in confidence, or for maintaining the authority and impartiality of the judiciary.

3. The right recognised by Article 3.*b* may not be subject to any restrictions other than such as are prescribed by law and are necessary in a democratic society, in the interests of national security or public safety, for the prevention of disorder or crime, for the protection of health or morals or for the protection of the rights and freedoms of others.

4. Any measure taken in accordance with the present article must be notified to the Secretary General of the Council of Europe, who shall inform the other Parties. The same procedure shall apply when such measures are revoked.

5. Nothing in this Convention shall be construed as limiting or derogating from any of the rights which may be guaranteed under the laws of any Party or under any other treaty to which it is a party.

Article 10

Each Party shall inform the Secretary General of the Council of Europe of any legislative provision or other measure adopted by the competent authorities on its territory which relates to its undertakings under the terms of this Convention.

Part III

Article 11

This Convention shall be open for signature by the member States of the Council of Europe. It is subject to ratification, acceptance or approval. Instruments of ratification, acceptance or approval shall be deposited with the Secretary General of the Council of Europe.

Article 12

1. This Convention shall enter into force on the first day of the month following the expiration of a period of three months after the date on which four member States of the Council of Europe have expressed their consent to be bound by the Convention, in accordance with the provisions of Article 11.

2. In respect of any member State which subsequently expresses its consent to be bound by it, the Convention shall enter into force on the first day of the month following the expiration of a period of three months after the date of the deposit of the instrument of ratification, acceptance or approval.

Article 13

1. After the entry into force of this Convention, the Committee of Ministers of the Council of Europe may invite any State not a member of the Council of Europe to accede to this Convention, by a decision taken by the majority provided for in Article 20.d of the Statute of the Council of Europe and by the unanimous vote of the representatives of the Contracting States entitled to sit on the Committee.

2. In respect of any acceding State, the Convention shall enter into force on the first day of the month following the expiration of a period of three months after the date of deposit of the instrument of accession with the Secretary General of the Council of Europe.

Article 14

Undertakings subsequently given by Parties to the Convention, in accordance with Article 1, paragraph 2, shall be deemed to be an integral part of the ratification, acceptance, approval or accession of the Party so notifying, and shall have the same effect as from the first day of the month following the expiration of a period of three months after the date of the receipt of the notification by the Secretary General.

Article 15

The provisions of this Convention shall apply to all the categories of local authorities existing within the territory of each Party. However, each Contracting State may, when depositing its instrument of ratification, acceptance, approval or accession, specify the categories of territorial authorities to which it intends to confine the scope of this Convention or which it intends to exclude from its scope.

Article 16

1.   Any State may at the time of signature or when depositing its instrument of ratification, acceptance, approval or accession specify the territory or territories to which this Convention shall apply.

2.   Any State may at any later date, by a declaration addressed to the Secretary General of the Council of Europe, extend the application of this Convention to any other territory specified in the declaration. In respect of such territory, the Convention shall enter into force on the first day of the month following the expiration of a period of three months after the date of receipt of such declaration by the Secretary General.

3.   Any declaration made under the two preceding paragraphs may, in respect of any territory specified in such declaration, be withdrawn by a notification addressed to the Secretary General. The withdrawal shall become effective on the first day of the month following the expiration of a period of six months after the date of receipt of such notification by the Secretary General.

Article 17

No reservation may be made in respect of the provisions of this Convention, other than that mentioned in Article 1, paragraph 1.

Article 18

1.   Any Party may at any time denounce this Convention by means of a notification addressed to the Secretary General of the Council of Europe.

2. Such denunciation shall become effective on the first day of the month following the expiration of a period of six months after the date of receipt of the notification by the Secretary General.

Article 19

The Secretary General of the Council of Europe shall notify the member States of the Council and any State which has acceded to this Convention of:

a. any signature;

b. the deposit of any instrument of ratification, acceptance, approval or accession;

c. any date of entry into force of this Convention in accordance with Articles 12, 13 and 16;

d. any notification received in application of the provisions of Article 1, paragraph 2;

e. any notification received in application of the provisions of Article 9, paragraph 4;

f. any other act, notification or communication relating to this Convention.

IN WITNESS WHEREOF the undersigned, being duly authorised thereto, have signed this Convention.

DONE at Strasbourg, this 5th day of February 1992, in English and French, both texts being equally authentic, in a single copy which shall be deposited in the archives of the Council of Europe. The Secretary General of the Council of Europe shall transmit certified copies to each member State of the Council of Europe and to any State invited to accede to this Convention.

34. Framework Convention for the Protection of National Minorities

Adopted at Strasbourg on 1 February 1995

The member States of the Council of Europe and the other States, signatories to the present framework Convention,

Considering that the aim of the Council of Europe is to achieve greater unity between its members for the purpose of safeguarding and realising the ideals and principles which are their common heritage;

Considering that one of the methods by which that aim is to be pursued is the maintenance and further realisation of human rights and fundamental freedoms;

Wishing to follow-up the Declaration of the Heads of State and Government of the member States of the Council of Europe adopted in Vienna on 9 October 1993;

Being resolved to protect within their respective territories the existence of national minorities;

Considering that the upheavals of European history have shown that the protection of national minorities is essential to stability, democratic security and peace in this continent;

Considering that a pluralist and genuinely democratic society should not only respect the ethnic, cultural, linguistic and religious identity of each person belonging to a national minority, but also create appropriate conditions enabling them to express, preserve and develop this identity;

Considering that the creation of a climate of tolerance and dialogue is necessary to enable cultural diversity to be a source and a factor, not a division, but of enrichment for each society;

Considering that the realisation of a tolerant and prosperous Europe does not depend solely on co-operation between States but also requires transfrontier co-operation between local and regional authorities without prejudice to the constitution and territorial integrity of each State;

Having regard to the Convention for the Protection of Human Rights and Fundamental Freedoms and the Protocols thereto;

Having regard to the commitments concerning the protection of national minorities in United Nations conventions and declarations and in the documents of the Conference on Security and Co-operation in Europe, particularly the Copenhagen Document of 29 June 1990;

Being resolved to define the principles to be respected and the obligations which flow from them, in order to ensure, in the member States and such other States as may become parties to the present instrument, the effective protection of national minorities and of the rights and freedoms of persons belonging to those minorities, within the rule of law, respecting the territorial integrity and national sovereignty of states;

Being determined to implement the principles set out in this framework Convention through national legislation and appropriate governmental policies,

Have agreed as follows:

Section I

Article 1

The protection of national minorities and of the rights and freedoms of persons belonging to those minorities forms an integral part of the international protection of human rights, and as such falls within the scope of international co-operation.

Article 2

The provisions of this framework Convention shall be applied in good faith, in a spirit of understanding and tolerance and in conformity with the principles of good neighbourliness, friendly relations and co-operation between States.

Article 3

1. Every person belonging to a national minority shall have the right freely to choose to be treated or not to be treated as such and no disadvantage shall result from this choice or from the exercise of the rights which are connected to that choice.

2. Persons belonging to national minorities may exercise the rights and enjoy the freedoms flowing from the principles enshrined in the present framework Convention individually as well as in community with others.

Section II

Article 4

1.   The Parties undertake to guarantee to persons belonging to national minorities the right of equality before the law and of equal protection of the law. In this respect, any discrimination based on belonging to a national minority shall be prohibited.

2.   The Parties undertake to adopt, where necessary, adequate measures in order to promote, in all areas of economic, social, political and cultural life, full and effective equality between persons belonging to a national minority and those belonging to the majority. In this respect, they shall take due account of the specific conditions of the persons belonging to national minorities.

3.   The measures adopted in accordance with paragraph 2 shall not be considered to be an act of discrimination.

Article 5

1.   The Parties undertake to promote the conditions necessary for persons belonging to national minorities to maintain and develop their culture, and to preserve the essential elements of their identity, namely their religion, language, traditions and cultural heritage.

2.   Without prejudice to measures taken in pursuance of their general integration policy, the Parties shall refrain from policies or practices aimed at assimilation of persons belonging to national minorities against their will and shall protect these persons from any action aimed at such assimilation.

Article 6

1.   The Parties shall encourage a spirit of tolerance and intercultural dialogue and take effective measures to promote mutual respect and understanding and co-operation among all persons living on their territory, irrespective of those persons' ethnic, cultural, linguistic or religious identity, in particular in the fields of education, culture and the media.

2.   The Parties undertake to take appropriate measures to protect persons who may be subject to threats or acts of discrimination, hostility or violence as a result of their ethnic, cultural, linguistic or religious identity.

Article 7

The Parties shall ensure respect for the right of every person belonging to a national minority to freedom of peaceful assembly, freedom of association, freedom of expression, and freedom of thought, conscience and religion.

Article 8

The Parties undertake to recognise that every person belonging to a national minority has the right to manifest his or her religion or belief and to establish religious institutions, organisations and associations.

Article 9

1. The Parties undertake to recognise that the right to freedom of expression of every person belonging to a national minority includes freedom to hold opinions and to receive and impart information and ideas in the minority language, without interference by public authorities and regardless of frontiers. The Parties shall ensure, within the framework of their legal systems, that persons belonging to a national minority are not discriminated against in their access to the media.

2. Paragraph 1 shall not prevent Parties from requiring the licensing, without discrimination and based on objective criteria, of sound radio and television broadcasting, or cinema enterprises.

3. The Parties shall not hinder the creation and the use of printed media by persons belonging to national minorities. In the legal framework of sound radio and television broadcasting, they shall ensure, as far as possible, and taking into account the provisions of paragraph 1, that persons belonging to national minorities are granted the possibility of creating and using their own media.

4. In the framework of their legal systems, the Parties shall adopt adequate measures in order to facilitate access to the media for persons belonging to national minorities and in order to promote tolerance and permit cultural pluralism.

Article 10

1. The Parties undertake to recognise that every person belonging to a national minority has the right to use freely and without interference his or her minority language, in private and in public, orally and in writing.

2. In areas inhabited by persons belonging to national minorities traditionally or in substantial numbers, if those persons so request and where such a request corresponds to a real need, the Parties shall endeavour to ensure, as far as possible, the conditions which would make it possible to use the minority language in relations between those persons and the administrative authorities.

3. The Parties undertake to guarantee the right of every person belonging to a national minority to be informed promptly, in a language which he or she understands, of the reasons for his or her arrest, and of the nature and cause of any accusation against him or her, and to defend himself or herself in this language, if necessary with the free assistance of an interpreter.

Article 11

1. The Parties undertake to recognise that every person belonging to a national minority has the right to use his or her surname (patronym) and first names in the minority language and the right to official recognition of them, according to modalities provided for in their legal system.

2. The Parties undertake to recognise that every person belonging to a national minority has the right to display in his or her minority language signs, inscriptions and other information of a private nature visible to the public.

3. In areas traditionally inhabited by substantial numbers of persons belonging to a national minority, the Parties shall endeavour, in the framework of their legal system, including, where appropriate, agreements with other States, and taking into account their specific conditions, to display traditional local names, street names and other topographical indications intended for the public also in the minority language when there is a sufficient demand for such indications.

Article 12

1. The Parties shall, where appropriate, take measures in the fields of education and research to foster knowledge of the culture, history, language and religion of their national minorities and of the majority.

2. In this context the Parties shall *inter alia* provide adequate opportunities for teacher training and access to textbooks, and facilitate contacts among students and teachers of different communities.

3. The Parties undertake to promote equal opportunities for access to education at all levels for persons belonging to national minorities.

Article 13

1. Within the framework for their education systems, the Parties shall recognise that persons belonging to a national minority have the right to set up and to manage their own private educational and training establishments.

2. The exercise of this right shall not entail any financial obligation for the Parties.

Article 14

1. The Parties undertake to recognise that every person belonging to a national minority has the right to learn his or her minority language.

2. In areas inhabited by persons belonging to national minorities traditionally or in substantial numbers, if there is sufficient demand, the Parties shall endeavour to ensure, as far as possible and within the framework of their education systems, that persons belonging to those minorities have adequate opportunities for being taught the minority language or for receiving instruction in this language.

3. Paragraph 2 of this article shall be implemented without prejudice to the learning of the official language or the teaching in this language.

Article 15

The Parties shall create the conditions necessary for the effective participation of persons belonging to national minorities in cultural, social and economic life and in public affairs, in particular those affecting them.

Article 16

The Parties shall refrain from measures which alter the proportions of the population in areas inhabited by persons belonging to national minorities and are aimed at restricting the rights and freedoms flowing from the principles enshrined in the present framework Convention.

Article 17

1. The Parties undertake not to interfere with the right of persons belonging to national minorities to establish and maintain free and peaceful contacts across frontiers with persons lawfully staying in other States, in particular those with whom they share an ethnic, cultural, linguistic or religious identity, or a common cultural heritage.

2. The Parties undertake not to interfere with the right of persons belonging to national minorities to participate in the activities of non-governmental organisations, both at the national and international levels.

Article 18

1. The Parties shall endeavour to conclude, where necessary, bilateral and multilateral agreements with other States, in particular neighbouring States, in order to ensure the protection of persons belonging to the national minorities concerned.

2. Where relevant, the Parties shall take measures to encourage transfrontier co-operation.

Article 19

The Parties undertake to respect and implement the principles enshrined in the present framework Convention making, where necessary, only those limitations, restrictions or derogations which are provided for in international legal instruments, in particular the Convention for the Protection of Human Rights and Fundamental Freedoms, in so far as they are relevant to the rights and freedoms flowing from the said principles.

Section III

Article 20

In the exercise of the rights and freedoms flowing from the principles enshrined in the present framework Convention, any person belonging to a national minority shall respect the national legislation and the rights of others, in particular those of persons belonging to the majority or to other national minorities.

Article 21

Nothing in the present framework Convention shall be interpreted as implying any right to engage in any activity or perform any act contrary to the fundamental principles of international law and in particular of the sovereign equality, territorial integrity and political independence of States.

Article 22

Nothing in the present framework Convention shall be construed as limiting or derogating from any of the human rights and fundamental freedoms which may be ensured under the laws of any Contracting Party or under any other agreement to which it is a Party.

Article 23

The rights and freedoms flowing from the principles enshrined in the present framework Convention, in so far as they are the subject of a corresponding provision in the Convention for the Protection of Human Rights and Fundamental Freedoms or in the Protocols thereto, shall be understood so as to conform to the latter provisions.

Section IV

Article 24

1.   The Committee of Ministers of the Council of Europe shall monitor the implementation of this framework Convention by the Contracting Parties.

2.   The Parties which are not members of the Council of Europe shall participate in the implementation mechanism, according to modalities to be determined.

Article 25

1.   Within a period of one year following the entry into force of this framework Convention in respect of a Contracting Party, the latter shall transmit to the Secretary General of the Council of Europe full information on the legislative and other measures taken to give effect to the principles set out in this framework Convention.

2.   Thereafter, each Party shall transmit to the Secretary General on a periodical basis and whenever the Committee of Ministers so requests any further information of relevance to the implementation of this framework Convention.

3.   The Secretary General shall forward to the Committee of Ministers the information transmitted under the terms of this Article.

Article 26

1.   In evaluating the adequacy of the measures taken by the Parties to give effect to the principles set out in this framework Convention the Committee of Ministers shall be assisted by an advisory committee, the members of which shall have recognised expertise in the field of the protection of national minorities.

2.   The composition of this advisory committee and its procedure shall be determined by the Committee of Ministers within a period of one year following the entry into force of this framework Convention.

Section V

Article 27

This framework Convention shall be open for signature by the member States of the Council of Europe. Up until the date when the Convention enters into force, it shall also be open for signature by any other State so invited by the Committee of Ministers. It is subject to ratification, acceptance or approval. Instruments of ratification, acceptance or approval shall be deposited with the Secretary General of the Council of Europe.

Article 28

1.   This framework Convention shall enter into force on the first day of the month following the expiration of a period of three months after the date on which twelve member States of the Council of Europe have expressed their consent to be bound by the Convention in accordance with the provisions of Article 27.

2.   In respect of any member State which subsequently expresses its consent to be bound by it, the framework Convention shall enter into force on the first day of the month following the expiration of a period of three months after the date of the deposit of the instrument of ratification, acceptance or approval.

Article 29

1.   After the entry into force of this framework Convention and after consulting the Contracting States, the Committee of Ministers of the Council of Europe may invite to accede to the Convention, by a decision taken by the majority provided for in Article 20.*d* of the Statute of the Council of Europe, any non-member State of the Council of Europe which, invited to sign in accordance with the provisions of Article 27, has not yet done so, and any other non-member State.

2.   In respect of any acceding State, the framework Convention shall enter into force on the first day of the month following the expiration of a period of three months after the date of the deposit of the instrument of accession with the Secretary General of the Council of Europe.

Article 30

1.   Any State may at the time of signature or when depositing its instrument of ratification, acceptance, approval or accession, specify the territory or territories for whose international relations it is responsible to which this framework Convention shall apply.

2.   Any State may at any later date, by a declaration addressed to the Secretary General of the Council of Europe, extend the application of this framework Convention to any other territory specified in the declaration. In respect of such territory the framework Convention shall enter into force on the first day of the month following the expiration of a period of three months after the date of receipt of such declaration by the Secretary General.

3.   Any declaration made under the two preceding paragraphs may, in respect of any territory specified in such declaration, be withdrawn by a notification addressed to the Secretary General. The withdrawal shall become effective on the first day of the month following the expiration of a period of three months after the date of receipt of such notification by the Secretary General.

Article 31

1.   Any Party may at any time denounce this framework Convention by means of a notification addressed to the Secretary General of the Council of Europe.

2.   Such denunciation shall become effective on the first day of the month following the expiration of a period of six months after the date of receipt of the notification by the Secretary General.

Article 32

The Secretary General of the Council of Europe shall notify the member States of the Council, other signatory States and any State which has acceded to this framework Convention, of:

a.   any signature;

b.   the deposit of any instrument of ratification, acceptance, approval or accession;

c.   any date of entry into force of this framework Convention in accordance with Articles 28, 29 and 30.

d.   any other act, notification or communication relating to this framework Convention.

IN WITNESS WHEREOF the undersigned, being duly authorised thereto, have signed this framework Convention.

DONE at Strasbourg, this 1st day of February 1995, in English and French, both texts being equally authentic, in a single copy which shall be deposited in the archives of the Council of Europe. The Secretary General of the Council of Europe shall transmit certified copies to each member State of the Council of Europe and to any State invited to sign or accede to this framework Convention.

35. European Convention on the Exercise
of Children's Rights

Adopted at Strasbourg on 25 January 1996

P REAMBLE

The member States of the Council of Europe and the other States signatory hereto,

Considering that the aim of the Council of Europe is to achieve greater unity between its members;

Having regard to the United Nations Convention on the rights of the child and in particular Article 4 which requires States Parties to undertake all appropriate legislative, administrative and other measures for the implementation of the rights recognised in the said Convention;

Noting the contents of Recommendation 1121 (1990) of the Parliamentary Assembly on the rights of the child;

Convinced that the rights and best interests of children should be promoted and to that end children should have the opportunity to exercise their rights, in particular in family proceedings affecting them;

Recognising that children should be provided with relevant information to enable such rights and best interests to be promoted and that due weight should be given to the views of children;

Recognising the importance of the parental role in protecting and promoting the rights and best interests of children and considering that, where necessary, states should also engage in such protection and promotion;

Considering, however, that in the event of conflict it is desirable for families to try to reach agreement before bringing the matter before a judicial authority,

Have agreed as follows:

Chapter I—Scope and object of the Convention and definitions

Article 1—Scope and object of the Convention

1.   This Convention shall apply to children who have not reached the age of 18 years.

2.   The object of the present Convention is, in the best interests of children, to promote their rights, to grant them procedural rights and to facilitate the exercise of these rights by ensuring that children are, themselves or through other persons or bodies, informed and allowed to participate in proceedings affecting them before a judicial authority.

3.   For the purposes of this Convention proceedings before a judicial authority affecting children are family proceedings, in particular those involving the exercise of parental possibilities such as residence and access to children.

4.   Every State, at the time of signature or when depositing its instrument of ratification, acceptance, approval or accession, by a declaration addressed to the Secretary General of the Council of Europe, specify at least three categories of family cases before a judicial authority to which this Convention is to apply.

5.   Any Party may, by further declaration, specify additional categories of family cases to which this Convention is to apply or provide information concerning the application of Article 5, paragraph 2 of Article 9, paragraph 2 of Article 10 and Article 11.

6.   Nothing in this Convention shall prevent Parties from applying rules more favourable to the promotion and the exercise of children's rights.

Article 2—Definitions

For the purposes of this Convention:

a. the term "judicial authority" means a court or an administrative authority having equivalent powers;

b. the term "holders of parental responsibilities" means parents and other persons or bodies entitled to exercise some or all parental responsibilities;

c. the term "representative" means a person, such as a lawyer, or a body appointed to act before a judicial authority on behalf of a child;

d. the term "relevant information" means information which is appropriate to the age and understanding of the child, and which will be given to enable the child to exercise his or her rights fully unless the provision of such information were contrary to the welfare of the child.

Chapter II—Procedural measures to promote the exercise of children's rights

A. Procedural rights of a child

Article 3—Right to be informed and to express his or her views in proceedings

A child considered by internal law as having sufficient understanding, in the case of proceedings before a judicial authority affecting him or her, shall be granted, and shall be entitled to request, the following rights:

    a. to receive all relevant information;

    b. to be consulted and express his or her views;

    c. to be informed of the possible consequences of compliance with these views and the possible consequences of any decision.

Article 4—Right to apply for the appointment of a special representative

1. Subject to Article 9, the child shall have the right to apply, in person or through other persons or bodies, for a special representative in proceedings before a judicial authority affecting the child where internal law precludes the holders of parental responsibilities from representing the child as a result of a conflict of interest with the latter.

2. States are free to limit the right in paragraph 1 to children who are considered by internal law to have sufficient understanding.

Article 5—Other possible procedural rights

Parties shall consider granting children additional procedural rights in relation to proceedings before a judicial authority affecting them, in particular:

    a. the right to apply to be assisted by an appropriate person of their choice in order to help them express their views;

    b. the right to apply themselves, or through other persons or bodies, for the appointment of a separate representative, in appropriate cases a lawyer;

    c. the right to appoint their own representative;

    d. the right to exercise some or all of the rights of parties to such proceedings.

B.   Role of judicial authorities

Article 6—Decision-making process

In proceedings affecting a child, the judicial authority, before taking a decision, shall:

a. consider whether it has sufficient information at its disposal in order to take a decision in the best interests of the child and, where necessary, it shall obtain further information, in particular from the holders of parental responsibilities;

b. in a case where the child is considered by internal law as having sufficient understanding:

—ensure that the child has received all relevant information;

—consult the child in person in appropriate cases, if necessary privately, itself or through other persons or bodies, in a manner appropriate to his or her understanding, unless this would be manifestly contrary to the best interests of the child;

—allow the child to express his or her views;

c. give due weight to the views expressed by the child.

Article 7—Duty to act speedily

In proceedings affecting a child the judicial authority shall act speedily to avoid any unnecessary delay and procedures shall be available to ensure that its decisions are rapidly enforced. In urgent cases the judicial authority shall have the power, where appropriate, to take decisions which are immediately enforceable.

Article 8—Acting on own motion

In proceedings affecting a child the judicial authority shall have the power to act on its own motion in cases determined by internal law where the welfare of a child is in serious danger.

Article 9—Appointment of a representative

1. In proceedings affecting a child where, by internal law, the holders of parental responsibilities are precluded from representing the child as a result of a conflict of interest between them and the child, the judicial authority shall have the power to appoint a special representative for the child in those proceedings.

2. Parties shall consider providing that, in proceedings affecting a child, the judicial authority shall have the power to appoint a separate representative, in appropriate cases a lawyer, to represent the child.

C.   Role of representatives

Article 10

1. In the case of proceedings before a judicial authority affecting a child the representative shall, unless this would be manifestly contrary to the best interests of the child:

a. provide all relevant information to the child, if the child is considered by internal law as having sufficient understanding;

b. provide explanations to the child if the child is considered by internal law as having sufficient understanding, concerning the possible consequences of compliance with his or her views and the possible consequences of any action by the representative;

c. determine the views of the child and present these views to the judicial authority.

2. Parties shall consider extending the provisions of paragraph 1 to the holders of parental responsibilities.

D.   Extension of certain provisions

Article 11

Parties shall consider extending the provisions of Articles 3, 4 and 9 to proceedings affecting children before other bodies and to matters affecting children which are not the subject of proceedings.

E.   National bodies

Article 12

1. Parties shall encourage, through bodies which perform, *inter alia*, the functions set out in paragraph 2, the promotion and the exercise of children's rights.

2. The functions are as follows:

a. to make proposals to strengthen the law relating to the exercise of children's rights;

b. to give opinions concerning draft legislation relating to the exercise of children's rights;

c. to provide general information concerning the exercise of children's rights to the media, the public and persons and bodies dealing with questions relating to children;

d. to seek the views of children and provide them with relevant information.

F. Other matters

Article 13—Mediation or other processes to resolve disputes

In order to prevent or resolve disputes or to avoid proceedings before a judicial authority affecting children, Parties shall encourage the provision of mediation or other processes to resolve disputes and the use of such processes to reach agreement in appropriate cases to be determined by Parties.

Article 14—Legal aid and advice

Where internal law provides for legal aid or advice for the representation of children in proceedings before a judicial authority affecting them, such provisions shall apply in relation to the matters covered by Articles 4 and 9.

Article 15—Relations with other international instruments

This Convention shall not restrict the application of any other international instrument with specific issues arising in the context of the protection of children and families, and to which a Party to this Convention is, or becomes, a Party.

Chapter III—Standing Committee

Article 16—Establishment and functions of the Standing Committee

1. A Standing Committee is set up for the purposes of this Convention.

2. The Standing Committee shall keep under review problems relating to this Convention. It may, in particular:

a. consider any relevant questions concerning the interpretation or implementation of the Convention. The Standing Committee's conclusions concerning the implementation of the Convention may take the form of a recommendation; recommendations shall be adopted by a three-quarters majority of the votes cast;

b. propose amendments to the Convention and examine those proposed in accordance with Article 20;

c. provide advice and assistance to the national bodies having the functions under paragraph 2 of Article 12 and promote international co-operation between them.

Article 17—Composition

1.   Each Party may be represented on the Standing Committee by one or more delegates. Each Party shall have one vote.

2.   Any State referred to in Article 21, which is not a Party to this Convention, may be represented in the Standing Committee by an observer. The same applies to any other State or to the European Community after having been invited to accede to the Convention in accordance with the provisions of Article 22.

3.   Unless a Party has informed the Secretary General of its objection at least one month before the meeting, the Standing Committee may invite the following to attend as observers at all its meetings or at one meeting or part of a meeting:

—any State not referred to in paragraph 2 above;

—the United Nations Committee on the Rights of the Child;

—the European Community;

—any international governmental body;

—any international non-governmental body with one or more functions mentioned under paragraph 2 of Article 12;

—any national governmental or non-governmental body with one or more functions mentioned under paragraph 2 of Article 12.

4.   The Standing Committee may exchange information with relevant organisations dealing with the exercise of children's rights.

Article 18—Meetings

1.   At the end of the third year following the date of entry into force of this Convention and, on his or her own initiative, at any time after this date, the Secretary General of the Council of Europe shall invite the Standing Committee to meet.

2.   Decisions may only be taken in the Standing Committee if at least one-half of the Parties are present.

3.   Subject to Articles 16 and 20 the decisions of the Standing Committee shall be taken by a majority of the members present.

4.   Subject to the provisions of this Convention the Standing Committee shall draw up its own rules of procedures and the rules of procedure of any working party it may set up to carry out all appropriate tasks under the Convention.

Article 19—Reports of the Standing Committee

After each meeting, the Standing Committee shall forward to the Parties and the Committee of Ministers of the Council of Europe a report on its discussions and any decisions taken.

Chapter IV—Amendments to the Convention

Article 20

1.   Any amendment to the articles of this Convention proposed by a Party or the Standing Committee shall be communicated to the Secretary General of the Council of Europe and forwarded by him or her, at least two months before the next meeting of the Standing Committee, to the member States of the Council of Europe, any signatory, any Party, any State invited to sign this Convention in accordance with the provisions of Article 21 and any State or the European Community invited to accede to it in accordance with the provisions of Article 22.

2.   Any amendment proposed in accordance with the provisions of the preceding paragraph shall be examined by the Standing Committee which shall submit the text adopted by a three-quarters majority of the votes cast to the Committee of Ministers for approval. After its approval, this text shall be forwarded to the Parties for acceptance.

3.   Any amendment shall enter into force on the first day of the month following the expiration of a period of one month after the date on which all Parties have informed the Secretary General that they have accepted it.

Chapter V—Final clauses

Article 21—Signature, ratification and entry into force

1.   This Convention shall be open for signature by the member States of the Council of Europe and the non-member States which have participated in its elaboration.

2. This Convention is subject to ratification, acceptance or approval. Instruments of ratification, acceptance or approval shall be deposited with the Secretary General of the Council of Europe.

3. This Convention shall enter into force on the first day of the month following the expiration of a period of three months after the date on which three States, including at least two member States of the Council of Europe, have expressed their consent to be bound by the Convention in accordance with the provisions of the preceding paragraph.

4. In respect of any signatory which subsequently expresses its consent to be bound by it, the Convention shall enter into force on the first day of the month following the expiration of a period of three months after the date of the deposit of its instrument of ratification, acceptance or approval.

Article 22—Non-member States and the European Community

1. After the entry into force of this Convention, the Committee of Ministers of the Council of Europe may, on its own initiative or following a proposal from the Standing Committee and after consultation of the Parties, invite any non-member State of the Council of Europe, which has not participated in the elaboration of the Convention, as well as the European Community to accede to this Convention by a decision taken by the majority provided for in Article 20, sub-paragraph *d* of the Statute of the Council of Europe, and by the unanimous vote of the representatives of the contracting States entitled to sit on the Committee of Ministers.

2. In respect of any acceding State or the European Community, the Convention shall enter into force on the first day of the month following the expiration of a period of three months after the date of deposit of the instrument of accession with the Secretary General of the Council of Europe.

Article 23—Territorial application

1. Any State may, at the time of signature or when depositing its instrument of ratification, acceptance, approval or accession, specify the territory or territories to which this Convention shall apply.

2. Any Party may, at any later date, by a declaration addressed to the Secretary General of the Council of Europe, extend the application of this Convention to any other territory specified in the declaration and for whose international relations it is responsible or on whose behalf it is authorised to give undertakings. In respect of such territory the Convention shall enter into force on the first day of the month following the expiration of a period of three months after the date of receipt of such declaration by the Secretary General.

3.   Any declaration made under the two preceding paragraphs may, in respect of any territory specified in such declaration, be withdrawn by a notification addressed to the Secretary General. The withdrawal shall become effective on the first day of the month following the expiration of a period of three months after the date of receipt of such notification by the Secretary General.

Article 24—Reservations

No reservation may be made to the Convention.

Article 25—Denunciation

1.   Any Party may at any time denounce this Convention by means of a notification addressed to the Secretary General of the Council of Europe.

2.   Such denunciation shall become effective on the first day of the month following the expiration of a period of three months after the date of receipt of notification by the Secretary General.

Article 26—Notifications

The Secretary General of the Council of Europe shall notify the member States of the Council, any signatory, any Party and any other State or the European Community which has been invited to accede to this Convention of:

a.   any signature;

b.   the deposit of any instrument of ratification, acceptance, approval or accession;

c.   any date of entry into force of this Convention in accordance with Articles 21 or 22;

d.   any amendment adopted in accordance with Article 20 and the date on which such an amendment enters into force;

e.   any declaration made under the provisions of Articles 1 and 23;

f.   any denunciation made in pursuance of the provisions of Article 25;

g.   any other act, notification or communication relating to this Convention.

IN WITNESS WHEREOF, the undersigned, being duly authorised thereto, have signed this Convention.

DONE at Strasbourg, this 25th day of January 1996, in English and French, both texts being equally authentic, in a single copy which shall be deposited in the archives of the Council of Europe. The Secretary General of the Council of Europe shall transmit certified copies to each member State of the Council of Europe, to the non-member States which have participated in the elaboration of this Convention, to the European Community and to any State invited to accede to this Convention.

36. Convention for the Protection of Human Rights and Dignity of the Human Being with regard to the Application of Biology and Medicine: Convention on Human Rights and Biomedicine

Adopted at Oviedo on 4 April 1997

Preamble

The member States of the Council of Europe, the other States and the European Community, Signatories hereto,

Bearing in mind the Universal Declaration of Human Rights proclaimed by the General Assembly of the United Nations on 10 December 1948;

Bearing in mind the Convention for the Protection of Human Rights and Fundamental Freedoms of 4 November 1950;

Bearing in mind the European Social Charter of 18 October 1961;

Bearing in mind the International Covenant on Civil and Political Rights and the International Covenant on Economic, Social and Cultural Rights of 16 December 1966;

Bearing in mind the Convention for the Protection of Individuals with regard to Automatic Processing of Personal Data of 28 January 1981;

Bearing also in mind the Convention on the Rights of the Child of 20 November 1989;

Considering that the aim of the Council of Europe is the achievement of a greater unity between its members and that one of the methods by which that aim is to be pursued is the maintenance and further realisation of human rights and fundamental freedoms;

Conscious of the accelerating developments in biology and medicine;

Convinced of the need to respect the human being both as an individual and as a member of the human species and recognising the importance of ensuring the dignity of the human being;

Conscious that the misuse of biology and medicine may lead to acts endangering human dignity;

Affirming that progress in biology and medicine should be used for the benefit of present and future generations;

Stressing the need for international co-operation so that all humanity may enjoy the benefits of biology and medicine;

Recognising the importance of promoting a public debate on the questions posed by the application of biology and medicine and the responses to be given thereto;

Wishing to remind all members of society of their rights and responsibilities;

Taking account of the work of the Parliamentary Assembly in this field, including Recommendation 1160 (1991) on the preparation of a convention on bioethics;

Resolving to take such measures as are necessary to safeguard human dignity and the fundamental rights and freedoms of the individual with regard to the application of biology and medicine,

Have agreed as follows:

Chapter I—General provisions

Article 1—Purpose and object

Parties to this Convention shall protect the dignity and identity of all human beings and guarantee everyone, without discrimination, respect for their integrity and other rights and fundamental freedoms with regard to the application of biology and medicine.

Each Party shall take in its internal law the necessary measures to give effect to the provisions of this Convention.

Article 2—Primacy of the human being

The interests and welfare of the human being shall prevail over the sole interest of society or science.

Article 3—Equitable access to health care

Parties, taking into account health needs and available resources, shall take appropriate measures with a view to providing, within their jurisdiction, equitable access to health care of appropriate quality.

Article 4—Professional standards

Any intervention in the health field, including research, must be carried out in accordance with relevant professional obligations and standards.

Chapter II—Consent

Article 5—General rule

An intervention in the health field may only be carried out after the person concerned has given free and informed consent to it.

This person shall beforehand be given appropriate information as to the purpose and nature of the intervention as well as on its consequences and risks.

The person concerned may freely withdraw consent at any time.

Article 6—Protection of persons not able to consent

1.   Subject to Articles 17 and 20 below, an intervention may only be carried out on a person who does not have the capacity to consent, for his or her direct benefit.

2.   Where, according to law, a minor does not have the capacity to consent to an intervention, the intervention may only be carried out with the authorisation of his or her representative or an authority or a person or body provided for by law.

The opinion of the minor shall be taken into consideration as an increasingly determining factor in proportion to his or her age and degree of maturity.

3.   Where, according to law, an adult does not have the capacity to consent to an intervention because of a mental disability, a disease or for similar reasons, the intervention may only be carried out with the authorisation of his or her representative or an authority or a person or body provided for by law.

The individual concerned shall as far as possible take part in the authorisation procedure.

4.   The representative, the authority, the person or the body mentioned in paragraphs 2 and 3 above shall be given, under the same conditions, the information referred to in Article 5.

5.   The authorisation referred to in paragraphs 2 and 3 above may be withdrawn at any time in the best interests of the person concerned.

Article 7—Protection of persons who have mental disorder

Subject to protective conditions prescribed by law, including supervisory, control and appeal procedures, a person who has a mental disorder of a serious nature may be subjected, without his or her consent, to an intervention aimed at treating his or her mental disorder only where, without such treatment, serious harm is likely to result to his or her health.

Article 8—Emergency situation

When because of an emergency situation the appropriate consent cannot be obtained, any medically necessary intervention may be carried out immediately for the benefit of the health of the individual concerned.

Article 9—Previously expressed wishes

The previously expressed wishes relating to a medical intervention by a patient who is not, at the time of the intervention, in a state to express his or her wishes shall be taken into account.

Chapter III—Private life and right to information

Article 10—Private life and right to information

1.   Everyone has the right to respect for private life in relation to information about his or her health.

2.   Everyone is entitled to know any information collected about his or her health. However, the wishes of individuals not to be so informed shall be observed.

3.   In exceptional cases, restrictions may be placed by law on the exercise of the rights contained in paragraph 2 in the interests of the patient.

Chapter IV—Human genome

Article 11—Non-discrimination

Any form of discrimination against a person on grounds of his or her genetic heritage is prohibited.

Article 12—Predictive genetic tests

Tests which are predictive of genetic diseases or which serve either to identity the subject as a carrier of a gene responsible for a disease or to detect a genetic predisposition or susceptibility to a disease may be performed only for health purposes or for scientific research linked to health purposes, and subject to appropriate genetic counselling.

Article 13—Interventions on the human genome

An intervention seeking to modify the human genome may only be undertaken for preventive, diagnostic or therapeutic purposes and only if its aim is not to introduce any modification in the genome of any descendants.

Article 14—Non-selection of sex

The use of techniques of medically assisted procreation shall not be allowed for the purpose of choosing a future child's sex, except where serious hereditary sex-related disease is to be avoided.

Chapter V—Scientific research

Article 15—General rule

Scientific research in the field of biology and medicine shall be carried out freely, subject to the provisions of this Convention and the other legal provisions ensuring the protection of the human being.

Article 16—Protection of persons undergoing research

Research on a person may only be undertaken if all the following conditions are met:

i. there is no alternative of comparable effectiveness to research on humans;

ii. the risks which may be incurred by that person are not disproportionate to the potential benefits of the research;

iii. the research project has been approved by the competent body after independent examination of its scientific merit, including assessment of the importance of the aim of the research, and multidisciplinary review of its ethical acceptability;

iv. the persons undergoing research have been informed of their rights and the safeguards prescribed by law for their protection;

v. the necessary consent as provided for under Article 5 has been given expressly, specifically and is documented. Such consent may be freely withdrawn at any time.

Article 17—Protection of persons not able to consent to research

1. Research on a person without the capacity to consent as stipulated in Article 5 may be undertaken only if all the following conditions are met:

   i. the conditions laid down in Article 16, sub-paragraphs i to iv, are fulfilled;

   ii. the results of the research have the potential to produce real and direct benefit to his or her health;

   iii. research of comparable effectiveness cannot be carried out on individuals capable of giving consent;

   iv. the necessary authorisation provided for under Article 6 has been given specifically and in writing; and

   v. the person concerned does not object.

   2. Exceptionally and under the protective conditions prescribed by law, where the research has not the potential to produce results of direct benefit to the health of the person concerned, such research may be authorised subject to the conditions laid down in paragraph 1, sub-paragraphs i, iii, iv and v above, and to the following additional conditions:

   i. the research has the aim of contributing, through significant improvement in the scientific understanding of the individual's condition, disease or disorder, to the ultimate attainment of results capable of conferring benefit to the person concerned or to other persons in the same age category or afflicted with the same disease or disorder or having the same condition;

   ii. the research entails only minimal risk and minimal burden for the individual concerned.

Article 18—Research on embryos in vitro

   1. Where the law allows research on embryos *in vitro*, it shall ensure adequate protection of the embryo.

   2. The creation of human embryos for research purposes is prohibited.

Chapter VI—Organ and tissue removal from living donors for transplantation purposes

Article 19—General rule

   1. Removal of organs or tissue from a living person for transplantation purposes may be carried out solely for the therapeutic benefit of the recipient and where there is no suitable organ or tissue available from a deceased person and no other alternative therapeutic method of comparable effectiveness.

2. The necessary consent as provided for under Article 5 must have been given expressly and specifically either in written form or before an official body.

Article 20—Protection of persons not able to consent to organ removal

1. No organ or tissue removal may be carried out on a person who does not have the capacity to consent under Article 5.

2. Exceptionally and under the protective conditions prescribed by law, the removal of regenerative tissue from a person who does not have the capacity to consent may be authorised provided the following conditions are met:

i. there is no compatible donor available who has the capacity to consent;

ii. the recipient is a brother or sister of the donor;

iii. the donation must have the potential to be life-saving for the recipient;

iv. the authorisation provided for under paragraphs 2 and 3 of Article 6 has been given specifically and in writing, in accordance with the law and with the approval of the competent body;

v. the potential donor concerned does not object.

Chapter VII—Prohibition of financial gain and disposal of a part of the human body

Article 21—Prohibition of financial gain

The human body and its parts shall not, as such, give rise to financial gain.

Article 22—Disposal of a removed part of the human body

When in the course of an intervention any part of a human body is removed, it may be stored and used for a purpose other than that for which it was removed only if this is done in conformity with appropriate information and consent procedures.

Chapter VIII—Infringements of the provisions of the Convention

Article 23—Infringement of the rights or principles

The Parties shall provide appropriate judicial protection to prevent or to put a stop to an unlawful infringement of the rights and principles set forth in this Convention at short notice.

Article 24—Compensation for undue damage

The person who has suffered undue damage resulting from an intervention is entitled to fair compensation according to the conditions and procedures prescribed by law.

Article 25—Sanctions

Parties shall provide for appropriate sanctions to be applied in the event of infringement of the provisions contained in this Convention.

Chapter IX—Relation between this Convention and other provisions

Article 26—Restrictions on the exercise of the rights

1. No restrictions shall be placed on the exercise of the rights and protective provisions contained in this Convention other than such as are prescribed by law and are necessary in a democratic society in the interest of public safety, for the prevention of crime, for the protection of public health or for the protection of the rights and freedoms of others.

2. The restrictions contemplated in the preceding paragraph may not be placed on Articles 11, 13, 14, 16, 17, 19, 20 and 21.

Article 27—Wider protection

None of the provisions of this Convention shall be interpreted as limiting or otherwise affecting the possibility for a Party to grant a wider measure of protection with regard to the application of biology and medicine than is stipulated in this Convention.

Chapter X—Public debate

Article 28—Public debate

Parties to this Convention shall see to it that the fundamental questions raised by the developments of biology and medicine are the subject of appropriate public discussion in the light, in particular, of relevant medical, social, economic, ethical and legal implications, and that their possible application is made the subject of appropriate consultation.

Chapter XI—Interpretation and follow-up of the Convention

Article 29—Interpretation of the Convention

The European Court of Human Rights may give, without direct reference to any specific proceedings pending in a court, advisory opinions on legal questions concerning the interpretation of the present Convention at the request of:

—the Government of a Party, after having informed the other Parties;

—the Committee set up by Article 32, with membership restricted to the Representatives of the Parties to this Convention, by a decision adopted by a two-thirds majority of votes cast.

Article 30—Reports on the application of the Convention

On receipt of a request from the Secretary General of the Council of Europe any Party shall furnish an explanation of the manner in which its internal law ensures the effective implementation of any of the provisions of the Convention.

Chapter XII—Protocols

Article 31—Protocols

Protocols may be concluded in pursuance of Article 32, with a view to developing, in specific fields, the principles contained in this Convention.

The Protocols shall be open for signature by Signatories of the Convention. They shall be subject to ratification, acceptance or approval. A Signatory may not ratify, accept or approve Protocols without previously or simultaneously ratifying, accepting or approving the Convention.

Chapter XIII—Amendments to the Convention

Article 32—Amendments to the Convention

1.   The tasks assigned to "the Committee" in the present article and in Article 29 shall be carried out by the Steering Committee on Bioethics

(CDBI), or by any other committee designated to do so by the Committee of Ministers.

2.   Without prejudice to the specific provisions of Article 29, each member State of the Council of Europe, as well as each Party to the present Convention which is not a member of the Council of Europe, may be represented and have one vote in the Committee when the Committee carries out the tasks assigned to it by the present Convention.

3.   Any State referred to in Article 33 or invited to accede to the Convention in accordance with the provisions of Article 34 which is not Party to this Convention may be represented on the Committee by an observer. If the European Community is not a Party it may be represented on the Committee by an observer.

4.   In order to monitor scientific developments, the present Convention shall be examined within the Committee no later than five years from its entry into force and thereafter at such intervals as the Committee may determine.

5.   Any proposal for an amendment to this Convention, and any proposal for a Protocol or for an amendment to a Protocol, presented by a Party, the Committee or the Committee of Ministers shall be communicated to the Secretary General of the Council of Europe and forwarded by him or her to the member States of the Council of Europe, to the European Community, to any Signatory, to any Party, to any State invited to sign this Convention in accordance with the provisions of Article 33 and to any State invited to accede to it in accordance with the provisions of Article 34.

6.   The Committee shall examine the proposal not earlier than two months after it has been forwarded by the Secretary General in accordance with paragraph 5. The Committee shall submit the text adopted by a two-thirds majority of the votes cast to the Committee of Ministers for approval. After its approval, this text shall be forwarded to the Parties for ratification, acceptance or approval.

7.   Any amendment shall enter into force, in respect of those Parties which have accepted it, on the first day of the month following the expiration of a period of one month after the date on which five Parties, including at least four member States of the Council of Europe, have informed the Secretary General that they have accepted it.

In respect of any Party which subsequently accepts it, the amendment shall enter into force on the first day of the month following the expiration of a period of one month after the date on which that Party has informed the Secretary General of its acceptance.

Chapter XIV—Final clauses

Article 33—Signature, ratification and entry into force

1. This Convention shall be open for signature by the member States of the Council of Europe, the non-member States which have participated in its elaboration and by the European Community.

2. This Convention is subject to ratification, acceptance or approval. Instruments of ratification, acceptance or approval shall be deposited with the Secretary General of the Council of Europe.

3. This Convention shall enter into force on the first day of the month following the expiration of a period of three months after the date on which five States, including at least four member States of the Council of Europe, have expressed their consent to be bound by the Convention in accordance with the provisions of paragraph 2 of the present article.

4. In respect of any Signatory which subsequently expresses its consent to be bound by it, the Convention shall enter into force on the first day of the month following the expiration of a period of three months after the date of the deposit of its instrument of ratification, acceptance or approval.

Article 34—Non-member States

1. After the entry into force of this Convention, the Committee of Ministers of the Council of Europe may, after consultation of the Parties, invite any non-member State of the Council of Europe to accede to this Convention by a decision taken by the majority provided for in Article 20, paragraph *d*, of the Statute of the Council of Europe, and by the unanimous vote of the representatives of the Contracting States entitled to sit on the Committee of Ministers.

2. In respect of any acceding State, the Convention shall enter into force on the first day of the month following the expiration of a period of three months after the date of deposit of the instrument of accession with the Secretary General of the Council of Europe.

Article 35—Territories

1. Any Signatory may, at the time of signature or when depositing its instrument of ratification, acceptance or approval, specify the territory or territories to which this Convention shall apply. Any other State may formulate the same declaration when depositing its instrument of accession.

2. Any Party may, at any later date, by a declaration addressed to the Secretary General of the Council of Europe, extend the application of this Convention to any other territory specified in the declaration and for whose

international relations it is responsible or on whose behalf it is authorised to give undertakings. In respect of such territory the Convention shall enter into force on the first day of the month following the expiration of a period of three months after the date of receipt of such declaration by the Secretary General.

3. Any declaration made under the two preceding paragraphs may, in respect of any territory specified in such declaration, be withdrawn by a notification addressed to the Secretary General. The withdrawal shall become effective on the first day of the month following the expiration of a period of three months after the date of receipt of such notification by the Secretary General.

Article 36—Reservations

1. Any State and the European Community may, when signing this Convention or when depositing the instrument of ratification, acceptance, approval or accession, make a reservation in respect of any particular provision of the Convention to the extent that any law then in force in its territory is not in conformity with the provision. Reservations of a general character shall not be permitted under this article.

2. Any reservation made under this article shall contain a brief statement of the relevant law.

3. Any Party which extends the application of this Convention to a territory mentioned in the declaration referred to in Article 35, paragraph 2, may, in respect of the territory concerned, make a reservation in accordance with the provisions of the preceding paragraphs.

4. Any Party which has made the reservation mentioned in this article may withdraw it by means of a declaration addressed to the Secretary General of the Council of Europe. The withdrawal shall become effective on the first day of the month following the expiration of a period of one month after the date of its receipt by the Secretary General.

Article 37—Denunciation

1. Any Party may at any time denounce this Convention by means of a notification addressed to the Secretary General of the Council of Europe.

2. Such denunciation shall become effective on the first day of the month following the expiration of a period of three months after the date of receipt of the notification by the Secretary General.

Article 38—Notifications

The Secretary General of the Council of Europe shall notify the member States of the Council, the European Community, any Signatory, any Party and any other State which has been invited to accede to this Convention of:

a. any signature;

b. the deposit of any instrument of ratification, acceptance, approval or accession;

c. any date of entry into force of this Convention in accordance with Articles 33 or 34;

d. any amendment or Protocol adopted in accordance with Article 32, and the date on which such an amendment or Protocol enters into force;

e. any declaration made under the provisions of Article 35;

f. any reservation and withdrawal of reservation made in pursuance of the provisions of Article 36;

g. any other act, notification or communication relating to this Convention.

IN WITNESS WHEREOF the undersigned, being duly authorised thereto, have signed this Convention.

DONE at Oviedo (Asturias), this 4th day of April 1997, in English and in French, both texts being equally authentic, in a single copy which shall be deposited in the archives of the Council of Europe. The Secretary General of the Council of Europe shall transmit certified copies to each member State of the Council of Europe, to the European Community, to the non-member States which have participated in the elaboration of this Convention, and to any State invited to accede to this Convention.

C. ORGANIZATION OF AFRICAN UNITY

37. OAU Convention Governing the Specific Aspects of Refugee Problems in Africa

Adopted at Addis Ababa on 10 September 1969

ENTRY INTO FORCE: 20 June 1974, in accordance with article XI

PREAMBLE

We, the Heads of State and Government, assembled in the city of Addis Ababa,

1. *Noting with concern* the constantly increasing numbers of refugees in Africa and desirous of finding ways and means of alleviating their misery and suffering as well as providing them with a better life and future,

2. *Recognizing* the need for an essentially humanitarian approach towards solving the problems of refugees,

3. *Aware*, however, that refugee problems are a source of friction among many Member States, and desirous of eliminating the source of such discord,

4. *Anxious* to make a distinction between a refugee who seeks a peaceful and normal life and a person fleeing his country for the sole purpose of fomenting subversion from outside,

5. *Determined* that the activities of such subversive elements should be discouraged, in accordance with the Declaration on the Problem of Subversion and Resolution on the Problem of Refugees adopted at Accra in 1965,

6. *Bearing* in mind that the Charter of the United Nations and the Universal Declaration of Human Rights have affirmed the principle that human beings shall enjoy fundamental rights and freedoms without discrimination,

7. *Recalling* Resolution 2312 (XXII) of 14 December 1967 of the United Nations General Assembly, relating to the Declaration on Territorial Asylum,

8. *Convinced* that all the problems of our continent must be solved in the spirit of the Charter of the Organization of African Unity and in the African context,

9. *Recognizing* that the United Nations Convention of 28 July 1951, as modified by the Protocol of 31 January 1967, constitutes the basic and universal instrument relating to the status of refugees and reflects the deep concern of States for refugees and their desire to establish common standards for their treatment,

10. *Recalling* Resolutions 26 and 104 of the OAU Assemblies of Heads of State and Government, calling upon Member States of the Organization who had not already done so to accede to the United Nations Convention of 1951 and to the Protocol of 1967 relating to the Status of Refugees, and meanwhile to apply their provisions to refugees in Africa,

11. *Convinced* that the efficiency of the measures recommended by the present Convention to solve the problem of refugees in Africa necessitates close and continuous collaboration between the Organization of African Unity and the Office of the United Nations High Commissioner for Refugees,

Have agreed as follows:

Article I.—DEFINITION OF THE TERM "REFUGEE"

1. For the purposes of this Convention, the term "refugee" shall mean every person who, owing to well-founded fear of being persecuted for reasons of race, religion, nationality, membership of a particular social group or political opinion, is outside the country of his nationality and is unable or, owing to such fear, is unwilling to avail himself of the protection of that country, or who, not having a nationality and being outside the country of his former habitual residence as a result of such events, is unable or, owing to such fear, is unwilling to return to it.

2. The term "refugee" shall also apply to every person who, owing to external aggression, occupation, foreign domination or events seriously disturbing public order in either part or the whole of his country of origin or nationality, is compelled to leave his place of habitual residence in order to seek refuge in another place outside his country of origin or nationality.

3. In the case of a person who has several nationalities, the term "a country of which he is a national" shall mean each of the countries of which he is a national, and a person shall not be deemed to be lacking the protection of the country of which he is a national if, without any valid reason based on well-founded fear, he has not availed himself of the protection of one of the countries of which he is a national.

4. This Convention shall cease to apply to any refugee if:

   (*a*) he has voluntarily re-availed himself of the protection of the country of his nationality, or

   (*b*) having lost his nationality, he has voluntarily re-acquired it, or

(c) he has acquired a new nationality, and enjoys the protection of the country of his new nationality, or

(d) he has voluntarily re-established himself in the country which he left or outside which he remained owing to fear of persecution, or

(e) he can no longer, because the circumstances in connection with which he was recognized as a refugee have ceased to exist, continue to refuse to avail himself of the protection of the country of his nationality, or

(f) he has committed a serious non-political crime outside his country of refuge after his admission to that country as a refugee, or

(g) he has seriously infringed the purposes and objectives of this Convention.

5. The provisions of this Convention shall not apply to any person with respect to whom the country of asylum has serious reasons for considering that:

(a) he has committed a crime against peace, a war crime, or a crime against humanity, as defined in the international instruments drawn up to make provision in respect of such crimes,

(b) he committed a serious non-political crime outside the country of refuge prior to his admission to that country as a refugee,

(c) he has been guilty of acts contrary to the purposes and principles of the Organization of African Unity,

(d) he has been guilty of acts contrary to the purposes and principles of the United Nations.

6. For the purposes of this Convention, the Contracting State of asylum shall determine whether an applicant is a refugee.

Article II.—ASYLUM

1. Member States of the OAU shall use their best endeavours consistent with their respective legislations to receive refugees and to secure the settlement of those refugees who, for well-founded reasons, are unable or unwilling to return to their country of origin or nationality.

2. The grant of asylum to refugees is a peaceful and humanitarian act and shall not be regarded as an unfriendly act by any Member State.

3. No person shall be subjected by a Member State to measures such as rejection at the frontier, return or expulsion, which would compel him to return to or remain in a territory where his life, physical integrity or liberty would be threatened for the reasons set out in Article I, paragraphs 1 and 2.

4. Where a Member State finds difficulty in continuing to grant asylum to refugees, such Member State may appeal directly to other Member States and through the OAU, and such other Member States shall in the

spirit of African solidarity and international co-operation take appropriate measures to lighten the burden of the Member State granting asylum.

5.   Where a refugee has not received the right to reside in any country of asylum, he may be granted temporary residence in any country of asylum in which he first presented himself as a refugee pending arrangement for his re-settlement in accordance with the preceding paragraph.

6.   For reasons of security, countries of asylum shall, as far as possible, settle refugees at a reasonable distance from the frontier of their country of origin.

Article III.—PROHIBITION OF SUBVERSIVE ACTIVITIES

1.   Every refugee has duties to the country in which he finds himself, which require in particular that he conforms with its laws and regulations as well as with measures taken for the maintenance of public order. He shall also abstain from any subversive activities against any Member State of the OAU.

2.   Signatory States undertake to prohibit refugees residing in their respective territories from attacking any State Member of the OAU, by any activity likely to cause tension between Member States, and in particular by use of arms, through the press, or by radio.

Article IV.—NON-DISCRIMINATION

Member States undertake to apply the provisions of this Convention to all refugees without discrimination as to race, religion, nationality, membership of a particular social group or political opinions.

Article V.—VOLUNTARY REPATRIATION

1.   The essentially voluntary character of repatriation shall be respected in all cases and no refugee shall be repatriated against his will.

2.   The country of asylum, in collaboration with the country of origin, shall make adequate arrangements for the safe return of refugees who request repatriation.

3.   The country of origin, on receiving back refugees, shall facilitate their re-settlement and grant them the full rights and privileges of nationals of the country, and subject them to the same obligations.

4.   Refugees who voluntarily return to their country shall in no way be penalized for having left it for any of the reasons giving rise to refugee situations. Whenever necessary, an appeal shall be made through national information media and through the Administrative Secretary-General of the OAU, inviting refugees to return home and giving assurance that the new

circumstances prevailing in their country of origin will enable them to return without risk and to take up a normal and peaceful life without fear of being disturbed or punished, and that the text of such appeal should be given to refugees and clearly explained to them by their country of asylum.

5.   Refugees who freely decide to return to their homeland, as a result of such assurances or on their own initiative, shall be given every possible assistance by the country of asylum, the country of origin, voluntary agencies and international and intergovernmental organizations to facilitate their return.

Article VI.—TRAVEL DOCUMENTS

1.   Subject to Article III, Member States shall issue to refugees lawfully staying in their territories travel documents in accordance with the United Nations Convention relating to the Status of Refugees and the Schedule and Annex thereto, for the purpose of travel outside their territory, unless compelling reasons of national security or public order otherwise require. Member States may issue such a travel document to any other refugee in their territory.

2.   Where an African country of second asylum accepts a refugee from a country of first asylum, the country of first asylum may be dispensed from issuing a document with a return clause.

3.   Travel documents issued to refugees under previous international agreements by States Parties thereto shall be recognized and treated by Member States in the same way as if they had been issued to refugees pursuant to this Article.

Article VII.—CO-OPERATION OF THE NATIONAL AUTHORITIES WITH THE ORGANIZATION OF AFRICAN UNITY

In order to enable the Administrative Secretary-General of the Organization of African Unity to make reports to the competent organs of the Organization of African Unity, Member States undertake to provide the Secretariat in the appropriate form with information and statistical data requested concerning:

(*a*) the condition of refugees,

(*b*) the implementation of this Convention, and

(*c*) laws, regulations and decrees which are, or may hereafter be, in force relating to refugees.

Article VIII.—CO-OPERATION WITH THE OFFICE OF THE UNITED
NATIONS HIGH COMMISSIONER FOR REFUGEES

1. Member States shall co-operate with the Office of the United
Nations High Commissioner for Refugees.

2. The present Convention shall be the effective regional complement in Africa of the 1951 United Nations Convention on the Status of
Refugees.

Article IX.—SETTLEMENT OF DISPUTES

Any dispute between States signatories to this Convention relating to
its interpretation or application, which cannot be settled by other means,
shall be referred to the Commission for Mediation, Conciliation and Arbitration of the Organization of African Unity, at the request of any one of the
parties to the dispute.

Article X.—SIGNATURE AND RATIFICATION

1. This Convention is open for signature and accession by all Member States of the Organization of African Unity and shall be ratified by signatory States in accordance with their respective constitutional processes.
The instruments of ratification shall be deposited with the Administrative
Secretary-General of the Organization of African Unity.

2. The original instrument, done if possible in African languages,
and in English and French, all texts being equally authentic, shall be deposited with the Administrative Secretary-General of the Organization of African Unity.

3. Any independent African State, Member of the Organization of
African Unity, may at any time notify the Administrative Secretary-General
of the Organization of African Unity of its accession to this Convention.

Article XI.—ENTRY INTO FORCE

This Convention shall come into force upon deposit of instruments of
ratification by one-third of the Member States of the Organization of African
Unity.

Article XII.—AMENDMENT

This Convention may be amended or revised if any Member State
makes a written request to the Administrative Secretary-General to that effect, provided however that the proposed amendment shall not be submitted
to the Assembly of Heads of State and Government for consideration until

all Member States have been duly notified of it and a period of one year has elapsed. Such an amendment shall not be effective unless approved by at least two-thirds of the Member States Parties to the present Convention.

Article XIII.—DENUNCIATION

1. Any Member State Party to this Convention may denounce its provisions by a written notification to the Administrative Secretary-General.

2. At the end of one year from the date of such notification, if not withdrawn, the Convention shall cease to apply with respect to the denouncing State.

Article XIV

Upon entry into force of this Convention, the Administrative Secretary-General of the OAU shall register it with the Secretary-General of the United Nations, in accordance with Article 102 of the Charter of the United Nations.

Article XV.—NOTIFICATIONS BY THE ADMINISTRATIVE SECRETARY-GENERAL OF THE ORGANIZATION OF AFRICAN UNITY

The Administrative Secretary-General of the Organization of African Unity shall inform all Members of the Organization:

(a) of signatures, ratifications and accessions in accordance with Article X,

(b) of entry into force, in accordance with Article XI,

(c) of requests for amendments submitted under the terms of Article XII,

(d) of denunciations, in accordance with Article XIII.

IN WITNESS WHEREOF we, the Heads of African State and Government, have signed this Convention.

38.   African Charter on Human and Peoples' Rights

Adopted at Nairobi on 26 June 1981

ENTRY INTO FORCE: 21 October 1986, in accordance with article 63

PREAMBLE

The African States members of the Organization of African Unity, Parties to the present convention entitled "African Charter on Human and Peoples' Rights",

Recalling Decision 115 (XVI) of the Assembly of Heads of State and Government at its Sixteenth Ordinary Session held in Monrovia, Liberia, from 17 to 20 July 1979 on the preparation of a "preliminary draft on an African Charter on Human and Peoples' Rights providing *inter alia* for the establishment of bodies to promote and protect human and peoples' rights";

Considering the Charter of the Organization of African Unity, which stipulates that "freedom, equality, justice and dignity are essential objectives for the achievement of the legitimate aspirations of the African peoples";

Reaffirming the pledge they solemnly made in Article 2 of the said Charter to eradicate all forms of colonialism from Africa, to co-ordinate and intensify their co-operation and efforts to achieve a better life for the peoples of Africa and to promote international co-operation having due regard to the Charter of the United Nations and the Universal Declaration of Human Rights;

Taking into consideration the virtues of their historical tradition and the values of African civilization which should inspire and characterize their reflection on the concept of human and peoples' rights;

Recognizing, on the one hand, that fundamental human rights stem from the attributes of human beings, which justifies their national and international protection, and on the other hand that the reality and respect of peoples' rights should necessarily guarantee human rights;

Considering that the enjoyment of rights and freedoms also implies the performance of duties on the part of everyone;

Convinced that it is henceforth essential to pay a particular attention to the right to development and that civil and political rights cannot be dissociated from economic, social and cultural rights in their conception as well as universality and that the satisfaction of economic, social and cultural rights is a guarantee for the enjoyment of civil and political rights;

Conscious of their duty to achieve the total liberation of Africa, the peoples of which are still struggling for their dignity and genuine independence, and undertaking to eliminate colonialism, neo-colonialism, apartheid, zionism and to dismantle aggressive foreign military bases and all forms of discrimination, particularly those based on race, ethnic group, colour, sex, language, religion or political opinion;

Reaffirming their adherence to the principles of human and peoples' rights and freedoms contained in the declarations, conventions and other instruments adopted by the Organization of African Unity, the Movement of Non-Aligned Countries and the United Nations;

Firmly convinced of their duty to promote and protect human and peoples' rights and freedoms taking into account the importance traditionally attached to these rights and freedoms in Africa;

Have agreed as follows:

PART I

RIGHTS AND DUTIES

CHAPTER I. HUMAN AND PEOPLES' RIGHTS

Article 1

The Member States of the Organization of African Unity Parties to the present Charter shall recognize the rights, duties and freedoms enshrined in this Charter and shall undertake to adopt legislative or other measures to give effect to them.

Article 2

Every individual shall be entitled to the enjoyment of the rights and freedoms recognized and guaranteed in the present Charter without distinction of any kind such as race, ethnic group, colour, sex, language, religion, political or any other opinion, national and social origin, fortune, birth or other status.

Article 3

1. Every individual shall be equal before the law.

2. Every individual shall be entitled to equal protection of the law.

Article 4

Human beings are inviolable. Every human being shall be entitled to respect for his life and the integrity of his person. No one may be arbitrarily deprived of this right.

Article 5

Every individual shall have the right to the respect of the dignity inherent in a human being and to the recognition of his legal status. All forms of exploitation and degradation of man, particularly slavery, slave trade, torture, cruel, inhuman or degrading punishment and treatment, shall be prohibited.

Article 6

Every individual shall have the right to liberty and to the security of his person. No one may be deprived of his freedom except for reasons and conditions previously laid down by law. In particular, no one may be arbitrarily arrested or detained.

Article 7

1. Every individual shall have the right to have his cause heard. This comprises:

(a) the right to an appeal to competent national organs against acts of violating his fundamental rights as recognized and guaranteed by conventions, laws, regulations and customs in force;

(b) the right to be presumed innocent until proved guilty by a competent court or tribunal;

(c) the right to defence, including the right to be defended by counsel of his choice;

(d) the right to be tried within a reasonable time by an impartial court or tribunal.

2. No one may be condemned for an act or omission which did not constitute a legally punishable offence at the time it was committed. No penalty may be inflicted for an offence for which no provision was made at the time it was committed. Punishment is personal and can be imposed only on the offender.

Article 8

Freedom of conscience, the profession and free practice of religion shall be guaranteed. No one may, subject to law and order, be submitted to measures restricting the exercise of these freedoms.

Article 9

1.   Every individual shall have the right to receive information.

2.   Every individual shall have the right to express and disseminate his opinions within the law.

Article 10

1.   Every individual shall have the right to free association provided that he abides by the law.

2.   Subject to the obligation of solidarity provided for in Article 29 no one may be compelled to join an association.

Article 11

Every individual shall have the right to assemble freely with others. The exercise of this right shall be subject only to necessary restrictions provided for by law, in particular those enacted in the interest of national security, the safety, health, ethics and rights and freedoms of others.

Article 12

1.   Every individual shall have the right to freedom of movement and residence within the borders of a State provided he abides by the law.

2.   Every individual shall have the right to leave any country including his own, and to return to his country. This right may only be subject to restrictions provided for by law for the protection of national security, law and order, public health or morality.

3.   Every individual shall have the right, when persecuted, to seek and obtain asylum in other countries in accordance with the laws of those countries and international conventions.

4.   A non-national legally admitted in a territory of a State Party to the present Charter may only be expelled from it by virtue of a decision taken in accordance with the law.

5.   The mass expulsion of non-nationals shall be prohibited. Mass expulsion shall be that which is aimed at national, racial, ethnic or religious groups.

Article 13

1.   Every citizen shall have the right to participate freely in the government of his country, either directly or through freely chosen representatives in accordance with the provisions of the law.

2.   Every citizen shall have the right of equal access to the public service of his country.

3.   Every individual shall have the right of access to public property and services in strict equality of all persons before the law.

Article 14

The right to property shall be guaranteed. It may only be encroached upon in the interest of public need or in the general interest of the community and in accordance with the provisions of appropriate laws.

Article 15

Every individual shall have the right to work under equitable and satisfactory conditions, and shall receive equal pay for equal work.

Article 16

1.   Every individual shall have the right to enjoy the best attainable state of physical and mental health.

2.   States Parties to the present Charter shall take the necessary measures to protect the health of their people and to ensure that they receive medical attention when they are sick.

Article 17

1.   Every individual shall have the right to education.

2.   Every individual may freely take part in the cultural life of his community.

3.   The promotion and protection of morals and traditional values recognized by the community shall be the duty of the State.

Article 18

1.   The family shall be the natural unit and basis of society. It shall be protected by the State which shall take care of its physical and moral health.

2.   The State shall have the duty to assist the family which is the custodian of morals and traditional values recognized by the community.

3.   The State shall ensure the elimination of every discrimination against women and also ensure the protection of the rights of the woman and the child as stipulated in international declarations and conventions.

4.   The aged and the disabled shall also have the right to special measures of protection in keeping with their physical or moral needs.

Article 19

All peoples shall be equal; they shall enjoy the same respect and shall have the same rights. Nothing shall justify the domination of a people by another.

Article 20

1.   All peoples shall have the right to existence. They shall have the unquestionable and inalienable right to self-determination. They shall freely determine their political status and shall pursue their economic and social development according to the policy they have freely chosen.

2.   Colonized or oppressed peoples shall have the right to free themselves from the bonds of domination by resorting to any means recognized by the international community.

3.   All peoples shall have the right to the assistance of the States Parties to the present Charter in their liberation struggle against foreign domination, be it political, economic or cultural.

Article 21

1.   All peoples shall freely dispose of their wealth and natural resources. This right shall be exercised in the exclusive interest of the people. In no case shall a people be deprived of it.

2.   In case of spoliation the dispossessed people shall have the right to the lawful recovery of its property as well as to an adequate compensation.

3.   The free disposal of wealth and natural resources shall be exercised without prejudice to the obligation of promoting international economic co-operation based on mutual respect, equitable exchange and the principles of international law.

4.   States Parties to the present Charter shall individually and collectively exercise the right to free disposal of their wealth and natural resources with a view to strengthening African unity and solidarity.

5.   States Parties to the present Charter shall undertake to eliminate all forms of foreign economic exploitation, particularly that practised by in-

ternational monopolies, so as to enable their peoples to fully benefit from the advantages derived from their national resources.

Article 22

1. All peoples shall have the right to their economic, social and cultural development with due regard to their freedom and identity and in the equal enjoyment of the common heritage of mankind.

2. States shall have the duty, individually or collectively, to ensure the exercise of the right to development.

Article 23

1. All peoples shall have the right to national and international peace and security. The principles of solidarity and friendly relations implicitly affirmed by the Charter of the United Nations and reaffirmed by that of the Organization of African Unity shall govern relations between States.

2. For the purpose of strengthening peace, solidarity and friendly relations, States Parties to the present Charter shall ensure that:

(a) any individual enjoying the right of asylum under Article 12 of the present Charter shall not engage in subversive activities against his country of origin or any other State Party to the present Charter;

(b) their territories shall not be used as bases for subversive or terrorist activities against the people of any other State Party to the present Charter.

Article 24

All peoples shall have the right to a general satisfactory environment favourable to their development.

Article 25

States Parties to the present Charter shall have the duty to promote and ensure through teaching, education and publication, the respect of the rights and freedoms contained in the present Charter and to see to it that these freedoms and rights as well as corresponding obligations and duties are understood.

Article 26

States Parties to the present Charter shall have the duty to guarantee the independence of the Courts and shall allow the establishment and improvement of appropriate national institutions entrusted with the promotion and protection of the rights and freedoms guaranteed by the present Charter.

CHAPTER II. DUTIES

Article 27

1. Every individual shall have duties towards his family and society, the State and other legally recognized communities and the international community.

2. The rights and freedoms of each individual shall be exercised with due regard to the rights of others, collective security, morality and common interest.

Article 28

Every individual shall have the duty to respect and consider his fellow beings without discrimination, and to maintain relations aimed at promoting, safeguarding and reinforcing mutual respect and tolerance.

Article 29

The individual shall also have the duty:

1. To preserve the harmonious development of the family and to work for the cohesion and respect of the family; to respect his parents at all times, to maintain them in case of need;

2. To serve his national community by placing his physical and intellectual abilities at its service;

3. Not to compromise the security of the State whose national or resident he is;

4. To preserve and strengthen social and national solidarity, particularly when the latter is threatened;

5. To preserve and strengthen the national independence and the territorial integrity of his country and to contribute to its defence in accordance with the law;

6. To work to the best of his abilities and competence, and to pay taxes imposed by law in the interest of the society;

7. To preserve and strengthen positive African cultural values in his relations with other members of the society, in the spirit of tolerance, dialogue and consultation and, in general, to contribute to the promotion of the moral well-being of society;

8. To contribute to the best of his abilities, at all times and at all levels, to the promotion and achievement of African unity.

PART II

MEASURES OF SAFEGUARD

CHAPTER I. ESTABLISHMENT AND ORGANIZATION OF THE AFRICAN
COMMISSION ON HUMAN AND PEOPLES' RIGHTS

Article 30

An African Commission on Human and Peoples' Rights, hereinafter called "the Commission", shall be established within the Organization of African Unity to promote human and peoples' rights and ensure their protection in Africa.

Article 31

1. The Commission shall consist of eleven members chosen from amongst African personalities of the highest reputation, known for their high morality, integrity, impartiality and competence in matters of human and peoples' rights, particular consideration being given to persons having legal experience.

2. The members of the Commission shall serve in their personal capacity.

Article 32

The Commission shall not include more than one national of the same State.

Article 33

The members of the Commission shall be elected by secret ballot by the Assembly of Heads of State and Government, from a list of persons nominated by the States Parties to the present Charter.

Article 34

Each State Party to the present Charter may not nominate more than two candidates. The candidates must have the nationality of one of the States

Parties to the present Charter. When two candidates are nominated by a State, one of them may not be a national of that State.

Article 35

1. The Secretary-General of the Organization of African Unity shall invite States Parties to the present Charter at least four months before the elections to nominate candidates.

2. The Secretary-General of the Organization of African Unity shall make an alphabetical list of the persons thus nominated and communicate it to the Heads of State and Government at least one month before the elections.

Article 36

The members of the Commission shall be elected for a six-year period and shall be eligible for re-election. However, the term of office of four of the members elected at the first election shall terminate after two years and the term of office of three others, at the end of four years.

Article 37

Immediately after the first election, the Chairman of the Assembly of Heads of State and Government of the Organization of African Unity shall draw lots to decide the names of those members referred to in Article 36.

Article 38

After their election, the members of the Commission shall make a solemn declaration to discharge their duties impartially and faithfully.

Article 39

1. In case of death or resignation of a member of the Commission, the Chairman of the Commission shall immediately inform the Secretary-General of the Organization of African Unity, who shall declare the seat vacant from the date of death or from the date on which the resignation takes effect.

2. If, in the unanimous opinion of other members of the Commission, a member has stopped discharging his duties for any reason other than a temporary absence, the Chairman of the Commission shall inform the Secretary-General of the Organization of African Unity, who shall then declare the seat vacant.

3. In each of the cases anticipated above, the Assembly of Heads of State and Government shall replace the member whose seat became vacant for the remaining period of his term unless the period is less than six months.

Article 40

Every member of the Commission shall be in office until the date his successor assumes office.

Article 41

The Secretary-General of the Organization of African Unity shall appoint the Secretary of the Commission. He shall also provide the staff and services necessary for the effective discharge of the duties of the Commission. The Organization of African Unity shall bear the cost of the staff and services.

Article 42

1. The Commission shall elect its Chairman and Vice-Chairman for a two-year period. They shall be eligible for re-election.

2. The Commission shall lay down its rules of procedure.

3. Seven members shall form the quorum.

4. In case of an equality of votes, the Chairman shall have a casting vote.

5. The Secretary-General may attend the meetings of the Commission. He shall neither participate in deliberations nor shall he be entitled to vote. The Chairman of the Commission may, however, invite him to speak.

Article 43

In discharging their duties, members of the Commission shall enjoy diplomatic privileges and immunities provided for in the General Convention on the Privileges and Immunities of the Organization of African Unity.

Article 44

Provision shall be made for the emoluments and allowances of the members of the Commission in the Regular Budget of the Organization of African Unity.

CHAPTER II. MANDATE OF THE COMMISSION

Article 45

The functions of the Commission shall be:

1. To promote human and peoples' rights and in particular:

(a) to collect documents, undertake studies and research on African problems in the field of human and peoples' rights, organize seminars, symposia and conferences, disseminate information, encourage national and local institutions concerned with human and peoples' rights, and should the case arise, give its views or make recommendations to Governments;

(b) to formulate and lay down principles and rules aimed at solving legal problems relating to human and peoples' rights and fundamental freedoms upon which African Governments may base their legislations;

(c) co-operate with other African and international institutions concerned with the promotion and protection of human and peoples' rights.

2. Ensure the protection of human and peoples' rights under conditions laid down by the present Charter.

3. Interpret all the provisions of the present Charter at the request of a State Party, an institution of the OAU or an African organization recognized by the OAU.

4. Perform any other tasks which may be entrusted to it by the Assembly of Heads of State and Government.

CHAPTER III. PROCEDURE OF THE COMMISSION

Article 46

The Commission may resort to any appropriate method of investigation; it may hear from the Secretary-General of the Organization of African Unity or any other person capable of enlightening it.

COMMUNICATION FROM STATES

Article 47

If a State Party to the present Charter has good reasons to believe that another State Party to this Charter has violated the provisions of the Charter, it may draw, by written communication, the attention of that State to the matter. This communication shall also be addressed to the Secretary-General of the OAU and to the Chairman of the Commission. Within three months of the receipt of the communication, the State to which the communication is addressed shall give the enquiring State written explanation or statement elucidating the matter. This should include as much as possible relevant information relating to the laws and rules of procedure applied and applicable and the redress already given or course of action available.

Article 48

If within three months from the date on which the original communication is received by the State to which it is addressed, the issue is not settled to the satisfaction of the two States involved through bilateral negotiation or by any other peaceful procedure, either State shall have the right to submit the matter to the Commission through the Chairman and shall notify the other States involved.

Article 49

Notwithstanding the provisions of Article 47, if a State Party to the present Charter considers that another State Party has violated the provisions of the Charter, it may refer the matter directly to the Commission by addressing a communication to the Chairman, to the Secretary-General of the Organization of African Unity and the State concerned.

Article 50

The Commission can only deal with a matter submitted to it after making sure that all local remedies, if they exist, have been exhausted, unless it is obvious to the Commission that the procedure of achieving these remedies would be unduly prolonged.

Article 51

1.   The Commission may ask the States concerned to provide it with all relevant information.

2.   When the Commission is considering the matter, States concerned may be represented before it and submit written or oral representations.

Article 52

After having obtained from the States concerned and from other sources all the information it deems necessary and after having tried all appropriate means to reach an amicable solution based on the respect of human and peoples' rights, the Commission shall prepare, within a reasonable period of time from the notification referred to in Article 48, a report stating the facts and its findings. This report shall be sent to the States concerned and communicated to the Assembly of Heads of State and Government.

Article 53

While transmitting its report, the Commission may make to the Assembly of Heads of State and Government such recommendations as it deems useful.

Article 54

The Commission shall submit to each Ordinary Session of the Assembly of Heads of State and Government a report on its activities.

OTHER COMMUNICATIONS

Article 55

1. Before each session, the Secretary of the Commission shall make a list of the communications other than those of States Parties to the present Charter and transmit them to the members of the Commission, who shall indicate which communications should be considered by the Commission.

2. A communication shall be considered by the Commission if a simple majority of its members so decide.

Article 56

Communications relating to human and peoples' rights referred to in Article 55 received by the Commission shall be considered if they:

1. Indicate their authors even if the latter request anonymity;

2. Are compatible with the Charter of the Organization of African Unity or with the present Charter;

3. Are not written in disparaging or insulting language directed against the State concerned and its institutions or to the Organization of African Unity;

4. Are not based exclusively on news disseminated through the mass media;

5. Are sent after exhausting local remedies, if any, unless it is obvious that this procedure is unduly prolonged;

6.   Are submitted within a reasonable period from the time local remedies are exhausted or from the date the Commission is seized of the matter; and

7.   Do not deal with cases which have been settled by the States involved in accordance with the principles of the Charter of the United Nations, or the Charter of the Organization of African Unity or the provisions of the present Charter.

Article 57

Prior to any substantive consideration, all communications shall be brought to the knowledge of the State concerned by the Chairman of the Commission.

Article 58

1.   When it appears after deliberations of the Commission that one or more communications apparently relate to special cases which reveal the existence of a series of serious or massive violations of human and peoples' rights, the Commission shall draw the attention of the Assembly of Heads of State and Government to these special cases.

2.   The Assembly of Heads of State and Government may then request the Commission to undertake an in-depth study of these cases and make a factual report, accompanied by its finding and recommendations.

3.   A case of emergency duly noticed by the Commission shall be submitted by the latter to the Chairman of the Assembly of Heads of State and Government who may request an in-depth study.

Article 59

1.   All measures taken within the provisions of the present Chapter shall remain confidential until such a time as the Assembly of Heads of State and Government shall otherwise decide.

2.   However, the report shall be published by the Chairman of the Commission upon the decision of the Assembly of Heads of State and Government.

3.   The report on the activities of the Commission shall be published by its Chairman after it has been considered by the Assembly of Heads of State and Government.

CHAPTER IV.   APPLICABLE PRINCIPLES

Article 60

The Commission shall draw inspiration from international law on human and peoples' rights, particularly from the provisions of various African instruments on human and peoples' rights, the Charter of the United Nations, the Charter of the Organization of African Unity, the Universal Declaration of Human Rights, other instruments adopted by the United Nations and by African countries in the field of human and peoples' rights as well as from the provisions of various instruments adopted within the Specialized Agencies of the United Nations of which the Parties to the present Charter are members.

Article 61

The Commission shall also take into consideration, as subsidiary measures to determine the principles of law, other general or special international conventions, laying down rules expressly recognized by Member States of the Organization of African Unity, African practices consistent with international norms on human and peoples' rights, customs generally accepted as law, general principles of law recognized by African States as well as legal precedents and doctrine.

Article 62

Each State Party shall undertake to submit every two years, from the date the present Charter comes into force, a report on the legislative or other measures taken with a view to giving effect to the rights and freedoms recognized and guaranteed by the present Charter.

Article 63

1.   The present Charter shall be open to signature, ratification or adherence of the Member States of the Organization of African Unity.

2.   The instruments of ratification or adherence to the present Charter shall be deposited with the Secretary-General of the Organization of African Unity.

3.   The present Charter shall come into force three months after the reception by the Secretary-General of the instruments of ratification or adherence of a simple majority of the Member States of the Organization of African Unity.

PART III

GENERAL PROVISIONS

Article 64

1. After the coming into force of the present Charter, members of the Commission shall be elected in accordance with the relevant Articles of the present Charter.

2. The Secretary-General of the Organization of African Unity shall convene the first meeting of the Commission at the Headquarters of the Organization within three months of the constitution of the Commission. Thereafter, the Commission shall be convened by its Chairman whenever necessary but at least once a year.

Article 65

For each of the States that will ratify or adhere to the present Charter after its coming into force, the Charter shall take effect three months after the date of the deposit by that State of its instrument of ratification or adherence.

Article 66

Special protocols or agreements may, if necessary, supplement the provisions of the present Charter.

Article 67

The Secretary-General of the Organization of African Unity shall inform Member States of the Organization of the deposit of each instrument of ratification or adherence.

Article 68

The present Charter may be amended if a State Party makes a written request to that effect to the Secretary-General of the Organization of African Unity. The Assembly of Heads of State and Government may only consider the draft amendment after all the States Parties have been duly informed of it and the Commission has given its opinion on it at the request of the sponsoring State. The amendment shall be approved by a simple majority of the States Parties. It shall come into force for each State which has accepted it in accordance with its constitutional procedure three months after the Secretary-General has received notice of the acceptance.

39. African Charter on the Rights and Welfare of the Child

Adopted at Addis Ababa on 11 July 1990

PREAMBLE

The African Member States of the Organization of African Unity, Parties to the present Charter entitled "African Charter on the Rights and Welfare of the Child",

Considering that the Charter of the Organization of African Unity recognizes the paramountcy of human rights and the African Charter on Human and Peoples' Rights proclaimed and agreed that everyone is entitled to all the rights and freedoms recognized and guaranteed therein, without distinction of any kind such as race, ethnic group, colour, sex, language, religion, political or any other opinion, national and social origin, fortune, birth or other status,

Recalling the Declaration on the Rights and Welfare of the African Child (AHG/ST.4 (XVI) Rev.1) adopted by the Assembly of Heads of State and Government of the Organization of African Unity at its Sixteenth Ordinary Session in Monrovia, Liberia, from 17 to 20 July 1979, which recognized the need to take all appropriate measures to promote and protect the rights and welfare of the African Child,

Noting with concern that the situation of most African children remains critical due to the unique factors of their socio-economic, cultural, traditional and developmental circumstances, natural disasters, armed conflicts, exploitation and hunger, and on account of the child's physical and mental immaturity he/she needs special safeguards and care,

Recognizing that the child occupies a unique and privileged position in the African society and that for the full and harmonious development of his personality the child should grow up in a family environment in an atmosphere of happiness, love and understanding,

Recognizing that the child, due to the needs of his physical and mental development, requires particular care with regard to health, physical, mental, moral and social development, and requires legal protection in conditions of freedom, dignity and security,

Taking into consideration the virtues of their cultural heritage, historical background and the values of the African civilization which should inspire and characterize their reflection on the concept of the rights and welfare of the child,

Considering that the promotion and protection of the rights and welfare of the child also implies the performance of duties on the part of everyone,

Reaffirming adherence to the principles of the rights and welfare of the child contained in the declarations, conventions and other instruments of the Organization of African Unity and of the United Nations and in particular the United Nations Convention on the Rights of the Child and the OAU Heads of State and Governments' Declaration on the Rights and Welfare of the African Child,

Have agreed as follows:

PART I.   RIGHTS AND DUTIES

CHAPTER ONE

RIGHTS AND WELFARE OF THE CHILD

Article 1.—Obligation of States Parties

1.   The Member States of the Organization of African Unity Parties to the present Charter shall recognize the rights, freedoms and duties enshrined in this Charter and shall undertake to take the necessary steps, in accordance with their constitutional processes and with the provisions of the present Charter, to adopt such legislative or other measures as may be necessary to give effect to the provisions of this Charter.

2.   Nothing in this Charter shall affect any provisions that are more conducive to the realization of the rights and welfare of the child contained in the law of a State Party or in any other international convention or agreement in force in that State.

3.   Any custom, tradition, or cultural or religious practice that is inconsistent with the rights, duties and obligations contained in the present Charter shall to the extent of such inconsistency be discouraged.

Article 2.—Definition of a child

For the purposes of this Charter, a child means every human being below the age of 18 years.

Article 3.—Non-discrimination

Every child shall be entitled to the enjoyment of the rights and freedoms recognized and guaranteed in this Charter irrespective of the child's or his/her parents' or legal guardians' race, ethnic group, colour, sex, language, religion, political or other opinion, national and social origin, fortune, birth or other status.

Article 4.—Best interests of the child

1.   In all actions concerning the child undertaken by any person or authority the best interests of the child shall be the primary consideration.

2.   In all judicial or administrative proceedings affecting a child who is capable of communicating his/her own views, an opportunity shall be provided for the views of the child to be heard either directly or through an impartial representative as a party to the proceedings, and those views shall be taken into consideration by the relevant authority in accordance with the provisions of appropriate law.

Article 5.—Survival and development

1.   Every child has an inherent right to life. This right shall be protected by law.

2.   States Parties to the present Charter shall ensure, to the maximum extent possible, the survival, protection and development of the child.

3.   The death sentence shall not be pronounced for crimes committed by children.

Article 6.—Name and nationality

1.   Every child shall have the right from his birth to a name.

2.   Every child shall be registered immediately after birth.

3.   Every child has the right to acquire a nationality.

4.   States Parties to the present Charter shall undertake to ensure that their constitutional legislation recognizes the principles according to which a child shall acquire the nationality of the State in the territory of which he has been born if, at the time of the child's birth, he is not granted nationality by any other State in accordance with its laws.

Article 7.—Freedom of expression

Every child who is capable of communicating his or her own views shall be assured the rights to express his opinions freely in all matters and to disseminate his opinions subject to such restrictions as are prescribed by laws.

Article 8.—Freedom of association

Every child shall have the right to free association and freedom of peaceful assembly in conformity with the law.

Article 9.—Freedom of thought, conscience and religion

1.   Every child shall have the right to freedom of thought, conscience and religion.

2.   Parents and, where applicable, legal guardians shall have a duty to provide guidance and direction in the exercise of these rights having regard to the evolving capacities and best interests of the child.

3.   States Parties shall respect the duty of parents and, where applicable, legal guardians to provide guidance and direction in the enjoyment of these rights subject to the national laws and policies.

Article 10.—Protection of privacy

No child shall be subject to arbitrary or unlawful interference with his privacy, family, home or correspondence, or to attacks upon his honour or reputation, provided that parents or legal guardians shall have the right to exercise reasonable supervision over the conduct of their children. The child has the right to the protection of the law against such interference or attacks.

Article 11.—Education

1.   Every child shall have the right to education.

2.   The education of the child shall be directed to:

(a)   the promotion and development of the child's personality, talents and mental and physical abilities to their fullest potential;

(b)   fostering respect for human rights and fundamental freedoms with particular reference to those set out in the provisions of various African instruments on human and peoples' rights and international human rights declarations and conventions;

(c)   the preservation and strengthening of positive African morals, traditional values and cultures;

(d)   the preparation of the child for responsible life in a free society, in the spirit of understanding, tolerance, dialogue, mutual respect and friendship among all peoples and ethnic, tribal and religious groups;

(e)   the preservation of national independence and territorial integrity;

(*f*) the promotion and achievement of African unity and solidarity;

(*g*) the development of respect for the environment and natural resources;

(*h*) the promotion of the child's understanding of primary health care.

3.   States Parties to the present Charter shall take all appropriate measures with a view to achieving the full realization of this right and shall in particular:

(*a*) provide free and compulsory basic education;

(*b*) encourage the development of secondary education in its different forms and to progressively make it free and accessible to all;

(*c*) make higher education accessible to all on the basis of capacity and ability by every appropriate means;

(*d*) take measures to encourage regular attendance at schools and the reduction of the drop-out rate;

(*e*) take special measures in respect of female, gifted and disadvantaged children, to ensure equal access to education for all sections of the community.

4.   States Parties to the present Charter shall respect the rights and duties of parents and, where applicable, of legal guardians to choose for their children schools other than those established by public authorities, which conform to such minimum standards as may be approved by the State, to ensure the religious and moral education of the child in a manner consistent with the evolving capacities of the child.

5.   States Parties to the present Charter shall take all appropriate measures to ensure that a child who is subjected to school or parental discipline shall be treated with humanity and with respect for the inherent dignity of the child and in conformity with the present Charter.

6.   States Parties to the present Charter shall take all appropriate measures to ensure that children who become pregnant before completing their education shall have an opportunity to continue with their education on the basis of their individual ability.

7.   No part of this Article shall be construed as to interfere with the liberty of individuals and bodies to establish and direct educational institutions subject to the observance of the principles set out in paragraph 2 of this Article and the requirement that the education given in such institutions shall conform to such minimum standards as may be laid down by the State.

Article 12.—Leisure, recreation and cultural activities

1.   States Parties recognize the right of the child to rest and leisure, to engage in play and recreational activities appropriate to the age of the child and to participate freely in cultural life and the arts.

2.   States Parties shall respect and promote the right of the child to fully participate in cultural and artistic life and shall encourage the provision of appropriate and equal opportunities for cultural, artistic, recreational and leisure activity.

Article 13.—Handicapped children

1.   Every child who is mentally or physically disabled shall have the right to special measures of protection in keeping with his physical and moral needs and under conditions which ensure his dignity and promote his self-reliance and active participation in the community.

2.   States Parties to the present Charter shall ensure, subject to available resources, to a disabled child and to those responsible for his care, assistance for which application is made and which is appropriate to the child's condition and in particular shall ensure that the disabled child has effective access to training, preparation for employment and recreation opportunities in a manner conducive to the child achieving the fullest possible social integration, individual development and his cultural and moral development.

3.   States Parties to the present Charter shall use their available resources with a view to achieving progressively the full convenience of the mentally and physically disabled person to movement and access to public highway buildings and other places to which the disabled may legitimately want to have access.

Article 14.—Health and health services

1.   Every child shall have the right to enjoy the best attainable state of physical, mental and spiritual health.

2.   States Parties to the present Charter shall undertake to pursue the full implementation of this right and in particular shall take measures:

   (*a*) to reduce infant and child mortality rate;

   (*b*) to ensure the provision of necessary medical assistance and health care to all children with emphasis on the development of primary health care;

   (*c*) to ensure the provision of adequate nutrition and safe drinking water;

(*d*) to combat disease and malnutrition within the framework of primary health care through the application of appropriate technology;

(*e*) to ensure appropriate health care for expectant and nursing mothers;

(*f*) to develop preventive health care and family life education and provision of service;

(*g*) to integrate basic health service programmes in national development plans;

(*h*) to ensure that all sectors of the society, in particular parents, children, community leaders and community workers, are informed and supported in the use of basic knowledge of child health and nutrition, the advantages of breast-feeding, hygiene and environmental sanitation and the prevention of domestic and other accidents;

(*i*) to ensure the meaningful participation of non-governmental organizations, local communities and the beneficiary population in the planning and management of a basic service programme for children;

(*j*) to support through technical and financial means the mobilization of local community resources in the development of primary health care for children.

Article 15.—Child labour

1. Every child shall be protected from all forms of economic exploitation and from performing any work that is likely to be hazardous or to interfere with the child's physical, mental, spiritual, moral, or social development.

2. States Parties to the present Charter shall take all appropriate legislative and administrative measures to ensure the full implementation of this Article which covers both the formal and informal sectors of employment and, having regard to the relevant provisions of the International Labour Organisation's instruments relating to children, States Parties shall in particular:

(*a*) provide, through legislation, minimum ages for admission to every employment;

(*b*) provide for appropriate regulation of hours and conditions of employment;

(*c*) provide for appropriate penalties or other sanctions to ensure the effective enforcement of this Article;

(*d*) promote the dissemination of information on the hazards of child labour to all sectors of the community.

Article 16.—Protection against child abuse and torture

1. States Parties to the present Charter shall take specific legislative, administrative, social and educational measures to protect the child from all forms of torture, inhuman or degrading treatment and especially physical or mental injury or abuse, neglect or maltreatment including sexual abuse, while in the care of a parent, legal guardian or school authority or any other person who has the care of the child.

2. Protective measures under this Article shall include effective procedures for the establishment of special monitoring units to provide necessary support for the child and for those who have the care of the child, as well as other forms of prevention, and for identification, reporting, referral, investigation, treatment and follow-up of instances of child abuse and neglect.

Article 17.—Administration of juvenile justice

1. Every child accused or found guilty of having infringed penal law shall have the right to special treatment in a manner consistent with the child's sense of dignity and worth and which reinforces the child's respect for human rights and fundamental freedoms of others.

2. States Parties to the present Charter shall in particular:

(*a*) ensure that no child who is detained or imprisoned or otherwise deprived of his/her liberty is subjected to torture or inhuman or degrading treatment or punishment;

(*b*) ensure that children are separated from adults in their place of detention or imprisonment;

(*c*) ensure that every child accused of infringing the penal law:

  (i) shall be presumed innocent until duly recognized guilty;

  (ii) shall be informed promptly in a language that he understands and in detail of the charge against him, and shall be entitled to the assistance of an interpreter if he or she cannot understand the language used;

  (iii) shall be afforded legal and other appropriate assistance in the preparation and presentation of his defence;

  (iv) shall have the matter determined as speedily as possible by an impartial tribunal and, if found guilty, be entitled to an appeal to a higher tribunal;

  (v) shall not be compelled to give testimony or confess guilt;

(*d*) prohibit the press and the public from the trial.

3. The essential aim of treatment of every child during the trial and also if found guilty of infringing the penal law shall be his or her reformation, re-integration into his or her family and social rehabilitation.

4. There shall be a minimum age below which children shall be presumed not to have the capacity to infringe the penal law.

Article 18.—Protection of the family

1. The family shall be the natural unit and basis of society. It shall enjoy the protection and support of the State for its establishment and development.

2. States Parties to the present Charter shall take appropriate steps to ensure equality of rights and responsibilities of spouses with regard to children during marriage and in the event of its dissolution. In case of dissolution, provision shall be made for the necessary protection of the child.

3. No child shall be deprived of maintenance by reference to the parents' marital status.

Article 19.—Parental care and protection

1. Every child shall be entitled to the enjoyment of parental care and protection and shall, whenever possible, have the right to reside with his or her parents. No child shall be separated from his parents against his will, except when a judicial authority determines, in accordance with the appropriate law, that such separation is in the best interest of the child.

2. Every child who is separated from one or both parents shall have the right to maintain personal relations and direct contact with both parents on a regular basis.

3. Where separation results from the action of a State Party, the State Party shall provide the child or, if appropriate, another member of the family with essential information concerning the whereabouts of the absent member or members of the family. States Parties shall also ensure that the submission of such a request shall not entail any adverse consequences for the person or persons in whose respect it is made.

4. Where a child is apprehended by a State Party, his parents or guardians shall, as soon as possible, be notified of such apprehension by that State Party.

Article 20.—Parental responsibilities

1. Parents or other persons responsible for the child shall have the primary responsibility for the upbringing and development of the child and shall have the duty:

(*a*) to ensure that the best interests of the child are their basic concern at all times;

(*b*) to secure, within their abilities and financial capacities, conditions of living necessary to the child's development; and

(*c*) to ensure that domestic discipline is administered with humanity and in a manner consistent with the inherent dignity of the child.

2.   States Parties to the present Charter shall in accordance with their means and national conditions take all appropriate measures:

(*a*) to assist parents and other persons responsible for the child and in case of need provide material assistance and support programmes particularly with regard to nutrition, health, education, clothing and housing;

(*b*) to assist parents and others responsible for the child in the performance of child-rearing and ensure the development of institutions responsible for providing care of children; and

(*c*) to ensure that the children of working parents are provided with care services and facilities.

Article 21.—Protection against harmful social and cultural practices

1.   States Parties to the present Charter shall take all appropriate measures to eliminate harmful social and cultural practices affecting the welfare, dignity, normal growth and development of the child and in particular:

(*a*) those customs and practices prejudicial to the health or life of the child; and

(*b*) those customs and practices discriminatory to the child on the grounds of sex or other status.

2.   Child marriage and the betrothal of girls and boys shall be prohibited and effective action, including legislation, shall be taken to specify the minimum age of marriage to be eighteen years and make registration of all marriages in an official registry compulsory.

Article 22.—Armed conflicts

1.   States Parties to this Charter shall undertake to respect and ensure respect for rules of international humanitarian law applicable in armed conflicts which affect the child.

2.   States Parties to the present Charter shall take all necessary measures to ensure that no child shall take a direct part in hostilities and refrain, in particular, from recruiting any child.

3.   States Parties to the present Charter shall, in accordance with their obligations under international humanitarian law, protect the civilian popula-

tion in armed conflicts and shall take all feasible measures to ensure the protection and care of children who are affected by armed conflicts. Such rules shall also apply to children in situations of internal armed conflicts, tension and strife.

Article 23.—Refugee children

1. States Parties to the present Charter shall take all appropriate measures to ensure that a child who is seeking refugee status or who is considered a refugee in accordance with applicable international or domestic law shall, whether unaccompanied or accompanied by parents, legal guardians or close relatives, receive appropriate protection and humanitarian assistance in the enjoyment of the rights set out in this Charter and other international human rights and humanitarian instruments to which the States are parties.

2. States Parties shall undertake to cooperate with existing international organizations which protect and assist refugees in their efforts to protect and assist such a child and to trace the parents or other close relatives of an unaccompanied refugee child in order to obtain information necessary for reunification with the family.

3. Where no parents, legal guardians or close relatives can be found, the child shall be accorded the same protection as any other child permanently or temporarily deprived of his family environment for any reason.

4. The provisions of this Article apply *mutatis mutandis* to internally displaced children whether through natural disaster, internal armed conflicts, civil strife, breakdown of economic and social order or howsoever caused.

Article 24.—Adoption

States Parties which recognize the system of adoption shall ensure that the best interest of the child shall be the paramount consideration and they shall:

(*a*) establish competent authorities to determine matters of adoption and ensure that the adoption is carried out in conformity with applicable laws and procedures and on the basis of all relevant and reliable information, that the adoption is permissible in view of the child's status concerning parents, relatives and guardians and that, if necessary, the appropriate persons concerned have given their informed consent to the adoption on the basis of appropriate counselling;

(*b*) recognize that inter-country adoption in those States which have ratified or adhered to the Convention on the Rights of the Child or this Charter may, as the last resort, be considered as an alternative means of child's care, if the child cannot be placed in a foster or an adoptive family or cannot in any suitable manner be cared for in the child's country of origin;

(*c*) ensure that the child affected by inter-country adoption enjoys safeguards and standards equivalent to those existing in the case of national adoption;

(*d*) take all appropriate measures to ensure that, in inter-country adoption, the placement does not result in trafficking or improper financial gain for those who try to adopt a child;

(*e*) promote, where appropriate, the objectives of this Article by concluding bilateral or multilateral arrangements or agreements, and endeavour within this framework to ensure that the placement of the child in another country is carried out by competent authorities or organs;

(*f*) establish a machinery to monitor the well-being of the adopted child.

Article 25.—Separation from parents

1.   Any child who is permanently or temporarily deprived of his family environment for any reason shall be entitled to special protection and assistance.

2.   States Parties to the present Charter:

(*a*) shall ensure that a child who is parentless, or who is temporarily or permanently deprived of his or her family environment, or who in his or her best interest cannot be brought up or allowed to remain in that environment, shall be provided with alternative family care, which could include, among others, foster placement, or placement in suitable institutions for the care of children;

(*b*) shall take all necessary measures to trace and re-unite children with parents or relatives where separation is caused by internal and external displacement arising from armed conflicts or natural disasters.

3.   When considering alternative family care of the child and the best interests of the child, due regard shall be paid to the desirability of continuity in a child's upbringing and to the child's ethnic, religious or linguistic background.

Article 26.—Protection against Apartheid and discrimination

1.   States Parties to the present Charter shall individually and collectively undertake to accord the highest priority to the special needs of children living under *Apartheid* and in States subject to military destabilization by the *Apartheid* regime.

2.   States Parties to the present Charter shall individually and collectively undertake to accord the highest priority to the special needs of chil-

dren living under regimes practising racial, ethnic, religious or other forms of discrimination as well as in States subject to military destabilization.

3. States Parties shall undertake to provide, whenever possible, material assistance to such children and to direct their efforts towards the elimination of all forms of discrimination and *Apartheid* on the African continent.

Article 27.—Sexual exploitation

States Parties to the present Charter shall undertake to protect the child from all forms of sexual exploitation and sexual abuse and shall in particular take measures to prevent:

(*a*) the inducement, coercion or encouragement of a child to engage in any sexual activity;

(*b*) the use of children in prostitution or other sexual practices;

(*c*) the use of children in pornographic activities, performances and materials.

Article 28.—Drug abuse

States Parties to the present Charter shall take all appropriate measures to protect the child from the use of narcotics and illicit use of psychotropic substances as defined in the relevant international treaties, and to prevent the use of children in the production and trafficking of such substances.

Article 29.—Sale, trafficking and abduction

States Parties to the present Charter shall take appropriate measures to prevent:

(*a*) the abduction, the sale of, or traffic in children for any purpose or in any form, by any person including parents or legal guardians of the child;

(*b*) the use of children in all forms of begging.

Article 30.—Children of imprisoned mothers

States Parties to the present Charter shall undertake to provide special treatment to expectant mothers and to mothers of infants and young children who have been accused or found guilty of infringing the penal law and shall in particular:

(*a*) ensure that a non-custodial sentence will always be first considered when sentencing such mothers;

(*b*) establish and promote measures alternative to institutional confinement for the treatment of such mothers;

(*c*) establish special alternative institutions for holding such mothers;

(*d*) ensure that a mother shall not be imprisoned with her child;

(*e*) ensure that a death sentence shall not be imposed on such mothers;

(*f*) ensure that the essential aim of the penitentiary system will be reformation, the integration of the mother to the family and social rehabilitation.

Article 31.—Responsibilities of the child

Every child shall have responsibilities towards his family and society, the State and other legally recognized communities and the international community. The child, subject to his age and ability, and such limitations as may be contained in the present Charter, shall have the duty:

(*a*) to work for the cohesion of the family, to respect his parents, superiors and elders at all times and to assist them in case of need;

(*b*) to serve his national community by placing his physical and intellectual abilities at its service;

(*c*) to preserve and strengthen social and national solidarity;

(*d*) to preserve and strengthen African cultural values in his relations with other members of the society, in the spirit of tolerance, dialogue and consultation and to contribute to the moral well-being of society;

(*e*) to preserve and strengthen the independence and the integrity of his country;

(*f*) to contribute to the best of his abilities, at all times and at all levels, to the promotion and achievement of African unity.

PART II

CHAPTER TWO

ESTABLISHMENT AND ORGANIZATION OF THE COMMITTEE ON THE RIGHTS AND WELFARE OF THE CHILD

Article 32.—The Committee

An African Committee of Experts on the Rights and Welfare of the Child hereinafter called "the Committee" shall be established within the Organization of African Unity to promote and protect the rights and welfare of the child.

Article 33.—Composition

1.   The Committee shall consist of 11 members of high moral standing, integrity, impartiality and competence in matters of the rights and welfare of the child.

2.   The members of the Committee shall serve in their personal capacity.

3.   The Committee shall not include more than one national of the same State.

Article 34.—Election

As soon as this Charter shall enter into force the members of the Committee shall be elected by secret ballot by the Assembly of Heads of State and Government from a list of persons nominated by the States Parties to the present Charter.

Article 35.—Candidates

Each State Party to the present Charter may nominate not more than two candidates. The candidates must have one of the nationalities of the States Parties to the present Charter. When two candidates are nominated by a State, one of them shall not be a national of that State.

Article 36

1.   The Secretary-General of the Organization of African Unity shall invite States Parties to the present Charter to nominate candidates at least six months before the elections.

2.   The Secretary-General of the Organization of African Unity shall draw up in alphabetical order a list of persons nominated and communicate it to the Heads of State and Government at least two months before the elections.

Article 37.—Term of office

1.   The members of the Committee shall be elected for a term of five years and may not be re-elected; however, the term of four of the members elected at the first election shall expire after two years and the term of six others, after four years.

2.   Immediately after the first election, the Chairman of the Assembly of Heads of State and Government of the Organization of African Unity shall draw lots to determine the names of those members referred to in paragraph 1 of this Article.

3. The Secretary-General of the Organization of African Unity shall convene the first meeting of the Committee at the Headquarters of the Organization within six months of the election of the members of the Committee, and thereafter the Committee shall be convened by its Chairman whenever necessary, at least once a year.

Article 38.—Bureau

1. The Committee shall establish its own Rules of Procedure.

2. The Committee shall elect its officers for a period of two years.

3. Seven Committee members shall form the quorum.

4. In case of an equality of votes, the Chairman shall have a casting vote.

5. The working languages of the Committee shall be the official languages of the OAU.

Article 39.—Vacancy

If a member of the Committee vacates his office for any reason other than the normal expiration of a term, the State which nominated that member shall appoint another member from among its nationals to serve for the remainder of the term—subject to the approval of the Assembly.

Article 40.—Secretariat

The Secretary-General of the Organization of African Unity shall appoint a Secretary for the Committee.

Article 41.—Privileges and immunities

In discharging their duties, members of the Committee shall enjoy the privileges and immunities provided for in the General Convention on the Privileges and Immunities of the Organization of African Unity.

CHAPTER THREE

MANDATE AND PROCEDURE OF THE COMMITTEE

Article 42.—Mandate

The functions of the Committee shall be:

(a) To promote and protect the rights enshrined in this Charter and in particular to:

(i) collect and document information, commission inter-disciplinary assessment of situations on African problems in the fields of the rights and welfare of the child, organize meetings, encourage national and local institutions concerned with the rights and welfare of the child, and where necessary give its views and make recommendations to Governments;

(ii) formulate and lay down principles and rules aimed at protecting the rights and welfare of children in Africa;

(iii) cooperate with other African, international and regional institutions and organizations concerned with the promotion and protection of the rights and welfare of the child;

(b) To monitor the implementation and ensure protection of the rights enshrined in this Charter;

(c) To interpret the provisions of the present Charter at the request of a State Party, an institution of the Organization of African Unity or any other person or institution recognized by the Organization of African Unity or any State Party;

(d) To perform such other tasks as may be entrusted to it by the Assembly of Heads of State and Government, the Secretary-General of the OAU and any other organs of the OAU, or the United Nations.

Article 43.—Reporting procedure

1. Every State Party to the present Charter shall undertake to submit to the Committee, through the Secretary-General of the Organization of African Unity, reports on the measures they have adopted which give effect to the provisions of this Charter and on the progress made in the enjoyment of these rights:

(a) within two years of the entry into force of the Charter for the State Party concerned; and

(b) thereafter, every three years.

2. Every report made under this Article shall:

(a) contain sufficient information on the implementation of the present Charter to provide the Committee with comprehensive understanding of the implementation of the Charter in the relevant country; and

(b) indicate factors and difficulties, if any, affecting the fulfilment of the obligations contained in the Charter.

3. A State Party which has submitted a comprehensive first report to the Committee need not, in its subsequent reports submitted in accordance

with paragraph 1 (*b*) of this Article, repeat the basic information previously provided.

Article 44.—Communications

1.   The Committee may receive communications from any person, group or non-governmental organization recognized by the Organization of African Unity, by a Member State or by the United Nations relating to any matter covered by this Charter.

2.   Every communication to the Committee shall contain the name and address of the author and shall be treated in confidence.

Article 45.—Investigations by the Committee

1.   The Committee may resort to any appropriate method of investigating any matter falling within the ambit of the present Charter, request from the States Parties any information relevant to the implementation of the Charter and may also resort to any appropriate method of investigating the measures a State Party has adopted to implement the Charter.

2.   The Committee shall submit to each Ordinary Session of the Assembly of Heads of State and Government, every two years, a report on its activities and on any communication made under Article 44 of this Charter.

3.   The Committee shall publish its report after it has been considered by the Assembly of Heads of State and Government.

4.   States Parties shall make the Committee's reports widely available to the public in their own countries.

CHAPTER FOUR

MISCELLANEOUS PROVISIONS

Article 46.—Sources of inspiration

The Committee shall draw inspiration from international law on human rights, particularly from the provisions of the African Charter on Human and Peoples' Rights, the Charter of the Organization of African Unity, the Universal Declaration of Human Rights, the Convention on the Rights of the Child and other instruments adopted by the United Nations and by African countries in the field of human rights, and from African values and traditions.

Article 47.—Signature, ratification or adherence

1.   The present Charter shall be open to signature by all the Member States of the Organization of African Unity.

2.   The present Charter shall be subject to ratification or adherence by Member States of the Organization of African Unity. The instruments of ratification or adherence to the present Charter shall be deposited with the Secretary-General of the Organization of African Unity.

3.   The present Charter shall come into force 30 days after the reception by the Secretary-General of the Organization of African Unity of the instruments of ratification or adherence of 15 Member States of the Organization of African Unity.

Article 48.—Amendment and revision of the Charter

1.   The present Charter may be amended or revised if any State Party makes a written request to that effect to the Secretary-General of the Organization of African Unity, provided that the proposed amendment is not submitted to the Assembly of Heads of State and Government for consideration until all the States Parties have been duly notified of it and the Committee has given its opinion on the amendment.

2.   An amendment shall be approved by a simple majority of the States Parties.

D. ORGANIZATION FOR SECURITY AND CO-OPERATION IN EUROPE

40. Helsinki Final Act
(Excerpt)

*Adopted at the Conference on Security and Co-operation in Europe,
Helsinki, on 1 August 1975*

Questions relating to Security in Europe

The States participating in the Conference on Security and Co-operation in Europe,

Reaffirming their objective of promoting better relations among themselves and ensuring conditions in which their people can live in true and lasting peace free from any threat to or attempt against their security,

Convinced of the need to exert efforts to make détente both a continuing and an increasingly viable and comprehensive process, universal in scope, and that the implementation of the results of the Conference on Security and Co-operation in Europe will be a major contribution to this process,

Considering that solidarity among peoples, as well as the common purpose of the participating States in achieving the aims as set forth by the Conference on Security and Co-operation in Europe, should lead to the development of better and closer relations among them in all fields and thus to overcoming the confrontation stemming from the character of their past relations, and to better mutual understanding,

Mindful of their common history and recognizing that the existence of elements common to their traditions and values can assist them in developing their relations, and desiring to search, fully taking into account the individuality and diversity of their positions and views, for possibilities of joining their efforts with a view to overcoming distrust and increasing confidence, solving the problems that separate them and cooperating in the interest of mankind,

Recognizing the indivisibility of security in Europe as well as their common interest in the development of co-operation throughout Europe and among themselves and expressing their intention to pursue efforts accordingly,

Recognizing the close link between peace and security in Europe and in the world as a whole and conscious of the need for each of them to make its contribution to the strengthening of world peace and security and to the

369

promotion of fundamental rights, economic and social progress and well-being of all peoples,

Have adopted the following:

1

(a) DECLARATION ON PRINCIPLES
GUIDING RELATIONS BETWEEN PARTICIPATING STATES

The participating States,

Reaffirming their commitment to peace, security and justice and the continuing development of friendly relations and co-operation,

Recognizing that this commitment, which reflects the interest and aspirations of peoples, constitutes for each participating State a present and future responsibility, heightened by experience of the past,

Reaffirming, in conformity with their membership in the United Nations and in accordance with the purposes and principles of the United Nations, their full and active support for the United Nations and for the enhancement of its role and effectiveness in strengthening international peace, security and justice, and in promoting the solution of international problems, as well as the development of friendly relations and co-operation among States,

Expressing their common adherence to the principles which are set forth below and are in conformity with the Charter of the United Nations, as well as their common will to act, in the application of these principles, in conformity with the purposes and principles of the Charter of the United Nations,

Declare their determination to respect and put into practice, each of them in its relations with all other participating States, irrespective of their political, economic or social systems as well as of their size, geographical location or level of economic development, the following principles, which all are of primary significance, guiding their mutual relations:

I. *Sovereign equality,*
respect for the rights inherent in sovereignty

The participating States will respect each other's sovereign equality and individuality as well as all the rights inherent in and encompassed by its sovereignty, including in particular the right of every State to juridical equality, to territorial integrity and to freedom and political independence. They will also respect each other's right freely to choose and develop its political, social, economic and cultural systems as well as its right to determine its laws and regulations.

Within the framework of international law, all the participating States have equal rights and duties. They will respect each other's right to define and conduct as it wishes its relations with other States in accordance with international law and in the spirit of the present Declaration. They consider that their frontiers can be changed, in accordance with international law, by peaceful means and by agreement. They also have the right to belong or not to belong to international organizations, to be or not to be a party to bilateral or multilateral treaties including the right to be or not to be a party to treaties of alliance; they also have the right to neutrality.

II. *Refraining from the threat or use of force*

The participating States will refrain in their mutual relations, as well as in their international relations in general, from the threat or use of force against the territorial integrity or political independence of any State, or in any other manner inconsistent with the purposes of the United Nations and with the present Declaration. No consideration may be invoked to serve to warrant resort to the threat or use of force in contravention of this principle.

Accordingly, the participating States will refrain from any acts constituting a threat of force or direct or indirect use of force against another participating State. Likewise they will refrain from any manifestation of force for the purpose of inducing another participating State to renounce the full exercise of its sovereign rights. Likewise they will also refrain in their mutual relations from any act of reprisal by force.

No such threat or use of force will be employed as a means of settling disputes, or questions likely to give rise to disputes, between them.

III. *Inviolability of frontiers*

The participating States regard as inviolable all one another's frontiers as well as the frontiers of all States in Europe and therefore they will refrain now and in the future from assaulting these frontiers.

Accordingly, they will also refrain from any demand for, or act of, seizure and usurpation of part or all of the territory of any participating State.

IV. *Territorial integrity of States*

The participating States will respect the territorial integrity of each of the participating States.

Accordingly, they will refrain from any action inconsistent with the purposes and principles of the Charter of the United Nations against the territorial integrity, political independence or the unity of any participating State, and in particular from any such action constituting a threat or use of force.

The participating States will likewise refrain from making each other's territory the object of military occupation or other direct or indirect measures of force in contravention of international law, or the object of acquisition by means of such measures or the threat of them. No such occupation or acquisition will be recognized as legal.

V.   *Peaceful settlement of disputes*

The participating States will settle disputes among them by peaceful means in such a manner as not to endanger international peace and security, and justice.

They will endeavour in good faith and a spirit of co-operation to reach a rapid and equitable solution on the basis of international law.

For this purpose they will use such means as negotiation, enquiry, mediation, conciliation, arbitration, judicial settlement or other peaceful means of their own choice including any settlement procedure agreed to in advance of disputes to which they are parties.

In the event of failure to reach a solution by any of the above peaceful means, the parties to a dispute will continue to seek a mutually agreed way to settle the dispute peacefully.

Participating States, parties to a dispute among them, as well as other participating States, will refrain from any action which might aggravate the situation to such a degree as to endanger the maintenance of international peace and security and thereby make a peaceful settlement of the dispute more difficult.

VI.   *Non-intervention in internal affairs*

The participating States will refrain from any intervention, direct or indirect, individual or collective, in the internal or external affairs falling within the domestic jurisdiction of another participating State, regardless of their mutual relations.

They will accordingly refrain from any form of armed intervention or threat of such intervention against another participating State.

They will likewise in all circumstances refrain from any other act of military, or of political, economic or other coercion designed to subordinate to their own interest the exercise by another participating State of the rights inherent in its sovereignty and thus to secure advantages of any kind.

Accordingly, they will, *inter alia*, refrain from direct or indirect assistance to terrorist activities, or to subversive or other activities directed towards the violent overthrow of the regime of another participating State.

VII. *Respect for human rights and fundamental freedoms, including the freedom of thought, conscience, religion or belief*

The participating States will respect human rights and fundamental freedoms, including the freedom of thought, conscience, religion or belief, for all without distinction as to race, sex, language or religion.

They will promote and encourage the effective exercise of civil, political, economic, social, cultural and other rights and freedoms all of which derive from the inherent dignity of the human person and are essential for his free and full development.

Within this framework the participating States will recognize and respect the freedom of the individual to profess and practise, alone or in community with others, religion or belief acting in accordance with the dictates of his own conscience.

The participating States on whose territory national minorities exist will respect the right of persons belonging to such minorities to equality before the law, will afford them the full opportunity for the actual enjoyment of human rights and fundamental freedoms and will, in this manner, protect their legitimate interests in this sphere.

The participating States recognize the universal significance of human rights and fundamental freedoms, respect for which is an essential factor for the peace, justice and well-being necessary to ensure the development of friendly relations and co-operation among themselves as among all States.

They will constantly respect these rights and freedoms in their mutual relations and will endeavour jointly and separately, including in co-operation with the United Nations, to promote universal and effective respect for them.

They confirm the right of the individual to know and act upon his rights and duties in this field.

In the field of human rights and fundamental freedoms, the participating States will act in conformity with the purposes and principles of the Charter of the United Nations and with the Universal Declaration of Human Rights. They will also fulfil their obligations as set forth in the international declarations and agreements in this field, including *inter alia* the International Covenants on Human Rights, by which they may be bound.

VIII.   *Equal rights and self-determination of peoples*

The participating States will respect the equal rights of peoples and their right to self-determination, acting at all times in conformity with the purposes and principles of the Charter of the United Nations and with the relevant norms of international law, including those relating to territorial integrity of States.

By virtue of the principle of equal rights and self-determination of peoples, all peoples always have the right, in full freedom, to determine, when and as they wish, their internal and external political status, without external interference, and to pursue as they wish their political, economic, social and cultural development.

The participating States reaffirm the universal significance of respect for and effective exercise of equal rights and self-determination of peoples for the development of friendly relations among themselves as among all States; they also recall the importance of the elimination of any form of violation of this principle.

IX.   *Co-operation among States*

The participating States will develop their co-operation with one another and with all States in all fields in accordance with the purposes and principles of the Charter of the United Nations. In developing their co-operation the participating States will place special emphasis on the fields as set forth within the framework of the Conference on Security and Co-operation in Europe, with each of them making its contribution in conditions of full equality.

They will endeavour, in developing their co-operation as equals, to promote mutual understanding and confidence, friendly and good-neighbourly relations among themselves, international peace, security and justice. They will equally endeavour, in developing their co-operation, to improve the well-being of peoples and contribute to the fulfilment of their aspirations through, *inter alia*, the benefits resulting from increased mutual knowledge and from progress and achievement in the economic, scientific, technological, social, cultural and humanitarian fields. They will take steps to promote conditions favourable to making these benefits available to all; they will take into account the interest of all in the narrowing of differences in the levels of economic development, and in particular the interest of developing countries throughout the world.

They confirm that governments, institutions, organizations and persons have a relevant and positive role to play in contributing toward the achievement of these aims of their co-operation.

They will strive, in increasing their co-operation as set forth above, to develop closer relations among themselves on an improved and more enduring basis for the benefit of peoples.

X. *Fulfilment in good faith of obligations under international law*

The participating States will fulfil in good faith their obligations under international law, both those obligations arising from the generally recognized principles and rules of international law and those obligations arising from treaties or other agreements, in conformity with international law, to which they are parties.

In exercising their sovereign rights, including the right to determine their laws and regulations, they will conform with their legal obligations under international law; they will furthermore pay due regard to and implement the provisions in the Final Act of the Conference on Security and Co-operation in Europe.

The participating States confirm that in the event of a conflict between the obligations of the Members of the United Nations under the Charter of the United Nations and their obligations under any treaty or other international agreement, their obligations under the Charter will prevail, in accordance with Article 103 of the Charter of the United Nations.

All the principles set forth above are of primary significance and, accordingly, they will be equally and unreservedly applied, each of them being interpreted taking into account the others.

The participating States express their determination fully to respect and apply these principles, as set forth in the present Declaration, in all aspects, to their mutual relations and co-operation in order to ensure to each participating State the benefits resulting from the respect and application of these principles by all.

The participating States, paying due regard to the principles above and, in particular, to the first sentence of the tenth principle, "Fulfilment in good faith of obligations under international law", note that the present Declaration does not affect their rights and obligations, nor the corresponding treaties and other agreements and arrangements.

The participating States express the conviction that respect for these principles will encourage the development of normal and friendly relations and the progress of co-operation among them in all fields. They also express the conviction that respect for these principles will encourage the development of political contacts among them which in turn would contribute to better mutual understanding of their positions and views.

The participating States declare their intention to conduct their relations with all other States in the spirit of the principles contained in the present Declaration.

. . .

41. Concluding Document of the Vienna Meeting 1986[1] of representatives of the participating States of the Conference on Security and Co-operation in Europe
(Excerpt)

CO-OPERATION IN HUMANITARIAN AND OTHER FIELDS

The participating States,

Considering that co-operation in humanitarian and other fields is an essential factor for the development of their relations,

Agreeing that their co-operation in these fields should take place in full respect for the principles guiding relations between participating States as set forth in the Final Act as well as for the provisions in the Madrid Concluding Document and in the present Document pertaining to those principles,

Confirming that, in implementing the provisions concerning co-operation in humanitarian and other fields in the framework of their laws and regulations, they will ensure that those laws and regulations conform with their obligations under international law and are brought into harmony with their CSCE commitments,

Recognizing that the implementation of the relevant provisions of the Final Act and of the Madrid Concluding Document requires continuous and intensified efforts,

Have adopted and will implement the following:

Human Contacts

(1)   In implementing the human contacts provisions of the Final Act, the Madrid Concluding Document and the present Document, they will fully respect their obligations under international law as referred to in the subchapter of the present Document devoted to principles, in particular that everyone shall be free to leave any country, including his own, and to return to his country, as well as their international commitments in this field.

---

[1] The meeting was held from 4 November 1986 to 17 January 1989.

(2)   They will ensure that their policies concerning entry into their territories are fully consistent with the aims set out in the relevant provisions of the Final Act, the Madrid Concluding Document and the present Document.

(3)   They will take the necessary steps to find solutions as expeditiously as possible, but in any case within six months, to all applications based on the human contacts provisions of the Final Act and the Madrid Concluding Document, outstanding at the conclusion of the Vienna Follow-up Meeting.

(4)   Thereafter they will conduct regular reviews in order to ensure that all applications based on the human contacts provisions of the Final Act and of the other aforementioned CSCE documents are being dealt with in a manner consistent with those provisions.

(5)   They will decide upon applications relating to family meetings in accordance with the Final Act and the other aforementioned CSCE documents in as short a time as possible and in normal practice within one month.

(6)   In the same manner they will decide upon applications relating to family reunification or marriage between citizens of different States, in normal practice within three months.

(7)   In dealing favourably with applications relating to family meetings, they will take due account of the wishes of the applicant, in particular on the timing and sufficiently long duration of such meetings, and on travelling together with other members of his family for joint family meetings.

(8)   In dealing favourably with applications relating to family meetings, they will also allow visits to and from more distant relatives.

(9)   In dealing favourably with applications relating to family reunification or marriage between citizens of different States, they will respect the wishes of the applicants on the country of destination ready to accept them.

(10)   They will pay particular attention to the solution of problems involving the reunification of minor children with their parents. In this context and on the basis of the relevant provisions of the Final Act and of the other aforementioned CSCE documents, they will ensure:

—That an application for this purpose submitted while the child is a minor will be dealt with favourably and expeditiously in order to effect the reunification without delay; and

—That adequate arrangements are made to protect the interests and welfare of the children concerned.

(11)   They will consider the scope for gradually reducing and eventually eliminating any requirement which might exist for travellers to obtain local currency in excess of actual expenditure, giving priority to persons

travelling for the purpose of family meetings. They will accord such persons the opportunity in practice to bring in or to take out with them personal possessions or gifts.

(12)   They will pay immediate attention to applications for travel of an urgent humanitarian nature and deal with them favourably as follows:

—They will decide within three working days upon applications relating to visits to a seriously ill or dying family member, travel to attend the funeral of a family member or travel by those who have a proven need of urgent medical treatment or who can be shown to be critically or terminally ill.

—They will decide as expeditiously as possible upon applications relating to travel by those who are seriously ill or by the elderly, and other travel of an urgent humanitarian nature.

They will intensify efforts by their local, regional and central authorities concerned with the implementation of the above, and ensure that charges for giving priority treatment to such applications do not exceed costs actually incurred.

(13)   In dealing with applications for travel for family meetings, family reunification or marriage between citizens of different States, they will ensure that acts or omissions by members of the applicant's family do not adversely affect the rights of the applicant as set forth in the relevant international instruments.

(14)   They will ensure that all documents necessary for applications based on the human contacts provisions of the Final Act and of the other aforementioned CSCE documents are easily accessible to the applicant. The documents will remain valid throughout the application procedure. In the event of a renewed application the documents already submitted by the applicant in connection with previous applications will be taken into consideration.

(15)   They will simplify practices and gradually reduce administrative requirements for applications based on the human contacts provisions of the Final Act and of the other aforementioned CSCE documents.

(16)   They will ensure that, when applications based on the human contacts provisions of the Final Act and of the other aforementioned CSCE documents are refused for reasons specified in the relevant international instruments, the applicant is promptly provided in writing with an official notification of the grounds on which the decision was based. As a rule and in all cases where the applicant so requests, he will be given the necessary information about the procedure for making use of any effective administrative or judicial remedies against the decision available to him as envisaged in the above-mentioned international instruments. In cases where exit for

permanent settlement abroad is involved, this information will be provided as part of the official notification foreseen above.

(17)   If in this context an individual's application for travel abroad has been refused for reasons of national security, they will ensure that, within strictly warranted time limits, any restriction on that individual's travel is as short as possible and is not applied in an arbitrary manner. They will also ensure that the applicant can have the refusal reviewed within six months and, should the need arise, at regular intervals thereafter so that any changes in the circumstances surrounding the refusal, such as time elapsed since the applicant was last engaged in work or duties involving national security, are taken into account. Before individuals take up such work or duties they will be formally notified if and how this could affect applications they might submit for such travel.

(18)   Within one year of the conclusion of the Vienna Follow-up Meeting they will publish and make easily accessible, where this has not already been done, all their laws and statutory regulations concerning movement by individuals within their territory and travel between States.

(19)   In dealing favourably with applications based on the human contacts provisions of the Final Act and of the other aforementioned CSCE documents, they will ensure that these are dealt with in good time in order, *inter alia*, to take due account of important family, personal or professional considerations significant for the applicant.

(20)   They will deal favourably with applications for travel abroad without distinction of any kind, such as race, colour, sex, language, religion, political or other opinion, national or social origin, property, birth, age or other status. They will ensure that any refusal does not affect applications submitted by other persons.

(21)   They will further facilitate travel on an individual or collective basis for personal or professional reasons and for tourism, such as travel by delegations, groups and individuals. To this end they will reduce the time for the consideration of applications for such travel to a minimum.

(22)   They will give serious consideration to proposals for concluding agreements on the issuing of multiple entry visas and the reciprocal easing of visa processing formalities, and consider possibilities for the reciprocal abolition of entry visas on the basis of agreements between them.

(23)   They will consider adhering to the relevant multilateral instruments as well as concluding complementary or other bilateral agreements, if necessary, in order to improve arrangements for ensuring effective consular, legal and medical assistance for citizens of other participating States temporarily on their territory.

(24)   They will take any necessary measures to ensure that citizens of other participating States temporarily on their territory for personal or professional reasons, *inter alia* for the purpose of participating in cultural, scientific and educational activities, are afforded appropriate personal safety, where this is not already the case.

(25)   They will facilitate and encourage the establishment and maintenance of direct personal contacts between their citizens as well as between representatives of their institutions and organizations through travel between States and other means of communication.

(26)   They will facilitate such contacts and co-operation among their peoples through such measures as direct sports exchanges on a local and regional level, the unimpeded establishment and implementation of town-twinning arrangements, as well as student and teacher exchanges.

(27)   They will encourage the further development of direct contacts between young people, as well as between governmental and non-governmental youth and student organizations and institutions; the conclusion between such organizations and institutions of bilateral and multilateral arrangements and programmes; and the holding on a bilateral and multilateral basis of educational, cultural and other events and activities by and for young people.

(28)   They will make further efforts to facilitate travel and tourism by young people, *inter alia* by recommending to those of their railway authorities which are members of the International Union of Railways (UIC) that they expand the Inter-Rail system to cover all their European networks and by recommending to those of their railway authorities which are not members of the UIC that they consider establishing similar facilities.

(29)   In accordance with the Universal Postal Convention and the International Telecommunication Convention, they will:

— Guarantee the freedom of transit of postal communication;

—Ensure the rapid and unhindered delivery of correspondence, including personal mail and parcels;

—Respect the privacy and integrity of postal and telephone communications; and

—Ensure the conditions necessary for rapid and uninterrupted telephone calls, including the use of international direct dialling systems, where they exist, and their development.

(30)   They will encourage direct personal contacts between the citizens of their States, *inter alia* by facilitating individual travel within their countries and by allowing foreigners to meet their citizens as well as, when invited to do so, to stay in private homes.

(31)   They will ensure that the status of persons belonging to national minorities or regional cultures on their territories is equal to that of other citizens with regard to human contacts under the Final Act and the other aforementioned CSCE documents and that these persons can establish and maintain such contacts through travel and other means of communication, including contacts with citizens of other States with whom they share a common national origin or cultural heritage.

(32)   They will allow believers, religious faiths and their representatives, in groups or on an individual basis, to establish and maintain direct personal contacts and communication with each other, in their own and other countries, *inter alia* through travel, pilgrimages and participation in assemblies and other religious events. In this context and commensurate with such contacts and events, those concerned will be allowed to acquire, receive and carry with them religious publications and objects related to the practice of their religion or belief.

(33)   They heard accounts of the Meeting of Experts on Human Contacts held in Bern from 15 April to 26 May 1986. Noting that no conclusions had been agreed upon at the Meeting, they regarded both the frankness of the discussion and the greater degree of openness in the exchanges as welcome developments. In this respect they noted the particular importance of the fact that proposals made at the Meeting had received further consideration at the Vienna Follow-up Meeting.

Information

(34)   They will continue efforts to contribute to an ever wider knowledge and understanding of life in their States, thus promoting confidence between peoples.

They will make further efforts to facilitate the freer and wider dissemination of information of all kinds, to encourage co-operation in the field of information and to improve the working conditions for journalists.

In this connection and in accordance with the International Covenant on Civil and Political Rights, the Universal Declaration of Human Rights and their relevant international commitments concerning seeking, receiving and imparting information of all kinds, they will ensure that individuals can freely choose their sources of information. In this context they will

—Ensure that radio services operating in accordance with the ITU Radio Regulations can be directly and normally received in their States; and

—Allow individuals, institutions and organizations, while respecting intellectual property rights, including copyright, to obtain, possess, reproduce and distribute information material of all kinds.

To these ends they will remove any restrictions inconsistent with the above-mentioned obligations and commitments.

(35)   They will take every opportunity offered by modern means of communication, including cable and satellites, to increase the freer and wider dissemination of information of all kinds. They will also encourage co-operation and exchanges between their relevant institutions, organizations and technical experts, and work towards the harmonization of technical standards and norms. They will bear in mind the effects of these modern means of communication on their mass media.

(36)   They will ensure in practice that official information bulletins can be freely distributed on their territory by the diplomatic and other official missions and consular posts of the other participating States.

(37)   They will encourage radio and television organizations, on the basis of arrangements between them, to broadcast live, especially in the organizing countries, programmes and discussions with participants from different States and to broadcast statements of and interviews with political and other personalities from the participating States.

(38)   They will encourage radio and television organizations to report on different aspects of life in other participating States and to increase the number of telebridges between their countries.

(39)   Recalling that the legitimate pursuit of journalists' professional activity will neither render them liable to expulsion nor otherwise penalize them, they will refrain from taking restrictive measures such as withdrawing a journalist's accreditation or expelling him because of the content of the reporting of the journalist or of his information media.

(40)   They will ensure that, in pursuing this activity, journalists, including those representing media from other participating States, are free to seek access to and maintain contacts with public and private sources of information and that their need for professional confidentiality is respected.

(41)   They will respect the copyright of journalists.

(42)   On the basis of arrangements between them, where necessary, and for the purpose of regular reporting, they will grant accreditation, where it is required, and multiple entry visas to journalists from other participating States, regardless of their domicile. On this basis they will reduce to a maximum of two months the period for issuing both accreditation and multiple entry visas to journalists.

(43)   They will facilitate the work of foreign journalists by providing relevant information, on request, on matters of practical concern, such as import regulations, taxation and accommodation.

(44)   They will ensure that official press conferences and, as appropriate, other similar official press events are also open to foreign journalists, upon accreditation, where this is required.

(45)   They will ensure in practice that persons belonging to national minorities or regional cultures on their territories can disseminate, have access to, and exchange information in their mother tongue.

(46)   They agree to convene an Information Forum to discuss improvement of the circulation of, access to and exchange of information; co-operation in the field of information; and the improvement of working conditions for journalists. The Forum will be held in London from 18 April to 12 May 1989. It will be attended by personalities from the participating States in the field of information. The agenda, timetable and other organizational modalities are set out in Annex VIII.

Co-operation and exchanges in the field of culture

(47)   They will promote and give full effect to their cultural co-operation, *inter alia* through the implementation of any relevant bilateral and multilateral agreements concluded among them in the various fields of culture.

(48)   They will encourage non-governmental organizations interested in the field of culture to participate, together with State institutions, in the elaboration and implementation of these agreements and specific projects, as well as in the elaboration of practical measures concerning cultural exchange and co-operation.

(49)   They will favour the establishment, by mutual agreement, of cultural institutes or centres of other participating States on their territory. Unhindered access by the public to such institutes or centres as well as their normal functioning will be assured.

(50)   They will assure unhindered access by the public to cultural events organized on their territory by persons or institutions from other participating States and ensure that the organizers can use all means available in the host country to publicize such events.

(51)   They will facilitate and encourage direct personal contacts in the field of culture, on both an individual and a collective basis, as well as contacts between cultural institutions, associations of creative and performing artists and other organizations in order to increase the opportunities for their citizens to acquaint themselves directly with the creative work in and from other participating States.

(52)   They will ensure the unimpeded circulation of works of art and other cultural objects, subject only to those restrictions which are aimed at preserving their cultural heritage, are based on respect for intellectual and

artistic property rights or derive from their international commitments on the circulation of cultural property.

(53)   They will encourage co-operation between and joint artistic endeavours of persons from different participating States who are engaged in cultural activities; as appropriate, facilitate specific initiatives to this end by such persons, institutions and organizations and encourage the participation of young people in such initiatives. In this context they will encourage meetings and symposia, exhibitions, festivals and tours by ensembles or companies, and research and training programmes in which persons from the other participating States may also freely take part and make their contribution.

(54)   The replacement of persons or groups invited to participate in a cultural activity will be exceptional and subject to prior agreement by the inviting party.

(55)   They will encourage the holding of film weeks including, as appropriate, meetings of artists and experts as well as lectures on cinematographic art; facilitate and encourage direct contacts between film directors and producers with a view to co-producing films; and encourage co-operation in the protection of film material and the exchange of technical information and publications about the cinema.

(56)   They will explore the scope for computerizing bibliographies and catalogues of cultural works and productions in a standard form and disseminating them.

(57)   They will encourage museums and art galleries to develop direct contacts, *inter alia* with a view to organizing exhibitions, including loans of works of art, and exchanging catalogues.

(58)   They will renew their efforts to give effect to the provisions of the Final Act and the Madrid Concluding Document relating to less widely spoken languages. They will also encourage initiatives aimed at increasing the number of translations of literature from and into these languages and improving their quality, in particular by the holding of workshops involving translators, authors and publishers, by the publication of dictionaries and, where appropriate, by the exchange of translators through scholarships.

(59)   They will ensure that persons belonging to national minorities or regional cultures on their territories can maintain and develop their own culture in all its aspects, including language, literature and religion; and that they can preserve their cultural and historical monuments and objects.

(60)   They heard accounts of the work done and the ideas advanced during the Cultural Forum held in Budapest from 15 October to 25 November 1985. Noting that no conclusions had been agreed upon at the Forum, they welcomed the fact that many of the useful ideas and proposals put forward there had received renewed consideration at the Vienna Follow-up

Meeting and that institutions and organizations in the participating States have based many activities on these ideas. They expressed their appreciation of the significant contributions made to the event by leading personalities in the field of culture, and noted, in the light of the experience gained, the importance of securing, both inside and outside future meetings of this nature, arrangements which would permit a freer and more spontaneous discussion.

(61)   Taking duly into account the originality and diversity of their respective cultures, they will encourage efforts to explore common features and to foster greater awareness of their cultural heritage. Accordingly they will encourage initiatives which may contribute to a better knowledge of the cultural heritage of the other participating States in all its forms, including regional aspects and folk art.

(62)   They agree to convene a Symposium on the Cultural Heritage of the CSCE participating States. The Symposium will take place in Cracow from 28 May to 7 June 1991. It will be attended by scholars and other personalities from the participating States who are engaged in cultural activities. The agenda, timetable and other organizational modalities are set out in Annex IX.

Co-operation and exchanges in the field of education

(63)   They will ensure access by all to the various types and levels of education without discrimination as to race, colour, sex, language, religion, political or other opinion, national or social origin, property, birth or other status.

(64)   In order to encourage wider co-operation in science and education, they will facilitate unimpeded communication between universities and other institutions of higher education and research. They will also facilitate direct personal contacts, including contacts through travel, between scholars, scientists and other persons active in these fields.

(65)   They will also ensure unimpeded access by scholars, teachers and students from the other participating States to open information material available in public archives, libraries, research institutes and similar bodies.

(66)   They will facilitate exchanges of schoolchildren between their countries on the basis of bilateral arrangements, where necessary, including meeting and staying with families of the host country in their homes, with the aim of acquainting schoolchildren with life, traditions and education in other participating States.

(67)   They will encourage their relevant government agencies or educational institutions to include, as appropriate, the Final Act as a whole in the curricula of schools and universities.

(68) They will ensure that persons belonging to national minorities or regional cultures on their territories can give and receive instruction on their own culture, including instruction through parental transmission of language, religion and cultural identity to their children.

(69) They will encourage their radio and television organizations to inform each other of the educational programmes they produce and to consider exchanging such programmes.

(70) They will encourage direct contacts and co-operation between relevant governmental institutions or organizations in the field of education and science.

(71) They will encourage further co-operation and contacts between specialized institutions and experts in the field of education and rehabilitation of handicapped children.

HUMAN DIMENSION OF THE CSCE

The participating States,

Recalling the undertakings entered into in the Final Act and in other CSCE documents concerning respect for all human rights and fundamental freedoms, human contacts and other issues of a related humanitarian character,

Recognizing the need to improve the implementation of their CSCE commitments and their co-operation in these areas which are hereafter referred to as the human dimension of the CSCE,

Have, on the basis of the principles and provisions of the Final Act and of other relevant CSCE documents, decided:

1. To exchange information and respond to requests for information and to representations made to them by other participating States on questions relating to the human dimension of the CSCE. Such communications may be forwarded through diplomatic channels or be addressed to any agency designated for these purposes;

2. To hold bilateral meetings with other participating States that so request, in order to examine questions relating to the human dimension of the CSCE, including situations and specific cases, with a view to resolving them. The date and place of such meetings will be arranged by mutual agreement through diplomatic channels;

3. That any participating State which deems it necessary may bring situations and cases in the human dimension of the CSCE, including those which have been raised at the bilateral meetings described in paragraph 2, to the attention of other participating States through diplomatic channels;

4. That any participating State which deems it necessary may provide information on the exchanges of information and the responses to its requests for information and to representations (paragraph 1) and on the results of the bilateral meetings (paragraph 2), including information concerning situations and specific cases, at the meetings of the Conference on the Human Dimension as well as at the main CSCE Follow-up Meetings.

The participating States decide further to convene a Conference on the Human Dimension of the CSCE in order to achieve further progress concerning respect for all human rights and fundamental freedoms, human contacts and other issues of a related humanitarian character. The Conference will hold three meetings before the next CSCE Follow-up Meeting.

The Conference will:

—Review developments in the human dimension of the CSCE including the implementation of the relevant CSCE commitments;

—Evaluate the functioning of the procedures described in paragraphs 1 to 4 and discuss the information provided according to paragraph 4;

—Consider practical proposals for new measures aimed at improving the implementation of the commitments relating to the human dimension of the CSCE and enhancing the effectiveness of the procedures described in paragraphs 1 to 4.

On the basis of these proposals, the Conference will consider adopting new measures.

The first Meeting of the Conference will be held in Paris from 30 May to 23 June 1989.

The second Meeting of the Conference will be held in Copenhagen from 5 to 29 June 1990.

The third Meeting of the Conference will be held in Moscow from 10 September to 4 October 1991.

The agenda, timetable and other organizational modalities are set out in Annex X.

The next main CSCE Follow-up Meeting, to be held in Helsinki, commencing on 24 March 1992, will assess the functioning of the procedures set out in paragraphs 1 to 4 above and the progress made at the Meetings of the Conference on the Human Dimension of the CSCE. It will consider ways of further strengthening and improving these procedures and will take appropriate decisions.

. . .

42. Document of the Copenhagen Meeting of the Conference on the Human Dimension of the Conference on Security and Co-operation in Europe (*29 June 1990*)
(Excerpt)

. . .

I

(1)   The participating States express their conviction that the protection and promotion of human rights and fundamental freedoms is one of the basic purposes of government, and reaffirm that the recognition of these rights and freedoms constitutes the foundation of freedom, justice and peace.

(2)   They are determined to support and advance those principles of justice which form the basis of the rule of law. They consider that the rule of law does not mean merely a formal legality which assures regularity and consistency in the achievement and enforcement of democratic order, but justice based on the recognition and full acceptance of the supreme value of the human personality and guaranteed by institutions providing a framework for its fullest expression.

(3)   They reaffirm that democracy is an inherent element of the rule of law. They recognize the importance of pluralism with regard to political organizations.

(4)   They confirm that they will respect each other's right freely to choose and develop, in accordance with international human rights standards, their political, social, economic and cultural systems. In exercising this right, they will ensure that their laws, regulations, practices and policies conform with their obligations under international law and are brought into harmony with the provisions of the Declaration on Principles and other CSCE commitments.

(5)   They solemnly declare that among those elements of justice which are essential to the full expression of the inherent dignity and of the equal and inalienable rights of all human beings are the following:

(5.1)   Free elections that will be held at reasonable intervals by secret ballot or by equivalent free voting procedure, under conditions which ensure in practice the free expression of the opinion of the electors in the choice of their representatives;

389

(5.2) A form of government that is representative in character, in which the executive is accountable to the elected legislature or the electorate;

(5.3) The duty of the government and public authorities to comply with the constitution and to act in a manner consistent with law;

(5.4) A clear separation between the State and political parties; in particular, political parties will not be merged with the State;

(5.5) The activity of the government and the administration as well as that of the judiciary will be exercised in accordance with the system established by law. Respect for that system must be ensured;

(5.6) Military forces and the police will be under the control of, and accountable to, the civil authorities;

(5.7) Human rights and fundamental freedoms will be guaranteed by law and in accordance with their obligations under international law;

(5.8) Legislation, adopted at the end of a public procedure, and regulations will be published, that being the condition for their applicability. Those texts will be accessible to everyone;

(5.9) All persons are equal before the law and are entitled without any discrimination to the equal protection of the law. In this respect, the law will prohibit any discrimination and guarantee to all persons equal and effective protection against discrimination on any ground;

(5.10) Everyone will have an effective means of redress against administrative decisions, so as to guarantee respect for fundamental rights and ensure legal integrity;

(5.11) Administrative decisions against a person must be fully justifiable and must as a rule indicate the usual remedies available;

(5.12) The independence of judges and the impartial operation of the public judicial service will be ensured;

(5.13) The independence of legal practitioners will be recognized and protected, in particular as regards conditions for recruitment and practice;

(5.14) The rules relating to criminal procedure will contain a clear definition of powers in relation to prosecution and the measures preceding and accompanying prosecution;

(5.15) Any person arrested or detained on a criminal charge will have the right, so that the lawfulness of his arrest or detention can be decided, to be brought promptly before a judge or other officer authorized by law to exercise this function;

(5.16) In the determination of any criminal charge against him, or of his rights and obligations in a suit at law, everyone will be entitled to a fair and public hearing by a competent, independent and impartial tribunal established by law;

(5.17) Any person prosecuted will have the right to defend himself in person or through prompt legal assistance of his own choosing or, if he does not have sufficient means to pay for legal assistance, to be given it free when the interests of justice so require;

(5.18) No one will be charged with, tried for or convicted of any criminal offence unless the offence is provided for by a law which defines the elements of the offence with clarity and precision;

(5.19) Everyone will be presumed innocent until proved guilty according to law;

(5.20) Considering the important contribution of international instruments in the field of human rights to the rule of law at a national level, the participating States reaffirm that they will consider acceding to the International Covenant on Civil and Political Rights, the International Covenant on Economic, Social and Cultural Rights and other relevant international instruments, if they have not yet done so;

(5.21) In order to supplement domestic remedies and better to ensure that the participating States respect the international obligations they have undertaken, the participating States will consider acceding to a regional or global international convention concerning the protection of human rights, such as the European Convention on Human Rights or the Optional Protocol to the International Covenant on Civil and Political Rights, which provide for procedures of individual recourse to international bodies.

(6) The participating States declare that the will of the people, freely and fairly expressed through periodic and genuine elections, is the basis of the authority and legitimacy of all government. The participating States will accordingly respect the right of their citizens to take part in the governing of their country, either directly or through representatives freely chosen by them through fair electoral processes. They recognize their responsibility to defend and protect, in accordance with their laws, their international human rights obligations and their international commitments, the democratic order freely established through the will of the people against the activities of persons, groups or organizations that engage in or refuse to renounce terrorism or violence aimed at the overthrow of that order or of that of another participating State.

(7) To ensure that the will of the people serves as the basis of the authority of government, the participating States will

(7.1) — hold free elections at reasonable intervals, as established by law;

(7.2) — permit all seats in at least one chamber of the national legislature to be freely contested in a popular vote;

(7.3) — guarantee universal and equal suffrage to adult citizens;

(7.4) — that they are counted and reported honestly with the official results made public;

(7.5) — respect the right of citizens to seek political or public office, individually or as representatives of political parties or organizations, without discrimination;

(7.6) — respect the right of individuals and groups to establish, in full freedom, their own political parties or other political organizations and provide such political parties and organizations with the necessary legal guarantees to enable them to compete with each other on a basis of equal treatment before the law and by the authorities;

(7.7) — ensure that law and public policy work to permit political campaigning to be conducted in a fair and free atmosphere in which neither administrative action, violence nor intimidation bars the parties and the candidates from freely presenting their views and qualifications, or prevents the voters from learning and discussing them or from casting their vote free of fear of retribution;

(7.8) — provide that no legal or administrative obstacle stands in the way of unimpeded access to the media on a non-discriminatory basis for all political groupings and individuals wishing to participate in the electoral process;

(7.9) — ensure that candidates who obtain the necessary number of votes required by law are duly installed in office and are permitted to remain in office until their term expires or is otherwise brought to an end in a manner that is regulated by law in conformity with democratic parliamentary and constitutional procedures.

(8) The participating States consider that the presence of observers, both foreign and domestic, can enhance the electoral process for States in which elections are taking place. They therefore invite observers from any other CSCE participating States and any appropriate private institutions and organizations who may wish to do so to observe the course of their national election proceedings, to the extent permitted by law. They will also endeavour to facilitate similar access for election proceedings held below the national level. Such observers will undertake not to interfere in the electoral proceedings.

II

(9) The participating States reaffirm that

(9.1) Everyone will have the right to freedom of expression including the right to communication. This right will include freedom to hold opinions and to receive and impart information and ideas without interference by public authority and regardless of frontiers. The exercise of this right may be subject only to such restrictions as are prescribed by law and are consistent with international standards. In particular, no limitation will be imposed on access to, and use of, means of reproducing documents of any kind, while respecting, however, rights relating to intellectual property, including copyright;

(9.2) Everyone will have the right of peaceful assembly and demonstration. Any restrictions which may be placed on the exercise of these rights will be prescribed by law and consistent with international standards;

(9.3) The right of association will be guaranteed. The right to form and—subject to the general right of a trade union to determine its own membership—freely to join a trade union will be guaranteed. These rights will exclude any prior control. Freedom of association for workers, including the freedom to strike, will be guaranteed, subject to limitations prescribed by law and consistent with international standards;

(9.4) Everyone will have the right to freedom of thought, conscience and religion. This right includes freedom to change one's religion or belief and freedom to manifest one's religion or belief, either alone or in community with others, in public or in private, through worship, teaching, practice and observance. The exercise of these rights may be subject only to such restrictions as are prescribed by law and are consistent with international standards;

(9.5) They will respect the right of everyone to leave any country, including his own, and to return to his country, consistent with a State's international obligations and CSCE commitments. Restrictions on this right will have the character of very rare exceptions, will be considered necessary only if they respond to a specific public need, pursue a legitimate aim and are proportionate to that aim, and will not be abused or applied in an arbitrary manner.

(9.6) Everyone has the right peacefully to enjoy his property either on his own or in common with others. No one may be deprived of his property except in the public interest and subject to the conditions provided for by law and consistent with international commitments and obligations.

(10) In reaffirming their commitment to ensure effectively the rights of the individual to know and act upon human rights and fundamental freedoms, and to contribute actively, individually or in association with others to their promotion and protection, the participating States express their commitment to

(10.1) — respect the right of everyone, individually or in association with others, to seek, receive and impart freely views and information on human rights and fundamental freedoms, including the rights to disseminate and publish such views and information;

(10.2) — respect the rights of everyone, individually or in association with others, to study and discuss the observance of human rights and fundamental freedoms and to develop and discuss ideas for improved protection of human rights and better means for ensuring compliance with international human rights standards;

(10.3) — ensure that individuals are permitted to exercise the right to association, including the right to form, join and participate effectively in non-governmental organizations which seek the promotion and protection of human rights and fundamental freedoms, including trade unions and human rights monitoring groups;

(10.4) — allow members of such groups and organizations to have unhindered access to and communication with similar bodies within and outside their countries and with international organizations, to engage in exchanges, contacts and co-operation with such groups and organizations and to solicit, receive and utilize for the purpose of promoting and protecting human rights and fundamental freedoms voluntary financial contributions from national and international sources as provided for by law.

(11)　　The participating States further affirm that, where violations of human rights and fundamental freedoms are alleged to have occurred, the effective remedies available include

(11.1) — the right of the individual to seek and receive adequate legal assistance;

(11.2) — the right of the individual to seek and receive assistance from others in defending human rights and fundamental freedoms, and to assist others in defending human rights and fundamental freedoms;

(11.3) — the right of individuals or groups acting on their behalf to communicate with international bodies with competence to receive and consider information concerning allegations of human rights abuses.

(12)　　The participating States, wishing to ensure greater transparency in the implementation of the commitments undertaken in the Vienna Concluding Document under the heading of the human dimension of the CSCE, decide to accept as a confidence-building measure the presence of observers sent by participating States and representatives of non-governmental organizations and other interested persons at proceedings before courts as provided for in national legislation and international law; it is understood that proceedings may only be held *in camera* in the circumstances prescribed by law and consistent with obligations under international law and international commitments.

(13)　　The participating States decide to accord particular attention to the recognition of the rights of the child, his civil rights and his individual freedoms, his economic, social and cultural rights, and his right to special protection against all forms of violence and exploitation. They will consider acceding to the Convention on the Rights of the Child, if they have not yet done so, which was opened for signature by States on 26 January 1990.

They will recognize in their domestic legislation the rights of the child as affirmed in the international agreements to which they are parties.

(14)   The participating States agree to encourage the creation, within their countries, of conditions for the training of students and trainees from other participating States, including persons taking vocational and technical courses. They also agree to promote travel by young people from their countries for the purpose of obtaining education in other participating States and to that end to encourage the conclusion, where appropriate, of bilateral and multilateral agreements between their relevant governmental institutions, organizations and educational establishments.

(15)   The participating States will act in such a way as to facilitate the transfer of sentenced persons and encourage those participating States which are not Parties to the Convention on the Transfer of Sentenced Persons, signed at Strasbourg on 21 November 1983, to consider acceding to the Convention.

(16)   The participating States

(16.1)   — reaffirm their commitment to prohibit torture and other cruel, inhuman or degrading treatment or punishment, to take effective legislative, administrative, judicial and other measures to prevent and punish such practices, to protect individuals from any psychiatric or other medical practices that violate human rights and fundamental freedoms and to take effective measures to prevent and punish such practices;

(16.2)   — intend, as a matter of urgency, to consider acceding to the Convention against Torture and Other Cruel, Inhuman or Degrading Treatment or Punishment, if they have not yet done so, and recognizing the competences of the Committee against Torture under articles 21 and 22 of the Convention and withdrawing reservations regarding the competence of the Committee under article 20;

(16.3)   — stress that no exceptional circumstances whatsoever, whether a state of war or a threat of war, internal political instability or any other public emergency, may be invoked as a justification of torture;

(16.4)   — will ensure that education and information regarding the prohibition against torture are fully included in the training of law enforcement personnel, civil or military, medical personnel, public officials and other persons who may be involved in the custody, interrogation or treatment of any individual subjected to any form of arrest, detention or imprisonment;

(16.5)   — will keep under systematic review interrogation rules, instructions, methods and practices as well as arrangements for the custody and treatment of persons subjected to any form of arrest, detention or imprisonment in any territory under their jurisdiction, with a view to preventing any cases of torture;

(16.6) — will take up with priority for consideration and for appropriate action, in accordance with the agreed measures and procedures for the effective implementation of the commitments relating to the human dimension of the CSCE, any cases of torture and other inhuman or degrading treatment or punishment made known to them through official channels or coming from any other reliable source of information;

(16.7) — will act upon the understanding that preserving and guaranteeing the life and security of any individual subjected to any form of torture and other inhuman or degrading treatment or punishment will be the sole criterion in determining the urgency and priorities to be accorded in taking appropriate remedial action; and, therefore, the consideration of any cases of torture and other inhuman or degrading treatment or punishment within the framework of any other international body or mechanism may not be invoked as a reason for refraining from consideration and appropriate action in accordance with the agreed measures and procedures for the effective implementation of the commitments relating to the human dimension of the CSCE.

(17)   The participating States

(17.1) — recall the commitment undertaken in the Vienna Concluding Document to keep the question of capital punishment under consideration and to co-operate within relevant international organizations;

(17.2) — recall, in this context, the adoption by the General Assembly of the United Nations, on 15 December 1989, of the Second Optional Protocol to the International Covenant on Civil and Political Rights, aiming at the abolition of the death penalty;

(17.3) — note the restrictions and safeguards regarding the use of the death penalty which have been adopted by the international community, in particular article 6 of the International Covenant on Civil and Political Rights;

(17.4) — note the provisions of the Sixth Protocol to the European Convention for the Protection of Human Rights and Fundamental Freedoms, concerning the abolition of the death penalty;

(17.5) — note recent measures taken by a number of participating States towards the abolition of capital punishment;

(17.6) — note the activities of several non-governmental organizations on the question of the death penalty;

(17.7) — will exchange information within the framework of the Conference on the Human Dimension on the question of the abolition of the death penalty and keep that question under consideration;

(17.8) — will make available to the public information regarding the use of the death penalty.

(18)   The participating States

(18.1) — note that the United Nations Commission on Human Rights has recognized the right of everyone to have conscientious objections to military service;

(18.2) — note recent measures taken by a number of participating States to permit exemption from compulsory military service on the basis of conscientious objections;

(18.3) — note the activities of several non-governmental organizations on the question of conscientious objections to compulsory military service;

(18.4) — agree to consider introducing, where this has not yet been done, various forms of alternative service, which are compatible with the reasons for conscientious objection, such forms of alternative service being in principle of a non-combatant or civilian nature, in the public interest and of a non-punitive nature;

(18.5) — will make available to the public information on this issue;

(18.6) — will keep under consideration, within the framework of the Conference on the Human Dimension, the relevant questions related to the exemption from compulsory military service, where it exists, of individuals on the basis of conscientious objections to armed service, and will exchange information on these questions.

(19) The participating States affirm that freer movement and contacts among their citizens are important in the context of the protection and promotion of human rights and fundamental freedoms. They will ensure that their policies concerning entry into their territories are fully consistent with the aims set out in the relevant provisions of the Final Act, the Madrid Concluding Document and the Vienna Concluding Document. While reaffirming their determination not to recede from the commitments contained in CSCE documents, they undertake to implement fully and improve present commitments in the field of human contacts, including on a bilateral and multilateral basis. In this context they will

(19.1) — strive to implement the procedures for entry into their territories, including the issuing of visas and passport and customs control, in good faith and without unjustified delay. Where necessary, they will shorten the waiting time for visa decisions, as well as simplify practices and reduce administrative requirements for visa applications;

(19.2) — ensure, in dealing with visa applications, that these are processed as expeditiously as possible in order, *inter alia*, to take due account of important family, personal or professional considerations, especially in cases of an urgent, humanitarian nature;

(19.3) — endeavour, where necessary, to reduce fees charged in connection with visa applications to the lowest possible level.

(20)   The participating States concerned will consult and, where appropriate, co-operate in dealing with problems that might emerge as a result of the increased movement of persons.

(21)   The participating States recommend the consideration, at the next CSCE Follow-up Meeting in Helsinki, of the advisability of holding a meeting of experts on consular matters.

(22)   The participating States reaffirm that the protection and promotion of the rights of migrant workers have their human dimension. In this context, they

(22.1) — agree that the protection and promotion of the rights of migrant workers are the concern of all participating States and that as such they should be addressed within the CSCE process;

(22.2) — reaffirm their commitment to implement fully in their domestic legislation the rights of migrant workers provided for in international agreements to which they are parties;

(22.3) — consider that, in future international instruments concerning the rights of migrant workers, they should take into account the fact that this issue is of importance for all of them;

(22.4) — express their readiness to examine, at future CSCE meetings, the relevant aspects of the further promotion of the rights of migrant workers and their families.

(23)   The participating States reaffirm their conviction expressed in the Vienna Concluding Document that the promotion of economic, social and cultural rights as well as of civil and political rights is of paramount importance for human dignity and for the attainment of the legitimate aspirations of every individual. They also reaffirm their commitment taken in the Document of the Bonn Conference on Economic Co-operation in Europe to the promotion of social justice and the improvement of living and working conditions. In the context of continuing their efforts with a view to achieving progressively the full realization of economic, social and cultural rights by all appropriate means, they will pay special attention to problems in the areas of employment, housing, social security, health, education and culture.

(24)   The participating States will ensure that the exercise of all the human rights and fundamental freedoms set out above will not be subject to any restrictions except those which are provided by law and are consistent with their obligations under international law, in particular the International Covenant on Civil and Political Rights, and with their international commitments, in particular the Universal Declaration of Human Rights. These restrictions have the character of exceptions. The participating States will ensure that these restrictions are not abused and are not applied in an arbitrary manner, but in such a way that the effective exercise of these rights is ensured.

Any restriction on rights and freedoms must, in a democratic society, relate to one of the objectives of the applicable law and be strictly proportionate to the aim of that law.

(25) The participating States confirm that any derogations from obligations relating to human rights and fundamental freedoms during a state of public emergency must remain strictly within the limits provided for by international law, in particular the relevant international instruments by which they are bound, especially with respect to rights from which there can be no derogation. They also reaffirm that

(25.1) — measures derogating from such obligations must be taken in strict conformity with the procedural requirements laid down in those instruments;

(25.2) — the imposition of a state of public emergency must be proclaimed officially, publicly, and in accordance with the provisions laid down by law;

(25.3) — measures derogating from obligations will be limited to the extent strictly required by the exigencies of the situation;

(25.4) — such measures will not discriminate solely on the grounds of race, colour, sex, language, religion, social origin or of belonging to a minority.

III

(26) The participating States recognize that vigorous democracy depends on the existence as an integral part of national life of democratic values and practices as well as an extensive range of democratic institutions. They will therefore encourage, facilitate and, where appropriate, support practical cooperative endeavours and the sharing of information, ideas and expertise among themselves and by direct contacts and co-operation between individuals, groups and organizations in areas including the following:

—constitutional law, reform and development,

—electoral legislation, administration and observation,

—establishment and management of courts and legal systems,

—the development of an impartial and effective public service where recruitment and advancement are based on a merit system,

—law enforcement,

—local government and decentralization,

—access to information and protection of privacy,

—developing political parties and their role in pluralistic societies,

—free and independent trade unions,

—cooperative movements,

—developing other forms of free associations and public interest groups,

—journalism, independent media, and intellectual and cultural life,

—the teaching of democratic values, institutions and practices in educational institutions and the fostering of an atmosphere of free enquiry.

Such endeavours may cover the range of co-operation encompassed in the human dimension of the CSCE, including training, exchange of information, books and instructional materials, cooperative programmes and projects, academic and professional exchanges and conferences, scholarships, research grants, provision of expertise and advice, business and scientific contacts and programmes.

(27)   The participating States will also facilitate the establishment and strengthening of independent national institutions in the area of human rights and the rule of law, which may also serve as focal points for coordination and collaboration between such institutions in the participating States. They propose that co-operation be encouraged between parliamentarians from participating States, including through existing inter-parliamentary associations and, *inter alia*, through joint commissions, television debates involving parliamentarians, meetings and round-table discussions. They will also encourage existing institutions, such as organizations within the United Nations system and the Council of Europe, to continue and expand the work they have begun in this area.

(28)   The participating States recognize the important expertise of the Council of Europe in the field of human rights and fundamental freedoms and agree to consider further ways and means to enable the Council of Europe to make a contribution to the human dimension of the CSCE. They agree that the nature of this contribution could be examined further in a future CSCE forum.

(29)   The participating States will consider the idea of convening a meeting or seminar of experts to review and discuss cooperative measures designed to promote and sustain viable democratic institutions in participating States, including comparative studies of legislation in participating States in the area of human rights and fundamental freedoms, *inter alia* drawing upon the experience acquired in this area by the Council of Europe and the activities of the Commission "Democracy through Law".

IV

(30)   The participating States recognize that the questions relating to national minorities can only be satisfactorily resolved in a democratic political framework based on the rule of law, with a functioning independent judiciary. This framework guarantees full respect for human rights and funda-

mental freedoms, equal rights and status for all citizens, the free expression of all their legitimate interests and aspirations, political pluralism, social tolerance and the implementation of legal rules that place effective restraints on the abuse of governmental power.

They also recognize the important role of non-governmental organizations, including political parties, trade unions, human rights organizations and religious groups, in the promotion of tolerance, cultural diversity and the resolution of questions relating to national minorities.

They further reaffirm that respect for the rights of persons belonging to national minorities as part of universally recognized human rights is an essential factor for peace, justice, stability and democracy in the participating States.

(31)   Persons belonging to national minorities have the right to exercise fully and effectively their human rights and fundamental freedoms without any discrimination and in full equality before the law.

The participating States will adopt, where necessary, special measures for the purpose of ensuring to persons belonging to national minorities full equality with the other citizens in the exercise and enjoyment of human rights and fundamental freedoms.

(32)   To belong to a national minority is a matter of a person's individual choice and no disadvantage may arise from the exercise of such choice.

Persons belonging to national minorities have the right freely to express, preserve and develop their ethnic, cultural, linguistic or religious identity and to maintain and develop their culture in all its aspects, free of any attempts at assimilation against their will. In particular, they have the right

(32.1)   — to use freely their mother tongue in private as well as in public;

(32.2)   — to establish and maintain their own educational, cultural and religious institutions, organizations or associations, which can seek voluntary financial and other contributions as well as public assistance, in conformity with national legislation;

(32.3)   — to profess and practise their religion, including the acquisition, possession and use of religious materials, and to conduct religious educational activities in their mother tongue;

(32.4)   — to establish and maintain unimpeded contacts among themselves within their country as well as contacts across frontiers with citizens of other States with whom they share a common ethnic or national origin, cultural heritage or religious beliefs;

(32.5)   — to disseminate, have access to and exchange information in their mother tongue;

(32.6) — to establish and maintain organizations or associations within their country and to participate in international non-governmental organizations.

Persons belonging to national minorities can exercise and enjoy their rights individually as well as in community with other members of their group. No disadvantage may arise for a person belonging to a national minority on account of the exercise or non-exercise of any such rights.

(33)	The participating States will protect the ethnic, cultural, linguistic and religious identity of national minorities on their territory and create conditions for the promotion of that identity. They will take the necessary measures to that effect after due consultations, including contacts with organizations or associations of such minorities, in accordance with the decision-making procedures of each State.

Any such measures will be in conformity with the principles of equality and non-discrimination with respect to the other citizens of the participating State concerned.

(34)	The participating States will endeavour to ensure that persons belonging to national minorities, notwithstanding the need to learn the official language or languages of the State concerned, have adequate opportunities for instruction of their mother tongue or in their mother tongue, as well as, wherever possible and necessary, for its use before public authorities, in conformity with applicable national legislation.

In the context of the teaching of history and culture in educational establishments, they will also take account of the history and culture of national minorities.

(35)	The participating States will respect the right of persons belonging to national minorities to effective participation in public affairs, including participation in the affairs relating to the protection and promotion of the identity of such minorities.

The participating States note the efforts undertaken to protect and create conditions for the promotion of the ethnic, cultural, linguistic and religious identity of certain national minorities by establishing, as one of the possible means to achieve these aims, appropriate local or autonomous administrations corresponding to the specific historical and territorial circumstances of such minorities and in accordance with the policies of the State concerned.

(36)	The participating States recognize the particular importance of increasing constructive co-operation among themselves on questions relating to national minorities. Such co-operation seeks to promote mutual understanding and confidence, friendly and good-neighbourly relations, international peace, security and justice.

Every participating State will promote a climate of mutual respect, understanding, co-operation and solidarity among all persons living on its territory, without distinction as to ethnic or national origin or religion, and will encourage the solution of problems through dialogue based on the principles of the rule of law.

(37)   None of these commitments may be interpreted as implying any right to engage in any activity or perform any action in contravention of the purposes and principles of the Charter of the United Nations, other obligations under international law or the provisions of the Final Act, including the principle of territorial integrity of States.

(38)   The participating States, in their efforts to protect and promote the rights of persons belonging to national minorities, will fully respect their undertakings under existing human rights conventions and other relevant international instruments and consider adhering to the relevant conventions, if they have not yet done so, including those providing for a right of complaint by individuals.

(39)   The participating States will co-operate closely in the competent international organizations to which they belong, including the United Nations and, as appropriate, the Council of Europe, bearing in mind their ongoing work with respect to questions relating to national minorities.

They will consider convening a meeting of experts for a thorough discussion of the issue of national minorities.

(40)   The participating States clearly and unequivocally condemn totalitarianism, racial and ethnic hatred, anti-semitism, xenophobia and discrimination against anyone as well as persecution on religious and ideological grounds. In this context, they also recognize the particular problems of Roma (gypsies).

They declare their firm intention to intensify the efforts to combat these phenomena in all their forms and therefore will

(40.1)   — take effective measures, including the adoption, in conformity with their constitutional systems and their international obligations, of such laws as may be necessary, to provide protection against any acts that constitute incitement to violence against persons or groups based on national, racial, ethnic or religious discrimination, hostility or hatred, including anti-semitism;

(40.2)   — commit themselves to take appropriate and proportionate measures to protect persons or groups who may be subject to threats or acts of discrimination, hostility or violence as a result of their racial, ethnic, cultural, linguistic or religious identity, and to protect their property;

(40.3)   — take effective measures, in conformity with their constitutional systems, at the national, regional and local levels to promote understanding and tolerance, particularly in the fields of education, culture and information;

(40.4) — endeavour to ensure that the objectives of education include special attention to the problem of racial prejudice and hatred and to the development of respect for different civilizations and cultures;

(40.5) — recognize the right of the individual to effective remedies and endeavour to recognize, in conformity with national legislation, the right of interested persons and groups to initiate and support complaints against acts of discrimination, including racist and xenophobic acts;

(40.6) — consider adhering, if they have not yet done so, to the international instruments which address the problem of discrimination and ensure full compliance with the obligations therein, including those relating to the submission of periodic reports;

(40.7) — consider, also, accepting those international mechanisms which allow States and individuals to bring communications relating to discrimination before international bodies.

V

(41) The participating States reaffirm their commitment to the human dimension of the CSCE and emphasize its importance as an integral part of a balanced approach to security and co-operation in Europe. They agree that the Conference on the Human Dimension of the CSCE and the human dimension mechanism described in the section on the human dimension of the CSCE of the Vienna Concluding Document have demonstrated their value as methods of furthering their dialogue and co-operation and assisting in the resolution of relevant specific questions. They express their conviction that these should be continued and developed as part of an expanding CSCE process.

(42) The participating States recognize the need to enhance further the effectiveness of the procedures described in paragraphs 1 to 4 of the section on the human dimension of the CSCE of the Vienna Concluding Document and with this aim decide

(42.1) — to provide in as short a time as possible, but no later than four weeks, a written response to requests for information and to representations made to them in writing by other participating States under paragraph 1;

(42.2) — that the bilateral meetings, as contained in paragraph 2, will take place as soon as possible, as a rule within three weeks of the date of the request;

(42.3) — to refrain, in the course of a bilateral meeting held under paragraph 2, from raising situations and cases not connected with the subject of the meeting, unless both sides have agreed to do so.

(43)   The participating States examined practical proposals for new measures aimed at improving the implementation of the commitments relating to the human dimension of the CSCE. In this regard, they considered proposals related to the sending of observers to examine situations and specific cases, the appointment of rapporteurs to investigate and suggest appropriate solutions, the setting up of a Committee on the Human Dimension of the CSCE, greater involvement of persons, organizations and institutions in the human dimension mechanism and further bilateral and multilateral efforts to promote the resolution of relevant issues.

They decide to continue to discuss thoroughly in subsequent relevant CSCE fora these and other proposals designed to strengthen the human dimension mechanism, and to consider adopting, in the context of the further development of the CSCE process, appropriate new measures. They agree that these measures should contribute to achieving further effective progress, enhance conflict prevention and confidence in the field of the human dimension of the CSCE.

. . .

43. Charter of Paris for a New Europe
(Excerpts)

Adopted at the Meeting of Heads of State or Government of the participating States
of the Conference on Security and Co-operation in Europe,
Paris, 21 November 1990

A new era of Democracy, Peace and Unity

We, the Heads of State or Government of the States participating in the Conference on Security and Co-operation in Europe, have assembled in Paris at a time of profound change and historic expectations. The era of confrontation and division of Europe has ended. We declare that henceforth our relations will be founded on respect and co-operation.

Europe is liberating itself from the legacy of the past. The courage of men and women, the strength of the will of the peoples and the power of the ideas of the Helsinki Final Act have opened a new era of democracy, peace and unity in Europe.

Ours is a time for fulfilling the hopes and expectations our peoples have cherished for decades: steadfast commitment to democracy based on human rights and fundamental freedoms; prosperity through economic liberty and social justice; and equal security for all our countries.

The Ten Principles of the Final Act will guide us towards this ambitious future, just as they have lighted our way towards better relations for the past fifteen years. Full implementation of all CSCE commitments must form the basis for the initiatives we are now taking to enable our nations to live in accordance with their aspirations.

HUMAN RIGHTS, DEMOCRACY AND RULE OF LAW

We undertake to build, consolidate and strengthen democracy as the only system of government of our nations. In this endeavour, we will abide by the following:

Human rights and fundamental freedoms are the birthright of all human beings, are inalienable and are guaranteed by law. Their protection and promotion is the first responsibility of government. Respect for them is an essential safeguard against an over-mighty State. Their observance and full exercise are the foundation of freedom, justice and peace.

Democratic government is based on the will of the people, expressed regularly through free and fair elections. Democracy has as its foundation respect for the human person and the rule of law. Democracy is the best safeguard of freedom of expression, tolerance of all groups of society, and equality of opportunity for each person.

Democracy, with its representative and pluralist character, entails accountability to the electorate, the obligation of public authorities to comply with the law and justice administered impartially. No one will be above the law.

We affirm that, without discrimination,

Every individual has the right to:

—Freedom of thought, conscience and religion or belief,

—Freedom of expression,

—Freedom of association and peaceful assembly,

—Freedom of movement;

No one will be:

—Subject to arbitrary arrest or detention,

—Subject to torture or other cruel, inhuman or degrading treatment or punishment;

Everyone also has the right:

—To know and act upon his rights,

—To participate in free and fair elections,

—To fair and public trial if charged with an offence, ·

—To own property alone or in association and to exercise individual enterprise,

—To enjoy his economic, social and cultural rights.

We affirm that the ethnic, cultural, linguistic and religious identity of national minorities will be protected and that persons belonging to national minorities have the right freely to express, preserve and develop that identity without any discrimination and in full equality before the law.

We will ensure that everyone will enjoy recourse to effective remedies, national or international, against any violation of his rights.

Full respect for these precepts is the bedrock on which we will seek to construct the new Europe.

Our States will co-operate and support each other with the aim of making democratic gains irreversible.

ECONOMIC LIBERTY AND RESPONSIBILITY

Economic liberty, social justice and environmental responsibility are indispensable for prosperity.

The free will of the individual, exercised in democracy and protected by the rule of law, forms the necessary basis for successful economic and social development. We will promote economic activity which respects and upholds human dignity.

Freedom and political pluralism are necessary elements in our common objective of developing market economies towards sustainable economic growth, prosperity, social justice, expanding employment and efficient use of economic resources. The success of the transition to market economy by countries making efforts to this effect is important and in the interest of us all. It will enable us to share a higher level of prosperity which is our common objective. We will co-operate to this end.

Preservation of the environment is a shared responsibility of all our nations. While supporting national and regional efforts in this field, we must also look to the pressing need for joint action on a wider scale.

FRIENDLY RELATIONS AMONG PARTICIPATING STATES

Now that a new era is dawning in Europe, we are determined to expand and strengthen friendly relations and co-operation among the States of Europe, the United States of America and Canada, and to promote friendship among our peoples.

To uphold and promote democracy, peace and unity in Europe, we solemnly pledge our full commitment to the Ten Principles of the Helsinki Final Act. We affirm the continuing validity of the Ten Principles and our determination to put them into practice. All the Principles apply equally and unreservedly, each of them being interpreted taking into account the others. They form the basis for our relations.

In accordance with our obligations under the Charter of the United Nations and commitments under the Helsinki Final Act, we renew our pledge to refrain from the threat or use of force against the territorial integrity or political independence of any State, or from acting in any other manner inconsistent with the principles or purposes of those documents. We recall that non-compliance with obligations under the Charter of the United Nations constitutes a violation of international law.

We reaffirm our commitment to settle disputes by peaceful means. We decide to develop mechanisms for the prevention and resolution of conflicts among the participating States.

With the ending of the division of Europe, we will strive for a new quality in our security relations while fully respecting each other's freedom of choice in that respect. Security is indivisible and the security of every participating State is inseparably linked to that of all the others. We therefore pledge to co-operate in strengthening confidence and security among us and in promoting arms control and disarmament.

We welcome the Joint Declaration of Twenty-Two States on the improvement of their relations.

Our relations will rest on our common adherence to democratic values and to human rights and fundamental freedoms. We are convinced that in order to strengthen peace and security among our States, the advancement of democracy, and respect for and effective exercise of human rights, are indispensable. We reaffirm the equal rights of peoples and their right to self-determination in conformity with the Charter of the United Nations and with the relevant norms of international law, including those relating to territorial integrity of States.

We are determined to enhance political consultation and to widen co-operation to solve economic, social, environmental, cultural and humanitarian problems. This common resolve and our growing interdependence will help to overcome the mistrust of decades, to increase stability and to build a united Europe.

We want Europe to be a source of peace, open to dialogue and to co-operation with other countries, welcoming exchanges and involved in the search for common responses to the challenges of the future.

. . .

Guidelines for the future

Proceeding from our firm commitment to the full implementation of all CSCE principles and provisions, we now resolve to give a new impetus to a balanced and comprehensive development of our co-operation in order to address the needs and aspirations of our peoples.

HUMAN DIMENSION

We declare our respect for human rights and fundamental freedoms to be irrevocable. We will fully implement and build upon the provisions relating to the human dimension of the CSCE.

Proceeding from the Document of the Copenhagen Meeting of the Conference on the Human Dimension, we will co-operate to strengthen democratic institutions and to promote the application of the rule of law. To that end, we decide to convene a seminar of experts in Oslo from 4 to 15 November 1991.

Determined to foster the rich contribution of national minorities to the life of our societies, we undertake further to improve their situation. We re-affirm our deep conviction that friendly relations among our peoples, as well as peace, justice, stability and democracy, require that the ethnic, cultural, linguistic and religious identity of national minorities be protected and conditions for the promotion of that identity be created. We declare that questions related to national minorities can only be satisfactorily resolved in a democratic political framework. We further acknowledge that the rights of persons belonging to national minorities must be fully respected as part of universal human rights. Being aware of the urgent need for increased co-operation on, as well as better protection of, national minorities, we decide to convene a meeting of experts on national minorities to be held in Geneva from 1 to 19 July 1991.

We express our determination to combat all forms of racial and ethnic hatred, anti-semitism, xenophobia and discrimination against anyone as well as persecution on religious and ideological grounds.

In accordance with our CSCE commitments, we stress that free movement and contacts among our citizens as well as the free flow of information and ideas are crucial for the maintenance and development of free societies and flourishing cultures. We welcome increased tourism and visits among our countries.

The human dimension mechanism has proved its usefulness, and we are consequently determined to expand it to include new procedures involving, *inter alia*, the services of experts or a roster of eminent persons experienced in human rights issues which could be raised under the mechanism. We shall provide, in the context of the mechanism, for individuals to be involved in the protection of their rights. Therefore, we undertake to develop further our commitments in this respect, in particular at the Moscow Meeting of the Conference on the Human Dimension, without prejudice to obligations under existing international instruments to which our States may be parties.

We recognize the important contribution of the Council of Europe to the promotion of human rights and the principles of democracy and the rule of law as well as to the development of cultural co-operation. We welcome moves by several participating States to join the Council of Europe and adhere to its European Convention on Human Rights. We welcome as well the readiness of the Council of Europe to make its experience available to the CSCE.

. . .

ECONOMIC CO-OPERATION

We stress that economic co-operation based on market economy constitutes an essential element of our relations and will be instrumental in the construction of a prosperous and united Europe. Democratic institutions and economic liberty foster economic and social progress, as recognized in the Document of the Bonn Conference on Economic Co-operation, the results of which we strongly support.

We underline that co-operation in the economic field, science and technology is now an important pillar of the CSCE. The participating States should periodically review progress and give new impulses in these fields.

We are convinced that our overall economic co-operation should be expanded, free enterprise encouraged and trade increased and diversified according to GATT rules. We will promote social justice and progress and further the welfare of our peoples. We recognize in this context the importance of effective policies to address the problem of unemployment.

We reaffirm the need to continue to support democratic countries in transition towards the establishment of market economy and the creation of the basis for self-sustained economic and social growth, as already undertaken by the Group of twenty-four countries. We further underline the necessity of their increased integration, involving the acceptance of disciplines as well as benefits, into the international economic and financial system.

We consider that increased emphasis on economic co-operation within the CSCE process should take into account the interests of developing participating States.

We recall the link between respect for and promotion of human rights and fundamental freedoms and scientific progress. Co-operation in the field of science and technology will play an essential role in economic and social development. Therefore, it must evolve towards a greater sharing of appropriate scientific and technological information and knowledge with a view to overcoming the technological gap which exists among the participating States. We further encourage the participating States to work together in order to develop human potential and the spirit of free enterprise.

We are determined to give the necessary impetus to co-operation among our States in the fields of energy, transport and tourism for economic and social development. We welcome, in particular, practical steps to create optimal conditions for the economic and rational development of energy resources, with due regard for environmental considerations.

We recognize the important role of the European Community in the political and economic development of Europe. International economic organizations such as the United Nations Economic Commission for Europe (ECE), the Bretton Woods Institutions, the Organisation for Economic Co-operation and Development (OECD), the European Free Trade Association (EFTA) and the International Chamber of Commerce (ICC) also have a significant task in promoting economic co-operation, which will be further enhanced by the establishment of the European Bank for Reconstruction and Development (EBRD). In order to pursue our objectives, we stress the necessity for effective coordination of the activities of these organizations and emphasize the need to find methods for all our States to take part in these activities.

...

CULTURE

We recognize the essential contribution of our common European culture and our shared values in overcoming the division of the continent. Therefore, we underline our attachment to creative freedom and to the protection and promotion of our cultural and spiritual heritage, in all its richness and diversity.

In view of the recent changes in Europe, we stress the increased importance of the Cracow Symposium and we look forward to its consideration of guidelines for intensified co-operation in the field of culture. We invite the Council of Europe to contribute to this Symposium.

In order to promote greater familiarity amongst our peoples, we favour the establishment of cultural centres in cities of other participating States as well as increased co-operation in the audio-visual field and wider exchange in music, theatre, literature and the arts.

We resolve to make special efforts in our national policies to promote better understanding, in particular among young people, through cultural exchanges, co-operation in all fields of education and, more specifically, through teaching and training in the languages of other participating States. We intend to consider first results of this action at the Helsinki Follow-up Meeting in 1992.

MIGRANT WORKERS

We recognize that the issues of migrant workers and their families legally residing in host countries have economic, cultural and social aspects as well as their human dimension. We reaffirm that the protection and promotion of their rights, as well as the implementation of relevant international obligations, is our common concern.

...

NON-GOVERNMENTAL ORGANIZATIONS

We recall the major role that non-governmental organizations, religious and other groups and individuals have played in the achievement of the objectives of the CSCE and will further facilitate their activities for the implementation of the CSCE commitments by the participating States. These organizations, groups and individuals must be involved in an appropriate way in the activities and new structures of the CSCE in order to fulfill their important tasks.

. . .

The original of the Charter of Paris for a New Europe, drawn up in English, French, German, Italian, Russian and Spanish, will be transmitted to the Government of the French Republic, which will retain it in its archives. Each of the participating States will receive from the Government of the French Republic a true copy of the Charter of Paris.

The text of the Charter of Paris will be published in each participating State, which will disseminate it and make it known as widely as possible.

The Government of the French Republic is requested to transmit to the Secretary-General of the United Nations the text of the Charter of Paris for a New Europe which is not eligible for registration under Article 102 of the Charter of the United Nations, with a view to its circulation to all the Members of the Organization as an official document of the United Nations.

The Government of the French Republic is also requested to transmit the text of the Charter of Paris to all the other international organizations mentioned in the text.

WHEREFORE, we, the undersigned High Representatives of the participating States, mindful of the high political significance we attach to the results of the Summit Meeting, and declaring our determination to act in accordance with the provisions we have adopted, have subscribed our signatures below. . .

44. Document of the Moscow Meeting of the Conference on the Human Dimension of the Conference on Security and Co-operation in Europe (*3 October 1991*)
(Excerpt)

. . .

I

(1)   The participating States emphasize that the human dimension mechanism described in paragraphs 1 to 4 of the section on the human dimension of the CSCE in the Vienna Concluding Document constitutes an essential achievement of the CSCE process, having demonstrated its value as a method of furthering respect for human rights, fundamental freedoms, democracy and the rule of law through dialogue and co-operation and assisting in the resolution of specific relevant questions. In order to improve further the implementation of the CSCE commitments in the human dimension, they decide to enhance the effectiveness of this mechanism and to strengthen and expand it as outlined in the following paragraphs.

(2)   The participating States amend paragraphs 42.1 and 42.2 of the Document of the Copenhagen Meeting to the effect that they will provide in the shortest possible time, but no later than ten days, a written response to requests for information and to representations made to them in writing by other participating States under paragraph 1 of the human dimension mechanism. Bilateral meetings, as referred to in paragraph 2 of the human dimension mechanism, will take place as soon as possible, and as a rule within one week of the date of the request.

(3)   A resource list comprising up to three experts appointed by each participating State will be established without delay at the CSCE Institution*. The experts will be eminent persons, preferably experienced in the field of the human dimension, from whom an impartial performance of their functions may be expected.

The experts will be appointed for a period of three to six years at the discretion of the appointing State, no expert serving more than two consecutive terms. Within four weeks after notification by the CSCE Institution of the appointment, any participating State may make reservations regarding no

---

* The Council will take the decision on the institution.

more than two experts to be appointed by another participating State. In such case, the appointing State may, within four weeks of being notified of such reservations, reconsider its decision and appoint another expert or experts; if it confirms the appointment originally intended, the expert concerned cannot take part in any procedure with respect to the State having made the reservation without the latter's express consent.

The resource list will become operational as soon as 45 experts have been appointed.

(4)   A participating State may invite the assistance of a CSCE mission, consisting of up to three experts, to address or contribute to the resolution of questions in its territory relating to the human dimension of the CSCE. In such case, the State will select the person or persons concerned from the resource list. The mission of experts will not include the participating State's own nationals or residents or any of the persons it appointed to the resource list or more than one national or resident of any particular State.

The inviting State will inform without delay the CSCE Institution when a mission of experts is established, which in turn will notify all participating States. The CSCE institutions will also, whenever necessary, provide appropriate support to such a mission.

(5)   The purpose of a mission of experts is to facilitate resolution of a particular question or problem relating to the human dimension of the CSCE. Such mission may gather the information necessary for carrying out its tasks and, as appropriate, use its good offices and mediation services to promote dialogue and co-operation among interested parties. The State concerned will agree with the mission on the precise terms of reference and may thus assign any further functions to the mission of experts, *inter alia* fact-finding and advisory services, in order to suggest ways and means of facilitating the observance of CSCE commitments.

(6)   The inviting State will co-operate fully with the mission of experts and facilitate its work. It will grant the mission all the facilities necessary for the independent exercise of its functions. It will, *inter alia*, allow the mission, for the purpose of carrying out its tasks, to enter its territory without delay, to hold discussions and to travel freely therein, to meet freely with officials, non-governmental organizations and any group or person from whom it wishes to receive information. The mission may also receive information in confidence from any individual, group or organization on questions it is addressing. The members of such missions will respect the confidential nature of their task.

The participating States will refrain from any action against persons, organizations or institutions on account of their contact with the mission of experts or of any publicly available information transmitted to it. The inviting State will comply with any request from a mission of experts to be accompanied by officials of that State if the mission considers this to be necessary to facilitate its work or guarantee its safety.

(7)   The mission of experts will submit its observations to the inviting State as soon as possible, preferably within three weeks after the mission has been established. The inviting State will transmit the observations of the mission, together with a description of any action it has taken or intends to take upon it, to the other participating States via the CSCE Institution no later than three weeks after the submission of the observations.

These observations and any comments by the inviting State may be discussed by the Committee of Senior Officials, which may consider any possible follow-up action. The observations and comments will remain confidential until brought to the attention of the Senior Officials. Before the circulation of the observations and any comments, no other mission of experts may be appointed for the same issue.

(8)   Furthermore, one or more participating States, having put into effect paragraphs 1 or 2 of the human dimension mechanism, may request that the CSCE Institution inquire of another participating State whether it would agree to invite a mission of experts to address a particular, clearly defined question on its territory relating to the human dimension of the CSCE. If the other participating State agrees to invite a mission of experts for the purpose indicated, the procedure set forth in paragraphs 4 to 7 will apply.

(9)   If a participating State (*a*) has directed an enquiry under paragraph 8 to another participating State and that State has not established a mission of experts within a period of ten days after the enquiry has been made, or (*b*) judges that the issue in question has not been resolved as a result of a mission of experts, it may, with the support of at least five other participating States, initiate the establishment of a mission of up to three CSCE rapporteurs. Such a decision will be addressed to the CSCE Institution, which will notify without delay the State concerned as well as all the other participating States.

(10)   The requesting State or States may appoint one person from the resource list to serve as a CSCE rapporteur. The requested State may, if it so chooses, appoint a further rapporteur from the resource list within six days after notification by the CSCE Institution of the appointment of the rapporteur. In such case the two designated rapporteurs, who will not be nationals or residents of, or persons appointed to the resource list by any of the States concerned, will by common agreement and without delay appoint a third rapporteur from the resource list. In case they fail to reach agreement within eight days, a third rapporteur who will not be a national or resident of, or a person appointed to the resource list by any of the States concerned, will be appointed from the resource list by the ranking official of the CSCE body designated by the Council. The provisions of the second part of paragraph 4 and the whole of paragraph 6 also apply to a mission of rapporteurs.

(11)   The CSCE rapporteur(s) will establish the facts, report on them and may give advice on possible solutions to the question raised. The report of the rapporteur(s), containing observations of facts, proposals or advice, will be submitted to the participating State or States concerned and, unless all the States concerned agree otherwise, to the CSCE Institution no later than three weeks after the last rapporteur has been appointed. The requested State will submit any observations on the report to the CSCE Institution, unless all the States concerned agree otherwise, no later than three weeks after the submission of the report.

The CSCE Institution will transmit the report, as well as any observations by the requested State or any other participating State, to all participating States without delay. The report may be placed on the agenda of the next regular meeting of the Committee of Senior Officials, which may decide on any possible follow-up action. The report will remain confidential until after that meeting of the Committee. Before the circulation of the report no other rapporteur may be appointed for the same issue.

(12)   If a participating State considers that a particularly serious threat to the fulfilment of the provisions of the CSCE human dimension has arisen in another participating State, it may, with the support of at least nine other participating States, engage the procedure set forth in paragraph 10. The provisions of paragraph 11 will apply.

(13)   Upon the request of any participating State the Committee of Senior Officials may decide to establish a mission of experts or of CSCE rapporteurs. In such case the Committee will also determine whether to apply the appropriate provisions of the preceding paragraphs.

(14)   The participating States or States that have requested the establishment of a mission of experts or rapporteurs will cover the expenses of that mission. In case of the appointment of experts or rapporteurs pursuant to a decision of the Committee of Senior Officials, the expenses will be covered by the participating States in accordance with the usual scale of distribution of expenses. These procedures will be reviewed by the Helsinki Follow-up Meeting of the CSCE.

(15)   Nothing in the foregoing will in any way affect the right of participating States to raise within the CSCE process any issue relating to the implementation of any CSCE commitment, including any commitment relating to the human dimension of the CSCE.

(16)   In considering whether to invoke the procedures in paragraphs 9 and 10 or 12 regarding the case of an individual, participating States should pay due regard to whether that individual's case is already *sub judice* in an international judicial procedure.

Any reference to the Committee of Senior Officials in this document is subject to the decision of that Committee and the Council.

II

(17)   The participating States

(17.1)   — condemn unreservedly forces which seek to take power from a representative government of a participating State against the will of the people as expressed in free and fair elections and contrary to the justly established constitutional order;

(17.2)   — will support vigorously, in accordance with the Charter of the United Nations, in case of overthrow or attempted overthrow of a legitimately elected government of a participating State by undemocratic means, the legitimate organs of that State upholding human rights, democracy and the rule of law, recognizing their common commitment to countering any attempt to curb these basic values;

(17.3)   — recognize the need to make further peaceful efforts concerning human rights, democracy and the rule of law within the context of security and co-operation in Europe, individually and collectively, to make democratic advances irreversible and prevent any falling below the standards laid down in the principles and provisions of the Final Act, the Vienna Concluding Document, the Document of the Copenhagen Meeting, the Charter of Paris for a New Europe and the present document.

(18)   The participating States recall their commitment to the rule of law in the Document of the Copenhagen Meeting and affirm their dedication to supporting and advancing those principles of justice which form the basis of the rule of law. In particular, they again reaffirm that democracy is an inherent element in the rule of law and that pluralism is important in regard to political organizations.

(18.1)   Legislation will be formulated and adopted as the result of an open process reflecting the will of the people, either directly or through their elected representatives.

(18.2)   Everyone will have an effective means of redress against administrative decisions, so as to guarantee respect for fundamental rights and ensure legal integrity.

(18.3)   To the same end, there will be effective means of redress against administrative regulations for individuals affected thereby.

(18.4)   The participating States will endeavour to provide for judicial review of such regulations and decisions.

(19)   The participating States

(19.1)   — will respect the internationally recognized standards that relate to the independence of judges and legal practitioners and the impartial operation of the public judicial service including, *inter alia*, the Universal Declaration of Human Rights and the International Covenant on Civil and Political Rights;

(19.2) — will, in implementing the relevant standards and commitments, ensure that the independence of the judiciary is guaranteed and enshrined in the constitution or the law of the country and is respected in practice, paying particular attention to the Basic Principles on the Independence of the Judiciary, which, *inter alia*, provide for

(i) prohibiting improper influence on judges;

(ii) preventing revision of judicial decisions by administrative authorities, except for the rights of the competent authorities to mitigate or commute sentences imposed by judges, in conformity with the law;

(iii) protecting the judiciary's freedom of expression and association, subject only to such restrictions as are consistent with its functions;

(iv) ensuring that judges are properly qualified, trained and selected on a non-discriminatory basis;

(v) guaranteeing tenure and appropriate conditions of service, including on the matter of promotion of judges, where applicable;

(vi) respecting conditions of immunity;

(vii) ensuring that the disciplining, suspension and removal of judges are determined according to law.

(20)   For the promotion of the independence of the judiciary, the participating States will

(20.1) — recognize the important function national and international associations of judges and lawyers can perform in strengthening respect for the independence of their members and in providing education and training on the role of the judiciary and the legal profession in society;

(20.2) — promote and facilitate dialogue, exchanges and co-operation among national associations and other groups interested in ensuring respect for the independence of the judiciary and the protection of lawyers;

(20.3) — co-operate among themselves through, *inter alia*, dialogue, contacts and exchanges in order to identify where problem areas exist concerning the protection of the independence of judges and legal practitioners and to develop ways and means to address and resolve such problems;

(20.4) — co-operate on an ongoing basis in such areas as the education and training of judges and legal practitioners, as well as the preparation and enactment of legislation intended to strengthen respect for their independence and the impartial operation of the public judicial service.

(21)   The participating States will

(21.1) — take all necessary measures to ensure that law enforcement personnel, when enforcing public order, will act in the public interest, respond to a specific need and pursue a legitimate aim, as well as use ways and means commensurate with the circumstances, which will not exceed the needs of enforcement;

(21.2) — ensure that law enforcement acts are subject to judicial control, that law enforcement personnel are held accountable for such acts, and that due compensation may be sought, according to domestic law, by the victims of acts found to be in violation of the above commitments.

(22) The participating States will take appropriate measures to ensure that education and information regarding the prohibition of excess force by law enforcement personnel as well as relevant international and domestic codes of conduct are included in the training of such personnel.

(23) The participating States will treat all persons deprived of their liberty with humanity and with respect for the inherent dignity of the human person and will respect the internationally recognized standards that relate to the administration of justice and the human rights of detainees.

(23.1) The participating States will ensure that

(i)   no one will be deprived of his liberty except on such grounds and in accordance with such procedures as are established by law;

(ii) anyone who is arrested will be informed promptly in a language which he understands of the reason for his arrest, and will be informed of any charges against him;

(iii) any person who has been deprived of his liberty will be promptly informed about his rights according to domestic law;

(iv) any person arrested or detained will have the right to be brought promptly before a judge or other officer authorized by law to determine the lawfulness of his arrest or detention, and will be released without delay if it is unlawful;

(v)   anyone charged with a criminal offence will have the right to defend himself in person or through legal assistance of his own choosing or, if he has not sufficient means to pay for legal assistance, to be given it free when the interests of justice so require;

(vi) any person arrested or detained will have the right, without undue delay, to notify or to require the competent authority to notify appropriate persons of his choice of his arrest, detention, imprisonment and whereabouts; any restriction in the exercise of this right will be prescribed by law and in accordance with international standards;

(vii) effective measures will be adopted, if this has not already been done, to provide that law enforcement bodies do not take undue advantage of the situation of a detained or imprisoned person for the purpose of compelling him to confess, or otherwise to incriminate himself, or to force him to testify against any other person;

(viii) the duration of any interrogation and the intervals between them will be recorded and certified, consistent with domestic law;

(ix) a detained person or his counsel will have the right to make a request or complaint regarding his treatment, in particular when torture or other cruel, inhuman or degrading treatment has been applied, to the authorities responsible for the administration of the place of detention and to higher authorities, and when necessary, to appropriate authorities vested with reviewing or remedial power;

(x) such request or complaint will be promptly dealt with and replied to without undue delay; if the request or complaint is rejected or in case of inordinate delay, the complainant will be entitled to bring it before a judicial or other authority; neither the detained or imprisoned person nor any complainant will suffer prejudice for making a request or complaint;

(xi) anyone who has been the victim of an unlawful arrest or detention will have a legally enforceable right to seek compensation.

(23.2) The participating States will

(i) endeavour to take measures, as necessary, to improve the conditions of individuals in detention or imprisonment;

(ii) pay particular attention to the question of alternatives to imprisonment.

(24) The participating States reconfirm the right to the protection of private and family life, domicile, correspondence and electronic communications. In order to avoid any improper or arbitrary intrusion by the State in the realm of the individual, which would be harmful to any democratic society, the exercise of this right will be subject only to such restrictions as are prescribed by law and are consistent with internationally recognized human rights standards. In particular, the participating States will ensure that searches and seizures of persons and private premises and property will take place only in accordance with standards that are judicially enforceable.

(25) The participating States will

(25.1) — ensure that their military and paramilitary forces, internal security and intelligence services, and the police are subject to the effective direction and control of the appropriate civil authorities;

(25.2) — maintain and, where necessary, strengthen executive control over the use of military and paramilitary forces as well as the activities of the internal security and intelligence services and the police;

(25.3) — take appropriate steps to create, wherever they do not already exist, and maintain effective arrangements for legislative supervision of all such forces, services and activities.

(26) The participating States reaffirm the right to freedom of expression, including the right to communication and the right of the media to collect, report and disseminate information, news and opinions. Any restriction in the exercise of this right will be prescribed by law and in accordance with international standards. They further recognize that independent media are essential to a free and open society and accountable systems of government and are of particular importance in safeguarding human rights and fundamental freedoms.

(26.1) They consider that the print and broadcast media in their territory should enjoy unrestricted access to foreign news and information services. The public will enjoy similar freedom to receive and impart information and ideas without interference by public authority regardless of frontiers, including through foreign publications and foreign broadcasts. Any restriction in the exercise of this right will be prescribed by law and in accordance with international standards.

(26.2) The participating States will not discriminate against independent media with respect to affording access to information, material and facilities.

(27) The participating States

(27.1) — express their intention to co-operate in the field of constitutional, administrative, commercial, civil and social welfare laws and other relevant areas, in order to develop, particularly in States where they do not yet exist, legal systems based on respect for human rights, the rule of law and democracy;

(27.2) — to this end, envisage the continuation and enhancement of bilateral and multilateral legal and administrative co-operation, *inter alia*, in the following fields:

—development of an efficient administrative system;
—assistance in formulating law and regulations;
—training of administrative and legal staff;
—exchange of legal works and periodicals.

(28) The participating States consider it important to protect human rights and fundamental freedoms during a state of public emergency, to take into account the relevant provisions of the Document of the Copenhagen Meeting, and to observe the international conventions to which they are parties.

(28.1) The participating States reaffirm that a state of public emergency is justified only by the most exceptional and grave circumstances, consistent with the State's international obligations and CSCE commitments. A state of public emergency may not be used to subvert the democratic constitutional order, nor aim at the destruction of internationally recognized human rights and fundamental freedoms. If recourse to force cannot be avoided, its use must be reasonable and limited as far as possible.

(28.2) A state of public emergency may be proclaimed only by a constitutionally lawful body, duly empowered to do so. In cases where the decision to impose a state of public emergency may be lawfully taken by the executive authorities, that decision should be subject to approval in the shortest possible time or to control by the legislature.

(28.3) The decision to impose a state of public emergency will be proclaimed officially, publicly, and in accordance with provisions laid down by law. The decision will, where possible, lay down territorial limits of a state of public emergency. The State concerned will make available to its citizens information, without delay, about which measures have been taken. The state of public emergency will be lifted as soon as possible and will not remain in force longer than strictly required by the exigencies of the situation.

(28.4) A de facto imposition or continuation of a state of public emergency not in accordance with provisions laid down by law is not permissible.

(28.5) The participating States will endeavour to ensure that the normal functioning of the legislative bodies will be guaranteed to the highest possible extent during a state of public emergency.

(28.6) The participating States confirm that any derogation from obligations relating to human rights and fundamental freedoms during a state of public emergency must remain strictly within the limits provided for by international law, in particular the relevant international instruments by which they are bound, especially with respect to rights from which there can be no derogation.

(28.7) The participating States will endeavour to refrain from making derogations from those obligations from which, according to international conventions to which they are parties, derogation is possible under a state of public emergency. Measures derogating from such obligations must be taken in strict conformity with the procedural requirements laid down in those instruments. Such measures will neither go further nor remain in force longer than strictly required by the exigencies of the situation; they are by nature exceptional and should be interpreted and applied with restraint. Such measures will not discriminate solely on the grounds of race, colour, sex, language, religion, social origin or of belonging to a minority.

(28.8) The participating States will endeavour to ensure that the legal guarantees necessary to uphold the rule of law will remain in force during a state of public emergency. They will endeavour to provide in their law for control over the regulations related to the state of public emergency, as well as the implementation of such regulations.

(28.9) The participating States will endeavour to maintain freedom of expression and freedom of information, consistent with their international obligations and commitments, with a view to enabling public discussion on the observance of human rights and fundamental freedoms as well as on the lifting of the state of public emergency. They will, in conformity with international standards regarding the freedom of expression, take no measures aimed at barring journalists from the legitimate exercise of their profession other than those strictly required by the exigencies of the situation.

(28.10) When a state of public emergency is declared or lifted in a participating State, the State concerned will immediately inform the CSCE Institution* of this decision, as well as of any derogation made from the State's international human rights obligations. The Institution will inform the other participating States without delay.

(29)   The participating States, recognizing their common interest in promoting contacts and the exchange of information amongst Ombudsmen and other institutions entrusted with similar functions of investigating individual complaints of citizens against public authorities, note with appreciation an offer by Spain to host a meeting of Ombudsmen.

(30)   The participating States suggest that the appropriate CSCE fora consider expanding the functions of the Office for Free Elections to enable it to assist in strengthening democratic institutions within the participating States.

(31)   The participating States acknowledge the extensive experience and expertise of the Council of Europe in the field of human rights. They welcome its contribution to strengthening democracy in Europe, including its readiness to make its experience available to the CSCE.

III

(32)   The participating States reaffirm their enduring commitment to the principles and provisions of the Final Act, the Vienna Concluding Document, and other relevant CSCE documents in which they undertook, *inter alia*, to respect human rights and fundamental freedoms and to ensure that they are guaranteed for all without distinction of any kind.

(33)   The participating States will remove all legal and other restrictions with respect to travel within their territories for their own nationals and foreigners, and with respect to residence for those entitled to permanent resi-

---

* The Council will take the decision on the institution.

dence, except those restrictions which may be necessary and officially declared for military, safety, ecological or other legitimate government interests, in accordance with their national laws, consistent with CSCE commitments and international human rights obligations. The participating States undertake to keep such restrictions to a minimum.

(34)   The participating States will adopt, where appropriate, all feasible measures to protect journalists engaged in dangerous professional missions, particularly in cases of armed conflict, and will co-operate to that effect. These measures will include tracing missing journalists, ascertaining their fate, providing appropriate assistance and facilitating their return to their families.

(35)   The participating States reaffirm that guaranteeing the freedom of artistic creation and preserving the cultural heritage form part of the human dimension of the CSCE. They consider that independent intellectual and cultural life is crucial for the maintenance of free societies and democratic institutions. They will implement their commitments in the cultural field, as laid down in the Document of the Cracow Symposium on the Cultural Heritage, and express the view that cultural issues, including cultural freedom, creativity and co-operation, should be further considered in the CSCE.

(36)   The participating States recall their commitment in the Vienna Concluding Document to keep the question of capital punishment under consideration and reaffirm their undertakings in the Document of the Copenhagen Meeting to exchange information on the question of the abolition of the death penalty and to make available to the public information regarding the use of the death penalty.

(36.1)   They note

(i) that the Second Optional Protocol to the International Covenant on Civil and Political Rights aiming at the abolition of the death penalty entered into force on 11 July 1991;

(ii) that a number of participating States have recently taken steps towards the abolition of capital punishment;

(iii) the activities of several non-governmental organizations concerning the question of the death penalty.

(37)   The participating States confirm the provisions and commitments of all CSCE documents, in particular the Document of the Copenhagen Meeting of the Conference on the Human Dimension of the CSCE, concerning questions relating to national minorities and the rights of persons belonging to them, and the Report of the Geneva CSCE Meeting of Experts on National Minorities, and call for their full and early implementation. They believe that, in particular, the use of the new and expanded CSCE

mechanisms and procedures will contribute to further protection and promotion of the rights of persons belonging to national minorities.

(38)   The participating States recognize the need to ensure that the rights of migrant workers and their families lawfully residing in the participating States are respected and underline their right to express freely their ethnic, cultural, religious and linguistic characteristics. The exercise of such rights may be subject to such restrictions as are prescribed by law and are consistent with international standards.

(38.1) They condemn all acts of discrimination on the ground of race, colour and ethnic origin, intolerance and xenophobia against migrant workers. They will, in conformity with domestic law and international obligations, take effective measures to promote tolerance, understanding, equality of opportunity and respect for the fundamental human rights of migrant workers and adopt, if they have not already done so, measures that would prohibit acts that constitute incitement to violence based on national, racial, ethnic or religious discrimination, hostility or hatred.

(38.2) They will adopt appropriate measures that would enable migrant workers to participate in the life of the society of the participating States.

(38.3) They note that issues which concern the human dimension of migrant workers residing on their territory could, as any other issue of the human dimension, be raised under the human dimension mechanism.

(38.4) They recommend that the CSCE in its future work on the human dimension consider appropriate means to hold focused discussions on all issues regarding migrant workers, including, *inter alia*, familiarization with the language and social life of the country concerned.

(39)   The participating States will

(39.1) — increase their preparedness and co-operate fully to enable humanitarian relief operations to be undertaken speedily and effectively;

(39.2) — take all necessary steps to facilitate speedy and unhindered access to the affected areas for such relief operations;

(39.3) — make the necessary arrangements for those relief operations to be carried out.

(40)   The participating States recognize that full and true equality between men and women is a fundamental aspect of a just and democratic society based on the rule of law. They recognize that the full development of society and the welfare of all its members require equal opportunity for full and equal participation of men and women. In this context they will

(40.1) — ensure that all CSCE commitments relating to the protection and promotion of human rights and fundamental freedoms are applied fully and without discrimination with regard to sex;

(40.2) — comply with the Convention on the Elimination of All Forms of Discrimination against Women (CEDAW), if they are parties, and, if they have not already done so, consider ratifying or acceding to this Convention; States that have ratified or acceded to this Convention with reservations will consider withdrawing them;

(40.3) — effectively implement the obligations in international instruments to which they are parties and take appropriate measures to implement the United Nations Nairobi Forward-looking Strategies for the Advancement of Women (FLS);

(40.4) — affirm that it is their goal to achieve not only *de jure* but de facto equality of opportunity between men and women and to promote effective measures to that end;

(40.5) — establish or strengthen national machinery, as appropriate, for the advancement of women in order to ensure that programmes and policies are assessed for their impact on women;

(40.6) — encourage measures effectively to ensure full economic opportunity for women, including non-discriminatory employment policies and practices, equal access to education and training, and measures to facilitate combining employment with family responsibilities for female and male workers; and will seek to ensure that any structural adjustment policies or programmes do not have an adversely discriminatory effect on women;

(40.7) — seek to eliminate all forms of violence against women, and all forms of traffic in women and exploitation of prostitution of women including by ensuring adequate legal prohibitions against such acts and other appropriate measures;

(40.8) — encourage and promote equal opportunity for full participation by women in all aspects of political and public life, in decision-making processes and in international co-operation in general;

(40.9) — recognize the vital role women and women's organizations play in national and international efforts to promote and enhance women's rights by providing, *inter alia*, direct services and support to women and encouraging a meaningful partnership between governments and these organizations for the purpose of advancing equality for women;

(40.10) — recognize the rich contribution of women to all aspects of political, cultural, social and economic life and promote a broad understanding of these contributions, including those made in the informal and unpaid sectors;

(40.11) — take measures to encourage that information regarding women and women's rights under international and domestic law is easily accessible;

(40.12) — develop educational policies, consistent with their constitutional systems, to support the participation of women in all areas of study and work, including non-traditional areas, and encourage and promote a greater understanding of issues relating to equality between men and women;

(40.13) — ensure the collection and analysis of data to assess adequately, monitor and improve the situation of women; these data should not contain any personal information.

(41)   The participating States decide

(41.1) — to ensure protection of the human rights of persons with disabilities;

(41.2) — to take steps to ensure the equal opportunity of such persons to participate fully in the life of their society;

(41.3) — to promote the appropriate participation of such persons in decision-making in fields concerning them;

(41.4) — to encourage services and training of social workers for the vocational and social rehabilitation of persons with disabilities;

(41.5) — to encourage favourable conditions for the access of persons with disabilities to public buildings and services, housing, transport, and cultural and recreational activities.

(42)   The participating States

(42.1) — affirm that human rights education is fundamental and that it is therefore essential that their citizens are educated on human rights and fundamental freedoms and the commitment to respect such rights and freedoms in domestic legislation and international instruments to which they may be parties;

(42.2) — recognize that effective human rights education contributes to combating intolerance, religious, racial and ethnic prejudice and hatred, including against Roma, xenophobia and anti-semitism;

(42.3) — will encourage their competent authorities responsible for education programmes to design effective human rights related curricula and courses for students at all levels, particularly students of law, administration and social sciences as well as those attending military, police and public service schools;

(42.4) — will make information on all CSCE human dimension provisions available to their educators;

(42.5) — will encourage organizations and educational establishments to co-operate in drawing up and exchanging human rights programmes at the national as well as the international level;

(42.6) — will seek to ensure that activities undertaken with a view to promoting human rights education in the broader sense take into account experience, programmes and forms of co-operation within existing international governmental and non-governmental bodies, such as the United Nations and the Council of Europe.

(43)   The participating States will recognize as NGOs those which declare themselves as such, according to existing national procedures, and will facilitate the ability of such organizations to conduct their activities freely on their territories; to that effect they will

(43.1)   — endeavour to seek ways of further strengthening modalities for contacts and exchanges of views between NGOs and relevant national authorities and governmental institutions;

(43.2)   — endeavour to facilitate visits to their countries by NGOs from within any of the participating States in order to observe human dimension conditions;

(43.3)   — welcome NGO activities, including, *inter alia*, observing compliance with CSCE commitments in the field of the human dimension;

(43.4)   — allow NGOs, in view of their important function within the human dimension of the CSCE, to convey their views to their own governments and the governments of all the other participating States during the future work of the CSCE on the human dimension.

(43.5)   During the future work of the CSCE on the human dimension, NGOs will have the opportunity to distribute written contributions on specific issues of the human dimension of the CSCE to all delegations.

(43.6)   The CSCE Secretariat will, within the framework of the resources at its disposal, respond favourably to requests by NGOs for non-restricted documents of the CSCE.

(43.7)   Guidelines for the participation of NGOs in the future work of the CSCE on the human dimension might, *inter alia*, include the following:

   (i) NGOs should be allotted common space at such meeting sites or in their immediate vicinity for their use as well as reasonable access, at their own expense, to technical facilities, including photocopying machines, telephones and fax machines;

  (ii) NGOs should be informed and briefed on openness and access procedures in a timely manner;

 (iii) delegations to CSCE meetings should be further encouraged to include or invite NGO members.

The participating States recommend that the Helsinki Follow-up Meeting consider establishing such guidelines.

. . .

45. Helsinki Document 1992 of the Conference on Security and Co-operation in Europe
(Excerpts)

Adopted at Helsinki on 10 July 1992

HELSINKI SUMMIT DECLARATION

Promises and problems of change

1.   We, the Heads of State or Government of the States participating in the Conference on Security and Co-operation in Europe, have returned to the birthplace of the Helsinki process, to give new impetus to our common endeavour.

. . .

6.   We welcome the commitment of all participating States to our shared values. Respect for human rights and fundamental freedoms, including the rights of persons belonging to national minorities, democracy, the rule of law, economic liberty, social justice and environmental responsibility are our common aims. They are immutable. Adherence to our commitments provides the basis for participation and co-operation in the CSCE and a cornerstone for further development of our societies.

7.   We reaffirm the validity of the guiding principles and common values of the Helsinki Final Act and the Charter of Paris, embodying responsibilities of States towards each other and of governments towards their people. These are the collective conscience of our community. We recognize our accountability to each other for complying with them. We underline the democratic rights of citizens to demand from their governments respect for these values and standards.

8.   We emphasize that the commitments undertaken in the field of the human dimension of the CSCE are matters of direct and legitimate concern to all participating States and do not belong exclusively to the internal affairs of the State concerned. The protection and promotion of the human rights and fundamental freedoms and the strengthening of democratic institutions continue to be a vital basis for our comprehensive security.

. . .

12.   This is a time of promise but also a time of instability and insecurity. Economic decline, social tension, aggressive nationalism, intolerance, xenophobia and ethnic conflicts threaten stability in the CSCE area. Gross violations of CSCE commitments in the field of human rights and fundamental freedoms, including those related to national minorities, pose a special threat to the peaceful development of society, in particular in new democracies.

There is still much work to be done in building democratic and pluralistic societies, where diversity is fully protected and respected in practice. Consequently, we reject racial, ethnic and religious discrimination in any form. Freedom and tolerance must be taught and practised.

. . .

43.   In order to foster our partnership, and to better manage change, we have today in Helsinki adopted an agenda for a strengthened and effective CSCE through the Helsinki Decisions. These decisions will be implemented fully and in good faith.

44.   We entrust the Council with the further steps which may be required to implement them. The Council may adopt any amendment to the decisions which it may deem appropriate.

45.   The full text of the Helsinki Document will be published in each participating State, which will make it known as widely as possible.

46.   The Government of Finland is requested to transmit to the Secretary-General of the United Nations the text of the Helsinki Document, which is not eligible for registration under Article 102 of the Charter of the United Nations, with a view to its circulation to all the members of the Organization as an official document of the United Nations.

. . .

HELSINKI DECISIONS

. . .

II

CSCE HIGH COMMISSIONER ON NATIONAL MINORITIES

(1)   The participating States decide to establish a High Commissioner on National Minorities.

Mandate

(2)   The High Commissioner will act under the aegis of the CSO[1] and will thus be an instrument of conflict prevention at the earliest possible stage.

(3)   The High Commissioner will provide "early warning" and, as appropriate, "early action" at the earliest possible stage in regard to tensions involving national minority issues which have not yet developed beyond an early warning stage, but, in the judgement of the High Commissioner, have the potential to develop into a conflict within the CSCE area, affecting peace, stability or relations between participating States, requiring the attention of and action by the Council or the CSO.

(4)   Within the mandate, based on CSCE principles and commitments, the High Commissioner will work in confidence and will act independently of all parties directly involved in the tensions.

(5 *a*)   The High Commissioner will consider national minority issues occurring in the State of which the High Commissioner is a national or a resident, or involving a national minority to which the High Commissioner belongs, only if all parties directly involved agree, including the State concerned.

(5 *b*)   The High Commissioner will not consider national minority issues in situations involving organized acts of terrorism.

(5 *c*)   Nor will the High Commissioner consider violations of CSCE commitments with regard to an individual person belonging to a national minority.

(6)   In considering a situation, the High Commissioner will take fully into account the availability of democratic means and international instruments to respond to it, and their utilization by the parties involved.

(7)   When a particular national minority issue has been brought to the attention of the CSO, the involvement of the High Commissioner will require a request and a specific mandate from the CSO.

Profile, appointment, support

(8)   The High Commissioner will be an eminent international personality with long-standing relevant experience from whom an impartial performance of the function may be expected.

---

[1] Committee of Senior Officials.

(9) The High Commissioner will be appointed by the Council by consensus upon the recommendation of the CSO for a period of three years, which may be extended for one further term of three years only.

(10) The High Commissioner will draw upon the facilities of the ODIHR[2] in Warsaw, and in particular upon the information relevant to all aspects of national minority questions available at the ODIHR.

Early warning

(11) The High Commissioner will:

(11 *a*) collect and receive information regarding national minority issues from sources described below (see Supplement paragraphs (23)-(25));

(11 *b*) assess at the earliest possible stage the role of the parties directly concerned, the nature of the tensions and recent developments therein and, where possible, the potential consequences for peace and stability within the CSCE area;

(11 *c*) to this end, be able to pay a visit, in accordance with paragraph (17) and Supplement paragraphs (27)-(30), to any participating State and communicate in person, subject to the provisions of paragraph (25), with parties directly concerned to obtain first-hand information about the situation of national minorities.

(12) The High Commissioner may during a visit to a participating State, while obtaining first-hand information from all parties directly involved, discuss the questions with the parties, and where appropriate promote dialogue, confidence and co-operation between them.

Provision of early warning

(13) If, on the basis of exchanges of communications and contacts with relevant parties, the High Commissioner concludes that there is a *prima facie* risk of potential conflict (as set out in paragraph (3)) he/she may issue an early warning, which will be communicated promptly by the Chairman-in-Office to the CSO.

(14) The Chairman-in-Office will include this early warning in the agenda for the next meeting of the CSO. If a State believes that such an early warning merits prompt consultation, it may initiate the procedure set out in Annex 2 of the Summary of Conclusions of the Berlin Meeting of the Council ("Emergency Mechanism").

(15) The High Commissioner will explain to the CSO the reasons for issuing the early warning.

---

[2] Office for Democratic Institutions and Human Rights.

Early action

(16)   The High Commissioner may recommend that he/she be authorized to enter into further contact and closer consultations with the parties concerned with a view to possible solutions, according to a mandate to be decided by the CSO. The CSO may decide accordingly.

Accountability

(17)   The High Commissioner will consult the Chairman-in-Office prior to a departure for a participating State to address a tension involving national minorities. The Chairman-in-Office will consult, in confidence, the participating State(s) concerned and may consult more widely.

(18)   After a visit to a participating State, the High Commissioner will provide strictly confidential reports to the Chairman-in-Office on the findings and progress of the High Commissioner's involvement in a particular question.

(19)   After termination of the involvement of the High Commissioner in a particular issue, the High Commissioner will report to the Chairman-in-Office on the findings, results and conclusions. Within a period of one month, the Chairman-in-Office will consult, in confidence, on the findings, results and conclusions the participating State(s) concerned and may consult more widely. Thereafter the report, together with possible comments, will be transmitted to the CSO.

(20)   Should the High Commissioner conclude that the situation is escalating into a conflict, or if the High Commissioner deems that the scope for action by the High Commissioner is exhausted, the High Commissioner shall, through the Chairman-in-Office, so inform the CSO.

(21)   Should the CSO become involved in a particular issue, the High Commissioner will provide information and, on request, advice to the CSO, or to any other institution or organization which the CSO may invite, in accordance with the provisions of Chapter III of this document, to take action with regard to the tensions or conflict.

(22)   The High Commissioner, if so requested by the CSO and with due regard to the requirement of confidentiality in his/her mandate, will provide information about his/her activities at CSCE implementation meetings on Human Dimension issues.

Supplement

Sources of information about national minority issues

(23)   The High Commissioner may:

(23 *a*) collect and receive information regarding the situation of national minorities and the role of parties involved therein from any source, including the media and non-governmental organizations with the exception referred to in paragraph (25);

(23 *b*) receive specific reports from parties directly involved regarding developments concerning national minority issues. These may include reports on violations of CSCE commitments with respect to national minorities as well as other violations in the context of national minority issues.

(24) Such specific reports to the High Commissioner should meet the following requirements:

—they should be in writing, addressed to the High Commissioner as such and signed with full names and addresses;

—they should contain a factual account of the developments which are relevant to the situation of persons belonging to national minorities and the role of the parties involved therein, and which have taken place recently, in principle not more than 12 months previously. The reports should contain information which can be sufficiently substantiated.

(25) The High Commissioner will not communicate with and will not acknowledge communications from any person or organization which practises or publicly condones terrorism or violence.

Parties directly concerned

(26) Parties directly concerned in tensions who can provide specific reports to the High Commissioner and with whom the High Commissioner will seek to communicate in person during a visit to a participating State are the following:

(26 *a*) governments of participating States, including, if appropriate, regional and local authorities in areas in which national minorities reside;

(26 *b*) representatives of associations, non-governmental organizations, religious and other groups of national minorities directly concerned and in the area of tension, which are authorized by the persons belonging to those national minorities to represent them.

Conditions for travel by the High Commissioner

(27) Prior to an intended visit, the High Commissioner will submit to the participating State concerned specific information regarding the intended purpose of that visit. Within two weeks the State(s) concerned will consult with the High Commissioner on the objectives of the visit, which may include the promotion of dialogue, confidence and co-operation between the parties. After entry the State concerned will facilitate free travel

and communication of the High Commissioner subject to the provisions of paragraph (25) above.

(28)   If the State concerned does not allow the High Commissioner to enter the country and to travel and communicate freely, the High Commissioner will so inform the CSO.

(29)   In the course of such a visit, subject to the provisions of paragraph (25) the High Commissioner may consult the parties involved, and may receive information in confidence from any individual, group or organization directly concerned on questions the High Commissioner is addressing. The High Commissioner will respect the confidential nature of the information.

(30)   The participating States will refrain from taking any action against persons, organizations or institutions on account of their contact with the High Commissioner.

High Commissioner and involvement of experts

(31)   The High Commissioner may decide to request assistance from not more than three experts with relevant expertise in specific matters on which brief, specialized investigation and advice are required.

(32)   If the High Commissioner decides to call on experts, the High Commissioner will set a clearly defined mandate and time-frame for the activities of the experts.

(33)   Experts will only visit a participating State at the same time as the High Commissioner. Their mandate will be an integral part of the mandate of the High Commissioner and the same conditions for travel will apply.

(34)   The advice and recommendations requested from the experts will be submitted in confidence to the High Commissioner, who will be responsible for the activities and for the reports of the experts and who will decide whether and in what form the advice and recommendations will be communicated to the parties concerned. They will be non-binding. If the High Commissioner decides to make the advice and recommendations available, the State(s) concerned will be given the opportunity to comment.

(35)   The experts will be selected by the High Commissioner with the assistance of the ODIHR from the resource list established at the ODIHR as laid down in the Document of the Moscow Meeting.

(36)   The experts will not include nationals or residents of the participating State concerned, or any person appointed by the State concerned, or any expert against whom the participating State has previously entered reservations. The experts will not include the participating State's own nation-

225

22525225

als or residents or any of the persons it appointed to the resource list, or more than one national or resident of any particular State.

Budget

(37)   A separate budget will be determined at the ODIHR, which will provide, as appropriate, logistical support for travel and communication. The budget will be funded by the participating States according to the established CSCE scale of distribution. Details will be worked out by the Financial Committee and approved by the CSO.

. . .

VI

THE HUMAN DIMENSION

(1)   The participating States conducted a useful review of implementation of CSCE commitments in the Human Dimension. They based their discussion on the new community of values established among them, as set forth by the Charter of Paris for a New Europe and developed by the new standards created within the CSCE in recent years. They noted major progress in complying with Human Dimension commitments, but recognized developments of serious concern and thus the need for further improvement.

(2)   The participating States express their strong determination to ensure full respect for human rights and fundamental freedoms, to abide by the rule of law, to promote the principles of democracy and, in this regard, to build, strengthen and protect democratic institutions, as well as to promote tolerance throughout society. To these ends, they will broaden the operational framework of the CSCE, including by further enhancing the ODIHR, so that information, ideas and concerns can be exchanged in a more concrete and meaningful way, including as an early warning of tension and potential conflict. In doing so, they will focus their attention on topics in the Human Dimension of particular importance. They will therefore keep the strengthening of the Human Dimension under constant consideration, especially in a time of change.

(3)   In this regard, the participating States adopt the following:

Framework for monitoring compliance with CSCE commitments and for promoting co-operation in the Human Dimension

(4)   In order to strengthen and monitor compliance with CSCE commitments as well as to promote progress in the Human Dimension, the par-

ticipating States agree to enhance the framework of their co-operation and to this end decide the following:

ENHANCED ROLE OF THE ODIHR

(5)   Under the general guidance of the CSO and in addition to its existing tasks as set out in the Charter of Paris for a New Europe and in the Prague Document on Further Development of CSCE Institutions and Structures, the ODIHR will, as the main institution of the Human Dimension:

(5 *a*) assist the monitoring of implementation of commitments in the Human Dimension by:

—serving as a venue for bilateral meetings under paragraph 2 and as a channel for information under paragraph 3 of the Human Dimension Mechanism as set out in the Vienna Concluding Document;

—receiving any comments from States visited by CSCE missions of relevance to the Human Dimension other than those under the Human Dimension Mechanism; it will transmit the report of those missions as well as eventual comments to all participating States with a view to discussion at the next implementation meeting or review conference;

—participating in or undertaking missions when instructed by the Council or the CSO;

(5 *b*) act as a clearing-house for information on:

—a state of public emergency according to paragraph 28.10 of the Document of the Moscow Meeting of the Conference on the Human Dimension;

—resource lists, and assistance, e.g. in the field of censuses or on democracy at a local and regional level, and the holding of national seminars on such issues;

(5 *c*) assist other activities in the field of the Human Dimension, including the building of democratic institutions by:

—fulfilling the tasks as defined in the "Programme of coordinated support for recently admitted participating States";

—arranging "Seminars on the democratic process" at the request of participating States. The same procedural provisions as set out in the "Programme of coordinated support for recently admitted participating States" will also apply to these seminars;

—contributing, within the resources at its disposal, to the preparation of seminars at the request of one or more participating States;

—providing, as appropriate, facilities to the High Commissioner on National Minorities;

—communicating, as appropriate, with relevant international and non-governmental organizations;

—consulting and cooperating with relevant bodies of the Council of Europe and those associated with it, and examining how they can contribute, as appropriate, to the ODIHR's activities. The ODIHR will also, at the request of participating States, supply them with information about programmes within the framework of the Council of Europe which are open to all participating States.

(6)   The activities on Human Dimension issues undertaken by the ODIHR may, *inter alia*, contribute to early warning in the prevention of conflicts.

HUMAN DIMENSION MECHANISM

(7)   In order to align the Human Dimension Mechanism with present CSCE structures and institutions the participating States decide that:

Any participating State which deems it necessary may provide information on situations and cases which have been the subject of requests under paragraphs 1 or 2 of the chapter entitled the "Human Dimension of the CSCE" of the Vienna Concluding Document or on the results of those procedures, to the participating States through the ODIHR—which can equally serve as a venue for bilateral meetings under paragraph 2—or diplomatic channels. Such information may be discussed at meetings of the CSO, at implementation meetings on Human Dimension issues and review conferences.

(8)   Procedures concerning the covering of expenses of expert and rapporteur missions of the Human Dimension Mechanism may be considered by the next review conference in the light of experience gained.

IMPLEMENTATION

Implementation meetings on Human Dimension issues

(9)   Every year in which a review conference does not take place, the ODIHR will organize a three-week meeting at expert-level of all participating States at its seat to review implementation of CSCE Human Dimension commitments. The meeting will perform the following tasks:

(9 *a*)   a thorough exchange of views on the implementation of Human Dimension commitments, including discussion on the information provided in accordance with paragraph 4 of the Human Dimension Mechanism and on the Human Dimension aspects of the reports of CSCE missions, as well as the consideration of ways and means of improving implementation;

(9 *b*)   an evaluation of the procedures for monitoring compliance with commitments.

(10)   The implementation meeting may draw to the attention of the CSO measures to improve implementation which it deems necessary.

(11)   The implementation meeting will not produce a negotiated document.

(12)   Written contributions and information material will be of a non-restricted or restricted character as indicated by the submitting State.

(13)   Implementation meetings will be organized to meet in formal and informal sessions. All formal sessions will be open. In addition, the participating States may decide, on a case-by-case basis, to open informal sessions.

(14)   The Council of Europe, the European Commission for Democracy through Law and the European Bank for Reconstruction and Development (EBRD), as well as other relevant international organizations and institutions, will be encouraged by the implementation meeting to attend and make contributions.

(15)   Non-governmental organizations having relevant experience in the field of the Human Dimension are invited to make written presentations to the implementation meeting, e.g. through the ODIHR, and may be invited by the implementation meeting, on the basis of their written presentations, to address specific questions orally as appropriate.

(16)   During two half days in the course of the implementation meeting no formal session will be scheduled in order to provide better opportunities for possible contacts with NGOs. To this purpose, a hall at the meeting site will be placed at the disposal of NGOs.

CSCE Human Dimension seminars

(17)   Under the general guidance of the CSO, the ODIHR will organize CSCE Human Dimension seminars which will address specific questions of particular relevance to the Human Dimension and of current political concern. The CSO will establish an annual work programme including the titles and dates of such seminars. The agenda and modalities of each seminar will be approved by the CSO at the latest three months before the seminar. In doing so, the CSO will take into account views expressed by the ODIHR. Unless otherwise decided, seminars will be held at the seat of the ODIHR and will not exceed one week. The work programme will take into account work by relevant international organizations and institutions.

(18)   These seminars will be organized in an open and flexible manner. Relevant international organizations and institutions may be invited to attend and to make contributions. So may NGOs with relevant experience. Independent experts attending the seminar as members of national delegations will also be free to speak in their own capacity.

(19)   CSCE seminars will be organized to meet in formal and informal sessions. All formal sessions will be open. In addition, the participating States may decide, on a case-by-case basis, to open informal sessions.

(20)   CSCE seminars will not produce a negotiated document or follow-up programmes.

(21)   Contributions by independent experts will be of a non-restricted character.

(22)   In order to launch the new CSCE Human Dimension seminars without delay, the participating States decide now at the Helsinki Follow-up Meeting that the ODIHR will organize the following four seminars:
—Migration
—Case Studies on National Minorities Issues: Positive Results
—Tolerance
—Free Media

These seminars will be held before 31 December 1993. The agenda and modalities of the seminars will be decided by the CSO. Seminars on migrant workers and on local democracy will be included in the first annual work programme of seminars. The financial implications of the seminar programme will be kept under consideration by the CSO.

Enhanced commitments and co-operation in the Human Dimension

NATIONAL MINORITIES

The participating States

(23)   Reaffirm in the strongest terms their determination to implement in a prompt and faithful manner all their CSCE commitments, including those contained in the Vienna Concluding Document, the Copenhagen Document and the Geneva Report, regarding questions relating to national minorities and rights of persons belonging to them;

(24)   Will intensify in this context their efforts to ensure the free exercise by persons belonging to national minorities, individually or in community with others, of their human rights and fundamental freedoms, including the right to participate fully, in accordance with the democratic decision-making procedures of each State, in the political, economic, social and cultural life of their countries including through democratic participation in decision-making and consultative bodies at the national, regional and local level, *inter alia*, through political parties and associations;

(25)   Will continue through unilateral, bilateral and multilateral efforts to explore further avenues for more effective implementation of their relevant CSCE commitments, including those related to the protection and

the creation of conditions for the promotion of the ethnic, cultural, linguistic and religious identity of national minorities;

(26)   Will address national minority issues in a constructive manner, by peaceful means and through dialogue among all parties concerned on the basis of CSCE principles and commitments;

(27)   Will refrain from resettling and condemn all attempts, by the threat or use of force, to resettle persons with the aim of changing the ethnic composition of areas within their territories;

(28)   Direct the ODIHR to organize, in spring 1993, a CSCE Human Dimension Seminar on Case Studies on National Minorities Issues: Positive Results.

INDIGENOUS POPULATIONS

The participating States

(29)   Noting that persons belonging to indigenous populations may have special problems in exercising their rights, agree that their CSCE commitments regarding human rights and fundamental freedoms apply fully and without discrimination to such persons.

TOLERANCE AND NON-DISCRIMINATION

The participating States

(30)   Express their concern over recent and flagrant manifestations of intolerance, discrimination, aggressive nationalism, xenophobia, anti-semitism and racism and stress the vital role of tolerance, understanding and co-operation in the achievement and preservation of stable democratic societies;

(31)   Direct the ODIHR to organize, in autumn 1992, a CSCE Human Dimension Seminar on Tolerance;

(32)   Will consider adhering to the International Convention on the Elimination of All Forms of Racial Discrimination, if they have not already done so;

(33)   Will consider taking appropriate measures within their constitutional framework and in conformity with their international obligations to assure to everyone on their territory protection against discrimination on racial, ethnic and religious grounds, as well as to protect all individuals, including foreigners, against acts of violence, including on any of these grounds. Moreover, they will make full use of their domestic legal processes, including enforcement of existing laws in this regard;

(34)   Will consider developing programmes to create the conditions for promoting non-discrimination and cross-cultural understanding which will focus on human rights education, grass-roots action, cross-cultural training and research;

(35)   Reaffirm, in this context, the need to develop appropriate programmes addressing problems of their respective nationals belonging to Roma and other groups traditionally identified as Gypsics and to create conditions for them to have equal opportunities to participate fully in the life of society, and will consider how to co-operate to this end.

MIGRANT WORKERS

The participating States

(36)   Restate that human rights and fundamental freedoms are universal, that they are also enjoyed by migrant workers wherever they live and stress the importance of implementing all CSCE commitments on migrant workers and their families lawfully residing in the participating States;

(37)   Will encourage the creation of conditions to foster greater harmony in relations between migrant workers and the rest of the society of the participating State in which they lawfully reside. To this end, they will seek to offer, *inter alia*, measures to facilitate the familiarization of migrant workers and their families with the languages and social life of the respective participating State in which they lawfully reside so as to enable them to participate in the life of the society of the host country;

(38)   Will, in accordance with their domestic policies, laws and international obligations seek, as appropriate, to create the conditions for promoting equality of opportunity in respect of working conditions, education, social security and health services, housing, access to trade unions as well as cultural rights for lawfully residing and working migrant workers.

REFUGEES AND DISPLACED PERSONS

The participating States

(39)   Express their concern over the problem of refugees and displaced persons;

(40)   Emphasize the importance of preventing situations that may result in mass flows of refugees and displaced persons and stress the need to identify and address the root causes of displacement and involuntary migration;

(41)   Recognize the need for international co-operation in dealing with mass flows of refugees and displaced persons;

(42)   Recognize that displacement is often a result of violations of CSCE commitments, including those relating to the Human Dimension;

(43)   Reaffirm the importance of existing international standards and instruments related to the protection of and assistance to refugees and will consider acceding to the Convention relating to the Status of Refugees and the Protocol, if they have not already done so;

(44)   Recognize the importance of the United Nations High Commissioner for Refugees and the International Committee of the Red Cross, as well as of non-governmental organizations involved in relief work, for the protection of and assistance to refugees and displaced persons;

(45)   Welcome and support unilateral, bilateral and multilateral efforts to ensure protection of and assistance to refugees and displaced persons with the aim of finding durable solutions;

(46)   Direct the ODIHR to organize, in early 1993, a CSCE Human Dimension Seminar on Migration, Including Refugees and Displaced Persons.

INTERNATIONAL HUMANITARIAN LAW

The participating States

(47)   Recall that international humanitarian law is based upon the inherent dignity of the human person;

(48)   Will in all circumstances respect and ensure respect for international humanitarian law including the protection of the civilian population;

(49)   Recall that those who violate international humanitarian law are held personally accountable;

(50)   Acknowledge the essential role of the International Committee of the Red Cross in promoting the implementation and development of international humanitarian law, including the Geneva Conventions and their relevant Protocols;

(51)   Reaffirm their commitment to extend full support to the International Committee of the Red Cross, as well as to the Red Cross and Red Crescent Societies, and to the United Nations organizations, particularly in times of armed conflict, respect their protective emblems, prevent the misuse of these emblems and, as appropriate, exert all efforts to ensure access to the areas concerned;

(52)   Commit themselves to fulfilling their obligation to teach and disseminate information about their obligations under international humanitarian law.

DEMOCRACY AT A LOCAL AND REGIONAL LEVEL

The participating States

(53)   Will endeavour, in order to strengthen democratic participation and institution building and in developing co-operation among them, to share their respective experience on the functioning of democracy at a local and regional level, and welcome against this background the Council of Europe information and education network in this field;

(54)   Will facilitate contacts and encourage various forms of co-operation between bodies at a local and regional level.

NATIONALITY

The participating States

(55)   Recognize that everyone has the right to a nationality and that no one should be deprived of his/her nationality arbitrarily;

(56)   Underline that all aspects of nationality will be governed by the process of law. They will, as appropriate, take measures, consistent with their constitutional framework not to increase statelessness;

(57)   Will continue within the CSCE the discussion on these issues.

CAPITAL PUNISHMENT

The participating States

(58)   Confirm their commitments in the Copenhagen and Moscow Documents concerning the question of capital punishment.

FREE MEDIA

The participating States

(59)   Direct the ODIHR to organize a CSCE Human Dimension Seminar on Free Media, to be held in 1993. The goal of the Seminar will be to encourage the discussion, demonstration, establishment of contacts and exchange of information between governmental representatives and media practitioners.

EDUCATION

The participating States

(60)   Would welcome, in view of the importance of education as to the dissemination of the ideas of democracy, human rights and democratic institutions, especially in a period of change, the organization to this end of a

seminar entitled "Education: Structures, Policies and Strategies" by the Council of Europe, open to all participating States.

COMPILATION OF HUMAN DIMENSION COMMITMENTS

The participating States

(61)   Welcome the drawing up of compilations of existing CSCE Human Dimension commitments in order to promote greater understanding for the implementation of these commitments.

DOMESTIC IMPLEMENTATION GUIDELINES

The participating States

(62)   Will promote, where appropriate, the drawing up of guidelines to assist the effective implementation of domestic legislation on human rights issues related to CSCE commitments.

· · ·

46. Document of the 1993 Rome Meeting of the Council of the Conference on Security and Co-operation in Europe
(Excerpts)

CSCE and the New Europe—Our Security is Indivisible

DECISIONS OF THE ROME COUNCIL MEETING

Adopted at the Conference on Security and Co-operation in Europe,
Rome, 1 December 1993

The CSCE Council held its Fourth Meeting in Rome from 30 November to 1 December 1993.

The Ministers expressed deep concern that threats to peace and stability proliferate and that crises, widespread violence and open confrontations persist. They strongly condemned the increasing violations of human rights and humanitarian law and the attempt of countries to acquire territories by the use of force. The increasing flow of refugees and appalling human suffering caused by armed conflicts must be urgently alleviated. The Ministers reiterated the personal accountability of those responsible for crimes against humanity.

Despite these events, there is encouraging progress in human rights, democracy and the rule of law in several parts of the CSCE area. The Ministers expressed satisfaction with the spread of free elections and development of democratic institutions registered in many participating States. The Ministers intended to ensure that the CSCE provides appropriate support for these efforts.

To promote the process of democratic change, the Ministers reiterated their determination to base their common action on solidarity, the comprehensive concept of security and freedom of choice of security relations. By utilizing the CSCE agreed set of standards and principles, participating States can demonstrate their unity of purpose and action and thus help to make security indivisible.

The Ministers agreed to strengthen the CSCE role as a pan-European and transatlantic forum for co-operative security as well as for political consultation on the basis of equality. The CSCE can be especially valuable as the first line of joint action on the underlying causes of conflict. At the heart of the CSCE efforts is the struggle to protect human rights and fundamental freedoms in the CSCE area.

The Ministers stressed the need to make wide use of CSCE capabilities in early warning and preventive diplomacy and to further integrate the human dimension in this endeavour. They commended the contribution of the High Commissioner on National Minorities to the development of these capabilities. They furthermore welcomed an increased role of the Office for Democratic Institutions and Human Rights in the human dimension, as well as the contributions of the CSCE missions in the field of conflict prevention and crisis management. The goal of further efforts should be to improve abilities to address potential crises at an early stage.

The Ministers also welcomed proposals to undertake jointly specific action to enhance stability.

In this respect the Ministers expressed appreciation for the presentation of the initiative for a Pact for Stability made by the European Union.

They also welcomed the proposed Partnership for Peace initiative being worked out among participants in the North Atlantic Co-operation Council.

The Ministers agreed to pursue the possibility of enhancing capabilities to apply CSCE crisis management arrangements on a case-by-case basis to situations involving third party forces when such arrangements are determined to be supportive of CSCE objectives.

The Ministers agreed to commit the necessary political, human and financial resources to the expanding operational tasks of the CSCE. They pledged to utilize the innovative means which the CSCE can bring to bear in dealing with the day-to-day challenges of change.

The Ministers also agreed to deepen the CSCE co-operation with the United Nations, as well as with European and transatlantic organizations. They welcomed all co-operative efforts by such organizations to make contributions toward stability.

The Ministers underlined the importance of the work of the Forum for Security Co-operation. They encouraged completion of the Programme for Immediate Action, including the proposal to establish a Code of Conduct.

Looking towards the Budapest Summit in December 1994, the Ministers determined to make their co-operation more concrete and effective through the action programme below. In so doing, the CSCE participating States will demonstrate that however varied their histories and backgrounds, their security is truly indivisible.

To give substance and direction to their commitments, the Ministers have agreed on an action programme to be implemented through the decisions which they have adopted today.

These decisions, *inter alia*, address the following issues:

(*a*) The situation in Bosnia-Herzegovina, Croatia and Yugoslavia (Serbia and Montenegro). Examination, as a complement to the efforts of the ICFY, of a CSCE contribution to regional security.

The responsibilities of the CSCE Mission in Georgia will be widened to include the promotion of human rights and the development of democratic institutions. A proposal will be elaborated on possible arrangements for CSCE liaison with and monitoring of the Joint Peacekeeping Forces established under the Sochi Agreement of 24 June 1992.

In Moldova, the work of the CSCE Mission will be intensified.

A new CSCE Mission will be sent to Tajikistan, to help build democratic institutions and processes there.

The remaining Russian troops will shortly complete their orderly withdrawal from the territories of the Baltic States as agreed.

(*b*) CSCE crisis management capabilities regarding situations involving third party military forces will be further considered.

(*c*) The role of the High Commissioner on National Minorities will be enhanced.

(*d*) The human dimension will be further integrated into the CSCE political consultation process; the ODIHR will be reinforced.

(*e*) The CSCE will play a more active role in promoting co-operation in the economic dimension.

(*f*) Co-operation and contacts with the United Nations and European and transatlantic organizations shall be improved.

(*g*) A Permanent Committee of the CSCE for political consultations and decision making will be created in Vienna, where also a new CSCE Secretariat with comprehensive tasks will be established. A decision on CSCE legal capacity was taken.

(*h*) Integration of recently admitted participating States will receive new impetus.

(*i*) Relations between the CSCE and non-participating Mediterranean States will be further developed.

(*j*) The role of the CSCE in combating aggressive nationalism, racism, chauvinism, xenophobia and anti-semitism will be strengthened.

III. HIGH COMMISSIONER ON NATIONAL MINORITIES

Bearing in mind the close interrelationship between questions relating to national minorities and conflict prevention, the Ministers encouraged the

High Commissioner on National Minorities (HCNM) to pursue his activities under his Mandate. They recognized the HCNM as an innovative and effective asset in early warning and preventive diplomacy. The Ministers stressed the importance of participating States co-operating fully with the High Commissioner and supporting follow-up and implementation of his recommendations. They welcomed the decision by the CSO to increase the resources available to the HCNM.

IV. THE HUMAN DIMENSION

1.   The Ministers reiterated that human dimension issues are fundamental to the comprehensive security concept of the CSCE. They noted that adherence to human dimension commitments remains to be consolidated in large parts of the CSCE area, and expressed particular concern that civilians continue to be the victims of atrocities in ongoing conflicts in the CSCE area. Concerned by the root causes of tension stemming from historical prejudices, the Ministers called for efforts, *inter alia*, through education, to promote tolerance and consciousness of belonging to a system of common values. The Ministers stressed that implementation of human dimension commitments must be a focus of attention in the CSCE's conflict prevention efforts.

2.   To this end the Ministers decided to strengthen the instruments of conflict prevention and early warning which are available within the human dimension of the CSCE. They emphasized the need in this context for enhanced co-operation and co-ordination with relevant international organizations such as the Council of Europe, as well as with non-governmental organizations.

The following decisions were taken:

3.   *The political consultation process and CSCE missions*

—In order to further political consideration and action under the human dimension, the decision-making bodies of the CSCE will consider human dimension issues on a regular basis as an integral part of deliberations relating to European security. Resources and information will be made available by the ODIHR in support of such consideration.

—Further emphasis will be given to human dimension issues in mandates of CSCE missions as well as in the follow-up of mission reports. To this end the ODIHR will be given an enhanced role in the preparation of CSCE missions, *inter alia*, in providing information and advice to missions in accordance with its expertise.

—In the context of conflict prevention and crisis management, the issue of mass migration, namely displaced persons and refugees, will be addressed, as appropriate, by the CSO and the Permanent Committee of the CSCE, taking into account the role of other relevant international bodies.

4. *Office for Democratic Institutions and Human Rights*

The Ministers decided to strengthen the ODIHR's functions and operations. *Inter alia*, the ODIHR will enhance its activities under its mandate in the following areas:

—the building of an expanded database of experts in fields relevant to the human dimension. Participating States and non-governmental organizations are requested to inform the ODIHR of experts available in fields relevant to the human dimension;

—enhancement of its role in comprehensive election monitoring;

—strengthened co-operation with relevant international organizations in order to co-ordinate activities and identify possible areas of joint endeavour;

—receiving information provided by NGOs having relevant experience in the human dimension field;

—serving as a point of contact for information provided by participating States in accordance with CSCE commitments;

—disseminating general information on the human dimension, and international humanitarian law.

The Ministers determined that in order to fulfil its new tasks, the ODIHR should be granted additional resources. They requested the CSO to consider the financial and administrative implications of strengthening the ODIHR as outlined above.

5. *Streamlining the Moscow Mechanism*

Recognizing the Moscow Mechanism as a significant inter-governmental instrument for follow-up within the human dimension, the Ministers agreed to develop its effectiveness and promote its use, by expanding the resource list and shortening time-frames under the mechanism. Also the Permanent Committee of the CSCE will be empowered to trigger the mechanism as well as to take follow-up action based on rapporteur's reports. To this end it was decided to modify the mechanism in accordance with annex A.

6. *Building on the work of the Implementation Meeting on Human Dimension Issues and the Human Dimension Seminars*

—The Ministers attached significance to the outcome of the first Implementation Meeting on Human Dimension Issues, as well as the human dimension seminars conducted. The results of the Implementation Meeting on Human Dimensions Issues were welcomed and the CSO and the Permanent Committee of the CSCE were tasked to consider relevant follow-up to them.

—Enhanced follow-up by the political bodies of the CSCE based on summaries of meetings and seminars in the human dimension will be sought. The ODIHR, in consultation with interested participating States, is invited to present further proposals for appropriate follow-up action resulting from human dimension seminars to forthcoming CSO or Permanent Committee meetings.

—The Ministers expressed their appreciation of the work carried out at the Seminar on Free Media to stimulate editorially independent broadcast media and a free press. They reiterated their commitment to safeguard freedom of expression, a basic human right, and stressed the necessity of independent media for a free and open society. To this end the Ministers decided that better use should be made of the CSCE human dimension instruments to promote open and diverse media, including exploring the possibility of utilizing CSCE missions.

—Human dimension seminars will be held before the Budapest Review Conference on the subjects of migrant workers, local democracy and, if time and the resources of the ODIHR permit, on Roma in the CSCE region. Other topics proposed in the course of the Implementation Meeting on Human Dimension Issues should be considered for inclusion in the programme of seminars for 1995 and thereafter.

VI. CO-OPERATION AND CONTACTS WITH THE UNITED NATIONS AS WELL AS WITH EUROPEAN AND TRANSATLANTIC ORGANIZATIONS AND INSTITUTIONS

1. The Ministers agreed that to pursue the CSCE objective of a stronger commitment to short and long term conflict prevention and crisis management requires improved consultations and co-ordination with international organizations.

2. They agreed that, to achieve this, CSCE efforts to further improve relations with the United Nations should be continued. The basis will be the "Framework for co-operation and co-ordination between the United Nations Secretariat and the Conference on Security and Co-operation in Europe", and CSCE's recently obtained observer status to the United Nations General Assembly. Furthermore, the Ministers agreed that establishing organized forms for consultations and co-operation with other European and Transatlantic institutions and organizations is essential to encourage a sense of wider community, as referred to in the Helsinki Summit Declaration. They also encouraged sub-regional organizations and arrangements to explore ways of supporting the CSCE.

3. The Ministers requested the Chairman-in-Office, assisted by the CSCE Troika and the Secretary General, as appropriate, to pursue talks with these institutions and organizations with a view to establishing improved arrangements for consultations and for co-ordination of activities. The Ministers requested the Chairman-in-Office to report to the Committee of Senior Officials on the evolution of these talks and to submit as appropriate proposals for co-operation arrangements.

VII. CSCE STRUCTURES AND OPERATIONS

1. The Ministers reaffirmed that significant enhancement of the political effectiveness and operational capability of the CSCE is critical to achieving the goals they have defined for it.

2. They recalled the two mutually supporting forms of action by the CSCE: those joint political decisions taken in accordance with consensus rules and direct action through agreed mechanisms activated by a limited number of participating States.

3. To ensure improved capabilities for day-to-day operational tasks of the CSCE, the Ministers created a permanent body for political consultations and decision-making in Vienna, the Permanent Committee of the CSCE.

4. The Ministers decided that the Permanent Committee should review the relevance and operation of existing mechanisms with a view to increasing their effectiveness.

5. The Ministers also endorsed the decision to establish a CSCE Secretariat in Vienna as an important step towards further efficiency in administrative and secretariat support services. Further evolution of CSCE's operational capabilities will be based on the overriding objective of a non-bureaucratic, cost-efficient and flexible administrative structure which can be adapted to changing tasks.

6. The Ministers considered also problems which have arisen because of a shortage of economic and human resources for CSCE operations, especially preventive diplomacy missions. They decided that the question of providing adequate resources, in the form of expertise as well as of finance, for the CSCE to fulfil its promise will be vigorously pursued.

7. Institutional arrangements for political consultation and decision-making.

7.1 In order to enhance the capacity of the CSCE area, the Ministers decided to create a permanent body consisting of representatives of the participating States for political consultations and decision-making in Vienna. The new body will be responsible for the day-to-day operational tasks of the

CSCE under the chairmanship of the Chairman-in-Office and will meet under the name of the Permanent Committee of the CSCE. The Permanent Committee will conduct comprehensive and regular consultations and, when the CSO is not in session, take decisions on all issues pertinent to the CSCE. The Permanent Committee will be responsible to the CSO, and undertake preliminary discussion of items suggested for the agenda of the CSO. The CSO will continued to lay down political guidelines and take key decisions between Council meetings.

7.2   With a view to strengthening the interrelation and complementarity of the CSCE decision-making process in the fields of arms control, disarmament and confidence and security-building, security co-operation and conflict prevention, the Ministers decided to dissolve the Consultative Committee of the Conflict Prevention Centre as set up by the Paris supplementary document and transfer its competence to the Permanent Committee and the Forum for Security Co-operation in the following way:

7.3   The Permanent Committee will, in addition to the mandate as above, hold the meetings of the participating States which may be convened under the mechanism on unusual military activities.

7.4   The Forum for Security Co-operation will, in addition to current tasks

—assume responsibility for the implementation of CSBMs,

—prepare seminars on military doctrine and such other seminars as may be agreed by the participating States,

—hold the annual implementation assessment meetings,

—provide the forum for discussion and clarification, as necessary, of information exchanged under agreed CSBMs.

8.   *CSCE Secretariat*

The Ministers endorsed the decision by the CSO to establish a CSCE Secretariat in Vienna with an office in Prague. The Secretariat will include departments for conference services, administration and budget, Chairman-in-Office support and the Conflict Prevention Centre.

9.   Ensuring necessary resources and expertise for the CSCE.

9.1   The Ministers agreed that additional efforts must be undertaken to provide financial resources and draw on available expertise, including that provided through non-governmental sources.

9.2   They also expressed concern about continued non-payment of assessed contributions by a large number of participating States. They noted that a co-operative undertaking such as the CSCE cannot flourish without mutual support by all participants.

9.3   The Ministers further pledged to make new efforts to identify suitable candidates for a roster to serve on CSCE missions in order to be able to make such candidates available rapidly.

9.4   Recalling the ministerial decision at Stockholm on the need to identify new sources of funding, the Ministers noted the importance of ensuring sufficient resources for CSCE operations, especially those in the field. They instructed the Permanent Committee to submit recommendations to the CSO for further action as soon as possible.

10.   *Staffing arrangements for the CSCE Institutions*

The Ministers have taken note with appreciation of the report of the ad hoc group on efficient management of CSCE resources, approved by the 23rd CSO Meeting. Regarding recruitment and appointment for senior CSCE positions, the Ministers took the following decisions:

—Candidates for the posts of Secretary General, High Commissioner on National Minorities and director of ODIHR will be nominated by participating States for appointment by the Council.

—Positions as heads of the departments within the CSCE Secretariat will be subject to open competition. These positions will be appointed by the Chairman-in-Office in consultation with the Secretary General. Other positions in the CSCE Secretariat will be appointed by the Secretary General, taking into account equal opportunity requirements and the diversity of the CSCE community.

—The Director of the ODIHR and the HCNM will appoint their respective senior staff in consultation with the Secretary General taking into account equal opportunity requirements and the diversity of the CSCE community.

—All CSCE positions will be budgeted for. Whenever possible participating States may consider seconding their nationals who have been successful in obtaining positions.

11.   The Ministers have taken note with appreciation of the report of the ad hoc Group of Legal and Other Experts. The Ministers adopted a decision on legal capacity and privileges and immunities that recommends implementation of the following three basic elements (CSCE/4-C/Dec.2):

—The CSCE participating States will, subject to their constitutional, legislative and related requirements, confer legal capacity on CSCE institutions in accordance with the provisions adopted by the Ministers;

—The CSCE participating States will, subject to their constitutional, legislative and related requirements, confer privileges and immunities on CSCE institutions, permanent missions of the participating States, representatives of participating States, CSCE officials and members of CSCE missions in accordance with the provisions adopted by the Ministers;

—The CSCE may issue CSCE Identity Cards in accordance with the form adopted by the Ministers.

X. DECLARATION ON AGGRESSIVE NATIONALISM, RACISM, CHAUVINISM, XENOPHOBIA AND ANTI-SEMITISM

1. Recalling their decisions taken at the Stockholm Council Meeting, the Ministers noted with deep concern the growing manifestations of aggressive nationalism, such as territorial expansionism, as well as racism, chauvinism, xenophobia and anti-semitism. These run directly counter to the principles and commitments of the CSCE.

2. The Ministers also noted that these phenomena can lead to violence, secessionism by the use of force and ethnic strife, and in their worst instances to the barbaric practices of mass deportation, ethnic cleansing and violence against innocent civilians.

3. Aggressive nationalism, racism, chauvinism, xenophobia and anti-semitism create ethnic, political and social tensions within and between States. They also undermine international stability and worldwide efforts to place universal human rights on a firm foundation.

4. The Ministers focused attention on the need for urgent action to enforce the strict observance of the norms of international humanitarian law, including the prosecution and punishment of those guilty of war crimes and other crimes against humanity.

5. The Ministers agreed that the CSCE must play an important role in these efforts. The clear standards of behaviour reflected in CSCE commitments include active support for the equal rights of all individuals in accordance with international law and for the protection of national minorities.

6. The Ministers decided to keep this issue high on the agenda of the CSCE and therefore decided:

—to task the Permanent Committee to study possible follow-up actions;

—to invite the High Commissioner on National Minorities, in light of his mandate, to pay particular attention to all aspects of aggressive nationalism, racism, chauvinism, xenophobia and anti-semitism;

—to request the ODIHR to pay special attention to these phenomena and to apply resources as necessary on addressing these problems.

47. Vienna Document 1994
(Excerpt)

Of the Negotiations on Confidence- and Security-Building Measures

Adopted at the Conference on Security and Co-operation in Europe,
Vienna, 28 November 1994

(1) Representatives of the participating States of the Conference on Security and Co-operation in Europe (CSCE), Albania, Armenia, Austria, Azerbaijan, Belarus, Belgium, Bosnia-Herzegovina, Bulgaria, Canada, Croatia, Cyprus, the Czech Republic, Denmark, Estonia, Finland, France, Georgia, Germany, Greece, the Holy See, Hungary, Iceland, Ireland, Italy, Kazakhstan, Kyrgyzstan, Latvia, Liechtenstein, Lithuania, Luxembourg, Malta, Moldova, Monaco, the Netherlands, Norway, Poland, Portugal, Romania, the Russian Federation, San Marino, Slovakia, Slovenia, Spain, Sweden, Switzerland, Tajikistan, Turkey, Turkmenistan, Ukraine, the United Kingdom, the United States of America, Uzbekistan and Yugoslavia*, met in Vienna in accordance with the provisions relating to the Conference on Confidence- and Security-Building Measures and Disarmament in Europe contained in the Concluding Documents of the Madrid, Vienna and Helsinki Follow-up Meetings of the CSCE. The delegation of the former Yugoslav Republic of Macedonia attended the meetings as an observer as from 1993.

(2) The Negotiations were conducted from 1989 to 1994.

(3) The participating States recalled that the aim of the Conference on Confidence- and Security-Building Measures and Disarmament in Europe is, as a substantial and integral part of the multilateral process initiated by the Conference on Security and Co-operation in Europe, to undertake, in stages, new, effective and concrete actions designed to make progress in strengthening confidence and security and in achieving disarmament, so as to give effect and expression to the duty of States to refrain from the threat or use of force in their mutual relations as well as in their international relations in general.

---

* On 13 December 1992 the CSCE Committee of Senior Officials agreed to maintain in force its decision of 8 July 1992 to suspend the participation of Yugoslavia in the CSCE and review it as appropriate.

(4) The participating States recognized that the mutually complementary confidence- and security-building measures which are adopted in the present document and which are in accordance with the mandates of the Madrid**, Vienna and Helsinki Follow-up Meetings of the CSCE serve by their scope and nature and by their implementation to strengthen confidence and security among the participating States.

(5)   The participating States recalled the declaration on Refraining from the Threat or Use of Force contained in paragraphs (9) to (27) of the Document of the Stockholm Conference and stressed its continuing validity as seen in the light of the Charter of Paris for a New Europe.

(6)   On 17 November 1990, the participating States adopted the Vienna Document 1990, which built upon and added to the confidence- and security-building measures contained in the Document of the Stockholm Conference 1986. On 4 March 1992, the participating States adopted the Vienna Document 1992, which built upon and added to the confidence- and security-building measures contained in the Vienna Document 1990.

(7)   In fulfilment of the Charter of Paris for a New Europe of November 1990 and the Programme for Immediate Action, set out in the Helsinki Document 1992, they continued the CSBM negotiations under the same mandate, and have adopted the present document which integrates a set of new confidence- and security-building measures with measures previously adopted.

** The zone of application for CSBMs under the terms of the Madrid mandate is set out in Annex 1.

48. Budapest Summit Declaration
(Excerpts)

Adopted at the Conference on Security and Co-operation in Europe,
Budapest, 6 December 1994

TOWARDS A GENUINE PARTNERSHIP IN A NEW ERA

1. We, the Heads of State or Government of the States participating in the Conference on Security and Co-operation in Europe, have met in Budapest to assess together the recent past, to consider the present and to look to the future. We do so as we approach the Fiftieth Anniversary of the end of World War II and the Twentieth Anniversary of the signing of the Helsinki Final Act, and as we commemorate the Fifth Anniversary of the fall of the Berlin Wall.

2. We believe in the central role of the CSCE in building a secure and stable CSCE community, whole and free. We reaffirm the principles of the Helsinki Final Act and subsequent CSCE documents. They reflect shared values which will guide our policies, individually and collectively, in all organizations and institutions to which we belong.

3. The CSCE is the security structure embracing States from Vancouver to Vladivostok. We are determined to give a new political impetus to the CSCE, thus enabling it to play a cardinal role in meeting the challenges of the twenty-first century. To reflect this determination, the CSCE will henceforth be known as the Organization for Security and Co-operation in Europe (OSCE).

4. The CSCE has been instrumental in overcoming barriers and in managing change throughout our region. Since we last met, there have been further encouraging developments. Most vestiges of the Cold War have disappeared. Free elections have been held and the roots of democracy have spread and struck deeper. Yet the path to stable democracy, efficient market economy and social justice is a hard one.

5. The spread of freedoms has been accompanied by new conflicts and the revival of old ones. Warfare in the CSCE region to achieve hegemony and territorial expansion continues to occur. Human rights and fundamental freedoms are still flouted, intolerance persists and discrimination against minorities is practised. The plagues of aggressive nationalism, ra-

459

cism, chauvinism, xenophobia, anti-semitism and ethnic tension are still widespread. Along with social and economic instability, they are among the main sources of crisis, loss of life and human misery. They reflect failure to apply the CSCE principles and commitments. This situation requires our resolute action. We must work together to ensure full respect for these principles and commitments as well as effective solidarity and co-operation to relieve suffering.

6.   We recognize that societies in the CSCE region are increasingly threatened by terrorism. We reiterate our unreserved condemnation of all acts and practices of terrorism, which cannot be justified under any circumstances. We reconfirm our determination to combat terrorism and our commitment for enhanced co-operation to eliminate this threat to security, democracy and human rights.

7.   The CSCE will be a forum where concerns of participating States are discussed, their security interests are heard and acted upon. We will further enhance its role as an instrument for the integration of these States in resolving security problems. Through the CSCE, we will build a genuine security partnership among all participating States, whether or not they are members of other security organizations. In doing so, we will be guided by the CSCE's comprehensive concept of security and its indivisibility, as well as by our commitment not to pursue national security interests at the expense of others. The CSCE's democratic values are fundamental to our goal of a community of nations with no divisions, old or new, in which the sovereign equality and the independence of all States are fully respected, there are no spheres of influence and the human rights and fundamental freedoms of all individuals, regardless of race, colour, sex, language, religion, social origin or of belonging to a minority, are vigorously protected.

8.   The CSCE will be a primary instrument for early warning, conflict prevention and crisis management in the region. We have agreed that the participating States may in exceptional circumstances jointly decide that a dispute will be referred to the United Nations Security Council on behalf of the CSCE. We have also decided to pursue more systematic and practical co-operation between the CSCE and European and other regional and transatlantic organizations and institutions that share its values and objectives.

9.   The CSCE has created new tools to deal with new challenges. In this regard, we welcome the entry into force of the Convention on Conciliation and Arbitration within the CSCE. We will further enhance the CSCE's role and capabilities in early warning, conflict prevention and crisis management, using, *inter alia*, CSCE peacekeeping operations and missions. We will provide consistent political support and adequate resources for CSCE efforts. We have agreed to strengthen the CSCE's political consultative and decision-making bodies and its executive action by the Chairman-in-Office, supported the Troika, as well as other CSCE procedures and institutions, in

particular the Secretary General and the Secretariat, the High Commissioner on National Minorities and the Office for Democratic Institutions and Human Rights. We have also decided to enhance our contacts and dialogue with the CSCE Parliamentary Assembly.

10.   Continuing the CSCE's norm-setting role, we have established a "Code of Conduct on Politico-Military Aspects of Security" that, *inter alia*, sets forth principles guiding the role of armed forces in democratic societies.

11.   We welcome the adoption by the CSCE Forum for Security Co-operation of substantial measures, including a new, developed Vienna Document 1994. A compendium of related measures is annexed to Decision V of the Budapest Document. In order to provide further momentum to arms control, disarmament and confidence- and security-building that adds to earlier decisions and agreements, we have directed it to continue its work in accordance with its mandate and to develop a framework which will serve as a basis for an agenda for establishing new measures of arms control, including in particular confidence- and security-building. We have also mandated it to address specific regional security problems, with special emphasis on longer-term stability in South-Eastern Europe.

12.   In view of the new threats posed by the proliferation of weapons of mass destruction, we have agreed on basic principles to guide our national policies in support of common non-proliferation objectives. We are strongly committed to the full implementation and indefinite and unconditional extension of the Treaty on the Non-Proliferation of Nuclear Weapons. We welcome the recent statements by the four nuclear-weapon-States in the CSCE region relating to nuclear testing as being consistent with negotiation of a comprehensive nuclear test-ban treaty. We urge that all signatories to the Convention on the Prohibition of Development, Production, Stockpiling or Use of Chemical Weapons and on their Destruction complete the ratification process in the shortest possible time. We also underline the importance of an early entry into force and implementation of the Treaty on Open Skies.

13.   In light of continuing rapid change, we deem it important to start discussion on a model of common and comprehensive security for our region for the twenty-first century, based on the CSCE principles and commitments. This discussion will take into account the CSCE's contribution to security, stability and co-operation. The Chairman-in-Office will present a progress report to the next Ministerial Council in 1995 in Budapest. The results of discussion on such a security model will be submitted to our next Summit Meeting in Lisbon in 1996.

14.   We confirm the significance of the Human Dimension in all the activities of the CSCE. Respect for human rights and fundamental freedoms, democracy and the rule of law is an essential component of security and co-operation in the CSCE regoin. It must remain a primary goal of CSCE action. Periodic reviews of implementation of our commitments, fundamental

throughout the CSCE, are critical in the Human Dimension. The enhanced capabilities of the Office for Democratic Institutions and Human Rights will continue to assist participating States, in particular those in transition. We underline the importance of human contacts in overcoming the legacy of old divisions.

15. We recognize that market economy and sustainable economic development are integral to the CSCE's comprehensive concept of security. We encourage the strengthening of co-operation to support the transition processes, regional co-operation and environmental responsibility. We welcome the role played by the relevant international organizations and institutions, such as the United Nations Economic Commission for Europe, OECD, EBRD and EIB, in support of the CSCE's economic dimension priorities. We are committed to enhancing the effectiveness of the Economic Forum and of the CSCE's other economic dimension activities. We ask the Chairman-in-Office to explore ways to integrate economic dimension issues into the tasks faced by the CSCE and report on progress at our next Summit Meeting.

16. We welcome the Declaration of Paris which launched the process aimed at the establishment of a Pact on Stability, as well as the intention expressed therein to entrust the CSCE with following the implementation of the Pact.

17. Strengthening security and co-operation in the Mediterranean is important for stability in the CSCE region. We welcome progress towards peace in the Middle East and its positive implications for European security. The common position adopted by Algeria, Egypt, Israel, Morocco and Tunisia on CSCE-Mediterranean relations encourages us to deepen the long-standing relationship and reinforce co-operation between the CSCE and the non-participating Mediterranean States.

18. We note with satisfaction the development of our relationship with Japan.

We welcome the interest of the Republic of Korea which has attended the CSCE Summit Meeting for the first time and of other States in the CSCE's experience and activities, and express our readiness to co-operate with them in areas of mutual interest.

19. In order to move towards a genuine partnership in a new era, we have today adopted the Budapest Decisions which will be implemented fully and in good faith.

20. We entrust the Ministerial Council with the further steps which may be required to implement them. The Council may adopt any amendment to the decisions which it may deem appropriate.

21. The full text of the Budapest Document will be published in each participating State, which will make it known as widely as possible.

22. The Government of Hungary is requested to transmit to the Secretary-General of the United Nations the text of the Budapest Document, which is not eligible for registration under Article 102 of the Charter of the United Nations, with a view to its circulation to all the members of the Organization as an official document of the United Nations.

Budapest, 6 December 1994

I

STRENGTHENING THE CSCE

1. The new era of security and co-operation in Europe has led to a fundamental change in the CSCE and to a dramatic growth in its role in shaping our common security area. To reflect this the CSCE will henceforth be known as the Organization for Security and Co-operation in Europe (OSCE). The change in name will be effective on 1 January 1995. As of this date, all references to the CSCE will henceforth be considered as references to the OSCE.

2. The participating States are determined to exploit its potential to the fullest, and agreed in that spirit on the following goals and objectives along with structural changes needed to strengthen the CSCE and make it as effective as possible. The purpose is to strengthen the CSCE's contribution to security, stability and co-operation in the CSCE region so that it plays a central role in the promotion of a common security space based on the principles of the Helsinki Final Act.

3. The Heads of State or Government have directed that the future role and functions of the CSCE will include the following:

4. — to make vigorous use of its norms and standards in shaping a common security area;

5. — to ensure full implementation of all CSCE commitments;

6. — to serve, based on consensus rules, as the inclusive and comprehensive forum for consultation, decision-making and co-operation in Europe;

7. — to enhance good-neighbourly relations through encouraging the conclusion of bilateral, regional and potential CSCE-wide agreements or arrangements between and among participating States;

8. — to strengthen further the CSCE's capacity and activity in preventive diplomacy;

9. — to further its principles and develop its capabilities in conflict resolution, crisis management and peacekeeping and in post-conflict rehabilitation, including assisting with reconstruction;

10. — to enhance security and stability through arms control, disarmament and confidence- and security-building throughout the CSCE region and at regional levels;

11. — to develop further CSCE work in the field of human rights and fundamental freedoms, and other areas of the human dimension;

12. — to promote co-operation among participating States to establish strong market-based economies throughout the CSCE region.

III

FURTHER DEVELOPMENT OF THE CAPABILITIES OF THE CSCE IN CONFLICT PREVENTION AND CRISIS MANAGEMENT

Confirming Chapter II of the Decisions of the Rome Council Meeting, the participating States request the Senior Council and the Permanent Council to pursue their work on this subject on the basis of the work carried out by the Permanent Committee and the Budapest Review Conference during 1994.

VIII

THE HUMAN DIMENSION

Introduction

1. In their review of implementation of CSCE commitments in the human dimension, the participating States based their discussion on the community of values established among them, which is reflected in the high standards created within the CSCE. During the discussion, it was noted that major progress had been made in compliance with human dimension commitments. The participating States acknowledged, however, that there was a serious deterioration in some areas and a need for action against the continuing violations of human rights and manifestations of aggressive nationalism,

such as territorial expansionism, as well as racism, chauvinism, xenophobia and anti-semitism, which continue to cause human suffering.

2. Human rights and fundamental freedoms, the rule of law and democratic institutions are the foundations of peace and security, representing a crucial contribution to conflict prevention, within a comprehensive concept of security. The protection of human rights, including the rights of persons belonging to national minorities, is an essential foundation of democratic civil society. Neglect of these rights has, in severe cases, contributed to extremism, regional instability and conflict. The participating States confirmed that issues of implementation of CSCE commitments are of legitimate and common concern to all participating States, and that the raising of these problems in the co-operative and result-oriented spirit of the CSCE was therefore a positive exercise. They undertook to encourage implementation of CSCE commitments through enhanced dialogue, implementation reviews and mechanisms. They will broaden the operational framework of the CSCE, in particular by enhancing the Office for Democratic Institutions and Human Rights (ODIHR), increasing its involvement in the work of the Permanent Council and mission activity, and furthering co-operation with international organizations and institutions active in human dimension areas.

3. The participation of non-governmental organizations (NGOs) was a welcome addition to the implementation review. In their statements, these organizations contributed ideas and raised issues of concern for participating States to take into consideration. They also informed the participating States of their activities, such as in the area of conflict prevention and resolution. The experience of the Budapest Review Conference invites further consideration with regard to promoting within the CSCE the dialogue between governments and NGOs of the participating States, in addition to State-to-State dialogue.

4. Reaffirming their commitments in the human dimension, the participating States, while considering it essential to concentrate their efforts on the implementation of existing CSCE commitments, decide to enhance the framework of their co-operation and to this end adopt the following:

ENHANCING COMPLIANCE WITH CSCE COMMITMENTS AND PROMOTING CO-OPERATION AND DIALOGUE IN THE HUMAN DIMENSION

Enhancing implementation

5. Building on the implementation review structures in the Helsinki Document 1992 and to improve human dimension implementation, the participating States will use the Permanent Council for an enhanced dialogue on the human dimension and for possible action in cases of non-implementation. To this end, the participating States decide that human di-

mension issues will be regularly dealt with by the Permanent Council. They will draw more widely on the possibilities offered by the Moscow Mechanism for examining or promoting the solution of questions relating to the human dimension on their territory.

6. They encourage the Chairman-in-Office to inform the Permanent Council of serious cases of alleged non-implementation of human dimension commitments, including on the basis of information from the ODIHR, reports and recommendations of the High Commissioner on National Minorities (HCNM), or reports of the head of a CSCE mission and information from the State concerned.

7. The participating States reconfirm their appreciation for the HCNM, who has, fully in line with his mandate, been able to focus on, and to successfully address a number of national minority issues, taking also into account specific situations of participating States and of parties directly concerned.

They encourage the HCNM to continue his present activities, and support him on taking up new and further ones, including those related to his recommendations. They will increase their efforts to implement these recommendations.

Role of the ODIHR

8. The ODIHR, as the main institution of the human dimension, in consultation with the Chairman-in-Office, will, acting in an advisory capacity, participate in discussions of the Senior Council and the Permanent Council, by reporting at regular intervals on its activities and providing information on implementation issues. It will provide supporting material for the annual review of implementation and, where necessary, clarify or supplement information received. Acting in close consultation with the Chairman-in-Office, the Director of the ODIHR may propose further action.

9. The participating States recognize the need for enhanced cooperation through the ODIHR with other international organizations and institutions active in the human dimension, including among others the United Nations High Commissioner for Human Rights, for the exchange of information, including reports, and for further developing of future-oriented activities, such as outlined in the present document.

10. The participating States decide to

—enhance the CSCE's co-operation with other international organizations and institutions, in particular UNHCR and IOM, with a view to contributing to UNHCR's preparation of a regional conference to address the problems of refugees, displaced persons, other forms of involuntary displacement and returnees in the countries of the Commonwealth of Independent States (CIS) and other interested neighbouring States, by establishing, after consultation in the informal Financial Committee, a temporary position, financed by voluntary contributions for a migration expert;

—task the ODIHR to act as a clearing-house for the exchange of information on media issues in the region, and encourage governments, journalists and NGOs to provide the ODIHR with information on the situation of the media.

11. The ODIHR will be consulted on a CSCE mission's mandate before adoption and will contribute to the follow-up of mission reports as decided by the Permanent Council. The ODIHR's knowledge of experts on the human dimension should be used to help to staff CSCE missions. These missions will also designate a mission member to liaise with the ODIHR and with NGOs on human dimension issues.

12. The ODIHR will plan an enhanced role in election monitoring, before, during and after elections. In this context, the ODIHR should assess the conditions for the free and independent functioning of the media.

The participating States request that co-ordination between the various organizations monitoring elections be improved, and task the ODIHR to consult all relevant organizations in order to develop a framework for co-ordination in this field.

In order to enhance election monitoring preparations and procedures, the ODIHR will also devise a handbook for election monitors and set up a rolling calendar for upcoming elections.

13. The provisions mentioned in the human dimension chapter of this document do not in any way constitute a change in the mandate of either the ODIHR or the HCNM.

ODIHR seminars

14. The number of large-scale human dimension seminars will as a rule be reduced to two per year. They will focus on topics which are of the broadest interest.

There will be more emphasis on regional seminars. Where appropriate they will form part of the Programme of Co-ordinated Support. These seminars should seek full participation from States in the region in which they are held. The ODIHR is requested to present to the Permanent Council a report on how to increase the effectiveness of human dimension seminars. Whilst these seminars will not produce a negotiated document, particular attention should be given to improving follow-up.

15. A large number of possible subjects for seminars, both large-scale and regional was suggested during the Review Conference. The Executive Secretariat kept a list, which will be passed on to the Permanent

Council. In conformity with the relevant provisions of the Helsinki Document 1992, the Permanent Council will establish an annual work programme including the titles, dates and venues of such seminars, taking into account the advice of the ODIHR and the HCNM.

16. The participating States welcomed the offer of Romania to host an International Seminar on Tolerance in Bucharest under the auspices of the ODIHR and the Council of Europe, in co-operation with UNESCO, in the context of the 1995 International Year of Tolerance.

Role of NGOs

17. The participating States and CSCE institutions will provide opportunities for increased involvement of NGOs in CSCE activities as foreseen in Chapter IV of the Helsinki Document 1992. They will search for ways in which the CSCE can best make use of the work and information provided by NGOs. The Secretary General is requested to make a study on how participation of NGOs can be further enhanced.

COMMITMENTS AND CO-OPERATION

Rule of law

18. The participating States emphasize that all action by public authorities must be consistent with the rule of law, thus guaranteeing legal security for the individual.

They also emphasize the need for protection of human rights defenders and look forward to the completion and adoption, in the framework of the United Nations, of the draft declaration on the "Right and Responsibility of Individuals, Groups and Organs of Society to Promote and Protect Universally Recognized Human Rights and Fundamental Freedoms".

Capital punishment

19. The participating States reconfirm their commitments in the Copenhagen and Moscow Documents concerning the question of capital punishment.

Prevention of torture

20. The participating States strongly condemn all forms of torture as one of the most flagrant violations of human rights and human dignity. They commit themselves to strive for its elimination. They recognize the importance in this respect of international norms as laid down in international treaties on human rights, in particular the United Nations Convention against

Torture and other Cruel, Inhuman or Degrading Treatment or Punishment and the European Convention for the Prevention of Torture and Inhuman or Degrading Treatment or Punishment. They also recognize the importance of national legislation aimed at eradicating torture. They commit themselves to inquire into all alleged cases of torture and to prosecute offenders. They also commit themselves to include in their educational and training programmes for law enforcement and police forces specific provisions with a view to eradicating torture. They consider that an exchange of information on this problem is an essential prerequisite. The participating States should have the possibility to obtain such information. The CSCE should in this context also draw on the experience of the Special Rapporteur on Torture and other Cruel, Inhuman or Degrading Treatment or Punishment established by the Commission on Human Rights of the United Nations and make use of information provided by NGOs.

National minorities

21.   The participating States confirm their determination consistently to advance the implementation of the provisions of the Final Act and all other CSCE documents relating to the protection of the rights of persons belonging to national minorities. They commend the work of the HCNM in this field.

22.   The participating States welcome the international efforts to improve protection of the rights of persons belonging to national minorities. They take note of the adoption, within the Council of Europe, of a Framework Convention on the Protection of National Minorities, which builds upon CSCE standards in this context. They stressed that the Convention is also open—by invitation—to signature by States which are not members of the Council of Europe and they may consider examining the possibility of becoming parties to this Convention.

Roma and Sinti

23.   The participating States decide to appoint within the ODIHR a contact point for Roma and Sinti (Gypsies) issues. The ODIHR will be tasked to:

—act as a clearing-house for the exchange of information on Roma and Sinti (Gypsies) issues, including information on the implementation of commitments pertaining to Roma and Sinti (Gypsies);

—facilitate contacts on Roma and Sinti (Gypsies) issues between participating States, international organizations and institutions and NGOs;

—maintain and develop contacts on these issues between CSCE institutions and other international organizations and institutions.

To fulfil these tasks, the ODIHR will make full use of existing resources. In this context they welcome the announcement made by some Roma and Sinti (Gypsies) organizations of their intention to make voluntary contributions.

24.   The participating States welcome the activities related to Roma and Sinti (Gypsies) issues in other international organizations and institutions, in particular those undertaken in the Council of Europe.

Tolerance and non-discrimination

25.   The participating States condemn manifestations of intolerance, and especially of aggressive nationalism, racism, chauvinism, xenophobia and anti-semitism, and will continue to promote effective measures aimed at their eradication. They request the ODIHR to continue to pay special attention to these phenomena, collecting information on their various manifestations in participating States. They will seek to strengthen or adopt appropriate legislation to this end and take the necessary measures to ensure that existing legislation is effectively implemented, in a way that would deter manifestations of these phenomena. They also stress that action to combat these phenomena should be seen as an integral part of integration policy and education. They condemn all crimes committed in the pursuit of so-called "ethnic cleansing" and will continue to give their effective support to the International War Crimes Tribunal for the former Yugoslavia in The Hague.

26.   They commend the Council of Europe's plan of action on racism, xenophobia, anti-semitism and intolerance. In following up the Rome Council's Declaration, CSCE institutions will explore possibilities for joint work with the Council of Europe, as well as the United Nations and other international organizations.

27.   Reaffirming their commitment to ensure freedom of conscience and religion and to foster a climate of mutual tolerance and respect between believers of different communities as well as between believers and non-believers, they expressed their concern about the exploitation of religion for aggressive nationalist ends.

Migrant workers

28.   The participating States reconfirm that human rights are universal and indivisible. They recognized that the protection and promotion of the rights of migrant workers have their human dimension. They underline the right of migrant workers to express freely their ethnic, cultural, religious and linguistic characteristics. The exercise of such rights may be subject to such restrictions as are prescribed by law and consistent with international standards.

29.   They decided that appropriate measures should be taken to better prevent racist attacks and other manifestations of violent intolerance against migrant workers and their families.

30.   They reconfirm their condemnation of all acts of discrimination on the ground of race, colour and ethnic origin, intolerance and xenophobia against migrant workers. They will, in conformity with domestic law and international obligations, continue to take effective measures to this end.

31.   They will continue to promote the integration of migrant workers in the societies in which they are lawfully residing. They recognize that a successful process of integration also depends on its active pursuit by the migrants themselves and decided therefore to encourage them in this regard.

Migration

32.   The participating States express their concern at mass migratory movements in the CSCE region, including millions of refugees and displaced persons, due mainly to war, armed conflict, civil strife and grave human rights violations. Taking into account the Rome Council Decisions 1993, they decide to expand their co-operation with appropriate international bodies in this respect.

They take note of efforts undertaken by UNHCR to prepare a regional conference to address the problems of refugees, displaced persons, other forms of involuntary displacement and returnees in the countries of the CIS and other interested neighbouring States.

International humanitarian law

33.   The participating States deeply deplore the series of flagrant violations of international humanitarian law that occurred in the CSCE region in recent years and reaffirm their commitment to respect and ensure respect for general international humanitarian law and in particular for their obligations under the relevant international instruments, including the 1949 Geneva Conventions and their additional protocols, to which they are a party.

34.   They emphasize the potential significance of a declaration on minimum humanitarian standards applicable in all situations and declare their willingness to actively participate in its preparation in the framework of the United Nations. They commit themselves to ensure adequate information and training within their military services with regard to the provisions of international humanitarian law and consider that relevant information should be made available.

35.   They highly value the developing co-operation between the CSCE and the International Committee of the Red Cross (ICRC), in particu-

lar in the case of CSCE missions, and welcome the readiness of the ICRC to develop this co-operation and commit themselves to further extend support to the ICRC, in particular by strengthening contacts already established between CSCE missions and the ICRC's delegations in the field.

Freedom of expression/Free media

36.		The participating States reaffirm that freedom of expression is a fundamental human right and a basic component of a democratic society. In this respect, independent and pluralistic media are essential to a free and open society and accountable systems of government. They take as their guiding principle that they will safeguard this right.

37.		They condemn all attacks on and harassment of journalists and will endeavour to hold those directly responsible for such attacks and harassment accountable.

38.		They further note that fomenting hatred and ethnic tension through the media, especially by governments, can serve as an early warning of conflict.

Freedom of movement/Human contacts/Cultural heritage

39.		The participating States will further encourage and facilitate human contacts, cultural and educational exchanges and co-operate in accordance with CSCE provisions. They will continue to implement their commitments in the cultural field, as laid down in the Document of the Cracow Symposium on the Cultural Heritage of the CSCE Participating States and other relevant CSCE documents. They will encourage public and private efforts aimed at the preservation of the cultural heritage in their States.

40.		They will encourage administrative authorities dealing with citizens of other States to fully implement the CSCE commitments concerning travel and will refrain from degrading treatment and other outrages against personal dignity. They will also consider the need for elaborating a document compiling relevant CSCE provisions.

41.		The Permanent Council will explore the possibility of holding informal meetings on the issues mentioned in the two preceding paragraphs.

PROGRAMME OF CO-ORDINATED SUPPORT

42.		The participating States, taking into account the progress achieved through the implementation of the Programme of Co-ordinated Support during the past two years under the co-ordination of the ODIHR, have decided that this programme should continue. The ODIHR and the Secretary General will continue to arrange meetings and seminars on CSCE-related matters to enable interested States to fulfil their CSCE commitments more easily. The participating States will continue to include representatives of these States in government-sponsored internships, study and training programmes so that levels of experience, knowledge and expertise can be raised.

43.   They agreed that the ability of the ODIHR to provide in-depth expertise on human dimension issues under the Programme of Co-ordinated Support should be further developed. In order to respond to requests for advice by newly independent States concerned on all aspects of democratization, they decided that using experts-at-large within the framework of the Programme of Co-ordinated Support would be a useful enhancement of the ODIHR's role.

E. ORGANIZATION OF THE ISLAMIC CONFERENCE

49. Resolution No. 49/19-P on the Cairo Declaration on Human Rights in Islam

The Nineteenth Islamic Conference of Foreign Ministers (Session of Peace, Interdependence and Development), held in Cairo, Arab Republic of Egypt, from 9-14 Muharram 1411H (31 July to 5 August 1990),

Keenly aware of the place of mankind in Islam as vicegerent of Allah on Earth;

Recognizing the importance of issuing a Document on Human Rights in Islam that will serve as a guide for Member States in all aspects of life;

Having examined the stages through which the preparation of this draft Document has, so far, passed and the relevant report of the Secretary General;

Having examined the Report of the Meeting of the Committee of Legal Experts held in Tehran from 26 to 28 December, 1989;

1. *Agrees* to issue the Cairo Declaration on Human Rights in Islam which will serve as a general guidance for Member States in the field of human rights.

50. The Cairo Declaration on Human Rights in Islam

Adopted at Cario on 5 August 1990

The Member States of the Organization of the Islamic Conference,

Reaffirming the civilizing and historical role of the Islamic Ummah which God made the best nation that has given mankind a universal and well-balanced civilization in which harmony is established between this life and the hereafter and knowledge is combined with faith; and the role that this Ummah should play to guide a humanity confused by competing trends and ideologies and to provide solutions to the chronic problems of this materialistic civilization.

Wishing to contribute to the efforts of mankind to assert human rights, to protect man from exploitation and persecution, and to affirm his freedom and right to a dignified life in accordance with the Islamic Shari'ah.

Convinced that mankind which has reached an advanced stage in materialistic science is still, and shall remain, in dire need of faith to support its civilization and of a self motivating force to guard its rights;

Believing that fundamental rights and universal freedoms in Islam are an integral part of the Islamic religion and that no one as a matter of principle has the right to suspend them in whole or in part or violate or ignore them in as much as they are binding divine commandments, which are contained in the Revealed Books of God and were sent through the last of His Prophets to complete the preceding divine messages thereby making their observance an act of worship and their neglect or violation an abominable sin, and accordingly every person is individually responsible—and the Ummah collectively responsible—for their safeguard.

Proceeding from the above-mentioned principles,

Declare the following:

Article 1

(a) All human beings form one family whose members are united by submission to God and descent from Adam. All men are equal in terms of basic human dignity and basic obligations and responsibilities, without any discrimination on the grounds of race, colour, language, sex, religious belief, political affiliation, social status or other considerations. True faith is the guarantee for enchancing such dignity along the path to human perfection.

(b) All human beings are God's subjects, and the most loved by Him are those who are most useful to the rest of His subjects, and no one has superiority over another except on the basis of piety and good deeds.

Article 2

(a) Life is a God-given gift and the right to life is guaranteed to every human being. It is the duty of individuals, societies and states to protect this right from any violation, and it is prohibited to take away life except for a Shari'ah prescribed reason.

(b) It is forbidden to resort to such means as may result in the genocidal annihilation of mankind.

(c) The preservation of human life throughout the term of time willed by God is a duty prescribed by Shari'ah.

(d) Safety from bodily harm is a guaranteed right. It is the duty of the state to safeguard it, and it is prohibited to breach it without a Shari'ah prescribed reason.

Article 3

(a) In the event of the use of force and in case of armed conflict, it is not permissible to kill non-belligerents such as old men, women and children. The wounded and the sick shall have the right to medical treatment; and prisoners of war shall have the right to be fed, sheltered and clothed. It is prohibited to mutilate dead bodies. It is a duty to exchange prisoners of war and to arrange visits or reunions of the families separated by the circumstances of war.

(b) It is prohibited to fell trees, to damage crops or livestock, and to destroy the enemy's civilian buildings and installations by shelling, blasting or any other means.

Article 4

Every human being is entitled to inviolability and the protection of his good name and honour during his life and after his death. The State and society shall protect his remains and burial place.

Article 5

(a) The family is the foundation of society, and marriage is the basis of its formation. Men and women have the right to marriage, and no restrictions stemming from race, colour or nationality shall prevent them from en-joying this right.

(b) Society and the State shall remove all obstacles to marriage and shall facilitate marital procedure. They shall ensure family protection and welfare.

Article 6

(a) Woman is equal to man in human dignity, and has rights to enjoy as well as duties to perform; she has her own civil entity and financial inde-pendence, and the right to retain her name and lineage.

(b) The husband is responsible for the support and welfare of the family.

Article 7

(a) As of the moment of birth, every child has rights due from the parents, society and the State to be accorded proper nursing, education and material, hygienic and moral care. Both the foetus and the mother must be protected and accorded special care.

(b) Parents and those in such like capacity have the right to choose the type of education they desire for their children, provided they take into consideration the interest and future of the children in accordance with ethi-cal values and the principles of the Shari'ah.

(c) Both parents are entitled to certain rights from their children, and relatives are entitled to rights from their kin, in accordance with the tenets of the Shari'ah.

Article 8

Every human being has the right to enjoy his legal capacity in terms of both obligation and commitment, should this capacity be lost or impaired, he shall be represented by his guardian.

Article 9

(a) The question for knowledge is an obligation and the provision of education is a duty for society and the State. The State shall ensure the avail-ability of ways and means to acquire education and shall guarantee educa-tional diversity in the interest of society so as to enable man to be acquainted with the religion of Islam and the facts of the Universe for the benefit of mankind.

(b) Every human being has the right to receive both religious and worldly education from the various institutions of, education and guidance, including the family, the school, the university, the media, etc., and in such an integrated and balanced manner as to develop his personality, strengthen his faith in God and promote his respect for and defence of both rights and obligations.

Article 10

Islam is the religion of unspoiled nature. It is prohibited to exercise any form of compulsion on man or to exploit his poverty or ignorance in order to convert him to another religion or to atheism.

Article 11

(a) Human beings are born free, and no one has the right to enslave, humiliate, oppress or exploit them, and there can be no subjugation but to God the Most-High.

(b) Colonialism of all types being one of the most evil forms of enslavement is totally prohibited. Peoples suffering from colonialism have the full right to freedom and self-determination. It is the duty of all States and peoples to support the struggle of colonized peoples for the liquidation of all forms of colonialism and occupation, and all States and peoples have the right to preserve their independent identity and exercise control over their wealth and natural resources.

Article 12

Every man shall have the right, within the framework of Shari'ah, to free movement and to select his place of residence whether inside or outside his country and if persecuted, is entitled to seek asylum in another country. The country of refuge shall ensure his protection until he reaches safety, unless asylum is motivated by an act which Shari'ah regards as a crime.

Article 13

Work is a right guaranteed by the State and society for each person able to work. Everyone shall be free to choose the work that suits him best and which serves his interests and those of society. The employee shall have the right to safety and security as well as to all other social guarantees. He may neither be assigned work beyond his capacity nor be subjected to compulsion or exploited or harmed in any way. He shall be entitled—without any discrimination between males and females—to fair wages for his work without delay, as well as to the holidays, allowances and promotions which he deserves. For his part, he shall be required to be dedicated and meticulous in his work. Should workers and employers disagree on any matter, the State shall intervene to settle the dispute and have the grievances redressed, the rights confirmed and justice enforced without bias.

Article 14

Everyone shall have the right to legitimate gains without monopolization, deceit or harm to oneself or to others. Usury (riba) is absolutely prohibited.

Article 15

(a) Everyone shall have the right to own property acquired in a legitimate way, and shall be entitled to the rights of ownership, without prejudice to oneself, others or to society in general. Expropriation is not permissible except for the requirements of public interest and upon payment of immediate and fair compensation.

(b) Confiscation and seizure of property is prohibited except for a necessity dictated by law.

Article 16

Everyone shall have the right to enjoy the fruits of his scientific, literacy, artistic or technical production and the right to protect the moral and material interests stemming therefrom, provided that such production is not contrary to the principles of Shari'ah.

Article 17

(a) Everyone shall have the right to live in a clean environment, away from vice and moral corruption, an environment that would foster his self-development and it is incumbent upon the State and society in general to afford that right.

(b) Everyone shall have the right to medical and social care, and to all public amenities provided by society and the State within the limits of their available resources.

(c) The State shall ensure the right of the individual to a decent living which will enable him to meet all his requirements and those of his dependents, including food, clothing, housing, education, medical care and all other basic needs.

Article 18

(a) Everyone shall have the right to live in security for himself, his religion, his dependents, his honour and his property.

(b) Everyone shall have the right to privacy in the conduct of his private affairs, in his home, among his family, with regard to his property and his relationships. It is not permitted to spy on him, to place him under surveillance or to besmirch his good name. The State shall protect him from arbitrary interference.

(c) A private residence is inviolable in all cases. It will not be entered without permission from its inhabitants or in any unlawful manner, nor shall it be demolished or confiscated and its dwellers evicted.

Article 19

(a) All individuals are equal before the law, without distinction between the ruler and the ruled.

(b) The right to resort to justice is guaranteed to everyone.

(c) Liability is in essence personal.

(d) There shall be no crime or punishment except as provided for in the Shari'ah.

(e) A defendant is innocent until his guilt is proven in a fair trial in which he shall be given all the guarantees of defence.

Article 20

It is not permitted without legitimate reason to arrest an individual, or restrict his freedom, to exile or to punish him. It is not permitted to subject him to physical or psychological torture or to any form of humiliation, cruelty or indignity. Nor is it permitted to subject an individual to medical or scientific experimentation without his consent or at the risk of his health or of his life. Nor is it permitted to promulgate emergency laws that would provide executive authority for such actions.

Article 21

Taking hostages under any form or for any purpose is expressly forbidden.

Article 22

(a) Everyone shall have the right to express his opinion freely in such manner as would not be contrary to the principles of the Shari'ah.

(*b*) Everyone shall have the right to express his opinion freely in such manner as would not be contrary to the principles of the Shari'ah.

(*b*) Everyone shall have the right to advocate what is right, and propagate what is good, and warn against what is wrong and evil according to the norms of Islamic Shari'ah.

(*c*) Information is a vital necessity to society. It may not be exploited or misused in such a way as may violate sanctities and the dignity of Prophets, undermine moral and ethical values or disintegrate, corrupt or harm society or weaken its faith.

(*d*) It is not permitted to arouse nationalistic or doctrinal hatred or to do anything that may be an incitement to any form of racial discrimination.

Article 23

(*a*) Authority is a trust; and abuse or malicious exploitation thereof is absolutely prohibited, so that fundamental human rights may be guaranteed.

(*b*) Everyone shall have the right to participate, directly or indirectly in the administration of his country's public affairs. He shall also have the right to assume public office in accordance with the provisions of Shari'ah.

Article 24

All the rights and freedoms stipulated in this Declaration are subject to the Islamic Shari'ah.

Article 25

The Islamic Shari'ah is the only source of reference for the explanation or clarification of any of the articles of this Declaration.